EAST ASIA'S GRAND STRATEGIES

EAST ASIA'S GRAND STRATEGIES

A Twelve-Case Comparison

RAMON PACHECO PARDO AND
JUNG H. PAK, EDITORS

GEORGETOWN UNIVERSITY PRESS / WASHINGTON, DC

Library of Congress Cataloging-in-Publication Data

Names: Pacheco Pardo, Ramon, editor. | Pak, Jung H., editor.
Title: East Asia's grand strategies : a twelve-case comparison / Ramon Pacheco Pardo and Jung H. Pak, editors.
Description: Washington, DC : Georgetown University Press, [2025] | Includes bibliographical references and index.
Identifiers: LCCN 2024051158 (print) | LCCN 2024051159 (ebook) | ISBN 9781647126254 (paperback) | ISBN 9781647126247 (hardcover) | ISBN 9781647126261 (ebook)
Subjects: LCSH: National security--East Asia. | East Asia--Strategic aspects. | East Asia--Foreign relations. | East Asia--Military policy.
Classification: LCC UA832.5 .E38 2025 (print) | LCC UA832.5 (ebook) | DDC 355/.03355--dc23/eng/20250209
LC record available at https://lccn.loc.gov/2024051158
LC ebook record available at https://lccn.loc.gov/2024051159

∞ This paper meets the requirements of ANSI/NISO Z39.48-1992 (Permanence of Paper).

EU GPSR Authorised Representative
LOGOS EUROPE, 9 rue Nicolas Poussin,
17000, LA ROCHELLE, France
E-mail: Contact@logoseurope.eu

26 25 9 8 7 6 5 4 3 2 First printing

Printed in the United States of America

Cover design by Erin Kirk
Interior design by Westchester Publishing Services

CONTENTS

TABLES

Introduction

Ramon Pacheco Pardo and Jung H. Pak

East Asia is a key center of global geopolitics. The region encompasses a third of world gross domestic product (GDP) and a third of the world's population, and its share of both has only grown in recent years. It is home to some of the biggest military spenders in the world, a legacy of the Cold War and the result of unresolved territorial disputes and historical disputes, among other reasons. Regional integration is deepening thanks to ASEAN+3 (Association of Southeast Asian Nations, plus China, South Korea, and Japan), ADMM-Plus (ASEAN Defence Ministers' Meeting, plus Australia, China, South Korea, Japan, India, New Zealand, Russia, and the United States), and the Regional Comprehensive Economic Partnership (RCEP) as key institutions. And the world's leading power, the United States, remains central to security, economic, and political developments in the region, owing to its post-World War II alliance system, including the four treaty alliances in this region. Post COVID-19 pandemic, East Asia's influence in the evolving global dynamics also grew thanks to its successful response to the health emergency and quicker economic recovery.

Despite the region's dynamism and increasing importance for international politics, how the states of East Asia calculate and pursue their interests is poorly understood. What is the grand strategy (GS) of each of the key powers in East Asia? This is the central question that informs and drives this edited volume. This volume sets out to answer it by analyzing the GSs of China, Indonesia, Japan, Malaysia, Myanmar, North Korea, Philippines, Singapore, South Korea, Taiwan,[1] Thailand, and Vietnam. These are the twelve biggest military spenders in East Asia.[2] They also include the eleven largest economies in the region.[3] North Korea, the only country not on this second list, is one of only nine countries in the world with nuclear weapons. In other words, the GSs of these powers have an impact on regional—when not global—geopolitics. Analyzing their GSs is necessary to better understand the recent history, present, and possible future of regional and global geopolitical dynamics.

Furthermore, these cases include a combination of great, middle, and small powers. Their analysis thus heeds recent calls to expand the study of GS beyond great powers and to concentrate on other cases that, while not as powerful, are also able to develop their own GS.[4] In addition, analyzing the GSs of these powers also supports the ongoing move to make the study of international relations more inclusive in terms of geographical scope—especially by focusing on countries and regions beyond "the West."[5]

Certainly, the study of GS has so far overwhelmingly prioritized the United States.[6] To an extent, this is understandable. The United States was one of the two superpowers during the Cold War and emerged from this confrontation as the world's hegemon. As a result the impact of Washington's behavior was strongly felt both in the United States itself and elsewhere. There was a need to understand the origins, evolution, and application in practice of Washington's GS. But while this remains true, it is also necessary to understand the GSs of other powers as well, particularly given the rise and growing assertiveness of China, with the perception of a decline in the relative power of the United States, and as other countries have become more assertive or at least sought more autonomy in their foreign policy. In the absence of such analysis, we cannot explain developments such as the unwillingness across East Asia to isolate China, territorial disputes between neighbors such as Japan and South Korea or in the South China Sea, or the fact that the region's last interstate clash was the Sino-Vietnamese skirmish of 1988—over thirty-five years ago.

When GS studies do set their sights on East Asia, they usually focus on China. Therefore, there is a growing literature analyzing China as a single case study,[7] as well as an increasing number of books comparing the GS of Asia's greatest power with other powers' GSs.[8] But China is usually compared with countries from outside East Asia, which in part suggests that Asia is a monolith, when that is hardly the case. There is also literature analyzing the GS of Japan.[9] But as is the case with China, Japan is not representative of the whole of East Asia. While it is understandable that the existing literature focuses on the study of the region's two biggest economies and military powers—and especially China as the only East Asian great power—their GSs do not represent the diversity of East Asia.[10]

This volume will focus on the period from 1980 to 2024. The starting point is the aftermath of two seminal events in contemporary East Asian history: the announcement of China's opening up in 1978 and the normalization of diplomatic relations between the United States and China in 1979.

Together with the end of the Cold War in 1991, another seminal development, these events marked a turning point with deep repercussions on the GS of powers across East Asia. The finishing point will be 2024, coinciding with the aftermath of the COVID-19 pandemic, the end of the Joe Biden administration following the tumultuous first Donald Trump administration in the United States, the reelection of Xi Jinping for a third term in China, and the implementation of RCEP. These four events are poised to have a strong impact on the international relations of East Asia and the evolution of the GS of powers in the region. By focusing on this period the volume adds to our knowledge about how the GSs of East Asian powers shaped and has been shaped by transformative regional and global dynamics.

Ultimately, the study of the GSs of twelve key East Asian cases during this period will contribute to a better understanding of the evolution of regional and global political, economic, and security developments at a time when the center of gravity of world politics is moving toward the region—or returning, depending on one's perspective. Arguably, this is the key defining phenomenon in twenty-first-century geopolitics. The United States, the European Union (EU), India, or Russia, never mind East Asia itself, have to accommodate this dynamic in their own GSs. Only by having a clear picture of the GS of the different powers across the region will this be possible.

WHAT IS GRAND STRATEGY?

Political scientists Thierry Balzacq and Ronald R. Krebs define GS as "a state's 'theory of victory,' explaining how the state will utilize its diverse means to advance and achieve national ends."[11] This is the definition that we adopt in this book. In other words, the contributors to this volume present and analyze the (long-term) goals that powers across East Asia want to achieve and the tools that they use to achieve them. For GS, whether clearly formulated and publicized or only visible by examining its practice, is posited to last decades and survive the vagaries of everyday events and politics.[12]

The concept of GS can trace its modern roots back to the eighteenth and nineteenth centuries. Foreign policy practitioners began to systematically collect their thoughts regarding how wars could be won and peace should be maintained. In other words, practitioners put together their thoughts on "strategy."[13] In 1929 military historian and theorist Basil Liddell Hart officially introduced the concept of "grand strategy" with his book *Strategy: The Indirect Approach*. He emphasized that the concept referred to winning wars but also to peace and to improving people's lives.[14] Throughout the Cold

War, the concept of GS lost its appeal as scholars focused on the study of "foreign policy" instead.[15] Following the end of the Cold War, the study of GS increased dramatically. Paul Kennedy's edited volume *Grand Strategies in War and Peace*, published in 1991, is widely credited with drawing renewed interest to the analysis of GS.[16]

Thirty years after Kennedy's volume and over ninety years since Liddell Hart's work, there is no universal agreement on the definition of GS. But most definitions of GS implicitly or explicitly draw on these two early definitions. According to Kennedy, "The crux of grand strategy lies therefore in *policy*, that is, in the capacity of the nation's leaders to bring together all of the elements, both military and non-military, for the preservation and enhancement of the nation's long-term (that is, in wartime *and* peacetime) best interests."[17] Meanwhile, Barry Posen posits that GS is "a state's theory about it can best 'cause' security for itself."[18] Synthesizing these two definitions, Nina Silove summarizes that GS "is long-term in scope, concerned with the state's most important priorities, and inclusive of all spheres of statecraft (military, diplomatic, and economic)."[19] These three key aspects—military, diplomatic, and economic—are almost universally adopted in the study of GS. They also underpin the analysis presented in this volume, as per the definition presented previously.

Scholars of GS may adopt similar definitions of GS, but they do not necessarily agree on what GS should examine. As Balzacq, Dombrowski, and Reich explain, scholarship on GS can be divided into two groups: the classicist approach and the international relations approach.[20] This distinction matters insofar as each approach focuses on particular sets of goals and draws attention to a narrower or wider range of instruments.

The classicist approach to GS draws inspiration from nineteenth-century discussions about (grand) strategy, therefore focusing on how the state can use military instruments to achieve its goals.[21] The logic behind this approach is that states have to prepare and, sometimes, fight wars. Therefore they have to strengthen their military capabilities in case they need to be deployed.[22] The number of interstate military conflicts have dramatically declined since the end of the Cold War.[23] But as classicists note, war remains possible. States therefore have to be ready to fight a war and have to prioritize potential threats and how to address them.[24] Certainly, even though interstate conflict has declined, the examples of Afghanistan, Armenia-Azerbaijan, Iraq, Libya, Russia-Ukraine, or Saudi Arabia-Yemen show that war between states, invasion by third parties, or a civil war in which external actors become involved are all very real possibilities.

The international relations approach broadens the scope of the classicist approach and is the one that we adopt in this book—in line with Balzacq,

Dombrowski, and Reich. Certainly the most popular definitions of GS referred to previously suggest that the international relations approach has become dominant. As Hal Brands posits, GS brings together the different elements of statecraft to its highest national objectives. These elements certainly include military capabilities, and national objectives undoubtedly involve winning a war if one takes place.[25] But as William Martel argues, GS is not and has never been about war or how to conduct it. He goes further by arguing that war can actually be considered a failure of GS.[26] While most proponents of an international relations approach to GS would not agree that war constitutes a failure of GS, they concur that GS cannot be reduced to war planning and conduct. After all, each state will define its interests—and potential threats—in a variety of ways and will mobilize a range of instruments depending on them.[27] Certainly climate change, energy, or trade are core interests of any state and have become securitized, including in East Asia.[28] They require the mobilization of diplomatic and economic instruments, not exclusively military means. This volume is therefore embedded in the international relations approach to GS, which arguably has become mainstream.

This takes us to one last aspect of the study of GS, which refers to what Silove identifies as three different research agendas. They include GS as a plan with a blueprint for action, GS as an organizing principle or principles giving direction to foreign policy, and GS as a pattern of behavior that applies over time.[29] This distinction may seem too arcane. After all, how can one distinguish between a blueprint for action and an organizing principle? Silove herself concedes that the difference is in the level of detail.[30] And Martel, for example, focuses on the overarching principle but certainly incorporates elements of a blueprint for action.[31] Even separating a pattern of behavior from a blueprint for action is complicated in practice. After all, patterns of behavior emerge from a state's strategic culture.[32] And strategic culture results from common ideas about strategy that result in a particular behavior.[33] The nexus between broader blueprints and even principles, on the one hand, and behavior on the other is inescapable. In this volume we concur with Balzacq, Dombrowski, and Reich that the study of GS requires analyzing principles, strategic planning, and behavior.[34]

In practice, the design and implementation of a GS may or may not entail a well-defined centralized institutional framework and may or may not be conscious.[35] To an extent this depends on the nature of the state. Both great powers, such as the United States or China, and their less powerful counterparts are capable of developing and implementing a GS. But their resources vary, which explains why some powers actively, consciously, and strategically devise and execute a GS while others are not necessarily aware that they are pursuing one.[36] In this volume we will see this work in practice. For some of the cases analyzed, their national (security) strategy is equivalent to their grand strategy. For others this is not the case. In the case of some powers, their long-term foreign policy as observed in practice is tantamount to their GS even if the principles and goals are not explicitly laid out in written form. The concluding chapter will briefly discuss the different ways in which the various East Asian powers analyzed in this book consciously or unconsciously formulate and deliver their GS, as explained by the contributors to this volume in their respective chapters.

FRAMEWORK OF ANALYSIS

Comparative studies need a solid framework of analysis to serve as the basis for the comparison. Otherwise the reader cannot see the similarities and differences across case studies. In the specific case of GS analysis, most literature focuses on a single case study developed in detail. Certainly there are studies comparing the GS of different states.[37] But their comparative element tends to be weak due to the absence of a well-defined framework allowing for systematic comparison across case studies.

This book adopts the framework of analysis laid out by Balzacq, Dombrowski, and Reich,[38] which is the work that has done the most in recent years to establish a method to compare the GSs of different states. As the authors note, taking an international relations approach to the analysis of GS has two implications. To begin with, different states with different institutional arrangements, resources, and geopolitical circumstances use GS instruments for different purposes and in different proportions.[39] In other words the diplomatic, economic, and military tools at the disposal of any given state will be deployed with specific goals in mind and with a wider or narrower scope—and this is contingent on the state's internal and external circumstances. This may seem logical. But it needs to be made clear. Otherwise dominance of the United States and a handful of great powers in GS scholarship may lead scholars to believe that their institutional arrangements are universal.

Furthermore, states will adjust their GS over time, and this adjustment will be contingent on the available instruments, evolving interests, and threats and opportunities related to regional and global security structures.[40] Certainly the fact that a state's GS evolves over the years is unsurprising. However, often existing literature assumes that GS remains constant over time. To an extent this stems from its focus on great powers, which have a wide range of instruments at their disposal and the ability to shape global politics in a way that smaller powers do not. Furthermore Balzacq, Dombrowski, and Reich draw attention to the importance of both regional and global structures.[41] As Barry Buzan and Ole Waever have convincingly argued, regional security structures matter as much as global geopolitical dynamics for most if not all states.[42] From this it follows that a state's GS evolves in response to both layers.

By using the framework advanced by Balzacq, Dombrowski, and Reich to articulate the cross-country comparative analysis and provide coherence to the different chapters, this volume will "examine both the international and domestic dimensions of formulating and implementing [a state's] grand strategy."[43] International relations scholarship drawing attention to the interplay between domestic and international dynamics when studying state behavior is of course not new. Five decades ago Graham Allison convincingly explained how bureaucratic politics lead to particular foreign policy decisions.[44] Foreign policy analysis scholars have long been calling to break down domestic-foreign boundaries.[45] Neoclassical realism has updated realist thought by emphasizing the centrality of domestic dynamics such as state-society relations, domestic political, regimes, strategic culture, or leaders' perceptions to determine how states react to international system dynamics.[46] The study of GS should follow from this persuasive move toward linking the domestic and the international to explain a state's behavior.

The external factors that Balzac, Dombrowski, and Reich suggest for consideration are as follows: (1) the type of third-party actors that domestic strategists have to deal with, including both nation-states and nonstate actors such as terrorist groups, insurgent, movements, nongovernmental organizations (NGOs), foundations, or firms; (2) the threats and opportunities available to them across a range of military, economic, diplomatic, and social dimensions; and (3) the types of conflicts they strategize against, whether conventional or nuclear, asymmetric, or hybrid.[47]

Regarding the domestic factors that Balzac, Dombrowski, and Reich lay out, they include (1) the source and types of national values collectively informing GS; (2) the influence of these values on policymakers' identification, interpretation, and definition of actors, threats, opportunities, and potential forms of conflict; (3) the way in which policymakers debate at the national level, both in terms of regional and international threats and opportunities; (4) the institutional process leading to the formulation of strategy; and (5) the combination of material and social resources strategists use to implement GS.[48]

This way Balzac, Dombrowski, and Reich—and by extension the contributors to this volume—are able to provide an interpretative analysis about how and why powers strategize to guarantee their security, for and against what they strategize, and the results of their choices.[49] This provides a holistic account of GS, which attends to its evolution over time by laying out how domestic factors influence the ways in which powers interact with and react to changing external factors. This framework is therefore sufficiently comprehensive and flexible to allow scholars to explain how and why a power settles on a particular GS, implements it, and modifies it or not.

In the specific case of East Asian powers, this volume lays out the two seminal overarching developments that created a different regional and global environment informing their GS. As a reminder, these were the announcement of China's opening up in 1978 together with the normalization of diplomatic relations between the United States and China one year later, and the end of the Cold War in 1991. But other developments—such as the rise of China and its evolving balance of power with the United States, the emergence of terrorist and insurgency groups across Southeast Asia, North Korea's development of nuclear weapons, several pandemics, or even the Asian financial crisis and global financial crisis—have also shaped the regional and global environment and affected the GS of the societies in the region.

As for the domestic factors informing GS across East Asia, the region is one of the most diverse in the world. Political systems include both democracies such as Japan, South Korea, or Taiwan and autocracies such as China or Vietnam.[50] Economies range from high-income countries including Japan, Singapore, or South Korea to low-income countries such as North Korea.[51] In terms of ethnic diversity, Indonesia and Thailand are among the most diverse countries in the world whereas Japan, South Korea, and North Korea are the most homogeneous.[52] And of course, as implied previously, the power capabilities in East Asia vary considerably, reflecting the region's range from great to middle to smaller powers. These data points suggest that the domestic factors informing the ways in which East Asian powers think about, develop, and implement GS can vary significantly from one case to another.

STRUCTURE OF THE VOLUME

This volume is divided into two sections. The first of them focuses on Northeast Asia. In chapter 1 Ketian Zhang analyzes the GS of China (People's

Republic of China; PRC). China's GS is a means-ends chain; that is, the use of all means available to ensure the core and important national interests laid out by the Chinese government. China's GS is influenced by both external and domestic factors. Regarding external factors, changes in the international system and China's perception of its security environment significantly affect China's calculation of the likelihood of major conflicts. Specifically China pays close attention to the capability and behavior of the US, the current hegemon. As for domestic factors, China prioritizes economic development and, therefore, takes economic costs and benefits into consideration when devising its GS. The survival of the Chinese Communist Party—regime legitimacy—is also a core concern driving Chinese GS. The end result is a GS whose goals are in tension with one another. On the one hand, Chinese GS aims at creating a stable international environment for its economic development, which dictates China to use economic inducement and diplomacy. On the other hand, the need to demonstrate that China is resolved to defend its national security, especially core security interests such as Taiwan, leads China to use negative means of statecraft, including coercion.

In chapter 2, Yuichi Hosoya analyzes the GS of Japan. Japan's role as the most important ally of the US in East Asia and the third biggest economic power in the world after the US and China are the key internal factors underpinning its GS. Japan's government published its first National Security Strategy in December 2013 based on its threat assessment of North Korea and its response to increasingly assertive Chinese military activities in the East China Sea. These are the external factors influencing Japan's contemporary GS. During the Cold War years the Soviet Union was the most immediate threat to Japan's national security. Japan's GS is generally labeled as the Yoshida doctrine, namely an economic-oriented approach with an emphasis on its alliance relationship with the US. However, after the end of the Cold War, Japan's GS has been transformed with a more proactive security policy. Prime Minister Shinzo Abe created Japan's National Security Council in 2013 and consolidated a new GS called the free and open Indo-Pacific (FOIP) strategy. Despite its limits in military power, Japan's GS has become an important driving force to create a coalition of like-minded liberal democracies in the region.

In chapter 3, Jung H. Pak and Ramon Pacheco Pardo analyze the GS of North Korea (Democratic People's Republic of Korea; DPRK). External factors informing its GS include the US, China, South Korea, and to an extent Japan and Russia as third-party actors; the (alleged) threat of a US strike or a South Korean invasion and the real threat of South Korea as an example of a democratic and open Korea that is an existential threat to the regime in Pyongyang are two threats that North Korea has to strategize against. Domestic factors informing its GS include an ideology (if not a reality) of self-reliance and loyalty to Kim Jong Un and his predecessors as core values, a closed and top-down decision-making process with limited input outside a small number of elites, and the prioritization of a strong military. Pyongyang's repression of its population, its alliance with China (albeit beset with mutual suspicion), its friendly and once superficial but growing relations with Russia, and coercion and diplomacy are tools the regime uses to implement GS. The result is a GS essentially underpinned by a strong nuclear and missile deterrent as the core elements to guard against external threats while reinforcing domestic legitimacy.

In chapter 4 Seong-ho Sheen analyzes the GS of South Korea (Republic of Korea; ROK). External factors informing its GS include North Korea, the US, China, and to an extent Japan and Russia as third-party actors, as well as the existential threat of a North Korea armed with nuclear, chemical, and biological weapons and ballistic missiles capable of delivering these weapons with increasing reliability, combined with massive but old conventional forces. The chapter will also discuss South Korea's geostrategic dilemma with growing US-China rivalry in the military as well as in other sectors. Domestic factors informing its GS include democratic transformation related to generational change in terms of ideology, gender, and demography, along with a rapidly aging society with a low birth rate; power transition from right-wing conservative to a new liberal progressive movement among Congress, media, and business; US-ROK alliance transformation with wartime operation control (OPCON); the domestic politics of Korea-Japan history disputes; the development of South Korea's new middle power roles in regional and world affairs; and its new drive for inter-Korean reconciliation and a peace regime on the Korean Peninsula. The result is a GS of peace building on the Korean Peninsula with inter-Korean engagement, denuclearization, ROK-US alliance transformation, hedging of US-China rivalry, reconfiguration of Korea-Japan relations, and a new northern policy with Russia backed by South Korea's growing middle power and maturing democracy.

In chapter 5, Chiung-Chiu Huang analyzes the GS of Taiwan (Republic of China; ROC). Because of its small size, Taiwan's foreign policymaking is profoundly shaped by the asymmetric power structure of East Asia. Taiwan perceives the influences (materially as well as ideationally) of mainland China as the biggest threat to its national security. Hence, managing the cross-Strait relationship is naturally the most important part of the Taiwanese policymakers' GS thinking. Meanwhile, the US has been viewed as the most important ally and supporter of Taiwan; Washington's responses to

Taiwan's actions in international arena matter greatly. The third and probably the most crucial factor influencing the Taiwanese policymakers' thinking about GS is the domestic politics and social atmosphere, including the need to strengthen the ruling legitimacy, the localization of Taiwanese national identity, the perceptions of China, the expectations of Taiwan's international status, and the political elites' striving for power and competitions for gaining dominance. The complicated entanglement of these factors contributes to the precarious and capricious essence of Taiwan's GS since the 1980s. This GS relies on manipulating domestic political discourses, serves temporary purposes only, and is more often than not instrumental and unfulfilled.

The second section covers Southeast Asia. In chapter 6, Muhamad Haripin analyzes the GS of Indonesia. External actors informing its GS include all of the regional major powers, in particular China, the US, and ASEAN; the most immediate threats are regarded to be primarily internal in nature such as from secessionist movements, violent communal conflicts, and terrorism that could be aided and exacerbated by external interventions from both state and nonstate actors. Lately Indonesia has also been increasingly concerned about maritime threats to security, particularly its territorial integrity around the South China Sea. The perennial search for national resilience, seen to be inextricably linked to regional resilience, has engendered a preference for a comprehensive security approach with an emphasis on economic development and regional cooperation. Ensuring Indonesia's and ASEAN's strategic autonomy, maximizing the benefits that the major powers have to offer while avoiding over-dependence on any external powers, has been central to Indonesia's GS. Domestic factors informing its GS include the doctrine of a "free and active" foreign policy that eschews military alliances and commits to nonalignment. There have been two different political systems: the authoritarian New Order government based on the dual function of the military (1966–98), and since the onset of Reformasi in 1998, a pluralistic democracy that is still in the process of consolidation. While the decision-making process was closed and top down, dominated by President Suharto and the army during the New Order period, the current democratic system has been characterized by the presence of multiple actors engaging in open debates and bureaucratic politics, often resulting in inconsistent and incoherent policies, though the military continues to be highly influential in matters relating to security. The result is a GS focused on enhancing the country's national resilience, particularly its territorial integrity and economic development as well as the stability and strategic autonomy of the ASEAN region. Diplomacy is Indonesia's primary tool, supported by a military still in the process of building a minimum essential force as a deterrence against potential external threats.

In chapter 7, Yew Meng Lai analyzes the GS of Malaysia as a "smaller state" seeking to advance its myriad of national interests in the context of the evolving regional order shaped by the changing power dynamics of the Cold War and post-Cold War eras. The external factors informing its GS include third-party actors, including the US, China, and, to an extent, Japan, as well as ASEAN, multilaterally and bilaterally in the guise of its member-states. Malaysia's behavior and preferences of action are likewise affected by correlated external challenges and opportunities, namely the Sino-American strategic competition manifesting in the context of the multiactor South China Sea maritime-territorial conflict; China's rise to regional preponderance and its growing assertiveness; and the existential, albeit nontraditional, cross-border security threats emanating from the Malaysia-Indonesia-Philippines "tri-border" region. Meanwhile domestic factors informing Malaysia's GS include an elite-centric decision-making process, commonly influenced by leadership idiosyncrasies and personality traits; a domestic political landscape shaped by ethnoreligious dynamics which saliently affect elite legitimation; developmental needs of an aspiring high-income economy; and small-state pragmatism, all of which serve to define its overarching foreign policy principles of nonalignment, neutrality, equidistance, and peaceful coexistence. Malaysia's strategic use of a combination of defense, diplomatic, legal, and economic tools to implement GS is essentially rooted as much in geopolitical and economic as in normative and ideational considerations. The result is a GS underpinned by strategic pragmatism tempered by a policy of hedging against the uncertainties of shifting power dynamics, relative power asymmetry, and great power rivalry in East Asia.

In chapter 8, Maung Aung Myoe analyzes the GS of Myanmar. Being a weak state, Myanmar's survival and security as a modern nation-state has been at the core of its GS. The geopolitical and geostrategic reality of Myanmar in the context of growing rivalry among regional and extra-regional great powers—particularly among the US, Russia, China, and India—have strongly influenced Myanmar's GS. Assessing the opportunities and challenges that result from the shift in the global distribution of power has been an important part of GS formulation and adjustment among political elites and the security establishment in Myanmar. Any possibility of spillover effects of a regional armed conflict or of fighting a proxy war has constantly informed Myanmar GS. In terms of domestic factors, historical and collective memory of anticolonial struggle and nationalist movement, a strategic culture of dealing with external security challenges in both precolonial and contemporary eras, and the preoccupation with internal armed challenges to the state as Myanmar's security predicament are critically shaping the country's GS. For all practical purposes, Myanmar's military establishment has exercised hegemony over conceptualizing, strategizing, and operationalizing the GS. With diplomacy as the most important instrument, Myanmar's GS is essentially a foreign policy strategy.

In chapter 9, Renato Cruz De Castro analyzes the GS of the Philippines. External factors informing its GS include the US, Japan, the member-states of ASEAN, and China. The emergence of China as a great power in East Asia and its maritime expansion in the South China Sea pushed the Philippines to shift its focus and attention away from internal security to external defense. Domestic factors include the ongoing communist and Islamic insurgencies that have diverted government attention and resources away from external defense, a liberal-democratic government that pays limited attention to defense matters and keeps the defense budget limited, and the absence of an industrial base that can support the build-up of a modern military. The result is a GS that is constrained by limited defense build-up, reliant on an alliance with the US and to a certain degree on a regional association (ASEAN), and recently, marked by efforts to appease China, an expanding revisionist power in the South China Sea.

In chapter 10, Ang Cheng Guan analyzes the GS of Singapore. Singapore's GS has been remarkably consistent since the country came into being in 1965. The chapter will consider Singapore's historical experience: its separation from Malaysia to form an independent country in 1965; its geographical location as a small, resource-poor, and trade-dependent country surrounded by very much larger and not always friendly neighbors; the make-up of the country as a predominantly ethnic Chinese country in a Malay/Islamic neighborhood; the mindset of the leadership—particularly the founding triumvirate, Lee Kuan Yew (the founding and longest serving prime minister), S. Rajaratnam (on foreign policy), and Goh Keng Swee (on defense policy)—as well as the changing external (regional and international) environment—a country which emerged from the cauldron of the Cold War and having to navigate the post-Cold War era. All of these factors informed or determined its GS, both its foreign and defense policies. With particular emphasis on empirical evidence from the 1980s to the present, this chapter will describe in particular Singapore's strategy with regard to its two immediate neighbors, Malaysia and Indonesia, and the two major/external powers—the United States and China. These are the four most important relationships. The chapter will also discuss the decision-making process.

In chapter 11, Pongphisoot Busbarat analyzes the GS of Thailand. The chapter examines the influence of Thailand's self-conception based on a historical understanding that Thailand is a pivotal state in Southeast Asia. This national self-conception informs Thailand's long-term strategy that aims to build and maintain its leading role in the region, especially in mainland Southeast Asia. This regional aspiration underpins Thailand's advocacy for regional development initiatives in which Thailand can play a central role. This strategy is shared across political spectra within Thai politics. As a result Thai policymakers tend to opt for engaging various external powers to participate in regional platforms, particularly those in which it designates itself as a key coordinator. In the context of regional power competition between China and the US, this strategy appears to be a major policy preference for Thailand to enmesh both powers into different types of cooperation. While this strategy aims to maintain the regional balance of power, it also helps preserve Thailand's leading role in the region. Therefore analyzing Thailand's regional aspiration offers a *longue durée* perspective on how the GS of Thailand is built, executed, and maintained.

In chapter 12, Dang Cam Tu analyzes the GS of Vietnam. The chapter examines the international and domestic dimensions of Vietnam's foreign policy formulation and implementation during the country's period of comprehensive reform (known as Doi Moi) that started in the early 1980s. While there is no formally-labeled GS in Vietnam, Hanoi's strategic responses to the contingencies of the domestic and external environment over the last thirty years through its integrated scheme of foreign policy interests, objectives, principles, tools, and resources suggests that it has made sense of external relations in grand strategic terms and employed what amounts to a GS for the purpose of ensuring its security and maximizing its interests. External factors informing Vietnam's foreign policy are largely associated with global and regional political, security, and economic changes and trends after the Cold War. They include strategies and relations of major powers, particularly China and the US; ASEAN's role in the emerging regional architecture; the prevalence of an East Asian model of economic development; the growth of globalization and regionalism; as well as traditional and nontraditional security challenges. Domestic factors include the need to shore up the legitimacy and leadership of the Communist Party of Vietnam, the new foreign policy thinking informed by a new worldview, and a greater role for diplomacy in the pursuit of national interests. These factors bring about a GS that is guided by the principles of independence, strategic autonomy, "being a friend to all and enemy to none," and an increasing sense of responsibility and credibility; prioritization of relations with neighboring countries and big powers; extensive and comprehensive international integration; and greater activism in multilateral arrangements, especially ASEAN and the

UN. The bottom line is that the foreign policy of Vietnam since the 1980s has been greatly influenced by the classical concept that considers diplomacy as the first line of defense and by the ability of policymakers in Hanoi to mobilize domestic resources and exploit the opportunities that external conditions have presented.

In the concluding chapter, Ramon Pacheco Pardo analyzes the findings of the previous twelve chapters using a comparative approach. The analysis will be guided by two tables. The first table will include the external factors affecting GS in each of the twelve powers analyzed, categorized according to the three dimensions outlined in this chapter. The second table will include the domestic factors in each of the cases, following from the five categories introduced in this chapter as well.

NOTES

We would like to thank three anonymous reviewers for their comments and suggestions about the whole edited volume. The opinions and characterizations in this piece are those of the author and do not necessarily represent those of the US government.

1. Throughout the edited volume, contributors referring to Taiwan in their chapters label it in accordance with their preferences and exercising their academic freedom. This should not be understood as necessarily representing the views of the US government.
2. IISS, *The Military Balance* (London: Routledge, 2020).
3. United Nations Strategic Division, *National Accounts—Analysis of Main Aggregates (AMA)* (2020), https://unstats.un.org/unsd/snaama
4. Balzacq, Thierry, Peter Dombrowski, and Simon Reich (eds.), *Comparative Grand Strategy: A Framework and Cases* (Oxford University Press, 2019); Hitchcock, William I., Melvyn P. Leffler, and Jeffrey W. Legro (eds.), *Shaper Nations: Strategies for a Changing World* (Harvard University Press, 2016); Taliaferro, Jeffrey W., Norrin M. Ripsman, and Steven E. Lobell (eds.), *The Challenge of Grand Strategy: The Great Powers and the Broken Balance Between the Wars* (Cambridge University Press, 2012).
5. Acharya, Amitav, and Barry Buzan, "Why Is There No Non-Western International Relations Theory? An Introduction," *International Relations of the Asia-Pacific* 7:3 (2007), 287–312; Bilgin, Pinar, and L.H.M. Ling, 'Transcultural Asia: Unlearning Colonial/Imperial Power Relations', *Perceptions: Journal of International Affairs* 19, no. 1 (2014): 1–8; Eun, Yong-Soo, "Opening Up the Debate over 'Non-Western' International Relations," *Politics* 39, no. 1 (2019): 4–17; Hutchings, Kim, 'Dialogue Between Whom? The Role of the West/Non-West Distinction in Promoting Global Dialogue in IR," *Millennium: Journal of International Studies* 39, no. 3 (2011): 639–47; Tickner, Arlene B., and Karen Smith (eds.), *International Relations from the Global South: World of Difference* (Routledge, 2020).
6. Art, Robert J., *A Grand Strategy for America* (Cornell University Press, 2003); Art, Robert J., *America's Grand Strategy and World Politics* (Routledge, 2009); Brands, Hal, *American Grand Strategy in the Age of Trump* (Brookings Institution Press, 2018); Brands, Hal, *What Good Is Grand Strategy? Power and Purpose in American Statecraft from*

Harry S. Truman to George W. Bush (Cornell University Press, 2014); Green, Michael, *By More than Providence: Grand Strategy and American Power in the Asia Pacific Since 1873* (Columbia University Press, 2019); Ikenberry, G. John, *Liberal Leviathan: The Origins, Crisis, and Transformations of American World Order* (Princeton University Press, 2011); Layne, Christopher, *The Peace of Illusions: American Grand Strategy from 1940 to the Present* (Cornell University Press, 2007); Lofflmann, Georg, *American Grand Strategy Under Obama: Competing Discourses* (Edinburgh University Press, 2017); Posen, Barry R., *Restraint: A New Foundation for U.S. Grand Strategy* (Cornell University Press, 2014); Selden, Zachary, *Alignment, Alliance, and American Grand Strategy* (University of Michigan Press, 2016); Thrall, A. Trevor, and Benjamin H. Friedman, *US Grand Strategy in the 21st Century: The Case for Restraint* (Routledge, 2018).
7. Danner, Lukas K., *China's Grand Strategy: Contradictory Foreign Policy?* (Palgrave Macmillan, 2018); Hyer, Eric, *The Pragmatic Dragon: China's Grand Strategy and Boundary Settlements* (UBC Press, 2015); Goldstein, Avery, *Rising to the Challenge: China's Grand Strategy and International Security* (Stanford University Press, 2005); Swaine, Michael D., and Ashley J. Tellis, *Interpreting China's Grand Strategy: Past, Present, and Future* (Rand Corporation, 2000); Ye, Zicheng, *Inside China's Grand Strategy: The Perspective from the People's Republic* (The University Press of Kentucky, 2011).
8. Balzacq, Dombrowski, and Reich, *Comparative Grand Strategy*; Hitchcock, Leffler, and Legro, *Shaper Nations*.
9. Samuels, Richard J., *Securing Japan: Tokyo's Grand Strategy and the Future of East Asia* (Cornell University Press, 2011).
10. More recently, one of the authors also published a monograph on South Korea's grand strategy: Pacheco Parod, Ramon, *South Korea's Grand Strategy: Making Its Own Destiny* (Columbia University Press, 2023).
11. Balzacq, Thierry, and Ronald R. Krebs, "The Enduring Appeal of Grand Strategy," in Balzacq, Thierry, and Ronald R. Krebs (eds.), *The Oxford Handbook of Grand Strategy* (Oxford University Press, 2021), 1.
12. Balzacq and Krebs, "Enduring Appeal," 3–4.
13. Strachan, Hew, "The Lost Meaning of Strategy," *Survival* 47, no. 3 (2005): 33–54.
14. Liddell Hart, Basil Henry, *Strategy: The Indirect Approach*, 3rd ed. (Faber and Faber, 1954).
15. Silove, Nina, "Beyond the Buzzword: The Three Meanings of 'Grand Strategy'," *Security Studies* 27, no. 1 (2018): 27.
16. Silove, "Beyond the Buzzword."
17. Kennedy, Paul M., "Grand Strategy in War and Peace: Toward a Broader Definition," in Kennedy, Paul M. (ed.), *Grand Strategies in War and Peace* (Yale University Press, 1991), 4.
18. Posen, Barry R., *The Sources of Military Doctrine: France, Germany, and Britain Between the World Wars* (Cornell University Press, 1984), 13.
19. Silove, "Beyond the Buzzword," 31.
20. Balzacq, Dombrowski, and Reich, *Comparative Grand Strategy*, 6.
21. Art, *A Grand Strategy for America*.
22. Balzacq, Dombrowski, and Reich, *Comparative Grand Strategy*, 7.
23. Pinker, Steven, *The Better Angels of Our Nature: Why Violence Has Declined* (Viking, 2011).
24. Posen, *Restraint: A New Foundation for U.S. Grand Strategy*.
25. Brands, *What Good Is Grand Strategy?*

26. Martel, William C., *Grand Strategy in Theory and Practice: The Need for an Effective America Foreign Policy* (Cambridge University Press, 2015).
27. Balzacq, Dombrowski and Reich, *Comparative Grand Strategy*, 7.
28. Pacheco Pardo, Ramon, and Jeffrey Reeves (eds.), *Non-Traditional Security in East Asia: A Regime Approach* (Imperial College Press, 2016).
29. Silove, "Beyond the Buzzword."
30. Silove, "Beyond the Buzzword,"39.
31. Martel, *Grand Strategy in Theory and Practice.*
32. Luttwak, Edward, *The Grand Strategy of the Byzantine Empire* (Harvard University Press, 2009).
33. Gray, Colin S., "Strategic Culture as Context: The First Generation Strikes Back," *Review of International Studies* 25, no. 1 (1999): 49–69.
34. Balzacq, Dombrowski, and Reich, *Comparative Grand Strategy*, 9.
35. Balzacq, Dombrowski, and Reich, *Comparative Grand Strategy*, 8.
36. Balzacq, Dombrowski, and Reich, *Comparative Grand Strategy*, 9.
37. Hitchcock, Leffler, and Legro, *Shaper Nations*; Kennedy, "Grand Strategy in War and Peace"; Taliaferro, Ripsman, and Lobell, *The Challenge of Grand Strategy*.
38. Balzacq, Dombrowski, and Reich, *Comparative Grand Strategy*, 15–16.
39. Balzacq, Dombrowski, and Reich, *Comparative Grand Strategy*, 8.
40. Balzacq, Dombrowski, and Reich, *Comparative Grand Strategy*, 8.
41. Balzacq, Dombrowski, and Reich, *Comparative Grand Strategy*, 8.
42. Buzan, Barry, and Ole Waever, *Regions and Powers: The Structure of International Security* (Cambridge University Press, 2009).
43. Balzacq, Dombrowski, and Reich, *Comparative Grand Strategy*, 15.
44. Allison, Graham T., *Essence of Decision: Explaining the Cuban Missile Crisis* (Little, Brown, 1971).
45. Rosenau, James N., *Along the Domestic-Foreign Frontier: Exploring Governance in a Turbulent World* (Cambridge University Press, 1997).
46. Taliaferro, Jeffrey W., Steven E. Lobell, and Norrin M. Ripsman, "Introduction: Neoclassical Realism, the State, and Foreign Policy," in Lobell, Steven E., Norrin M. Ripsman, and Jeffrey W. Taliaferro, Jeffrey (eds.), *Neoclassical Realism, the State, and Foreign Policy* (Cambridge University Press, 2012), 1–41.
47. Balzacq, Dombrowski, and Reich, *Comparative Grand Strategy*, 15–16.
48. Balzacq, Dombrowski, and Reich, *Comparative Grand Strategy*, 16.
49. Balzacq, Dombrowski, and Reich, *Comparative Grand Strategy*, 16.
50. Center for Systemic Peace, *The Polity Project* (2020), https://www.systemicpeace.org/polityproject.html
51. World Bank, *The World by Income and Region* (2020), https://datatopics.worldbank.org/world-development-indicators/the-world-by-income-and-region.html
52. Fisher, Max, "A Revealing Map of the Most and Least Ethnically Diverse Countries," *The Washington Post*, 16 May 2013.

PART I

Northeast Asia

CHAPTER 1

China

Ketian Zhang

China's grand strategy has always been of theoretical and empirical interest to both academics and scholars alike.[1]

As a rising power, China's grand strategy intrigues scholars of international relations. Are rising powers' grand strategies similar to or different from hegemons'? How is China's grand strategy similar to or different from those of other rising powers in history? Can China's grand strategy tell us anything about the future trajectory of a rising power?

Analyzing China's grand strategy is important also due to its real-world significance. Changes or continuities in China's grand strategy might be crucial in predicting degrees of peace and stability in the Asia-Pacific region. Analyzing Chinese grand strategy is particularly critical given the current speculation in the media about China's present-day behavior, which believes that China is embracing a new brand of aggressive diplomacy, especially during COVID-19.[2] Yet, it remains to be seen whether China's grand strategy has changed drastically or not during the Xi Jinping era.

This chapter therefore describes and analyzes China's grand strategy during the period of its reform and opening-up eras. It specifically seeks to answer two questions: what is China's grand strategy, and what factors affect China's grand strategy? In line with other chapters in this book, grand strategy is conceptualized as a means-ends chain, that is, the use of comprehensive means of statecraft to achieve a set of priorities laid out by the state.

Using primary Chinese-language sources such as Chinese government documents and reports as well as speeches from Chinese leaders, some of which are internal, I argue that China's grand strategy employs the use of diplomatic, economic, gray-zone, and military means to ensure China's core and important interests. China's grand strategy is driven by both internal and external factors. Regarding external factors, changes in the international system and China's perception of its security environment significantly affect China's calculation of the likelihood of major conflicts. Specifically, China pays close attention to the capability and behavior of the United States, the current hegemon. As for domestic factors, China prioritizes economic development and therefore takes economic costs and benefits into consideration when devising its grand strategy. The survival of the Chinese Communist Party—regime legitimacy—is also a core concern driving Chinese grand strategy. Despite leadership style differences, Xi Jinping's China is similarly affected by the aforementioned factors. The content and operationalization of China's grand strategy have remained stable. In short, there is more continuity than there is change.

In the upcoming section, I describe China's strategic priorities—the "ends" part of China's grand strategy. I then turn toward analyzing the external and internal factors that influence China's grand strategy. The subsequent section explores how China implements its grand strategy, i.e., the "means" component to its grand strategy. The final section of this chapter concludes by discussing whether there were any changes to China's grand strategy in the period following COVID-19.

STRATEGIC PRIORITIES

China has a clear set of priorities and an interest hierarchy, coined as "core interests" and "important national interests." These priorities were made explicit by then Chinese State Councilor Dai Bingguo in 2010, who stated officially that China's core interests including, first, regime security, including the Chinese Communist Party's (CCP) rule second, territorial integrity and security and, third, continuous economic and social development (singling out Taiwan as a core interest).[3] These rights, according to Dai, are inalienable and shall not be encroached upon.[4] This hierarchy of China's national interests remained unchanged even after Xi Jinping came to power.

Regime Security

As an authoritarian state, China's most important priority has been for its leaders to maintain the power of the CCP, which has remained a priority even throughout the reform and opening-up era of the post-1978 period. During the 13th CCP Party Congress in 1987, Deng Xiaoping noted that China must adhere to the "four basic principles," with the core being "upholding the CCP's rule" (*hexin shi jianchi dangde lingdao*).[5] Deng repeatedly emphasized that "[maintaining] stability trumps everything," which meant the stable rule of the CCP and its regime security.

Deng's successors, including Xi Jinping, followed his step and emphasis on regime security. Jiang Zemin, Hu Jintao, and Xi Jinping all explicitly stated that China should never give up on its four basic principles.[6] China's annual government work reports also reflect such prioritization.[7] As such, regime security is the most pressing concern among the three strategic priorities, suggesting that authoritarian states such as China might prioritize regime security over external security.

Sovereignty

Territorial sovereignty, issues related to Taiwan, and issues related to Tibet constitute the core or most important national interests in China, which include national security as well as internal regime stability. The first official reference to Taiwan as among China's core interests appeared in the report of a meeting between Foreign Minister Tang Jiaxuan and US Secretary of State Colin Powell on 19 January 2003.[8] In a previously internal speech made by President Hu Jintao—on the international situation and foreign affairs—during the Central Foreign Affairs Conference (*zhongyang waishi huiyi*) in August 2006, Hu also reaffirmed Taiwan as one of China's core interests.[9]

Of course Taiwan has, for a long time, been the single most important foreign policy issue for China. For example, Chinese paramount leader Deng Xiaoping stated to former US president Ford on 23 March 1981 that "the Taiwan issue" was the only issue between the United States and China and similarly told US Secretary of State Haig on June 16, 1981, that "the Taiwan issue" such as arms sales was one of China's most critical policies, namely, national unification (*sheji dao zhongguo zuida de zhengce zhiyi*).[10]

The first official reference to Tibet as one of China's core interests appeared when Vice President Zeng Qinghong stated on April 23, 2006, that Tibet involved China's core interests.[11] Jeffrey Bader, former senior director for Asian affairs on the National Security Council during the Obama administration, also noted that in the first few months of the Obama administration in 2009, the Chinese informed the United States of their "core concerns," namely, their claimed sovereignty over Taiwan and Tibet.[12]

Chinese leaders explicitly affirm that Taiwan and Tibet are their core interests. While China has been vague about whether the South and East

China Sea maritime territorial disputes concern its core interests, they do not deny that these maritime disputes are of importance to their national security interests.[13]

Therefore, if China were to be involved in militarized conflicts at all, it is most likely that these three sets of issues would constitute a majority of coercion by China. Meanwhile Taiwan and Tibet are explicitly stated as China's core interests, whereas any individual territorial dispute—be it maritime or land-based—is not explicitly stated in Chinese official documents as a core interest.

Tibet and particularly Taiwan are therefore high-stake issues, and the stakes over issues such as territorial disputes are lower when compared with that of Taiwan and Tibet. As President Hu Jintao stated during the internal Central Foreign Affairs Conference in August 2006, it is necessary to differentiate between "core interests" and "important interests"—core interests should be defended with resolution and without compromise, whereas important interests leave room for maneuver, and China should strive to get the best results.[14]

More recently, President Xi Jinping coined Taiwan as the "core of the core interests."[15] China has repeatedly demonstrated that it will not shy away from using military coercion when it comes to tackling cross-Strait issues, such as that of US leaders' visits to Taiwan.[16]

Economic and Social Development

Economic development has been the focus of China's grand strategy during the reform and opening-up period after 1978.

In 1987 Deng Xiaoping stated that China should make "economic development the focus" (*yi jingji jianshe weizhongxin*), serving as a guiding principle for subsequent Chinese leaders.[17] Other key official documents, for example, such as China's annual government work report, also suggests the centrality of economic development in China's overall strategy, despite the conventional wisdom in grand strategy studies that external security tends to be the focus or priority of states.[18] In the 1988 government work report, it was stated that "national defence should take into account the overall framework of economic development" and should be "subsumed in the overall planning of national economic and social development."[19]

To summarize, China's strategic priorities constitute what Xi Jinping calls "comprehensive national security," with "political" or regime security being the key.[20] It demonstrates that China has a clear interest hierarchy, external security is not as crucial as regime security, and that China views grand strategy in a comprehensive manner, conceptualizing political and economic security as part of it. Of course, China has other national interests and foreign policy goals, including ensuring a stable Korean Peninsula, tackling nontraditional security issues such as counterterrorism and climate change, and engaging in multilateralism.

These foreign policy objectives, however, are not ranked as high as its three strategic priorities. The third and fourth sections of this chapter will examine the external and internal factors that drive China's grand strategy to focus on regime security, sovereignty, and economic development in greater detail.

EXTERNAL FACTORS

Changes in the international system and China's perception of its security environment significantly affect its speculation of major conflicts, which in turn affects China's grand strategic priorities and the ends it uses to achieve them. The following section discusses how third-party actors, threats and opportunities from international security and economic systems, along with the various types of conflicts that affect its grand strategic calculations.

Third-Party Actors

China pays close attention to the capability and behavior of the United States, the current hegemon. For example, not only does the Chinese Ministry of Foreign Affairs track the overall external environment, but it also makes detailed assessments of the United States, particularly regarding its posture and capability in the Asia-Pacific region. One case study on China's use of coercion in the South China Sea (a kind of means toward its grand strategic ends) indicates that the Chinese foreign ministry tracks US national security documents and analyzes the level of US commitment and capability in Southeast Asia.[21]

In the 1990s China viewed the United States to have reduced its resources in Southeast Asia, and because of the ensuing geopolitical vacuum, China used military coercion more than nonmilitary coercion.[22] Beginning in the 2000s, however, the foreign ministry noted that the United States began to increase its resources and commitment in the Asia-Pacific region. For fear of a militarized conflict with the United States, Chinese coercion in the South China Sea, therefore, tends to be nonmilitarized or gray-zone.[23] China's national defense white papers also note increased US presence and strengthened alliances in the Asia-Pacific region.[24]

Another case study involves China's military strategy, a crucial component of the "means" aspect to China's grand strategy. Taylor Fravel argues that China shifted its military strategic guideline in 1993, instructing the People's Liberation Army (PLA) to fight "local wars under modern high technology conditions," underscoring the quality, not quantity, of military modernization.[25]

This shift arose due to two critical factors: one was the changing international security landscape making small- and medium-sized local conflicts instead of total wars, and the other was changes in the nature of warfare, with the US performance in the Gulf War in the early 1990s being a wakeup call for Chinese leaders.[26] In other words China watches US behavior closely and responds in kind by adapting components of its grand strategy to the changing international environment as well as US behavior.

Subsequently, official Chinese documents track China's external environment on an annual basis through what Deng calls the "international situation." For example, *China's Foreign Affairs,* a book-length document published annually by the Chinese Ministry of Foreign Affairs, makes assessments about the international system, including an annual analysis on whether the international system is heading toward multipolarity or moving back to US hegemony.[27] Similarly China's biannual national defense white paper tracks changes in the international system as well as the Asia-Pacific region.[28] As noted in the previous section, sovereignty is one of China's grand strategic objectives. Changing assessments over China's external environments and its US resolve also affect the means China uses to respond to sovereignty issues.

Threats and Opportunities

As mentioned previously, the US plays a key role in China's grand strategic calculation, because it poses significant threats to China's national security, which official Chinese documents coin as "the US hegemony."

However, it is not just the international security landscape but also the global economic system, China's bilateral economic relations with the United States, and new nontraditional security threats that affect China's grand strategy, providing both threats and opportunities. Some prime examples include the 2008 global financial crisis, the US-China trade war, and the COVID-19 pandemic. These external economic and public health factors heightened China's perception of economic vulnerability, especially the dependence on external markets and technology, thereby having an impact on the means China utilizes to achieve its grand strategic priorities.

For a long time since China began reform and opening in 1978, the focus had been on exporting, foreign direct investment, and foreign technology transfer. China needed Organisation for Economic Co-operation and Development (OECD) countries, especially the United States, for their markets, capital, and advanced technology. At times China even had to sacrifice a tough stance on Taiwan, one of the core-interest issues, for a smoother economic relationship with the United States. For instance, the United States sold 150 F-16 jet fighters to Taiwan, a significant breach from its past behavior, which China viewed as adversely threatening its core interest concerning Taiwan. When contemplating a proper response to US arms sales in 1992, Deng Xiaoping endorsed the foreign ministry report that "China needed to give priority to economic interests" and that if China retaliated with trade sanctions, "a cycle of mutual retaliation could unleash a trade war in which *China would lose most*." The report concluded that "China should *do everything it could to avoid the deterioration of Sino-U.S. economic relations*."[29]

In more recent years, however, changes in the international economic landscape forced China to make adjustments to the means to achieve economic development. One critical event was the 2008 global financial crisis, which had an adverse impact on China's exports—a key driver to China's economic development. In response to the global economic downturn, China began to strive for transitioning its economic growth mode from export oriented to domestic consumption (*neixu*), as indicated by China's annual government work reports. Prior government work reports in the post-1978 period emphasized increasing exports, attracting foreign direct investment, and broadening external markets. The 2009 Chinese government work report was the first time when "expanding domestic consumption" was emphasized and made the "first priority," and subsequent reports continued to stress domestic consumption.[30]

This trend stressing domestic consumption heightened in the Xi Jinping regime, primarily because of the trade war between China and the United States as well as the shock from COVID-19. The former convinced Chinese leaders of the potential danger of depending too much on the United States. The latter further highlighted the vulnerability of a globalized production and supply chain that China is part of, since COVID-19 limited both economic growth and the exchange of goods and services across borders. Therefore in 2020 Xi Jinping raised the notion of a dual circulation development model—internal and external circulation—with internal circulation being the priority (*guonei daxunhuan wei zhuti, guonei guoji shuangxunhuan*), stating explicitly that the rationale had to do with COVID-19, protectionism from the United States, and a global economic recession.[31] By internal circulation, Xi means domestic-oriented consumption and production. Admittedly, Xi has not given up on external circulation—external trade and financial relations—yet the focus is internal circulation while ensuring supply chain security (*chanyelian renxing he anquan shuiping*).[32] Therefore changes in the international political economic environment shapes how China pursues economic growth, which is one of the major grand strategic objectives as examined in the previous section.

Types of Conflicts

Related to the threats from the United States and changes in the international security landscape, the types of conflicts affect China's defense posture and strategic prioritization. During the Cold War period and when Mao Zedong was China's leader, the bipolar international system, especially the US-Soviet rivalry, influenced China's grand strategic thinking. China emphasized forming coalitions or alliances against a principal adversary, with the 1950s focusing on threats from the United States and the 1960s the threats from the Soviet Union.[33] China's strategic assessment viewed the external environment as harsh and conflict-prone due to the US-Soviet competition. Viewing a world war as unavoidable, China's grand strategy focused on national defense against external conflicts. The "three-line" defense was one prime example.[34] The focus of industrial development was geared toward a defense build-up.

Toward the end of the Cold War, however, the détente between the Soviet Union and the United States significantly changed Chinese leaders' assessment of China's external environment and the likelihood of conflict. In 1984 Deng Xiaoping noted that "new factors preventing a world war have been on the rise."[35] Deng added in 1985 and 1987 respectively that it was possible to avoid a world war and that the general "international situation" (*guoji xingshi*) made long-term peace possible.[36] Therefore China's strategic prioritization shifted to focusing more on economic development, which leads to the guideline that "economic development is the first priority," as discussed in the previous section. Although national defense was still one of the strategic priorities, China's military guideline changed in accordance with the more relaxed external environment, which focused on modernization during peacetime instead of war-time preparation while making an impressive one-million-person reduction of the military.[37]

In short China assesses the international political environment carefully. It especially pays attention to US policies and postures in the Asia-Pacific region, using these assessments to guide its grand strategy in terms of both specific means and the prioritization of ends.

INTERNAL FACTORS

Internal factors also affect China's grand strategy, including national values, the institutional process, and material resources.

National Values

Since China is a single-party authoritarian system, the national value, at the core, really is the CCP's value. Although some might indicate that Xi's slogans such as "national rejuvenation" or "the China dream" constitutes an important Chinese national value, these slogans are not what the CCP values the most. Instead the most critical factor is Chinese leaders' concern about regime security, which emphasizes maintaining internal stability (*wei-wen*). As Bates Gill notes, although the CCP also seeks to "tell China's story well" at the international stage and to build up its "international narrative (or discourse) power," the legitimacy of the CCP remains the most crucial driving factor of China's foreign policy.[38] In other words all of China's grand strategic means and ends are geared toward ensuring the survival and domestic legitimacy of the CCP.

As a single-party authoritarian regime, the CCP always needs to maintain regime legitimacy. The concern for internal regime security, however, was not as pressing prior to the 1989 Tiananmen incident and the collapse of the Soviet Union in 1991. Before 1989 central Chinese government documents rarely mentioned "stability" (*wending*); after 1989, however, key Chinese leaders have begun to drastically increase the emphasis on "social stability" (*shehui wending*).[39] The change was due to the Tiananmen incident. The frequency of key CCP documents mentioning stability became ever higher in the 2000s.[40]

Not only was the lesson from the Tiananmen incident everlasting, but the collapse of the Soviet Union also continues to remind CCP leaders of the importance of regime legitimacy. Xi Jinping reportedly told CCP officials internally in 2012 that China should continue to learn the profound lesson from the collapse of the Soviet Union, emphasizing regime legitimacy.[41] Xi's speeches on "comprehensive national security" continue to place political security (*zhengzhi anquan*) as the first priority.[42] Just recently, Minister of Public Security Zhao Kezhi told the provincial police chiefs in a meeting in January 2021 to prioritize security and social stability in their work this year, making sure all the major events will go well to celebrate the 100th anniversary of the CCP.[43] Therefore domestic regime legitimacy has a crucial impact on the content of China's grand strategy. Despite increasing China's global footprint and utilizing various foreign policy tools, China at the current stage is still more internally focused.

Institutional Process

Given China's authoritarian political system, the decision-making regarding its grand strategy is highly controlled at the central leadership level. The paramount leader, the CCP's chairman, has the greatest power over grand strategic decisions. For example, as mentioned in the previous sections, it was the Chinese leader Deng Xiaoping that made the decision to focus on maintaining stable economic relations with the United States in 1992 despite US weapons sales to Taiwan. It was also Xi Jinping that made the key decision to focus on internal transition in response to the US-China trade conflicts and COVID-19.

Material Resources: Economic Development as a Driving Factor

Concerns about regime legitimacy also explain why China prioritizes economic development. As Avery Goldstein notes, "in charge of a developmental state whose legitimacy depends in large measure on sustaining economic growth and improving the people's living standards, no leader of the CCP is likely to embrace foreign policies that he thinks might jeopardize the country's prosperity."[44] This focus on economic development over national defense has to do with regime security being the core of the three strategic priorities; for an authoritarian state such as China, if its economy stagnates, there is a greater risk of social instability, which in turn might endanger the stable rule of the CCP. Moreover, without a growing economy, the defense budget will be negatively affected, too. Speech evidence from Chinese presidents in the post-Cold War era also confirmed the centrality of economic development in China's grand strategy, as shown in Table 1.1.

Table 1.1. Speeches of Chinese Leaders in the Post-Cold War Period

Leader	Date of Speech	Content of Speech
Deng Xiaoping	18 January–21 February 1992[45]	The key is economic development.
Jiang Zemin	12 October 1992[46]	The Party should uphold the basic line and continue to uphold economic development as the focus (*jixu zhuazhu jingji jianshe zhege zhongxin*).
	13 January 1993[47]	We need to concentrate our effort on developing our national economy.
	12 July 1993[48]	The fundamental purpose of our foreign policy is to serve our reform and economic development.
	21 July 1998[49]	Regarding the fundamental mission of socialism, we raised the notion of focusing on economic development (*yi jingji jianshe weizhongxin*).
	18 December 1998[50]	Regardless of what we may be facing, economic development as the focus should not be shaken (*buneng dongyao heyingxiang jingji jianshe zhege zhongxin*).
	11 October 2000[51]	Development is the way to go (*fazhan shi yingdaoli*). Our important lesson is that regardless of what happens and as long as it is not a large-scale foreign invasion, we must always uphold economic development as the focus.
	2 April 2001[52]	The key is to uphold economic development as the focus.
	25 February 2002[53]	Uphold economic development as the focus. Development is the way to go.
	14 October 2002[54]	Nowadays, many leaders of developing countries have realized that economic and social development is the first and foremost mission of regime legitimacy and national development (*gaohao jingjishehui fazhan shi zhizheng xingguo de shouyao renwu*).
	8 November 2002[55]	The fundamental is to uphold economic development as the focus.
Hu Jintao	24 July 2000[56]	Prioritizing the economy and focusing on development has become a worldwide trend (*jingji youxian fazhan weizhong yijing chengwei dangjin shijie chaoliu*).

(*continued*)

Table 1.1 (*continued*)

Leader	Date of Speech	Content of Speech
	2 September 2002[57]	We must concentrate our effort on doing well domestically, especially in economic development. Development is the "first priority" for Party legitimacy, and national development and development here means economic development as the focus (*fazhan shi zhizheng xingguo de diyi yaowu*).
	25 August 2003[58]	Our nation currently is and will for a long time remain in the initial stage of socialism. This basic national condition determines that we must keep development as the "first priority" for Party legitimacy and national development. The fundamental mission of foreign policy is to serve economic development.
	20 August 2006[59]	Foreign affairs conduct must uphold economic development as the focus (*waishi gongzuo bixu jianchi jingji jianshe weizhongxin*). The primary national interests are development interest and security interest (*fazhan liyi he anquan liyi*). Development is the foundation for security.
	2 March 2007[60]	We must keep growth as the "first priority" for Party legitimacy and national development. We must uphold economic development as the focus.
	17 December 2007[61]	We must always remember that the key to solving all of China's problems is development (*fazhan shi jiejue zhongguo suoyou wenti de guanjian*). We must keep development as the "first priority" for Party legitimacy and national development. We must uphold economic growth as the focus.
	19 September 2008[62]	We should further keep development as the "first priority" for Party legitimacy and national development.
	17 July 2009[63]	Our primary mission in the current stage is to keep development as the "first priority" for Party legitimacy and national development. We must resolutely uphold economic development as the focus.
	18 October 2010[64]	We must uphold development, the "first priority."

Table 1.1

Leader	Date of Speech	Content of Speech
	8 November 2012[65]	We must firmly uphold economic development as the focus.
Xi Jinping	Post-2012[66]	We must always uphold economic development as the focus.
	Post-2012[67]	We must uphold economic development as the focus. Development is the key and foundation to solving all problems in China. We must further keep development as the "first priority" for Party legitimacy and national development.
	17 November 2012[68]	We must uphold economic development as the focus.
	12 November 2013[69]	Economic development is still the central work for the Party.
	27 March 2013[70]	We will continue to keep development as the "first priority" and economic development as the focus.
	11 January 2021[71]	We must correctly manage the relationship between independence and opening up and cooperation (*kaifang hezuo*). We must keep opening up while ensuring security.
	21 July 2024[72]	We must emphasize the coordination between development and security (*tongchou anquan he fazhan*). National security is the important basis for China's modernization.

In other words, subsequent Chinese presidents Jiang Zemin, Hu Jintao, and Xi Jinping have been following Deng's guiding principle. Despite media claims that Xi acts differently, it is clear from the primary evidence given previously that China's grand strategy has been stable and demonstrates continuity in prioritizing economic development.

In short, China's grand strategy reflects the cautious calculation from Chinese leaders regarding their external and internal environments. As Xi Jinping himself reasoned in an internal speech: "We are a large country. We must not make mistakes on fundamental issues. If we do, it will be irremediable."[73]

OPERATIONALIZATION OF GRAND STRATEGY

The result is a grand strategy whose goals are in tension with one another. On the one hand, China needs to create a stable international environment for its economic development, which dictates China to use means such as economic inducement and bilateral and multilateral diplomacy. On the other hand, the need to demonstrate that China is resolved to defend China's national security, especially core interests on sovereignty such as Taiwan, leads China to use negative means of statecraft such as coercion. The following passages detail China's combination of "carrots and sticks" when implementing its grand strategy, including diplomatic, economic, gray-zone, and military statecraft.

Carrots: Reassurance Tactics

The literature on power transition tends to predict China's behavior as a rising power to be aggressive.[74] A rising power, however, needs to send reassurance signals while it is still in the process of rising. According to Michael Glosny, a rising power can minimize the severity of the balancing response in two ways: preventing the other powers from concluding that the rising power is a threat and "using its power to provide them benefits and protect their interests."[75] China's logic of using reassurance tactics follows Glosny's arguments: since two of the strategic priorities are regime security and economic development, China needs a peaceful external environment to facilitate its economic growth. Its tactics include diplomatic, economic, and military statecraft.

Diplomatically, China has been using several policies to reduce tension with its neighbors and to improve its international image. China adopted the "good neighbor" policy during the Hu Jintao administration. It began to improve bilateral relationships and establish various levels of "partnership" to "facilitate economic and security coordination and to offset the United States' system of regional alliances," with one prime example being the Treaty of Good-Neighbourliness and Friendly Cooperation that China signed with Russia in 2001.[76] Multilaterally, China began to engage ASEAN and helped initiate the ASEAN +3 mechanism, a series of yearly meetings among the ten ASEAN countries plus China, Japan, and South Korea.[77] In Central Asia, meanwhile, China led the establishment of the region's first multilateral group, the Shanghai Cooperation Organization, which was founded to settle long-standing territorial disputes and to demilitarize borders but now stresses counterterrorism cooperation and regional trade.[78] More recently China helped form the Asian Infrastructure Investment Bank (AIIB), a multilateral development bank focused on developing Asia.[79] China even utilized the latest COVID-19 strain to promote the so-called vaccine diplomacy, distributing Chinese-made vaccines to many developing countries in the world, especially those hard-hit by the pandemic in Africa and Asia.[80]

Economically, China has increased its use of economic statecraft, especially economic inducement, in various regions in the world. For example, to reduce concerns from ASEAN countries about China's entry into the World Trade Organization (WTO) and to expand China's export market, China and ASEAN signed the China-ASEAN Free Trade Free Agreement in 2002.[81] China's global economic presence went beyond Asia. In Latin America, China provided development assistance, including concessional finance, grants, technical assistance, and aid. China became Latin America's second-most important trading partner, second-most important source of Foreign Direct Investment (FDI), and top source of development assistance, having provided more than $141 billion in development.[82] In Africa, China surpassed the United States as Africa's largest trade partner in 2009.[83] China is a destination for 15 to 16 percent of sub-Saharan Africa's exports and the source of 14 to 21 percent of the region's imports.[84] China exports a range of machinery, transportation, communications equipment, as well as manufactured goods to African countries.[85] In the Middle East, China tried to forge stable economic relationships with Middle Eastern countries for access to oil and natural gas. More recently, in addition to improving foreign trade relations via import and export, China initiated the Belt and Road Initiative (BRI) that focused on infrastructure development and cooperation. It is important to note, however, that China's use of economic statecraft, including the BRI, is shaped by its grand strategic priorities. The origin of the BRI, for example, was not the media-portrayed geopolitical competition, but rather domestic challenges for China to continue its economic growth, including decreasing GDP growth rates, poor corporate performance, and industrial overcapacities.[86]

Finally, China also resorts to military diplomacy, despite the conventional wisdom that the Chinese military is reserved only for the use of force. For example, China's national defense white paper noted in 2013 that since 2002, the PLA had held twenty-eight joint exercises and thirty-four joint trainings with more than thirty countries, including counterterrorism as well as exercises involving all service branches.[87] Even in the South China Sea, where China has territorial disputes with some of the ASEAN members, China and ASEAN held the first joint naval exercise in 2018.[88] The United States and China also maintain a stable military-to-military (mil-mil) relationship with bilateral military exchanges and joint exercises. US-China mil-mil dialogues and exchanges include "high-level visits of defence officials, longstanding dialogues, military academic exchanges, and functional exchanges."[89] For instance, amid the US-China trade war, the Chinese and US militaries took part in a joint disaster relief training exercise in Hawaii in November 2019.[90]

Sticks: Coercive and Deterrence Tactics

In addition to reassurance tactics, China also utilizes coercion and deterrence, both of which are negative means of statecraft. By coercion, I mean the use or threats of negative means of statecraft to force the target state to change behavior.

Diplomatically, China has used diplomatic sanctions, which include terminating or pausing senior-level exchanges, temporarily closing consulates, and recalling ambassadors. For example, China sanctioned Norway for awarding the Nobel Peace Prize to Chinese political dissident Liu Xiaobo by pausing senior-level exchanges and denying the Norwegian prime minister a visa to visit China.[91] Of course, Chinese diplomatic sanctions are nothing new. China has been exercising this tool for grand strategic priorities since the 1990s, especially regarding Taiwan. In 1992 China imposed harsh diplomatic sanctions against France by closing the French consulate in Guangzhou, China, over the French weapons sale of 60 Mirage-2000 jet fighters to Taiwan.[92] In 1995 China recalled its ambassador to the United States due to the US State Department granting a visa for then Taiwanese President Lee Teng-hui to visit the United States.[93]

Notable, however, is China's more recent assertive and aggressive public diplomacy in traditional and public media. For instance, in response to the Japanese leader's visit to the Yasukuni shrine, the Chinese ambassador to the United Kingdom, Liu Xiaoming, wrote in an op-ed in Britain's *Daily Telegraph* in early 2014: "If militarism is like the haunting Voldemort of Japan, the Yasukuni shrine in Tokyo is a kind of horcrux, representing the darkest parts of that nation's soul."[94] Voldemort is the antagonist of the popular British novel series *Harry Potter*. More recently, Chinese ministry of foreign affairs spokesperson Zhao Lijian posted unfounded claims on the origins of COVID-19 from the US military on his official Twitter account.[95] Although these public relations tactics on traditional and social media do not appear to have a clear coercive target, they are clearly negative and aggressive.

Economically, China has been resorting to economic sanctions, defined as "instructions by the government to certain actors to withdraw from trade or financial relations so as to force the target to change a foreign policy the coercer dislikes."[96] For example, China used a "banana ban" against the Philippines in 2012 over maritime territorial disputes around the Scarborough Shoal in the South China Sea.[97] China imposed a month-long embargo against Philippine banana exports to China.[98] When French and German leaders met with the Dalai Lama, the Tibetan spiritual leader, China froze Airbus orders and cancelled large-scale contracts with these two countries.[99] It is important to note, however, that China's use of economic sanctions is not a recent phenomenon. China has been utilizing economic sanctions since the Cold War, even when it was a weaker economic power.[100]

Similarly, in 1992 China imposed economic sanctions over French weapons sales to Taiwan. China imposed a ban on French wheat exports to China, awarding a subway bid in China's southern city of Guangzhou to Germany, freezing a French project to build a nuclear power plant in China.[101] This sanctions episode was effective in forcing a foreign policy change in France, yet not all cases of Chinese economic sanctions were successful. William Norris notes that the effectiveness of Chinese sanctions partially depends on whether the state is able to control and direct the behavior of Chinese economic actors.[102] China does not utilize coercion every time an issue threatening its strategic priorities arises. This restraint is due, in large part, to concerns about its dependence on the target state's market or technology and capital supply, especially if the target is the United States.[103] As mentioned in the previous section, however, as China strives to transition from an export-oriented economy to a domestic-consumption-oriented one, China's dependence on foreign markets and supply might lessen in the future, which may in turn suggest that China could be using coercion more frequently.

One interesting kind of statecraft that China has been using more frequently, especially in the post-2000s, is gray-zone coercion. Gray-zone coercion straddles nonmilitary tactics, such as diplomatic and economic sanctions, and military coercion. It is the use of physical violence by government agencies to force the target state to change its behavior.[104] Similar to military coercion, gray-zone coercion inflicts damage on the target state. The difference, however, is that gray-zone coercion utilizes the civilian government agencies to inflict such damage, not the military. China resorts to gray-zone coercion mostly in maritime territorial disputes. For example, China used its maritime surveillance ships to block Philippine naval ships during the 2012 Scarborough Shoal incident.[105] In 2014 China used its coast guard ships to ram Vietnamese vessels during the Sino-Vietnamese standoff over China's Haiyang Shiyou 981 oil rig operating in disputed waters in the Paracel Islands.[106] The rationale for using these civilian law enforcement ships instead of naval ships is to avoid crisis escalation. In particular, China worries that if it uses military coercion against the Philippines, it might cause the United States to respond with military force, given the Philippines is an ally to the United States.[107] Being nonmilitarized, gray-zone coercion allows states to claim plausible deniability: States can deny that they are using military force, thus reducing the likelihood of military escalation triggered by defense treaty commitments.[108] China's use of the so-called "maritime militia" in the South China Sea is the same logic.[109]

Finally, China does use military means of statecraft, including the use of force, coercion, and deterrence. China used actual military force more frequently during the Cold War, especially regarding territorial disputes.[110] In the post-Cold War period, China rarely uses military force directly. The frequency of Chinese military coercion also decreased in the post-Cold War period, with the majority of Chinese military coercion taking place in the 1990s over maritime disputes in the South China Sea as well as China's relations with Taiwan.[111]

Nevertheless China has been utilizing its military for deterrence purposes in accordance with its grand strategic priorities, including regime security and sovereignty. Chinese sources stress that "the armed forces should provide important and powerful guarantees for the consolidation of the party's ruling position."[112] For example, the PLA 27th, 38th, and 65th Group armies are located around Beijing to "defend the capital from attack and to maintain political stability."[113] Externally the Chinese PLA is tasked with defending the state's "sovereignty and maritime rights."[114] For example, the Chinese PLA navy regularly patrols the South and East China Seas. China launched its DF-26 antiship ballistic missiles in the South China Sea as a warning to the United States in August 2020.[115] The army patrols the Sino-Indian land border. Regarding Taiwan, China has short- and medium-range missiles deployed opposite Taiwan in its Fujian province and has equipped the PLA with the more advanced J-20 jet fighters, Type 052-D destroyers, and DF-26 intermediate ballistic missiles.[116] The purpose is mainly deterrence—to deter Taiwan from declaring *de jure* independence—while being prepared for the actual use of force should Taiwan go ahead with formal independence.

As for strategic deterrence, China has been focusing on modernizing the quality of its nuclear weapons instead of quantity, developing a secure second-strike capability by improving the reliability, survivability, and penetrability of its nuclear arsenal.[117] In particular China seeks to make its nuclear arsenal more mobile by more advanced road-mobile intercontinental ballistic missiles (ICBMs), especially through the development of DF-41, a multiple independently targetable reentry vehicle (MIRV)-capable, road-mobile ICBM.[118]

CONCLUSION

In conclusion, this chapter argues that China's grand strategy is a means-ends chain. China has a clear interest hierarchy and a set of strategic priorities: regime security, territorial integrity and security, and continuous economic and social development. China uses a combination of diplomatic, economic, gray-zone, and military means to ensure its core and important interests. China's grand strategy is driven by both internal and external factors. Regarding external factors, changes in the international system and China's perception of its security environment significantly affect China's calculation of the likelihood of major conflicts. China particularly pays close attention to the capability and behavior of the United States, the current hegemon. As for domestic factors, the survival of the Chinese Communist Party—regime legitimacy—is a core concern driving Chinese grand strategy. It is important to note that China's strategic priorities as well as the factors influencing China's grand strategy have not witnessed dramatic shifts in the Xi Jinping regime. In other words, there is consistency and continuity in China's grand strategy in the post-Cold War era.

There are several theoretical and policy implications. First, in contrast to the conventional literature on US grand strategy that focuses on external factors, it is crucial to acknowledge that internal dynamics are highly relevant for authoritarian states such as China and North Korea. Internal security—regime security of the CCP—is of key concern to Chinese leaders. Changes in China's domestic political environment have a profound impact on China's grand strategy.

Relatedly, despite the association between security interests and grand strategy in US-centric literature, internal economic development is an important strategic priority, as seen also in the North Korea chapter. Japan similarly also incorporates economic security as part of its grand strategy—comprehensive security.[119] In fact, when the United States was still a rising power, internal economic development was a critical strategic priority that John Quincy Adams proposed.[120]

Moreover, although China is increasing its global footprint via diplomatic, economic, and military statecraft, China's strategic priorities demonstrate an internally oriented focus: regime security, sovereignty, and economic development. The empirical evidence presented in this chapter does not support media claims that China's goal is to take over the entire world, either through military expansion or exporting its authoritarian model.[121] Despite the media's claims that Xi Jinping's regime is different, China's grand strategy has exhibited relative continuity and stability. It is, therefore, critical to use primary sources and speech evidence to support claims about any state's grand strategy. One cannot make convincing claims about China's grand strategy without utilizing primary Chinese-language documents and sources.

Finally, because China's grand strategic priorities include both economic development and national security, there is an inherent tension. Economic development requires a stable external environment, which dictates China to use reassurance tactics. Defending China's sovereignty, however, requires China to at times resort to coercion. Therefore, what we see is a rising China sending multiple, sometimes conflicting, signals to its external and internal audience.[122] Predicting into the future, however, if COVID-19 proves to be a turning point for China to become more internal-consumption driven, it is possible that China may be less restrained when it comes to using coercive means to achieve its strategic ends in the future.

NOTES

1. Part of this chapter is adapted from Zhang, Ketian, "Bringing the Economy Back In: Economic Development and China's Grand Strategy," *Journal of Indo-Pacific Affairs*, January 2022.
2. Westcott, Ben, and Steven Jiang, "China Is Embracing a New Brand of Foreign Policy. Here's What Wolf Warrior Diplomacy Means," *CNN*, May 29, 2020; Chellaney, Brahma, "China Risks Imperial Overstretch with Post-Pandemic Aggression," *Nikkei Asia*, June 10, 2020.
3. Dai Bingguo, "Zhongguo guowu weiyuan daibingguo: jianchi zou heping fazhan daolu" ["China Should Continue the Path of Peaceful Development"], *Central People's Government of the People's Republic of China*, December 6, 2010, http://www.gov.cn/ldhd/2010-12/06/content_1760381.htm. Dai first expressed the aforementioned written statements verbally in 2009. See Li Jing and Wu Qingcai, *Xinhua News Agency*, July 28, 2009, http://www.chinanews.com/gn/news/2009/07-29/1794984.shtml
4. Dai, "Zhongguo guowu weiyuan daibingguo."
5. Zhan Shu, "Jianchi sixiang jiben yuanze, renheshihou wodoumeiyou dangguobu" [I Have Never Given Up on Holding the Four Basic Principles], *Zhongguo jijjian jiancha bao* [China Rules and Inspection Paper], May 22, 2018.
6. See China's *Renmin Wang* [*People Website*], the official website of the Chinese Communist Party, hereafter *People Website*, "Yige zhongxin, liangge jiben dian" [One centre and two basic points], http://theory.people.com.cn/GB/40557/350432/350699/index.html

7. Chinese State Council, "Annual China's Government Work Report," reports prior to 2013 can be accessed at http://www.gov.cn/2013zfbgjjd/lnzf.htm, reports from 2014–2020 can be accessed at http://www.gov.cn/guowuyuan/2020zfgzbg.htm. I thank my research assistant, Yulin Wu, for compiling and comparing the reports.
8. *People's Daily,* January 21, 2003.
9. Hu Jintao, *Hu Jintao wenxuan [Hu Jintao's Selected Works]* (People's Press, 2016), 510. Hu's speech during this conference was previously not made public.
10. Leng Rong and Wang Zuoling (eds.), *Deng Xiaoping nianpu [Deng Xiaoping's Chronology 1975–1997]* (Zhongyang wenxian chubanshe [Central Documentation Press], 2004), 723, 749.
11. *People's Daily,* April 23, 2006. However, as early as the 1992 PRC white paper on Tibet stated that "there is no room for haggling" on the fundamental principle that "Tibet is an inalienable part of China." See footnote 34 of Swaine, Michael D., "China's Assertive Behaviour Part One: On 'Core Interests," Carnegie Endowment, http://carnegieendowment.org/files/CLM34MS_FINAL.pdf
12. Bader, Jeffrey A., *Obama and China's Rise: An Insider's Account of America's Asia Strategy* (Brookings Institution Press, 2012), 49.
13. Interview, Beijing, January 7, 2015.
14. Hu Jintao, *Hu Jintao's Selected Works,* 519. See also Hu Jintao, *Hu Jintao wenxuan disan juan [Hu Jintao's Selected Works Vol. 3]* (People's Press, 2016), 237.
15. China's Ministry of Foreign Affairs spokesperson, May 2, 2024, https://www.mfa.gov.cn/web/fyrbt_673021/202405/t20240502_11292335.shtml
16. For more information on China's military coercion over cross-Strait relations, see Ketian Zhang, *China's Gambit: The Calculus of Coercion* (Cambridge University Press, 2024).
17. "Deng Xiaoping tongzhi shouxian tichu dangde shisanda quedingle zhetiao jiben Luxian" ["Deng Xiaoping Raised This Basic Principle, and the CCP's 13th Party Congress Confirmed This Principle"], *People Website,* http://theory.people.com.cn/GB/40557/350432/350699/index.html
18. See, for example, Posen, Barry, *Restraint: A New Foundation for U.S. Grand Strategy* (Cornell University Press, 2014).
19. China's State Council, *1988 nian zhengfu gongzuo baogao [Government Work Report of 1988]*, http://www.gov.cn/test/2006-02/16/content_200865.htm
20. Xi Jinping, "Xi Jinping tan zongti guojia anquan" ["Xi Jinping Talks About Comprehensive National Security"], *People Website,* April 14, 2020, http://cpc.people.com.cn/n1/2020/0414/c164113-31673157.html
21. Zhang, "Cautious Bully."
22. Zhang, "Cautious Bully."
23. Zhang, "Cautious Bully."
24. See China's Ministry of National Defense, http://www.mod.gov.cn/regulatory/node_47121.htm. I thank Yulin Wu for the research assistance in compiling the documents.
25. Fravel, *Active Defence.*
26. Fravel, *Active Defence.*
27. See Zhang, Ketian, "Cautious Bully: Reputation, Resolve, and Beijing's Use of Coercion in the South China Sea," *International Security,* 44, no. 1 (2019): 117–59.
28. For China's biannual national defense white papers, see China's Ministry of National Defence, http://www.mod.gov.cn/regulatory/node_47121.htm (accessed January 27, 2021). I thank Yulin Wu for the research assistance in compiling the documents.

29. Tian Chen, "Foreign Ministry's Secret Report on Sino-U.S. Relations," *Zheng ming*, 1 November 1992, qtd. in Garver, J. W., *Face Off: China, the United States, and Taiwan's Democratization* (University of Washington Press, 2011). Another source that corroborates this report was John Garver's personal communication with Hong Kong sources; one former US State Department official also agreed that economics was the number one concern for Deng at that time and that Deng was aware that China was not in a position to coerce the United States, because it needed US markets, technology, and business investment: Interview KZ-#121, Washington, DC, March 1, 2017.
30. Chinese State Council, "Annual China's Government Work Report," reports prior to 2013 can be accessed at http://www.gov.cn/2013zfbgjjd/lnzf.htm, reports from 2014–2020 can be accessed at http://www.gov.cn/guowuyuan/2020zfgzbg.htm. I thank my undergraduate research assistant, Yulin Wu, for compiling and comparing the reports.
31. Wang Zihui, "Kan Xi Jinping zhe jici zhongyao jianghua, nongdong daxunhuan shuangxunhuan" ["Understanding the General Circulation and Dual Circulation from Xi Jinping's Several Important Speeches"], *Xinhua News*, September 5, 2020. For additional official documents, see Pei, Minxin, "China's Fateful Inward Turn: Beijing's New Economic Strategy as Spelled Out by the Resolution of the CCP Central Committee's 5th Plenum," *China Leadership Monitor*, December 16, 2020.
32. Xi Jinping, "Kaichuang woguo gaozhiliang fazhan xinjumian" ["Creating the New Era of China's High Quality Development"], *Qiushi*, June 15, 2024, https://www.gov.cn/yaowen/liebiao/202406/content_6957469.htm
33. See Goldstein, Avery, *Rising to the Challenge: China's Grand Strategy and International Security* (Stanford University Press, 2005), 21; Chen, Jian, *China's Road to the Korean War: The Making of the Sino-American Confrontation* (Columbia University Press, 1995); Lüthi, Lorenz M., *The Sino-Soviet Split: Cold War in the Communist World* (Princeton University Press, 2008).
34. Fravel, M. Taylor, *Active Defence: China's Military Strategy Since 1949* (Princeton University Press, 2019).
35. Jiang Yanyu, "Gaige kaifang Deng Xiaiping dui Mao Zedong junshi zhanlue sixiang de jicheng" ["The Continuities in Deng Xiaoping Regarding Mao's Military Strategic Thinking During the Reform and Opening Up Era"], *People Website,* August 12, 2014, http://www.cssn.cn/zgs/zgs_jl/201408/t20140813_1289164_1.shtml
36. Jiang Yanyu, "The Continuities in Deng Xiaoping."
37. Jiang Yanyu, "The Continuities in Deng Xiaoping"; see also Fravel, *Active Defence.*
38. Gill, Bates, *Daring to Struggle: China's Global Ambitions Under Xi Jinping* (Oxford University Press, 2022).
39. Wang Juyang, "Fanghuan weiran: gaigekaifang yilai yukongxing weiwen zhengce dexingqi—jiyu 315fen zhongyao wenjian de fenxi" ["The Rise of Pre-emptive Strategy to Maintain Social Stability in Post-Reform China—Evidence from 315 Central Documents"], *Shehui Kexue* [*Social Science*], no. 4, 2019.
40. Wang Juyang, "The Rise of Pre-emptive Strategy."
41. Chubailiang, "Xi Jinping jinggao zhonggong jiqu qiansulian jiaoxun" ["Xi Jinping Warned that the CCP Should Heed Lessons from the Former Soviet Union"], *The New York Times*, February 15, 2013.
42. Xi Jinping, "Xi Jinping tan zongti guojia anquan" ["Xi Jinping Talks About Comprehensive National Security"].

43. Zhao Kezhi, "Bawo xinfazhan jieduan, tuidong gaozhiliang fazhan yiquebao guojia zhengzhianquan he shehuiwending de youyi chengji qingzhu jiandang 100 zhounian" ["Grasping the New Development and Pushing for High-Quality Development so as to Ensure the National Political Security and Social Stability During the 100th Year Anniversary Celebration of the Founding of the CCP"], *Phoenix News*, January 19, 2021.
44. Goldstein, Avery, "China's Foreign Policy and the Leadership Transition: Prospects for Change Under the Fifth Generation," in Rozman, Gilbert, ed., *China's Foreign Policy: Who Makes It, and How Is It Made?* (Palgrave Macmillan, 2012), 45.
45. "Deng's Main Talking Points While in Wuchang, Shenzhen, Zhuhai, and Shanghai," in *Deng Xiaoping Wenxuan [Selected Works of Deng Xiaoping], Vol. 3* (People's Press, 1994), 375; this is also corroborated by Bo Yibo's statement, see *Bo Yibo Wenxuan [Selected Works of Bo Yibo]* (People's Press, 1992), 526. Bo stated on 22 December 1990 that unless there was a large-scale foreign invasion, China should always uphold economic development as the focus.
46. Jiang Zemin's report during the 14th Party Congress, in *Jiang Zemin Wenxuan [Selected Works of Jiang Zemin], Vol. 1* (People's Press, 2006), 217.
47. Jiang's speech during an enlarged meeting of the Central Military Commission, in *Selected Works of Jiang Zemin, Vol. 1*, 284.
48. Jiang's speech during the 8th meeting of foreign diplomats, in *Selected Works of Jiang Zemin, Vol. 1*, 314.
49. *Selected Works of Jiang Zemin, Vol. 2*, 193.
50. *Selected Works of Jiang Zemin, Vol. 2*, 253.
51. Jiang's speech during the fifth plenum of the 15th Party Congress, in *Selected Works of Jiang Zemin, Vol. 3*, 118, 124.
52. Jiang's speech during the national conference on social security work, in *Selected Works of Jiang Zemin, Vol. 3*, 214.
53. *Selected Works of Jiang Zemin, Vol. 3*, 444.
54. Jiang's meeting with the UN Secretary General, in *Selected Works of Jiang Zemin, Vol. 3*, 520.
55. Jiang's report during the 16th Party Congress, in *Selected Works of Jiang Zemin, Vol. 3*, 544.
56. Hu's speech when visiting Indonesia, in *Hu Jintao Wenxuan [Selected Works of Hu Jintao], Vol. 1* (People's Press, 2016), 450.
57. *Selected Works of Hu Jintao, Vol. 1*, 556, 559.
58. During a symposium with foreign diplomats, in *Selected Works of Hu Jintao, Vol. 2*, 87.
59. Part of Hu's speech during the central foreign affairs conference, in *Selected Works of Hu Jintao, Vol. 2*, 508–509. It was not previously public.
60. *Selected Works of Hu Jintao, Vol. 2*, 578.
61. Hu's speech with newly elected politburo members, in *Selected Works of Hu Jintao, Vol. 3*, 3.
62. *Selected Works of Hu Jintao, Vol. 3*, 95.
63. Hu's speech during the 11th meeting of foreign diplomats, in *Selected Works of Hu Jintao, Vol. 3*, 237.
64. Hu's speech during the fifth plenum of the 17th Party Congress, in *Selected Works of Hu Jintao, Vol. 3*, 439.
65. Hu's report during the 18th Party Congress, in *Selected Works of Hu Jintao, Vol. 3*, 618.

66. Xi Jinping's speech, "Xinde lishi tiaojian xia zhiguo lizheng zongfanglue" ["The General Guideline of Governance Under New Conditions], *People Website*, 22 April 2016, http://theory.people.com.cn/n1/2016/0422/c40531-28296007.html
67. Xi Jinping's speech, "Zhudong shiying, bawo, yinling, jingji fazhan xichangtai" ["Proactively Grasp, Adapt, and Lead the New Normal of Economic Development"], *People Website*, 3 May 2016, http://theory.people.com.cn/n1/2016/0503/c40531-28319669.html
68. Xi Jinping, *Xi Jinping tan zhiguo lizheng ["On Governance"]* (Foreign Languages Press, 2014), 11.
69. Xi's speech during the third plenum of the 18th Party Congress, in *On Governance*, 93.
70. Xi's speech during the fifth meeting of BRIC leaders, in *On Governance*, 326.
71. Xi Jinping, "Kaichuang woguo gaozhiliang fazhan xinjumian" ["Creating the New Era of China's High Quality Development"].
72. Xi Jinping, "Guanyu zhonggong zhongyang jinyibu quanmian shenhua gaige tuijin zhongguoshi xiandaihua de guiding de shuoming" ["A Elaboration on the Decision to Further Deepen Reform and Promote China-Styled Modernization], *Xinhua News*, 21 July 2024, https://www.gov.cn/yaowen/liebiao/202407/content_6963773.htm
73. Chubailiang, "Xi Jinping jinggao zhonggong jiqu qiansulian jiaoxun" ["Xi Jinping Warned that the CCP Should Heed Lessons from the Former Soviet Union"].
74. For example, Gilpin, Robert, *War and Change in International Politics* (Cambridge University Press, 1981).
75. Glosny, Michael, "The Grand Strategies of Rising Powers: Reassurance, Coercion, and Balancing Responses," Ph.D. dissertation: Massachusetts Institute of Technology, 2012, 13.
76. Medeiros, Evan S., and M. Taylor Fravel, "China's New Diplomacy," *Foreign Affairs*, November 2003.
77. Medeiros and Fravel, "China's New Diplomacy."
78. Medeiros and Fravel, "China's New Diplomacy."
79. Official website of the AIIB, https://www.aiib.org/en/about-aiib/index.html
80. Chinese Ministry of Foreign Affairs (hereafter MFA) press conference, January 20, 2021, http://m.news.cctv.com/2021/01/20/ARTI9cU3M97BOVvABQIJRXlD210120.shtml
81. Zhang, "Cautious Bully."
82. Myers, Margaret, "China in Latin America: Major Impacts and Avenues for Constructive Engagement, A U.S. Perspective," *China Research Center*, 19, no. 1 (2020).
83. Albert, Eleanor, "China in Africa," *Council on Foreign Relations*, July 12, 2017.
84. Albert, "China in Africa."
85. Albert, "China in Africa."
86. Ye, Min, *The Belt Road and Beyond: State-Mobilized Globalization in China: 1998–2018* (Cambridge University Press, 2020), 44.
87. Ministry of National Defence, "Zhongguo wuzhuang Liliang de duoyanghua yunyong" ["The Multi-use of China's Armed Forces"], April 16, 2013, http://www.mod.gov.cn/regulatory/2013-04/16/content_4617811.htm
88. Zhou, Laura, "China Embarks on First Joint Naval Drills with ASEAN as US Tensions Simmer in South China Sea," *South China Morning Post*, October 22, 2018.
89. Congressional Research Service, "U.S.-China Military-to-Military Relations," *In Focus*, January 4, 2021.

90. Wu, Wendy, "Chinese Troops Head to Hawaii for Joint Disaster Relief Exercise with US Military," *South China Morning Post*, November 13, 2019.
91. Zhang, Ketian V., "Chinese Non-military Coercion—Tactics and Rationale," *Brookings Institution*, January 22, 2019.
92. Zhang, Ketian, "China Is Pushing Back Against Taiwan for These Three Reasons," *Washington Post/Monkey Cage*, April 8, 2019.
93. Zhang, "China Is Pushing Back."
94. Wee, Sui-Lee, and Hui Li, "China-Japan 'Voldemort' Attacks Up Ante in Propaganda War," *Reuters*, January 7, 2014.
95. Galbraith, Andrew, "Twitter Flags China Spokesman's Tweet on COVID-19," *Reuters*, May 28, 2020.
96. Zhang, "Cautious Bully," 121.
97. For more information, see Zhang, Ketian, "Just Do It: Explaining the Characteristics and Rationale of Chinese Economic Sanctions," *Texas National Security Review* 7, no. 3 (Summer 2024), https://tnsr.org/2024/06/just-do-it-explaining-the-characteristics-and-rationale-of-chinese-economic-sanctions/
98. Zhang, "Just Do It."
99. See Zhang, Ketian, "Calculating Bully: Explaining Chinese Coercion," Ph.D. dissertation, Massachusetts Institute of Technology, 2018.
100. Zhang, Shuguang, *Beijing's Economic Statecraft During the Cold War, 1949–1991* (Johns Hopkins University Press, 2014).
101. Zhang, "China Is Pushing Back."
102. Norris, William J., *Chinese Economic Statecraft: Commercial Actors, Grand Strategy, and State Control* (Cornell University Press, 2016).
103. Zhang, "China Is Pushing Back."
104. Zhang, "Cautious Bully," 122.
105. Zhang, "Cautious Bully," 122.
106. Zhang, "Calculating Bully."
107. Zhang, "Cautious Bully."
108. Zhang, "Cautious Bully," 122.
109. For more on the maritime militia, see Erickson, Andrew S., and Ryan D. Martinson, *China's Maritime Grey Zone Operations* (Naval Institute Press, 2019).
110. Fravel, M. Taylor, *Strong Borders, Secure Nation: Cooperation and Conflict in China's Territorial Disputes* (Princeton University Press, 2008).
111. Zhang, "Calculating Bully."
112. Fravel, M. Taylor, "China's Search for Military Power," *The Washington Quarterly* 31, no. 3 (2008).
113. Fravel, "China's Search for Military Power," 131.
114. China's Ministry of National Defence, "Xinshidai de zhongguo guofang baipishu quanwen" ["China's National Defense White Paper in a New Era"], July 27, 2019, http://www.mod.gov.cn/regulatory/2019-07/24/content_4846424.htm
115. Huang, Kristin, "Chinese Military Fires 'Aircraft-Carrier Killer' Missile into South China Sea in 'Warning to the United States'," *South China Morning Post*, August 26, 2020.
116. Huang, "Chinese Military Fires 'Aircraft-Carrier Killer' Missile."
117. Fravel, M. Taylor, and Evan S. Medeiros, "China's Search for Assured Retaliation: The Evolution of Chinese Nuclear Strategy and Force Structure," *International Security* 35, no. 2 (2010), 48–87.

118. US Department of Defense, "Annual Report to Congress: Military and Security Developments Involving the People's Republic of China 2019," May 2019, https://media.defense.gov/2019/May/02/2002127082/-1/-1/1/2019_CHINA_MILITARY_POWER_REPORT.pdf
119. Samuels, Richard J., *Securing Japan: Tokyo's Grand Strategy and the Future of East Asia* (Cornell University Press, 2007).
120. Edel, Charles N., *Nation Builder: John Quincy Adams and the Grand Strategy of the Republic* (Harvard University Press, 2014).
121. For more evidence refuting the claim that China aims at exporting authoritarianism, see Weiss, Jessica Chen, "A World Safe for Autocracy? China's Rise and the Future of Global Politics," *Foreign Affairs*, July/August 2019.
122. On multiple signaling, see Xiaoyu Pu, *Rebranding China: Contested Status Signaling in the Changing Global Order* (Stanford University Press, 2019).

CHAPTER 2

Japan

Yuichi Hosoya

Japan occupies an important place in the international politics of East Asia, as it is the third largest economy in the world, trailing only the United States and China. It is also the most important ally of the United States in East Asia. Although the United States and China are two leading powers that will decide the future trajectory of East Asian regional order, Japan's influence should not be underestimated.

At the same time, Japan has experienced a turbulent path in the twentieth century. Before and during the Second World War, the Japanese empire had established a huge sphere of influence in the region, mostly within the Korean peninsula, Taiwan, and Manchuria. After its defeat, mainly at the hands of the United States, Japan was reborn as a new nation-state with a pacifist constitution and a more limited territory. Its complex national identity seems to be one of the major factors that makes it difficult (though not impossible) for Japan to present a clear and long-term grand strategy when faced with its domestic and international constraints.[1]

Japan's grand strategic policies during the Cold War are generally understood as part of the "Yoshida doctrine," which was named after Prime Minister Shigeru Yoshida, who concluded the US-Japan security treaty of September 1951.[2] On his own foreign policy position, Prime Minister Yoshida said that "we remain, and should not change, our doctrine to place Japan's basic policy onto the good relationship with America."[3] The Yoshida doctrine is generally defined as "non-militarism to guide a nonaggressive, low-cost postwar Japanese security policy" based on the US-Japan alliance diplomacy.[4] Shinichi Kitaoka, a leading expert of Japanese political history, also wrote that "Yoshida's path of prioritizing the economy and adopting only minimal rearmament would serve as the basis for Japan's postwar development."[5] Thus, based on this Yoshida doctrine, postwar Japan set the US-Japan alliance at the center of its grand strategy.

In this chapter, it will be argued that Japan's postwar grand strategy, namely the Yoshida doctrine, was updated and transformed during the first and second Shinzo Abe administrations, evolving from its historical perspective. The grand strategy of the Abe administration, namely the Abe doctrine, was crystalized in Japan's first National Security Strategy document, published in December 2013.[6] At the same time, Prime Minister Abe initiated the establishment and development of Japan's National Security Council as well as a National Security Secretariat, which radically transformed the institutional process of making and implementing Japan's grand strategy.[7]

However, we can also see some important continuities in Japan's grand strategy as it evolved from the Yoshida doctrine to the Abe doctrine. By analyzing the essence of Japan's grand strategy, we can more deeply understand how Japan is positioning itself in the East Asian and global strategic environment.

STRATEGIC PRIORITIES

Japanese grand strategy has includes a number of long-standing strategic priorities. They include maintaining the country's alliance with the United States, maintaining the balance of power in East Asia, and maintaining Japan's own economic growth.

Maintaining the Alliance with the United States

Japan's relationship with the United States has long been placed at the center of Japan's grand strategy. As article 9 of the Constitution of Japan stipulates a pacifist tradition,[8] Japan needs to rely on the American security commitment for the benefit of Japan's defense as well as to the benefit of peace and stability in the East Asia region. Due to the alliance, Japan is restricted to become a militarist power that would threaten or destroy peace and stability in East Asia. Thus, Japan's grand strategy cannot be fully independent from American security strategy in the region. In other words, Japan's grand strategy is closely and strongly tied within the US-Japan alliance.

The alliance between Tokyo and Washington also accrues huge benefits to Japan. Kazuya Sakamoto has argued that "the joining of hands with

America in security affairs was extremely effective for Japanese security," since "the United States possessed both the desire and the ability to forward deploy its powerful might from its naval, air, and ground in East Asia, which was indispensable for Japan's defense."[9] Following the Second World War, the intensification of the Cold War confrontation in East Asia, including both China and the Soviet Union, strengthened the value of the alliance with the United States for Japan, especially since the constitution of Japan prevented the country from sufficiently re-arming.

However, it was not an easy process in Japanese politics to place the alliance at the core of Tokyo's grand strategy in the 1950s and 1960s. Both Yoshida's political rivals within the ruling party, the Liberal Democratic Party (LDP), and the main opposition party, the Japan Socialist Party (JSP), became hostile to the basic position of Yoshida's diplomacy centered around the US-Japan alliance. In different ways and according to their own positions, they expected a more independent foreign and defense policy, separate from the global strategy of the United States.

Nevertheless, the Yoshida doctrine had another dimension. During these decades, Japan needed to concentrate on its effort to accelerate postwar reconstruction and economic growth. Japan's reliance on its alliance with the United States allowed Tokyo to reduce its defense spending. Besides, Japan could benefit from open access to the American markets by maintaining its alliance with the United States. Thus, Sakamoto also wrote that "the United States, with its overwhelming economic might, established and led an international liberal economic system, which helped Japan recover and grow economically."[10]

Anti-American nationalism was largely mitigated and the Japanese began to accept the US alliance as the foundation of their country's postwar foreign and defense policy after their country overcame the 1960 security treaty crisis (when the alliance with the United States had been put into question). In 1967, the Japanese government thus declared the "Three Non-Nuclear Principles," which reflected a broad overall approval of the Yoshida doctrine.[11] The principles were nonpossession, non-production, and nonintroduction of nuclear weapons (in Japanese territory),[12] and it dated back to the Allied occupation of Japan in the post–Second World War phase. At this time, Japan therefore decided to be covered by American extended deterrence while abandoning its own development of nuclear weapons.

In 1976 the Japanese government issued its first National Defense Program Outline.[13] This is generally regarded as the foundation of Japan's security strategy, and the basic framework of this strategy continued to be effective until 2010. That year, the Democratic Party of Japan (DPJ) government introduced the new security concept of "dynamic defense force" (*do-teki boeiryoku*).

In the National Defense Program Outline of 1976, the Japanese government established and defined that "the equilibrium between the superpowers and the existence of the Japan-U.S. security arrangement seems to play a major role in maintaining international stability, and in preventing full-scale aggression against Japan."[14] The National Defense Program Outline therefore reaffirmed that the US-Japan alliance was an integral part of Japan's security strategy, and the following Guidelines for Japan-U.S. Defense Cooperation of 1978 defined the outline of the division of labor between Japan's Self-Defense Forces and the US forces in defending Japan.[15] Established in 1954 and comprising ground, maritime and air units,[16] the Self-Defense Forces were Japan's armed forces but were limited to protecting Japan's territory with no possibility of international deployment.

Up until today, the US-Japan alliance has thus been placed at the center of Japan's grand strategy from the Yoshida doctrine until the Abe doctrine. In Japan's National Security Strategy of 2013, the government maintained that "For more than 60 years, the Japan-U.S. Alliance, with the Japan-U.S. security arrangements at its core, has played an indispensable role for peace and security in Japan as well as peace and stability in the Asia-Pacific region."[17]

Maintaining the Balance of Power

Following the end of the Second World War in 1945, Japan needed to radically transform its imperial grand strategy. As mentioned previously, the Japanese constitution, approved in 1946 and coming into effect in 1947, clearly redefined Japan's national identity as a peace-loving country moving away from its militaristic and imperialist past. This redefinition has informed Japan's grand strategy for decades.

However, at the same time, it was widely understood in Japanese government circles that Japan should not create a power vacuum in East Asia, as this would destabilize the balance of power in the region. Successive US administrations have also demanded over the decades that the Japanese government make sufficient efforts to rearm the country. Therefore, Narushige Michishita wrote that, "There are two major objectives in Japan's grand strategy," and "the first is to maintain the balance of power in the face of a rising China by strengthening security cooperation with the countries such as the United States, Australia, Southeast Asian countries, India, and South Korea."[18]

Japan's rearmament is mainly for the purpose of maintaining the balance of power in the East Asian region and not for the purpose of expanding its sphere of influence as it did before 1945 by establishing the "Great East Asian Coprosperity Sphere" during the imperial era. Thus, Japan has aimed to contribute to the balance of power by developing its own Self-Defense Forces, introduced previously. The US-Japan alliance has been an indispensable component of pursuing this strategic goal as well.

Maintaining Japan's Economic Growth

In addition to maintaining the regional balance of power, Michishita argued that bringing about economic prosperity, peace, and stability in East Asia via cooperation with the countries in the region has been the second major objective in Japan's grand strategy.[19] This includes cooperation with China as well, at least in the area of economics as a means to bring about economic prosperity.

The strategy behind Japan's pursuit of economic growth was strongly tied with Tokyo's alliance strategy based upon the Yoshida doctrine. Yoshida recognized that Japan should prioritize its economic reconstruction over rearmament in the post–Second World War decades. Therefore, he resisted strong American demands for rapid Japanese rearmament, claiming that the state of the economy and public opinion made such an undertaking impossible.[20] The US government began to accept this Yoshida strategy in the beginning of the 1950s, as it thought that it would be better to have a stronger Japanese economy to prevent communists sympathizers within the country from gaining broader support. The Japanese economy around this time was still very fragile, and the US government needed to support the continuation of Japan's economic reconstruction and economic growth to prevent the spread of communism in the country and, more broadly, across East Asia.

Since then, postwar Japan's grand strategy has focused on the use of economic statecraft tools, rather than simple reliance on military options. Maaike Okano-Heijmans and Takaaki Asano appropriately explained that "Since the end of the Second World War, Japan's so-called 'peace constitution' and the security guarantee by the United States provided Japanese policy-makers with a unique chance to focus on economic development and to openly emphasize economic, rather than military, means to project and exert power in its relations with other countries."[21] In other words, "in a system that was largely dominated by the United States and European countries, Japan has chiefly employed economic diplomacy as a means to secure broader national interests—including economic prosperity, political stability and national security."[22] This has been a trademark tool of Japanese grand strategy for decades.

To conceptualize this Japanese strategic culture, Prime Minister Masayoshi Ohira began to use a new notion of "comprehensive security" in the 1970s.[23] While Japanese public opinion tended to be averse to militarization, the Japanese government strived to promote "comprehensive security," in which economic measures also played an important role to provide for the security of Japan. Partly based upon this sort of approach toward security, the Japanese government substantially increased its spending on Official Development Assistance (ODA) in the 1980s and 1990s. This way, Japan became one of the largest providers of total ODA globally, including toward Southeast Asia.[24]

In summary, Japan has developed its own grand strategy focusing on several important goals based upon the Yoshida doctrine dating back to the postwar years. Michishita argued that "maintaining the balance of power" and "bringing about economic prosperity, and peace and stability, in the region" are the two major objectives in Japan's grand strategy.[25] This tradition of postwar Japan's grand strategy has been informed by both external and domestic factors, and these will be explained in the following sections.

EXTERNAL FACTORS

Japan's grand strategy has been constructed taking into consideration both external and domestic factors. After the defeat of the Japanese empire in 1945, the great powers fighting together in the Grand Alliance, and in particular the United States and the Soviet Union, greatly expanded their influence in East Asia. These two superpowers occupied the southern and northern parts of the Korean Peninsula right after the end of the Second World War, respectively. The Korean War that broke out in June 1950 then resulted in the consolidation of the dividing line between the West and the East in Northeast Asia, right next to Japan in the Korean Peninsula.

As the predominant power that defeated and occupied Japan, the United Stated held an exceptional position in the country postwar that was unmatched by any other power. The San Francisco Peace Treaty of September 8, 1951,[26] which reestablished relations between Tokyo and the Allied Powers, was essentially drafted by the US government, and even the postwar Japanese constitution was largely designed by American officials. In addition, the US government played a predominant role in the creation of the Japanese Self-Defense Forces in 1954. Thus, the United States should be considered as the principal actor that influences Japan's grand strategy to this day.

Third-Party Actors

The United States is the key external factor for Japan. In Japan's major strategic documents such as the National Defense Program Outline of 1976, the National Defense Program Outline of 1996, the National Defense Program Guidelines of 2005, the National Defense Program Guidelines of 2011, and the National Security Strategy of 2013 and others, the United States occupies a special place in Tokyo's foreign, defense and security strategies. One of the key reasons for this is that Japan alone cannot respond to any Russian (previously Soviet) or Chinese full-scale attacks if war happens. Japan's Self-Defense Forces can only deter these threats if and when US forces would engage in that war, based on article 5 of the US–Japan security treaty signed in 1960.[27] The importance of defense cooperation between Japan's Self-Defense Forces and their American counterparts is one of the most important continuities that has lasted over the seven decades since the end of the Second World War.

The two governments began to consider the possibility of more consultation and coordination between the two military forces in the 1970s. After the end of the Vietnam War, the US government expected that its allies should play a larger role in their own defense but also in their own region. The Security Consultative Committee between the two governments already in place had played an important role in coordinating their defense policies through deep and regular consultation. The 17th Security Consultative Committee on November 27, 1978, approved the Guidelines for U.S.–Japan Defense Cooperation (also known as "the Guidelines"),[28] and this became the foundation of their defense cooperation moving forward.

After the end of the Cold War, the Japanese government felt that Japan needed to contribute more to defense cooperation with the United States. However, Japan showed no intention to develop and possess nuclear weapons, following from the Three Non-Nuclear Principles, nor to amend article 9 of its constitution, which limits Japan's defense activities to this date—even after the Cold War ended. The U.S.-Japan Joint Declaration on Security, issued by US President Bill Clinton and Prime Minister Ryutaro Hashimoto in April 1996,[29] reaffirmed that Japan continued to rely on its alliance partnership with the United States, following questions about the future of the alliance after the end of the Cold War. The two leaders agreed that "the foundation for our cooperation remain firm, and this partnership will remain vital in the twenty-first century."[30]

Thus, the US-Japan alliance continues to be the foundation of Japan's grand strategy. In the National Security Strategy of 2013, the Japanese government maintained the following: "The Japan-U.S. Alliance is the cornerstone of Japan's security."[31] In other words, American grand strategy remains an integral part of Japan's strategic thinking. Following this line of thought, Japan's grand strategy must be in harmony with American global strategy.

With the strengthening and expansion of Chinese military power in recent decades, the US and Japanese governments agreed to strengthen the alliance and to deepen cooperation. In addition, the two powers extended this cooperation to other like-minded democracies in this region, such as Australia and India. Thus, the so-called Quad, or Quadrilateral Security Dialogue, was developed as an important foundation of cooperation among liberal democracies in the Indo-Pacific region, with the US-Japan alliance at its core.[32]

The Soviet Union (or Russia) remained another key factor. The main function of the US-Japan alliance during the Cold War years was to contain the expansion of the Soviet military activities in the Asia-Pacific region. In the 1970s and 1980s the Soviet Union's armed forces posed a serious threat to Japan's territory as well as the sea lines of communication that stretch from Japan all the way to the Middle East.

Thus Christopher Hughes wrote that "during the late 1970s and 1980s, the enhanced common threat of the USSR forced a convergence of Japanese and US strategic interests."[33] This threat ran in parallel to the evolution of US-Japan defense cooperation during this period. The rise of the Soviet threat was a main external factor that informed Japan's grand strategy around this time. Since the demise of the Soviet Union in 1991, Japan began to revise its previous threat perception as well as the direction of its defense policy. As a result, the threat of the Soviet Union has been replaced by North Korea and China since the 1990s.

North Korea is therefore yet another important factor for Japan. Soon after the positive feelings that came together with end of the Cold War, the Japanese people became disillusioned by a series of crises in East Asia. In particularly, the North Korean nuclear and missile crisis of 1993–94 awakened Japanese people to "the collapse of the security myth."[34] In 1993 North Korean leader Kim Il-sung announced the start of his country's nuclear development program to defend his own nation. The birth of a nuclear North Korea in contravention of the Treaty on the Nonproliferation of

Nuclear Weapons (NPT) would become a nightmare scenario for Japanese security—including by potentially igniting nuclear proliferation across Northeast Asia—but Japan did not have sufficient tools to affect this development.[35] This crisis resulted in a reaffirmation of the validity and utility of the US-Japan alliance even after the end of the Cold War.

Prime Minister Junichiro Koizumi decided to visit Pyongyang to meet with North Korean Chairman Kim Jong-il, the successor of his father Kim Il-sung, in September 2001.[36] The Japanese government strived to promote rapprochement between Japan and North Korea with this surprising summit meeting, especially in consideration that Tokyo and Pyongyang were—and are—yet to normalize diplomatic relations. The summit resulted in the Pyongyang Declaration.[37] To this date, the Japanese government continues to prioritize engagement as the optimum policy toward North Korea, preferable to a direct military action.[38] From Tokyo's perspective, it would be a great asset for East Asia security if North Korea became more cooperative in strengthening the security environment in this region.

However, due to multiple political reasons, Japan-North Korean negotiations were unsuccessful.[39] As a result, the Pyongyang Declaration was not implemented. Instead, the North Korean government resumed its nuclear development program, and regional and global tensions followed from this. Thus Japan's National Defense Program Guidelines of 2011, for example, explained that "North Korea's military activities constitute an immediate and grave destabilizing factor to regional security" and that "they also pose a serious challenge to international non-proliferation efforts."[40]

Furthermore Japan's Security Consultative Committee of 2013 argued that "North Korea has enhanced the capability of WMDs [weapons of mass destruction] including nuclear weapons and that of ballistic missiles" and that "these concerns pose a serious challenge to the entire international community from the viewpoint of the non-proliferation of WMD and related materials."[41] The National Defense Program Guidelines of 2011 and Security Consultative Committee of 2013 demonstrate that throughout the 2010s Japan became more proactive in facing security threats, compared to the 1990s, which was the time of the "collapse of the security myth."

North Korea had been the main threat perception within Japanese grand strategy circles until the 2010s. However, since then, China has emerged as the most pressing security concern, which largely defines Japan's grand strategy as of the 2020s. Beijing's economic, diplomatic, and especially military rise is the key threat against which Japanese decision-makers strategize today.

China, therefore, is another crucial external factor for Japan. In the 1990s the Japanese government did not regard China as a security threat or a challenge in its official documents. For example, the National Defense Program Guidelines of 1996 maintained that "uncertainty and unpredictability" in the Korean Peninsula were a security conundrum, but there was no reference to China in the section on the "International Situation" affecting Japanese security.[42] Around this time, there was hope in Japan that Tokyo could help bring Beijing into the international community, similarly to the line of thought in the United States and Europe. The thinking therefore was that Japan should enhance its engagement policy toward China, and not its containment policy. Furthermore the Japanese government even took the lead internationally in helping China to avoid isolation after the Tiananmen Square incident of June 1989,[43] when Chinese troops shot on pro-democracy protesters.

As Hughes wrote, it would be appropriate to argue that "Japanese policymakers first became concerned about China as a serious military threat in the post-Cold War period."[44] However, Japan continued to maintain its engagement policy toward China for two decades after the Tiananmen Square incident. When Prime Minister Abe visited Beijing in October 2006 to meet with Chinese President Hu Jintao, the two governments agreed on "a mutually beneficial relationship based on common strategic interests" in the joint statement issued after their summits.[45] The two sides took the then-rational decision to make efforts to benefit from mutual economic interdependence, and China became Japan's biggest trading partner in 2009.

However, a Chinese trawler collision incident in the Senkaku Islands in September 2010 radically transformed this bilateral relationship. A Chinese trawler collided with several Japanese Coast Guard patrol boats off the islands, resulting in a diplomatic incident when the trawler and its crew were detained before being released after ten days.[46] This incident seriously damaged the Japan-China "mutually beneficial relationship based on common strategic interests" and initiated a subsequently deeply rooted threat perception about Chinese maritime activities around Japanese territorial waters. This is shared by Japanese policymakers and the general public.

This change in perceptions was explicitly laid out in the way that China was described in the National Defense Program Guidelines of 2010 and the National Security Strategy of 2013. With regard to the National Defense Program Guidelines of 2010, the Japanese government stated that "China has been expanding and intensifying its maritime activities in the surrounding waters" and that "these trends, together with insufficient transparency over China's military forces and its security policy, are of concern for the regional and global community."[47] Three years later, the Japanese government mentioned the following in the National Security Strategy of 2013: "China has rapidly expanded and intensified its activities in the seas and airspace around Japan, including intrusion into Japan's territorial waters and airspace around the Senkaku Islands."[48] Thus a rapid Chinese military buildup together with its more assertive military activities, including in and near Japanese territorial waters, has become a central external factor that defines the outline of Japanese grand strategy.

Threats and Opportunities

There are several important elements that form part of Japan's threat perceptions. The first of these is the changing balance of power in East Asia and also at the global levels. Starting with the early Cold War years and all the way until today, the Japanese government has been aware of the changes in the balance of power in the East Asian region, as this could easily damage and destroy peace and stability in Japan's own neighborhood.

The Sino-Japanese rapprochement of the 1970s and the 1980s—Japan normalized diplomatic relations with China in 1972, seven years before the United States[49]—was possible largely due to the Soviet Union becoming more assertive militarily in East Asia. This was the main reason driving normalization between Tokyo and Beijing. Following the Sino-Soviet border conflict of 1969—when Chinese and Soviet soldiers exchanged fired across the border, threatening escalation between the two nuclear powers[50]—China became closer to the United States and Japan as a means to guard against the growing Soviet threat. On the other hand, after China repaired its diplomatic relations with the Soviet Union/Russia from the late 1980s, China has felt less need to be work together with the United States and Japan. These strategic trends undoubtedly influenced Japanese official thinking on its strategic necessities.

With the rapid rise of the Chinese economy and military power in the 1990s and the 2000s, China had become less cautious on its territorial disputes with Japan in the East China Sea. Even as the Japanese government had remained committed to its engagement policy toward China until the Senkaku incident of 2010, the Chinese government expanded its strategic and territorial interests in both the South China Sea and the East China Sea. This can be considered a key consequence of the changing balance of power in the region, with a rising China boosting its relative power.

Territorial disputes are another important threat for Tokyo to consider as part of its security policy and grand strategy. Japan's territorial disputes with its neighbors are closely linked with the changing balance of power in the region as well. This is an important external factor that guides the direction of Japan's grand strategy. The growing sense of the relative decline in Japanese power throughout the 2010s is considered to have made the peaceful resolution to these disputes even more difficult. Instead, from a Japanese perspective China tends to have started to rely more on its power play. At the same time, China's Ministry of Foreign Affairs has lost influence in Beijing's foreign policymaking throughout this period, further compounding the sense of threat perception among Tokyo's decision-makers.

Sea lines of communication are another threat that Japan has to consider. In the National Security Strategy of 2013, the Japanese government argued that "Japan as a maritime state has achieved economic growth through maritime trade and development of marine resources, and has pursued 'Open and Stable Seas.'"[51] Japan's national security and prosperity are largely decided by Japan's control of sea lines of communication.

Euan Graham wrote in his comprehensive book on the sea lines of communication that "the extent to which sea lines of communication have historically been perceived by Japanese policymakers as core security concerns in a large part reflects the economic importance to Japan in maintaining inward-bound shipments of fuels, metal ores, other raw materials and food, as well as outward-bound exports of manufactured goods."[52] Securing Japan's sea lines of communication thus becomes a key component of Japan's grand strategy, as was the case prior to the Second World War.

These external factors largely define the outline of Japan's grand strategy. But, at the same time, domestic factors also influence its essence in different ways.

DOMESTIC FACTORS

There are several domestic factors influencing Japan's grand strategy. Together with the external factors described above, they serve to explain the key tenets behind the country's grand strategy—both its continuities as well as its changes.

National Values

After the end of the Second World War, Japan started a process to reconstruct its fundamental values. Japan's empire was placed at the top during the prewar Japanese value system. But the postwar democratization and reconstruction process taking place in the country has fundamentally transformed postwar Japan's national identity in a way that still prevails today.

Pacifism is a central value for Japanese grand strategy. The constitution of Japan provides the normative foundation of postwar Japan's national values. In particular, article 9 on the "Renunciation of War" has informed and resulted in Japan's basic defense posture. This is the so-called "exclusively defense-oriented policy" (*senshu boei*), which prohibits Japan from possessing certain types of military equipment that could be deemed as offensive in nature, such as long-range ballistic missiles.[53] Pacifism, or a national value as being a peace-loving nation, has become one of the most important normative foundations for Japanese grand strategy to this day.

Liberal values are also crucial for Japan's grand strategy. Together with the postwar pacifist tradition just described, Japan also embraces some of the universal values that have been the basis for the postwar liberal international order. Nobukatsu Kanehara, who was the Deputy Secretary-General of the National Security Council under Abe between 2014 and 2019, wrote in his book on "Security Strategy" that modern states have three fundamental national interests, namely "national security," "national prosperity," and "national values."[54] According to Kanehara, Japan's national strategy needs to be based not just on its own national interests but also on universal values, which are placed at the foundation of the liberal international order, such as human rights and the rule of law. Kanehara played a central role in drafting the National Security Strategy of 2013 as a close foreign policy advisor to Abe.

In the National Security Strategy of 2013, the Japanese government posited that "the maintenance and protection of an international order based on rules and universal values, such as freedom, democracy, respect for fundamental human rights, and the rule of law, are likewise in Japan's national interests."[55] Thus Japan's National Security Strategy of 2013 underlines the importance of values in defending Japan's national interests. This emphasis on values marks one of the most important features of this strategy document, strongly informing Tokyo's grand strategy.

Influence of These Values

The emphasis upon the importance of values naturally resulted in Japan's orientation toward security cooperation with like-minded democracies. Thus, Abe strived to create the Quad with the United States, Australia, and India.[56] Unlike his predecessors, Abe frequently made public his strong interest in promoting Japan's partnership with India. India is the largest democracy in the world, and Abe stressed the importance of increasing the role of India in regional and international politics.

On the other hand, it has become clearer that Japan's cooperation with (communist) China has some limits as Tokyo and Beijing are representatives of different political ideologies. In this way, Abe's foreign policy during his first and second administrations are often summarized as a "value-oriented diplomacy."[57] This foreign policy stance has a clear contrast with the "Yoshida Doctrine," which focuses on the importance of Japan's economic growth and the reliance upon American military force but deemphasizes the role of values.

While the norms of pacifism and prosperity have been the core of the Yoshida doctrine, universal values such as freedom, democracy, human rights, and the rule of law became the essence of the Abe doctrine, or "value-oriented diplomacy." The Abe doctrine also uses the key phrase of "proactive contribution to peace based on international cooperation," which was kept in Japan's National Security Strategy of December 2022.[58] This refers to Japan moving from self-defense to take a more active role in regional and global affairs. As of 2024, there is much broader support in Japan for Tokyo to make a greater contribution to international peace and stability. In this sense, pursuing Japan's own economic prosperity should not be the only strategic goal of the country.

Institutional Process

Japan has a cabinet system at the heart of its political process. The cabinet with a prime minister who is *prima inter pares* decides, and the majority party within Japan's National Diet forms the government. However, there are several institutional problems in the Japanese political system. Some examples include the excessive power of the Upper House, the weakness of the Prime Minister's Office, and frequent cabinet reshuffles. All of them have prevented the Japanese government from having strong political leadership,[59] thus there are frequent changes in prime minister.

Historically, it has not been easy for the Japanese government to coordinate interdepartmental rivalries across and within different ministries and even within the cabinet. This has been changing with the establishment of the National Security Council in December 2013, and the National Security Secretariat, dating back to early 2014.[60] Tokyo has been able to formulate and articulate its national strategy more clearly thanks to both. The National

Security Council, in particular, was created with the expectation that it will serve as a "control tower" enabling the government to adopt a more comprehensive approach in addressing various security issues.[61]

OPERATIONALIZATION OF GRAND STRATEGY

It is often said that Japan has not had a grand strategy post-1945. In other words, this would mean that Japan has not had a grand strategy following the end of the Japanese empire. This could be considered partly true, as there is no single official document that presents Japan's comprehensive national strategy covering defense, diplomacy, and economic policy, as well as other relevant policy areas. Instead, as noted previously, the National Defense Program outlines and the National Security Strategy are generally regarded as Japan's official documents that present its evolving strategic vision over time.

Having said that and as discussed earlier, certain Japanese political leaders such as Yoshida Shigeru and Shinzo Abe have presented strategic visions that became clear and apparent in their speeches and writings. Thus, the Yoshida doctrine and the Abe doctrine are generally regarded as Japan's major strategic doctrines in the postwar years, meaning the decades since the Second World War. We have seen the continuities but also the evolution and transformation in Japan's grand strategy from the Yoshida doctrine to the Abe doctrine in the previous sections.

At the same time, it can also be argued that the "Arc of Freedom and Prosperity" was a major foreign policy speech that presented a comprehensive and coherent strategic vision, akin to Japan's operationalization of its contemporary grand strategy.[62] This speech was delivered by Foreign Minister Taro Aso on November 30, 2006, during the first Abe administration (2006–07). It can probably be said that Japan's grand strategy was operationalized in this foreign policy speech by Aso in a comprehensive way for the first time.[63]

Nobukatsu Kanehara, then the director of the Policy Coordination Division at the Foreign Policy Bureau of the Ministry of Foreign Affairs, played a significant role in designing this speech in 2006. Kanehara has argued that in this speech Aso articulated that "Japan is no longer a small defeated nation," as Yoshida presupposed half a century previously, so "it needs to stand up to do something good to the international community to which it owes today's prosperity."[64] Kanehara's thought on Japan's renewed and evolved grand strategy laid the groundwork for a new thinking in Japanese diplomacy and foreign policy.

Aso is one of Yoshida's grandsons, and he radically transformed his grandfather's strategic doctrine with his speech. The speech was launched at a Japanese foreign policy think tank, the Japan Institute of International Affairs (JIIA),[65] which was established by his grandfather Yoshida. In this important speech, Aso spoke of two new important diplomatic concepts, namely the "value-oriented diplomacy" and the "arc of freedom and prosperity." Aso was proud of these "new bases for our foreign policy." The central theme of his speech was to place "emphasis on the universal values such as democracy, freedom, human rights, the rule of law, and the market economy as we advance our diplomatic endeavors." More concretely, he argued that Japan "wants to design an 'arc of freedom and prosperity' along the outer rim of the Eurasian continent." In this speech, Aso tried to combine "value-oriented diplomacy" with a new geopolitical strategy in the Eurasian continent.[66]

As this grand strategy was based on the "value-oriented diplomacy," it was natural for the first Abe administration to promote security cooperation among like-minded democracies. Thus, Abe was the main force behind the creation of the Quad with the United States, Australia, and India. In particular, it was essential for Abe to gain the support from India to operationalize this new strategic vision. Thus, on August 22, 2007, Abe visited India[67] and made a long and energetic speech at the Parliament of the Republic of India. In the speech, he that said the partnership between these two countries was "an association in which we share fundamental values such as freedom, democracy, and the respect for basic human rights as well as strategic interests." Abe declared that the "Strategic Global Partnership of Japan and India is pivotal for" the success of the "arc of freedom and prosperity."[68] However, due largely to Abe's health problems, he stepped down from the post of prime minister in 2007, and his successor, Prime Minister Yasuo Fukuda, developed a much more East Asian-oriented diplomacy that was considerably different from Abe's maritime strategy.[69]

Lavina Lee of Macquarie University appropriately summarized that "Japan's first attempt to engender deeper strategic cooperation between Japan, Australia, India and the United States—the Quadrilateral Dialogue (QD) of 2007—was a short-lived experiment that ultimately failed to gain traction in the face of strong Chinese opposition and the loss of office by its major proponents in Australia, Japan and the US."[70] Lee also pointed out that "Prime Minister Abe was widely acknowledged as the main protagonist behind the QD, with firm support from the Bush Administration, particularly US Vice President Dick Cheney."[71]

These strategic initiatives that the first Abe administration presented were later resurrected via the free and open Indo-Pacific (FOIP) vision,[72] which Abe launched a decade later by himself during this second administration (2012–20). This was the longest tenure by a Japanese prime minister since the end of the Second World War.[73] Arguably, the FOIP is the most successful operationalization of Japan' grand strategy since the beginning of its modernization in the middle of the nineteenth century.[74] It laid the foundations of the concept of an Indo-Pacific region, and this vision has been supported by most of the major democracies such as the United States, Australia, India, South Korea, and the EU, as well as organizations such as NATO, among others.

Thus Japan's renewed and updated grand strategy has been mainly operationalized during the first and second Abe administrations of 2006–07 and 2012–20. Japan's grand strategy is the result of the integration of its own geopolitical and normative visions. Fumio Kishida's administration then worked in the creation of a new national security strategy, which revised the previous National Security Strategy of 2013. Economic security occupied a special place in the National Security Strategy of 2022.[75] This continued to be the case as of 2024.[76] Overall, however, the National Security Strategy built on the grand strategy laid out during the Abe years. Having said that, Japan needs a more integrated strategy that will cover other areas such as health, digitalization, and intelligence, among others.

CONCLUSION

It would be a little difficult to find a single, appropriate official document in which we can find the essence of the grand strategy of Japan, unlike other leading world powers.

But this chapter shows how the National Defense Program and the National Security Strategy (the latter reinforced by the most recent National Security Strategy of 2022) in particular present the core of Japan' grand strategy.

In addition, we can see the historical evolution of Japanese grand strategy in its transformation through the Yoshida doctrine to the Abe doctrine. While there are continuities between the two of them, there are also some important differences. The establishment of the National Security Council in December 2013 and the National Secretary Secretariat in January 2014 supported the government to create a whole-of-the-government approach to a Japanese grand strategy.

However, the postwar national value of pacifism has been an important hurdle that made the creation of a comprehensive grand strategy more difficult than was the case in other leading powers across the world. This helps explain why Japan arguably still needs a much more comprehensive strategy that would serve to clarify its strategic goals and strategic tools. This would also help promote the transparency of Japan's security policy as well as strengthening its security partnerships.

As argued in this chapter, Japan underwent and experienced a U-turn from prewar militarism to postwar pacifism. At the same time, Japan's grand strategy has been formulated in response to the threat that emerged in each period of time. Abe's value-oriented diplomacy integrated national and universal values in its grand strategy. The next question would be about how long the Abe doctrine survives.

NOTES

1. Yuichi Hosoya, "Japan's National Identity in Postwar Diplomacy: Three Basic Principles," in Gilbert Rozman (ed.), *East Asian National Identities: Common Roots and Chinese Exceptionalism* (Stanford University Press, 2012).
2. Security Treaty between the United States and Japan, September 8, 1951, https://avalon.law.yale.edu/20th_century/japan001.asp
3. Shigeru Yoshida, *Kaiso Junen*, vol. 1 (Chuokoronshinsha, 1998), 33–34. Also see Yuichi Hosoya, *Gaiko: Tabunmei Jidai no Taiwa to Kousyou [Diplomacy: The Dialogue and Negotiations across Civilizations]* (Yuhikaku, 2007). Edited one volume translation of Yoshida Memoirs; see Shigeru Yoshida, *Yoshida Shigeru: Last Meiji Man*, edited by Hiroshi Nara (Rowan & Littlefield, 2007).
4. Richard J. Samuels, *Securing Japan: Tokyo's Grand Strategy and the Future of East Asia*, (Cornell University Press, 2007), 29; it is widely accepted that Masataka Kosaka, professor of international politics at Kyoto University, first positively reappraised the diplomatic doctrine of Shigeru Yoshida, though the original word was first used by Masashi Nishihara, then professor at National Defense Academy, Japan. See Masataka Kosaka, *Saisyo Yoshida Shigeru* (Chuokoronsha, 1968).
5. Shinichi Kitaoka, *The Political History of Modern Japan: Foreign Relations and Domestic Politics*, translated by Robert D. Eldridge with Graham Leonard (Kindle edition, Routledge, 2018), Chapter 13.
6. Yuichi Hosoya, "Japan's National Security Strategy and the Japan-US Alliance," in Nakasone Peace Institute (ed.), *The Japan-US Alliance of Hope: Asia-Pacific Maritime Security* (JPIC, 2016).
7. Yuichi Hosoya, "The Role of Japan's National Security Council," AJISS-Commentary, No. 199, June 17, 2013.
8. The Constitution of Japan, official English text (November 3, 1946) https://japan.kantei.go.jp/constitution_and_government_of_japan/constitution_e.html
9. Kazuya Sakamaoto, "Conditions of an Independent State: Japanese Diplomacy in the 1950s," in Makoto Iokibe (ed.), *The Diplomatic History of Postwar Japan*, translated by Robert D. Eldridge (Kindle edition, Routledge, 2011), Chapter 2.
10. Sakamaoto, "Conditions of an Independent State."

11. Makoto Iokibe, "Conclusion: What Was Postwar Japanese Diplomacy?" in Iokibe (ed.), *The Diplomatic History of Postwar Japan.*
12. Ministry of Foreign Affairs of Japan, "Three Non-Nuclear Principles," December 11, 1967, https://www.mofa.go.jp/policy/un/disarmament/nnp/index.html
13. National Defense Program Outline, October 29, 1976, official English text, https://worldjpn.net/documents/texts/docs/19761029.O1E.html
14. "Appendix A: National Defense Program Outline," in Akihiro Sado, *The Self-Defense Forces and Postwar Politics in Japan,* translated Makito Noda (Kindle edition, JPIC, 2017).
15. "Appendix C: The Guidelines for Japan-U.S. Defense Cooperation," in Sado, *The Self-Defense Forces and Postwar Politics in Japan.*
16. For more details, see "Japan Air Self-Defense Force," https://www.mod.go.jp/asdf/English_page/; "Japan Ground Self-Defense Force," https://www.mod.go.jp/gsdf/english/index.html; and Japan Maritime Self-Defense Force, https://www.mod.go.jp/msdf/en/
17. Cabinet Secretariat of Japan, *National Security Strategy of Japan* (December 17, 2013), 20.
18. Narushige Michishita, "Japan's Grand Strategy for a Free and Open Indo-Pacific," in Robert J. Pekkanen and Saadia M. Pekkanen (eds.), *The Oxford Handbook of Japanese Politics* (Kindle edition, Oxford University Press, 2022), Chapter 25.
19. Michishita, "Japan's Grand Strategy."
20. Kitaoka, *The Political History of Modern Japan,* Chapter 13.
21. Maaike Okano-Heijmans and Takaaki Asano, "Economic Diplomacy," in Mary M. McCarthy (ed.), *Routledge Handbook of Japanese Foreign Policy* (Kindle edition, Routledge, 2018), Chapter 16.
22. Okano-Heijmans and Asano, "Economic Diplomacy."
23. Sado, *The Self-Defense Forces and Postwar Politics in Japan,* Chapter 8, "What Comprehensive Security Is."
24. Data about the evolution and increase in Japanese ODA is available from OECD, "Development Co-Operation Profiles—Japan," https://www.oecd-ilibrary.org/sites/b8cf3944-en/index.html?itemId=/content/component/5e331623-en&_csp_=b14d4f60505d057b456dd1730d8fcea3&itemIGO=oecd&itemContentType=chapter
25. Michishita, "Japan's Grand Strategy for a Free and Open Indo-Pacific," Chapter 25.
26. Treaty of Peace with Japan (with Two Declarations), September 8, 1951, official English text, https://treaties.un.org/doc/publication/unts/volume%20136/volume-136-i-1832-english.pdf
27. Treaty of Mutual Cooperation and Security between Japan and the United States of America January 19, 1960, https://www.mofa.go.jp/region/n-america/us/q&a/ref/1.html
28. Guidelines for Japan-U.S. Defense Cooperation, https://japan2.usembassy.gov/pdfs/wwwf-mdao-defense-guidelines1978.pdf
29. Ministry of Foreign Affairs of Japan, "Japan-U.S. Joint Declaration on Security—Alliance for the 21st Century," April 17, 1996, https://www.mofa.go.jp/region/n-america/us/security/security.html
30. Ministry of Foreign Affairs of Japan, "Japan-U.S. Joint Declaration on Security."
31. Cabinet Secretariat of Japan, *National Security Strategy of Japan* 2013, 20.
32. For more information about the Quad, see Ministry of Foreign Affairs of Japan, "Japan-Australia-India-U.S. (Quad) Meetings," September 27, 2022, https://www.mofa.go.jp/fp/nsp/page1e_000396.html

33. Christopher W. Hughes, *Japan's Re-emergence as a "Normal" Military Power* (Kindle edition, Routledge, 2006), Chapter 1.
34. Makoto Iokibe, "Japanese Diplomacy after the Cold War," in Iokibe (ed.), *The Diplomatic History of Postwar Japan,* Chapter 6.
35. North Korea was the first member of the NPT to first announce withdrawal and finally withdraw from the NPT, as well as the first NPT member to develop its own nuclear weapons, in contravention of the treaty.
36. Ministry of Foreign Affairs of Japan, "Prime Minister Junichiro Koizumi's Visit to North Korea," September 17, 2002, https://www.mofa.go.jp/region/asia-paci/n_korea/pmv0209/index.html
37. Japan-DPRK Pyongyang Declaration, September 17, 2002, official English text, https://www.mofa.go.jp/region/asia-paci/n_korea/pmv0209/pyongyang.html
38. Hughes, *Japan's Re-emergence as a "Normal" Military Power,* Chapter 2.
39. Iokibe, "Japanese Diplomacy after the Cold War."
40. "Appendix G: National Defense Program Guidelines for FY 2011 and Beyond," December 17, 2010, in Sado, *The Self-Defense Forces and Postwar Politics in Japan.*
41. Cabinet Secretariat of Japan, *National Security Strategy of Japan* (2013), 12.
42. "Appendix D: National Defense Program Outline in and after FY 1996," December 1995, in Sado, *The Self-Defense Forces and Postwar Politics in Japan.*
43. Ryosei Kokubun, Yoshihide Soeya, Akio Takahara, and Shin Kawashima, *Japan-China Relations in the Modern Era,* trans. Keith Krulak (Kindle edition, Routledge, 2017), Chapter 5, "Japan-China Relations in the 1990s: Rise of China and Increase of Frictions."
44. Hughes, *Japan's Re-emergence as a "Normal" Military Power,* Chapter 2.
45. Kokubun, Soeya, Takahara, and Kawashima, *Japan-China Relations in the Modern Era,* Chapter 6, "Japan-China Relations at the Start of the Twenty-First Century: The Rocky Path to a Strategic Mutually Beneficial Relationship."
46. Kokubun, Soeya, Takahara, and Kawashima, *Japan-China Relations in the Modern Era.*
47. "Appendix G: National Defense Program Guidelines for FY 2011 and Beyond," December 17, 2010.
48. Cabinet Secretariat of Japan, *National Security Strategy of Japan* (2013), 12–13.
49. "Joint Communique of the Government of Japan and the Government of the People's Republic of China," September 29, 1972, official English text https://www.mofa.go.jp/region/asia-paci/china/joint72.html
50. For official documents from the Chinese, Soviet, and other governments related to the Sino-Soviet border clash of 1969, see Wilson Center Digital Archive, "Sino-Soviet Border Conflict, 1969," https://digitalarchive.wilsoncenter.org/topics/sino-soviet-border-conflict-1969
51. Cabinet Secretariat of Japan, *National Security Strategy of Japan* (2013), 12–13.
52. Euan Graham, *Japan's Sea Lane Security 1940–2004: A Matter of Life and Death?* (Kindle edition, Routledge, 2006), Chapter 1, "Japan's Maritime Trade and Trade Routes."
53. Hughes, *Japan's Re-emergence as a "Normal" Military Power,* Chapter 1.
54. Nobukatsu Kanehara, *Anzenhosho Senryaku* (Nikkei Shimbun, 2021), Chapter 8.
55. Cabinet Secretariat of Japan, *National Security Strategy of Japan* (2013), 4.
56. Ministry of Foreign Affairs of Japan, "Japan-Australia-India-U.S. (Quad) Meetings."
57. Yuichi Hosoya, "FOIP 2.0: The Evolution of Japan's Free and Open Indo-Pacific Strategy," *Asia-Pacific Review* 26, no. 1 (2019), 18–28.

58. Cabinet Secretariat of Japan, *National Security Strategy of Japan*, December 16, 2022, official English translation, https://www.cas.go.jp/jp/siryou/221216anzenhoshou/nss-e.pdf
59. Yuichi Hosoya, "The Evolution of Japan's 'Leadership Deficit,'" Ryo Sahashi and James Gannon (eds.), *Looking for Leadership: The Dilemma of Political Leadership in Japan* (Kindle edition, JCIE, 2015), Chapter 2.
60. Ministry of Defense of Japan, *2023 Defense White Paper* (Ministry of Defense of Japan, 2023), 3.
61. Hosoya, "The Role of Japan's National Security Council."
62. Yuichi Hosoya, "The Rise and Fall of Japan's Grand Strategy: The 'Arc of Freedom and Prosperity' and the Future Asian Order," *Asia-Pacific Review* 18, no.1 (2011), 13–24.
63. For in-depth analysis of the "arc of freedom and prosperity" concept and its links to Japan's grand strategy and foreign policy and defense thinking, see Yuichi Hosoya, "Japan's Two Strategies for East Asia: The Evolution of Japan's Diplomatic Strategy," *Asia-Pacific Review*, 20, no. 2 (2013), 146–156; and Hosoya, "The Rise and Fall of Japan's Grand Strategy."
64. Nobukatsu Kanehara, "Japan's Grand Strategy in the 21st Century," speech at JICC, Washington, DC, January 27, 2005.
65. The Japan Institute of International Affairs, "Home," https://www.jiia.or.jp/en/
66. Hosoya, "The Rise and Fall of Japan's Grand Strategy," 18.
67. Ministry of Foreign Affairs of Japan, "Prime Minister Shinzo Abe Visit to Indonesia, India and Malaysia," August 2007, https://www.mofa.go.jp/region/asia-paci/pmv0708/index.html
68. Ministry of Foreign Affairs of Japan, "Prime Minister Shinzo Abe Visit," 19.
69. Ministry of Foreign Affairs of Japan, "Speech by H.E. Mr. Yasuo Fukuda, Prime Minister of Japan: When the Pacific Ocean Becomes an 'Inland Sea': Five Pledges to a Future Asia that 'Acts Together,'" May 22, 2008, https://www.mofa.go.jp/region/asia-paci/speech0805-2f.pdf
70. Lavina Lee, "Abe's Democratic Security Diamond and New Quadrilateral Initiative: An Australian Perspective," *The Journal of East Asian Affairs* 30, no. 2 (Fall/Winter 2016), 3.
71. Lee, "Abe's Democratic Security Diamond."
72. Ministry of Foreign Affairs of Japan, "Free and Open Indo-Pacific," April 24, 2023, https://www.mofa.go.jp/policy/page25e_000278.html
73. Prime Minister's Office of Japan, "Previous Prime Ministers," https://japan.kantei.go.jp/past_cabinet/index.html
74. For an in-depth analysis of FOIP and its place in Japanese grand strategy and security and foreign policy, see Hosoya, "FOIP 2.0." For an analysis of FOIP with specific reference to Japan-United States relations, see Yuichi Hosoya, "Helping the US Lead Again: Japan's Vision of a Free and Open Indo-Pacific," *Global Asia* 16, no. 1 (2021), 52–56.
75. *National Security Strategy of Japan*, 2022.
76. Ministry of Defense of Japan, "Defense of Japan 2024," https://www.mod.go.jp/j/press/wp/wp2024/pdf/DOJ2024_Digest_EN.pdf

CHAPTER 3

North Korea

Jung H. Pak[1] and Ramon Pacheco Pardo

North Korea's grand strategy is informed and shaped by the Korean Peninsula's long history of invasion from its neighbors China and Japan, annexation and eventual colonization by the latter from 1905, division by the US and the Soviet Union in 1945, and war in 1950. North Korea's national priorities since then have reflected a keen awareness of its weakness—a result of its unfortunate geography among larger, more powerful countries—as well as Korea's internecine conflicts, peasant and soldier rebellions, and failed reform efforts that made it more vulnerable to external forces. Kim Il Sung, the former anti-Japanese guerrilla fighter, emerged from that crucible of high-stakes geopolitics as the leader of North Korea with the backing of his patron, the Soviet Union. Harnessing that traumatic history of domination by foreign powers and a desire for autonomy and stability, Kim generated and perpetuated a foundational national narrative that placed himself at the center of the country's identity and as the only guarantor of its survival.

That national narrative of defeat but strength and autonomy under the Kims—Kim Il Sung (1948–94), Kim Jong Il (1994–2011), and Kim Jong Un (2011–present)—serve as the anchor of the regime's security strategy. Indeed, even as the regime depended on outside powers for political and economic support, the regime's distrust of external actors and the necessity of internal strength to withstand foreign interference were reinforced through the decades. In the 1970s the North's only treaty ally China opened up its economy and normalized relations with the United States—North Korea's enemy during the Korean War. Pyongyang's sense of betrayal was deepened when Beijing established diplomatic relations with Seoul in 1992. Meanwhile the Soviet Union collapsed with the closing of the Cold War, ending the generous aid from Moscow and the Eastern European bloc. Without outside assistance, North Korea's economy, which had been robust until the 1960s, buckled under the weight of an inefficient centralized economy, poor management and corruption, and natural disasters.

This chapter describes North Korea's grand strategy (GS). Surrounded by more powerful countries, betrayed by allies, and profoundly aware of its economic weakness and reliant on repression, the regime—specifically, the Kim family—has prioritized its survival above all else. Thus, given its history and the geopolitical realities of the region, as well as the Kims' dependence on violence and fear to maintain internal control, North Korea's GS has been fairly consistent over the decades. We start by analyzing North Korea's strategic priorities, which include the pursuit of nuclear weapons, economic development without reform, and the meta goal of reunification under its own terms. We then examine the external factors informing North Korea's GS. Even as North Korea's strategic view has remained relatively unchanged, these external factors have been dynamic owing to China's rise, Russia's relative decline, South Korea's growing wealth and influence in regional affairs, the evolution of the US-South Korea alliance, and the intensification of the US-China rivalry in recent years. Finally we focus on the domestic factors underpinning the country's GS and how North Korea has operationalized its GS as a result of these priorities and factors. The conclusion describes the key aspects of North Korean GS.

STRATEGIC PRIORITIES

North Korea's strategic priorities include independent security through a strong military, particularly through the possession of nuclear weapons, economic development without extensive reform or global integration, and the meta goal of Korean reunification under its own terms, which has become an unachievable ideal. The external shockwaves of China's opening up, Beijing's diplomatic normalization with Washington in the 1970s and with Seoul in the 1992, as well as the end of the Cold War in the early 1990s probably reinforced the importance of achieving these goals, even as reunification and prosperity became more unattainable in part due to the regime's insistence—and success—in developing nuclear weapons.

Development of an Independent Nuclear Deterrent

North Korea began exploring the idea of a nuclear weapons program as early as the 1950s, when it requested and received some assistance from the

Soviet Union, which provided training for North Korean scientists, helped build a nuclear research center, and signed a nuclear cooperation agreement. In 1958 the United States deployed nuclear weapons in South Korea to deter North Korean aggression and reassure Seoul about US commitment to its defense, undoubtedly strengthening Kim Il Sung's belief that North Korea should also possess nuclear weapons.[2] Pyongyang's dogged pursuit of nuclear weapons capabilities, despite Moscow and Beijing's criticism and reluctance to assist, reflected its deepening insecurity about the reliability of its two sponsors, fears about South Korea's growing wealth and military and its alliance with the United States, and qualms about the regime's long-term prospects for its conventional military capabilities and its economy, especially after the 1970s. That commitment deepened after the collapse of communism and the attendant aid from Moscow and the Soviet bloc. North Korea's increasingly straitened economic circumstances and the deterioration of its aging armaments placed increasing importance on the nuclear weapons program to compensate for those deficiencies.

Pyongyang's development of its nuclear weapons program led to the first North Korea nuclear crisis in 1993–94 after it announced withdrawal from the Treaty on Nonproliferation of Nuclear Weapons (NPT) and expelled International Atomic Energy Agency inspectors who were there to monitor the North's nuclear facilities.[3] This prompted the United States to consider military options to stop the suspected covert nuclear weapons program. The crisis was seemingly resolved in October 1994 when Kim Jong Il, who had succeeded his father who died earlier that year, signed the Agreed Framework with Washington.[4] But a second nuclear crisis followed from 2002 when US officials confronted the regime about its covert uranium enrichment program and North Korea announced and then withdrew from the NPT.[5]

Kim Il Sung and Kim Jong Il meanwhile continued to pay lip service to denuclearization. North and South Korea had signed a joint declaration in January 1992 committing to "denuclearization of the Korean Peninsula."[6] Kim Jong Il in the Agreed Framework with the United States reiterated his country's commitment to denuclearization. In September 2005 Pyongyang once again "committed to abandoning all nuclear weapons and existing nuclear programmes and returning, at an early date, to the Treaty on the Non-Proliferation of Nuclear Weapons and to IAEA safeguards."[7] Nevertheless the regime secretly advanced its capabilities, indicating that it continued to see possession of a nuclear program as a high strategic priority despite the promise of diplomatic relations with the United States and costs incurred as a result of sanctions and international opprobrium.

Kim Jong Un accelerated the development of the nuclear weapons program upon coming to power in late 2011 after his father's sudden death. He elevated its importance in 2012 when the regime codified North Korea's nuclear weapons status by adding the fifth amendment to its 1972 constitution, which praised the late Kim for developing North Korea into a "nuclear state."[8] Adding to Kim Jong Il's two nuclear tests in 2006 and 2009, the younger Kim carried out four increasingly more powerful nuclear tests, as well as tests of multiple intercontinental ballistic missiles (ICBM) that theoretically would allow Pyongyang to launch a nuclear strike on the US mainland. Under the young dictator the ballistic missiles became more diverse, more reliable, and more dangerous. In announcing the *byungjin* or parallel development policy in March 2013,[9] Kim emphasized development of North Korea's nuclear program as one of Pyongyang's two priorities—economic development being the other. In his New Year speech of 2017, Kim stated that North Korea had "achieved the status of a nuclear power."[10] Following the third ICBM test in November 2017, the North Korean leader declared that his country had "finally realized the great historic cause of completing the state nuclear force."[11] In his New Year message of 2018, he said he would focus on "the perfecting of the North Korean nuclear forces."[12] And in September 2024 North Korean media published pictures of Kim touring the country's uranium enrichment facilities. This was interpreted, among others, as a North Korean message that the country should be accepted as a nuclear power whose weapons are nonnegotiable.[13] While Kim Jong Un made it clear in his statements and with his actions that the nuclear program was a deterrent against the United States, he was also acknowledging its centrality to North Korea's national identity, sovereignty, and ultimately, his legacy.

Independent Economic Development

Despite, or perhaps because of, its economic dependence on its Russia and China, North Korea advanced the ideology of *juche*, roughly meaning "self-reliance." Kim Il Sung introduced the concept in a December 1955 speech.[14] Subsequent speeches, including a crucial one in April 1965 in which he laid out the principles behind juche,[15] asserted North Korea's independence in the political, security, and economic spheres. An amalgamation of Christianity (via missionaries), the imperial cult of the emperor (via Japanese colonialists), Confucianism (via China), communism (via Russia and especially Stalin's cult of personality), and filial piety, juche as an ideology aimed at highlighting Kim's Koreanness and harnessing the people's nationalism and xenophobia after the Korean War to bolster his position as the *suryong,* or the unitary leader of North Korea.[16]

Infinitely adaptable to justify whatever policies Kim Il Sung and his successors adopted, it nevertheless acknowledged the regime's understanding of economic independence as critical to political independence. The party daily noted in 1963, "Economic dependence on foreign forces entails political dependence on those forces. Economic subordination leads to political subordination."[17] This sentiment was echoed repeatedly in the ensuing decades, as in 1981 the paper asserted that economic independence served as the "material basis" and guiding principle of juche and that it was necessary in "successfully accelerating socialist and communist construction . . . ,"[18] even as the North's economic fortunes were in a downward spiral.

The amplification of the rhetoric of self-reliance became more important as the reality of attaining that goal became more elusive. Engaged in economic competition with South Korea, which was growing wealthier and more knitted into the international financial system, the Kim regime sought to show its "independent" economic development and prove the superiority and egalitarianism of the North Korean-style socialist system. In practice, however, Pyongyang played China against the Soviet Union throughout the Cold War to extract economic benefits.[19] Since the mid-1990s onward, the nuclear weapons program expanded the regime's ability to conduct brinkmanship and coercive diplomacy for economic gain, and indeed the maneuvering space provided by the nuclear weapons program became more vital because of the collapse of the communist bloc in the early 1990s.[20]

The juche concept was useful for the regime during the famine in North Korea between 1995 and 1998, during which hundreds of thousands of people perished.[21] The famine—the result of economic mismanagement, unsustainable agricultural practices and bad policies, and the Kim Jong Il regime's unwillingness to adopt reforms—laid bare the dependence of Pyongyang on foreign assistance and its inability to take care of its people.[22] Dubbed "the arduous march" to give it a revolutionary flavor, the regime evoked the country's exceptionalism and exhorted the people to fend for themselves in the spirit of self-reliance rather than relying on the state's depleted public distribution system. As a result, grassroots-driven markets or *jangmadang* started to take hold, sparking a culture of licit and illicit entrepreneurship by state and nonstate actors.[23]

While Kim Jong Il promised to usher in a "strong and prosperous nation" by the centennial of his father Kim Il Sung's birthday in April 2012, it was his son, Kim Jong Un, who more decisively linked the nuclear weapons program to economic development.[24] As part of his byungjin policy, Kim emphasized that economic development is compatible with nuclear weapons development,[25] a contrast to his father's military-first policy and famine days of want and despair.

Yet nuclear weapons development has been counterproductive to economic prosperity. Since its first nuclear test in 2006, the regime has lost trade partners, turned off by the Kim family's threats and missile and nuclear tests. Sanctions and international opprobrium have increased North Korea's isolation while deepening Pyongyang's dependence on Beijing—its only real remaining partner—for political and economic aid.

Reunification under North Korea's Terms

Since the division of the Korean Peninsula in 1945 by the United States and the Soviet Union, the two Koreas have seen each other as illegitimate and sought to eliminate their existential rival. Pyongyang and Seoul built up their military with the help of their respective sponsors, the Soviet Union and the United States, making the 38th parallel one of the most dangerous spots in the world. Soon after the partition, Kim Il Sung sought to make reunification a reality in 1950, making the Korean conflict the first "hot" war in the emerging Cold War.

Despite the North's catastrophic defeat, Kim and his successors did not relinquish this goal. The preamble of the December 1972 North Korean constitution—which replaced the original 1948 constitution and still applies today—enshrines Korean reunification as the ultimate goal of the Kim family and, by definition, the North Korean state: "The great Comrades Kim Il Sung and Kim Jong Il are the sun of the nation and the lodestar of national reunification. Regarding the reunification of the country as the supreme national task, they devoted all their efforts and care for its realization."[26]

Over time, however, the realities of Pyongyang's deteriorating economic and geopolitical fortunes while Seoul became increasingly rich and democratic made North Korea's vision of reunification an increasingly aspirational one. Nevertheless, that did not completely dampen Kim Il Sung and Kim Jong Il's appetite for trying to weaken their successful southern neighbor. Acknowledging changing geopolitics and its own straitened circumstances, Pyongyang employed a mix of diplomacy and terroristic acts aimed at shoring up its position and trying to erode Seoul's. In July 1972 the regime joined with South Korea to issue the first-ever joint communiqué.

The document emphasized "the common desire of achieving the peaceful unification of the nation," but also that "a great national unity as one people shall be sought first, transcending differences in ideas, ideologies, and systems."[27] In 1991 North Korea joined the United Nations. It then signed the Inter-Korean Basic Agreement reaffirming the 1972 call for reunification but also stating that "the South and the North shall recognize and respect each other's systems."[28] And in 1992 Pyongyang introduced an extensive amendment to the 1972 constitution in support of peaceful—rather than "revolutionary"—reunification.[29] In 2024 North Korea seemingly moved away from its goal of reunification when Kim Jong Un announced that South Korea should be defined as its "invariable principal enemy" rather than as a partner for reconciliation and reunification. At the same time, however, Kim also made the point that North Korea should be ready to occupy South Korea and thus reunify the Korean Peninsula by force were war to break out in the Korean Peninsula.[30] In other words, the goal remained even if the means had changed.

Yet these diplomatic moves were driven not by a desire for rapprochement and genuine peace, but aimed at reducing its insecurity and exploring potential opportunities amid geopolitical changes. The 1972 joint communiqué, for example, was issued just months after US President Richard Nixon visited China, opening a process leading to eventual Sino-American diplomatic normalization.[31] In fact, in the 1970s, the regime was building up its military, which the US Central Intelligence Agency (CIA) at the time assessed was part of an approach to strengthen "the North as a revolutionary base for reunification."[32] Pyongyang sought to open channels of potential influence in South Korea and undermine the government in Seoul and exploit perceived cracks in the US-South Korea alliance. Diplomacy was accompanied by acts of terrorism. The 1960s to the 1980s were marked by violent North Korean activities: an unsuccessful infiltration of the South Korean presidential Blue House, the shooting down of a US reconnaissance plane, and an attack against a South Korean delegation in Burma that killed almost the entire cabinet.[33]

Even as each successive Kim evoked the revolutionary past and a unified future, the vision has become increasingly dim. North Korea's demonstration of its nuclear weapons capabilities has come at the expense of economic development and integration with the international community. North Korea has deepened its isolation and made reunification under its terms a more distant ideal, but its approach is ultimately aimed at guaranteeing the survival of the Kim family dynasty and its control of the regime above all else.

EXTERNAL FACTORS

As a weak power, North Korea's GS is inevitably affected by external factors, particularly its immediate neighborhood. This reflects the fact that North Korea has little influence in global affairs and therefore its core strategic priorities do not aim to shape the international system as may be the case for China or the United States. Even at the regional level, North Korea has very limited influence beyond the Korean Peninsula. Nevertheless the regime's possession of nuclear weapons and growing cyber capabilities give it strategic relevance beyond Northeast Asia. Moreover, the US alliance relationships with South Korea and Japan and the intensification of US-China rivalry provide both risks and opportunities for Pyongyang.

Third-Party Actors

Pyongyang's GS is affected, above all, by state actors. It is not at risk from terrorist or insurgent groups, and its links with NGOs or firms—by regime design—are fairly limited.

South Korea is a key factor in North Korean grand strategy. From North Korea's perspective, no state is more important than South Korea, which claims that "the territory of the Republic of Korea shall consist of the Korean peninsula and its adjacent islands," according to its constitution.[34] Similar to Pyongyang, Seoul also sees unification on its terms as one of its core strategic priorities.

China and the United States are two other key factors. The centrality of Beijing and Washington can be traced back to the Korean War, for the United States led the UN forces that almost defeated North Korea, and China was the country whose support guaranteed North Korea's survival.[35] As the two most economic and militarily powerful countries in East Asia, China and the US shape the region like no other countries do. But from the North's perspective, its border with China and the presence of US troops in South Korea serve as a physical reminder of the importance of maneuvering between the two powers.

Japan and Russia are important factors as well. From a North Korean perspective, Russia's importance had decreased since the collapse of the Soviet Union.[36] But North Korea's shared border with Moscow and the latter's role as one of five permanent members of the UN Security Council made it worthwhile for Pyongyang to maintain ties to Moscow as a source of diplomatic and economic support. Furthermore, Russo-North Korean relations received a boost after Russia's invasion of Ukraine in 2022 and Pyongyang's subsequent decision to transfer weapons and provide diplomatic support to Moscow.[37] Eventually, North Korea would also send troops to fight together with the Russian military.[38] A "comprehensive strategic partnership" between Pyongyang and Moscow in 2024 and the two countries' anti-US and anti-West alignment suggest potential for expanded economic and security ties, but it remains unclear how this relationship will evolve. As for Japan, although it had relatively robust trade ties with North Korea until the 2000s, it now has negligible trade links with the North and has had little success in establishing substantive diplomatic links. But the US-Japan alliance and Tokyo's political and economic strength—as well as its history as the former colonial power on the Korean Peninsula—makes it a potential threat.[39]

Threats and Opportunities

As a small country surrounded by richer, more militarily advanced nations, North Korea sees proximate threats to the survival of the Kim dynasty and its sovereignty. However, Pyongyang has been able to take the initiative in its regional relationships and exploit national priorities of its adversaries toward driving wedges between and among US allies and North Korea's neighbors while wresting political and economic concessions. Thus North Korea's opportunities paradoxically are embedded in its perceived and real threats.

United States is a threat, from a North Korean perspective. Pyongyang sees Washington as its greatest military threat and uses that threat to justify the regime's nuclear weapons pursuit, repressive political system, and refusal to open up the economy. The US-South Korea alliance puts the world's most powerful military just several dozen miles away from North Korea. The collapse of the Soviet Union made the United States the undisputed hegemon throughout the 1990s and 2000s, further heightening the sense that Washington was a threat to North Korea's survival. Almost every US president considered plans to conduct military action against North Korea; the Bill Clinton and George W. Bush administrations came close to launching strikes on North Korea.[40] During the Korean War, President Truman even considered using nuclear weapons against the country.[41]

But the regime has also harnessed the memory of the Korean War and the fact of US power as tools for sustaining its own control of the country. The Kim leaders have continually harkened back to the wartime past, revitalizing and exaggerating US brutality and malevolent intentions. For the current leader Kim Jong Un—who could not be temporally placed in the wartime past given his youth—magnifying his blood connection to his grandfather and guerrilla fighter Kim Il Sung and amplifying the Korean war for the younger generations while highlighting the looming US peril, serve to legitimize dynastic succession of the Kims. The need for defense also provides justification for the country's isolation and poverty and the siphoning of North Korea's scarce resources toward its military program.[42]

Despite the anti-American rhetoric, Pyongyang has sporadically engaged in nuclear negotiations with the United States—culminating in the Agreed Framework (1994), Six-Party Talks Joint Statement (2005), Leap Day agreement (2012), and Singapore communiqué (2018)—that have had little success in taming North Korea's ambitions but afforded the regime time to covertly advance its weapons programs; defuse tension, usually after a North Korea provocation such as a nuclear or ballistic missile test; and try to split the US from its allies.[43] In alternating cycles of belligerence and aggression with pivots toward dialogue and diplomacy, Pyongyang has been able to keep Washington on the back foot.

South Korea is another threat, from a North Korean perspective. Washington's expansive alliance with South Korea and the latter's economic success and respected international position pose an existential threat to Pyongyang. Though North Korea's economy was better than the South's throughout the 1950s and 1960s, by the 1980s, it had become clear that South Korea had "won" the competition, its hosting of the 1988 Olympics serving as a "coming out" party.[44] South Korea's economy was bigger, and central and Eastern European states were breaking ranks with the communist bloc to normalize relations with the country. A vibrant democracy and a global and technology powerhouse, South Korea has become a key player in global institutions. It also has a more modern and powerful military than North Korea.[45]

Despite South Korea's outpacing of North Korea across the range of issues and development and its possession of soft and hard power across the globe, it also presents an opportunity for North Korea. Seoul's desire for rapprochement across both conservative and progressive presidential administrations offer tantalizing avenues for Pyongyang to use calibrated engagement to reap the benefits of South Korea's wealth. For example, Kim Jong Il and Kim Jong Un have opportunistically used the administrations of pro-engagement South Korean presidents—Kim Dae-jung and Roh Moo-hyun (1998–2008) and then under also liberal president Moon Jae-in (2017–22)—to advance the regime's goals, whether it is to launder its reputation after provocative acts or to gain monetary benefits as during the era of Sunshine Policy, when it was revealed that the Kim Dae-jung administration had secretly funneled half a billion US dollars to the Kim regime prior to the first inter-Korean summit in 2000. Conservative president Park Geun-hye early in her administration tried unsuccessfully to build a process for "trust-building."[46] Kim Jong Un in recent years has used summits with president Moon Jae-in to try to enlarge the perceived policy divergences between President Moon and President Trump.

Thus, rich and influential South Korea, aligned with the most powerful country in the world, the United States, still poses an existential threat to the poorer North. But Pyongyang has been able to maintain the initiative through belligerence and dialogue. By honing in on Seoul's own meta-goal of reunification and the constraints on its actions as a result of its alliance with Washington and its international and economic position, North Korea's leaders have ensured their survival and expanded their policy space using tools of coercion and diplomacy.[47]

China and Russia are potential threats for North Korea, but also opportunities. Abandonment by China and to a lesser extent Russia is another potential threat informing Pyongyang's GS. Throughout the Cold War, Kim Il Sung exploited Sino-Soviet competition to extract economic concessions that allowed the North Korean economy to prosper, probably reinforcing Kim's adventurism in the form of terrorist attacks against South Korea.[48] Furthermore, both China and the Soviet Union signed military treaty alliances with North Korea during the Cold War. But the collapse of the Soviet Union in 1991 put an end to its alliance with North Korea, and China's decision to normalize diplomatic relations with South Korea in 1992 signaled to Pyongyang that even its only remaining treaty ally was not reliable.[49] While the treaty alliance with Beijing continues to be in place, poor relations between Xi Jinping and Kim Jong Un and debates in China regarding the potential drawbacks of the alliance highlight for Pyongyang that it cannot trust Beijing, even though ties have warmed since 2018.[50]

Nevertheless, the shared border and the formal treaty alliance with China have yielded benefits for Pyongyang. For one, China's growing economic and military power in the past two decades has provided opportunities for North Korea. Chinese leaders' desire to develop its poor northeast, adjacent to North Korea, have been a boon for the market generation that has emerged since the famine of the 1990s and those who rely on the cross-border trade and smuggling for their livelihood, and in some cases get wealthy doing so. China's share of North Korea's total trade has risen accordingly—accounting for over 95 percent in 2019—even as trade with other former partners like Japan, South Korea, and India has dissipated.[51]

Beijing, for its part, regards North Korea as a buffer state against US troops stationed in South Korea. Seeing US and South Korean pressure on the North as driving the Kim regime's belligerence, Chinese leaders have prioritized regional stability, even if it is at the expense of North Korean denuclearization. This explains China's tolerance for North Korea despite the tension sown by Pyongyang's actions, US and South Korean shows of force and imposition of mounting sanctions, and the North's defiance of Chinese leaders' wishes. China has used its veto power at the UN Security Council over the years to prevent the imposition of even more sanctions as a result of the North's nuclear and ballistic missile tests.[52] Given the history of China's actions vis-à-vis North Korea-related issues, Pyongyang almost certainly sees Beijing's concern for North Korean internal and regional stability as a way to play its patron against Washington.

While the heyday of its relationship with Moscow is long gone, Russia's proximity and the leadership's desire to avoid marginalization in Korean Peninsula issues offers another opportunity for Pyongyang. Following Beijing's lead, Moscow has sought to ease UN Security Council sanctions after North Korea's nuclear or missile tests and at times undermining the sanctions regime.[53] Although North Korea and Russia have minimal trade and investment links,[54] President Vladimir Putin since coming to power has devoted more attention to Russia's Far East—the region bordering North Korea. This has made Moscow become more involved in Korean Peninsula affairs than in the 1990s.[55] Thus, even though North Korea's expectations for relations with Russia had been low, it kept ties at least lukewarm to keep open potential opportunities, such as the "comprehensive strategic partnership" and the weapons trade driven in part by Russia's war against Ukraine. For North Korea, Moscow is a useful partner for Pyongyang, particularly as a hedge against over-reliance on Beijing.

Japan is another threat for North Korea to consider. Japanese colonial rule of the Korean Peninsula has cast a long shadow in Tokyo's relations with Pyongyang. Although Japan and South Korea established diplomatic ties in 1965, Pyongyang does not have formal relations with Tokyo. There was a thaw in the early 2000s, when North Korea's Kim Jong Il and Japanese Prime Minister Koizumi met twice for summits and discussed normalization, economic aid from Japan, and North Korea's extension of its then-moratorium on missile testing and commitment to its international commitments regarding nuclear weapons development. But Kim Jong Il's admission that the North in the 1970s and 1980s abducted Japanese citizens unleashed anger in Japan and calls for Pyongyang to release the individuals or send back their remains. Since then the regime's nuclear weapons and ballistic missile programs as well as the abductions issue have cooled bilateral relations, although the two sides have dabbled in occasional diplomacy.[56] The current

Kim has largely ignored Tokyo—he has yet to meet with the Japanese prime minister as of January 2021—and he sees value in poor Seoul-Tokyo ties, which hamper regional and global cooperation on pressuring Pyongyang on its nuclear weapons program.

Types of Conflict

North Korea's GS mainly focuses on two preparations for two types of conflict. The first is a potential military strike by the United States, along with its ally South Korea. North Korea's attack against the South in 1950 led to US bombings that devastated the country, and American and South Korean troops pushed the North Korean military all the way to the Yalu river dividing the Korean Peninsula from China.[57] North Korea has also seen demonstration of US military power since the wars in Southeast Asia during the Cold War and invasions in countries such as Afghanistan in 2001 and Iraq in 2003 during the war on terror. Over the decades, South Korea has provided military and other support, as in the US wars in Vietnam, Iraq, Afghanistan, and in counter-piracy operations in the Middle East and Africa.[58] In Pyongyang's view, it needs to fortify its border with South Korea—thousands of artillery systems are arrayed along the northern side of the 38th parallel—and its nuclear weapons program to deter an attack against the North, given the examples of Libya and Iraq.[59]

Internal conflict, supported and fueled by external forces, also factors into North Korea's GS. To preserve the unitary power of the leader, the regime has an infrastructure of repression that punishes any criticism of the Kim family, cultivates an environment of suspicion, and operates a siloed bureaucracy to prevent coups. Border crackdowns and severe punishment for possession of South Korea-derived media reveal the extent of fear that the regime has for outside information penetrating the country.

DOMESTIC FACTORS

Domestic factors are as important as the external ones to understand North Korea's GS. Since its foundation, the country has been a dictatorship led by a single family: the Kims. The remarkable degree of continuity over a period expanding more than seven decades has resulted in Pyongyang developing a series of long-lasting values and decision-making structures. Even though they have been affected by domestic and international developments, the essence of these values and structures has not changed. In contrast, material resources have changed from the 1970s onward—and especially since the end of the Cold War.

National Values

As discussed previously, juche combines elements of both Korean history and mistrust toward others, both domestically and internationally. According to North Korean revisionism dating back to the 1950s, the Korean War was a "glorious revolutionary struggle against the imperialist aggressors."[60] In other words, the Korean War was an attempt by the United States to eliminate North Korea and spread its imperialism across Asia, even though it was Kim Il Sung who attacked the south in June 1950.

In particular, juche was seen as an expression of North Korean independence within the socialist camp and signaled the country's move away from universal Marxism-Leninism, even if it shares its focus on politics conceived as a struggle between the oppressors and the oppressed. By the 1990s reference to this Soviet-inspired ideology had almost disappeared from public discourse, with the complete removal of the mention of Marxism-Leninism from the North's 2009 constitution.[61] Meanwhile, the Confucianism and filial piety elements are evident in juche, in its focus on the society over the individual and portrayal of Kim Il Sung as the father figure to whom the North Korean people must remain loyal for the sake of the country.[62]

Kim Il Sung was not just suspicious of the outside world; he was profoundly aware of inside threats and took early measures to stamp out disloyalty and perceived and real challenges to his rule. In the 1950s, Kim developed a *songbun* system that categorized every individual into three main castes—core, wavering or basic, and hostile—based on their family background. One's songbun is inherited and can be downgraded according to the individuals' or their family's behavior and their demonstrated loyalty to Kim.[63] The system incentivized human rights violations, a culture of surveillance, and a cult of personality of the Kim leaders.

Juche was a malleable ideological tool. Following the collapse of the Soviet Union, Kim Jong Il supplemented juche by linking it to the concepts of *songun* ("military first"). Introduced by Kim Jong Il in 1995, songun placed the military at the center of North Korean politics, economics, and society. The military thus became both the embodiment and the mechanism to implement North Korea's self-reliant revolution.[64] Songun's centrality to Kim's conception of juche was demonstrated when it was added to the North Korean constitution in 2009.[65] Kim Jong Un reframed juche as byungjin, promising both military strength through nuclear weapons and economic development. Byungjin reflected Kim's optimism that the North could have both nuclear weapons and prosperity, in contrast to the dark days of sacrifice during the famine and in the ensuing years.[66]

Influence of These Values

The influence of juche on North Korean policymakers' views about actors, threats, opportunities, and potential forms of conflict is two-fold. To begin with, juche means that the Kim family is North Korea and North Korea is the Kim family. Centering the state on the cult of personality of Kim Il Sung also elevated the bloodline, which has been used to legitimize and transfer the people's loyalty to Kim Jong Il and Kim Jong Un, the only two dynastic successions in the communist world.[67]

Institutionalization and incentivization of the cult of personality and fear of the outside world into the social, cultural, and political fabric mean that any threat to the Kim family is considered a threat to North Korea itself. Were the Kim family to stop ruling North Korea, the country itself would disappear in its current terms, at least in constitutional terms.[68] Therefore the pervasiveness of internal and external threats requires extreme vigilance and loyalty to the Kim regime.

The Way in Which Policymakers Debate

Policymaking in North Korea is dominated by the Kim family and is personality-driven.[69] The three Kims have exercised near absolute dictatorial power. They have also purged any potential challenger to their rule; Kim Jong Un during his tenure purged, demoted, and disappeared hundreds of party and military officials.[70] As a result, decision-making in North Korea is top-down and dominated by the leader. There is probably little room for debate and for other officials to share their views and challenge the decisions taken by the leader, a result of the groupthink that the regime has cultivated over the decades.

Institutional Process

North Korea's formal institutions and processes provide an aura of legitimacy to the Kim regime. While the institutional processes are opaque, the Kims have understood the importance of designating themselves with appropriate military and party titles and demonstrating democratic practices, such as voting. From 1948 to 1998 the premier or president was the leader of North Korea. Only Kim Il Sung and Kim Jong Il upon his father's death held this position. The State Affairs Commission (SAC)—replacing the National Defence Commission as the ultimate decision-making body—has been the main policymaking institution in North Korea dating back to the 1998 constitution amendment, when Kim Il Sung was named eternal president.[71] Kim Jong Il and Kim Jong Un have been the only two chairmen of the SAC dating back to the amendment. In the most recent party congress, Kim Jong Un was "elected" the general secretary, further elevating his status. The Supreme People's Assembly, the main legislative body, is a rubber-stamp organization.[72] North Koreans vote for the members of the assembly, almost all of whom belong to the party.[73] In practice, however, the institutional policymaking process is less formalized since any debate on policy depends on direct access to Kim. In other words, power depends on access to the leader.

Material Resources

North Korea's material resources to implement its GS are military in nature for the most part. Pyongyang has a nuclear program including dozens of nuclear warheads plus a wide range of ballistic missiles—including intercontinental-range—that are increasingly more reliable and more mobile, potentially allowing it to launch a strike on any of its neighbors plus the US mainland.[74] In addition North Korea reportedly has up to 5,000 tons of chemical weapons, one of the largest stockpiles globally. North Korean agents used a nerve agent to kill Kim's half-brother Kim Jong Nam at an airport in Malaysia in February 2017. Pyongyang is also believed to be in possession of biological weapons.[75]

In terms of conventional capabilities, North Korea has almost 1.2 million active military personnel, making Pyongyang's military the fourth largest force in the world. In addition, North Korea has at least 4,300 tanks, over 1,300 aircraft, more than 70 submarines, and 300 helicopters. Plus, North Korea also is in possession of over 21,000 artillery. Thousands of them are in the inter-Korean border, pointed at South Korean territory.[76] In recent years Pyongyang has also developed asymmetric warfare capabilities in the form of a cyberwarfare unit, which includes as many as 6,000 hackers and support staff.[77]

In sheer numbers the North Korean military is impressive by global standards. But it is less technologically advanced than the military capabilities of its immediate neighbors or the United States. Furthermore, possession of nuclear weapons in and of itself is not exceptional in northeast Asia. China and Russia are both nuclear powers, and Japan and South Korea are protected by Washington's nuclear umbrella. Also, Pyongyang's military budget is dwarfed by its neighbors'.[78] Therefore North Korea's focus on strengthening its military resources since the end of the Cold War has yielded impressive capabilities in absolute terms—but North Korea has been losing ground against its neighbors on which its GS focuses in relative terms. The only exception is its nuclear weapons program, further increasing its value to the regime. Recognizing his military's deficiencies, Kim Jong Un has made selective investments into certain military capabilities in recent years, including artillery, special operations forces, training, and professionalization of the services.

Pyongyang's economic capabilities are unimpressive. North Korea is one of the poorest countries across East Asia—a region that has four of the eleven biggest economies in the world, China, Japan, South Korea, and Russia—measured as GDP per capita.[79] Trade with China, cybertheft, arms exports, illicit activities, and foreign aid are the backbone of the North Korean economy.

The diplomatic resources of North Korea are also poor. Since the collapse of the communist bloc and the increasing irrelevance of the non-aligned movement from the 1990s, North Korea has become more isolated than before. North Korea as of 2024 has fewer than 50 embassies across the world, the lowest number in Northeast Asia with the exception of Taiwan.[80] Its diplomats are required to pay for their upkeep and are charged with generating revenue—through arms sales, smuggling, and fraud, for example—to send back to Pyongyang. It is absent or secondary at best in most regional and multilateral institutions, even if it participates in security forums such as the ASEAN Regional Forum (ARF) and the Council for Security Cooperation in the Asia Pacific (CSCAP) or the United Nations system. North Korean nationals do not hold leadership roles in any regional or multilateral institution.

OPERATIONALIZATION OF GRAND STRATEGY

To implement its GS, North Korea has used brinkmanship and coercive diplomacy while bolstering ideological and repressive control to advance the regime's narrative of independence. These methods have compensated for the country's relative weakness and preserved the Kims' grip on power and North Korea's autonomy, and they can be categorized into two separate but interdependent sets of actions.

North Korea has a range of domestic capabilities at its disposal. Pyongyang has doggedly pursued the development of nuclear weapons and used them to extract material benefits. The North's current primary concern is to deter a US attack and invasion, but below the level of actual conflict, the regime has sought to normalize its possession of nuclear weapons, test its technologies and make advancements based on those tests, and obtain tacit international acceptance of the regime's claimed status.

In the early years of the program Kim Jong Il used satellite launch vehicle (SLV) tests to try to dilute (unsuccessfully) international condemnation for testing intercontinental ballistic missile technologies. Claiming North Korea's right to "peaceful uses of space," Kim would then use international criticism and sanctions as evidence of the "hostile" nature of outside powers and to justify testing of nuclear weapons and additional ballistic missile tests and pull out of negotiations as it did in 2009 when it quit the multilateral Six-Party Talks on North Korea's nuclear weapons program.[81]

Having inherited an advanced nuclear weapons program, Kim Jong Un was determined to make serious and significant new progress as he embarked on his leadership of the country. Conducting scores of new designs of ballistic missiles and progressively testing more powerful nuclear weapons, Kim aimed to show that he was aggressive and determined to assert the North's status, despite doubts about his age and inexperience when he first came to power as a 27-year-old.[82] Under Kim the North has improved and diversified the ballistic missile program and made progress on credibly threatening the United States with intercontinental ballistic missiles.[83] These demonstrations have had the effect of showing and projecting the North's military power and strategic relevance and reinforcing Kim's power and solidifying his status as the sole leader and defender of the North Korean state.

North Korea has also made use of diplomacy for political and economic gain. Pyongyang has long sought ways to legitimize itself in the eyes of its domestic and external audiences. Pyongyang tried to maintain strong diplomatic links within the communist bloc and touted its part in the non-aligned movement, which were useful networks to present the regime as the legitimate representative of the Korean people.[84] The North joined the UN in 1991 and established diplomatic relations with most Western countries throughout the 1990s and early 2000s.[85] And it engaged in dialogue with the United States in those years, in part to explore options for economic and political benefits.

North Korea has tried to operationalize this goal through high-profile bilateral summits, particularly with the big regional players. Kim Jong Il had summits with his South Korean counterpart in 2000 and 2007.[86] Although a meeting with US President Bill Clinton in the late 1990s never happened,

Kim Jong Il met with Secretary of State Madeleine Albright in Pyongyang in 2000.[87] Finally, in 2018 and 2019 Kim Jong Un held two summits and a meeting with US President Donald Trump,[88] three summits with South Korea's Moon Jae-in,[89] five with China's Xi Jinping,[90] and three with Russia's Vladimir Putin,[91] lending Kim an aura of respectability and international standing.

Diplomacy is also useful for Pyongyang in its efforts to find sources of revenue and economic partners. In the 1990s Japan was North Korea's largest trading partner. During the 2000s China and South Korea vied for this position. In the case of South Korea, the inter-Korean summit of 2000 paved the way for two joint economic projects: the Kaesong industrial zone involving North Korean labor and South Korean capital, and the Mount Kumgang tourism zone for South Korean tourists.[92] Pyongyang also sought to attract aid and investment from Western countries with which it had normalized relations, as well as with a resurgent Russia. And Kim Jong Il held summits with Japanese Prime Minister Koizumi Junichiro to shore up bilateral relations and elicit Japanese aid.[93] Kim Jong Un has sought to mend ties to Beijing since 2018 to mitigate the effects of international sanctions and to attract investors and tourists. Furthermore Kim has also made use of Russia's need to get missiles, troops and other military support to continue its 2022 invasion of Ukraine to play the country against China to maximize its gains, as it did during the Cold War.

The North has used diplomacy to try to extract economic concessions in exchange for its nuclear concessions. The result of North Korea's economic underdevelopment and its belligerence has been overreliance in China to sustain the regime. Wary of dependence, North Korea has targeted engagement with the United States to dampen international appetite for sanctions implementation and to gain access to international markets and funds from multilateral economic institutions, while providing reversible or insignificant concessions on its nuclear weapons program.[94]

CONCLUSION

North Korea is a weak power in a region that includes the two most powerful countries in the international system (China and the United States), a more prosperous and stronger "half" (South Korea), and two influential stakeholder powers (Japan and Russia). Aware of its weakness, Pyongyang has enacted a consistent GS designed to ensure survival as an independent state with the Kim dynasty at the helm. Measured by this yardstick, North Korea has been successful in its GS. The Kims have ruled North Korea since its foundation in 1948, even as economic success and international reputation remain elusive.

The three key goals pursued by North Korea over the decades include development of an increasingly more dangerous nuclear weapons program, independent economic development as a means to avoid dependence on external benefactors, and the meta-goal of reunification under the North's terms.

These goals are informed by several external factors. These include the existential threat that South Korea poses as a more successful competitor, the US-ROK alliance that puts the world's most powerful military at North Korea's door, and potential abandonment by China and Russia. External factors also include the opportunities that come from Pyongyang's formal alliance with Beijing, relatively good relations with Moscow, and sporadic cordial relations with South Korea. The other external factors that Pyongyang need to consider are the types of conflict it has to prepare for, namely, a potential military strike by the United States together with South Korea and information penetration that might erode the regime's control on its people.

Internal factors informing North Korea's GS include above all the national value of juche—with its focus on political independence, economic self-reliance, and self-defense. As a consequence of juche and the centrality of the Kims to the very notion of North Korea as an independent state, policymaking debate and institutional processes are essentially subsumed and driven by the preferences of the Kim in power. In terms of material resources, Pyongyang mainly relies on its military given the inadequacy of its economic and diplomatic tools.

Lacking the diplomatic and economic tools to influence external actors and unwilling to loosen its grip on its people, North Korea has had to rely on demonstration of its nuclear weapons capabilities and occasional pivots to diplomacy to operationalize its GS. Pyongyang's preferred method of operationalizing its GS has been relatively consistent since after the Cold War—when its nuclear efforts began to bear fruit—suggesting that Kim Jong Un and his potential successors will continue to prioritize the possession of nuclear weapons as their only means of maintaining power and strategic relevance.

NOTES

1. The opinions and characterizations in this piece are those of the author and do not necessarily represent those of the US government.
2. IISS, *North Korea's Weapons Programmes: A Net Assessment* (Palgrave Macmillan, 2004).
3. KCNA, "KCNA Detailed Report on Circumstances of DPRK's Withdrawal from NPT," KCNA, January 22, 2003.
4. Agreed Framework of 21 October 1994 between the United States of America and the Democratic People's Republic of Korea, Geneva, October 21, 1994.

5. KCNA, "KCNA Detailed Report on Circumstances of DPRK's Withdrawal from NPT."
6. Joint Declaration of the Denuclearization of the Korean Peninsula, January 20, 1992.
7. Joint Statement of the Fourth Round of the Six-Party Talks, Beijing, September 19, 2005.
8. The Socialist Constitution of the Democratic People's Republic of Korea, Pyongyang, December 27, 1972, last amended August 29, 2019.
9. KCNA, "Report on Plenary of WPK Committee," KCNA, March 31, 2013.
10. KCNA, "Kim Jong Un Makes New Year Address," KCNA, January 1, 2017.
11. KCNA, "Rodong Sinmun Hails Successful Test-fire of Hwasong-15," KCNA, November 30, 2017.
12. KCNA, "Kim Jong Un Makes New Year Address," KCNA, January 1, 2018.
13. Hyunsu Yim and Josh Smith, "North Korea Shows First Photos of Uranium Enrichment Site," Reuters, September 13, 2024.
14. Kim Il Sung, "On Eliminating Dogmatism and Formalism and Establishing Juche in Ideological Work," in *Kim Il Sung: Works 9* (Foreign Languages Publishing House, 1981), 402–25.
15. Kim Il Sung, "On Socialist Construction in the Democratic People's Republic of Korea and the South Korean Revolution," in *Kim Il Sung: Works 19* (Foreign Languages Publishing House, 1984), 236–84.
16. Jung H. Pak, *Becoming Kim Jong Un* (Penguin Random House, 2020), 23–24.
17. Rodong Sinmun, April 11, 1963.
18. Rodong Sinmun, November 25, 1981.
19. Ramon Pacheco Pardo, *North Korea-US Relations from Kim Jong Il to Kim Jong Un* (Routledge), 18–19.
20. Pacheco Pardo, *North Korea-US Relations*, 28–29.
21. Kongdan Oh and Ralph Hassig, "North Korea between Collapse and Reform," *Asian Survey*, 39, no. 2 (1999), 301.
22. Pak, *Becoming Kim Jong Un*, 52–56.
23. Young Chul Chung, "North Korean Reform and Opening: Dual Strategy and 'Silli (Practical) Socialism'," *Pacific Affairs* 77, no.2 (2004), 283–304.
24. Pak, *Becoming Kim Jong Un*, 89–96.
25. KCNA, "Report on Plenary of WPK Committee," KCNA, March 31, 2013.
26. The Socialist Constitution of the People's Republic of Korea.
27. The July 4 South-North Joint Communiqué, July 4, 1972.
28. Agreement on Reconciliation, Non-Aggression and Exchanges and Cooperation between the South and the North, December 13, 1991.
29. Dae-Jyu Yoon, "The Constitution of North Korea: Its Changes and Implications," *Fordham International Law Journal* 27, no. 4 (2003), 1289–1305.
30. Yonhap News Agency, "NK Leader Calls for Defining S. Korea as 'No. 1 Hostile Country' in Constitution," Yonhap News Agency, January 16, 2024.
31. *The New York Times*, "Excerpts from the Messages and Toasts Opening Full U.S.-Chinese Diplomatic Ties," *The New York Times*, January 2, 1979.
32. U.S. Central Intelligence Agency, "North Korean Military Capabilities and Intentions," Special National Intelligence Estimate, May 23, 1979, https://www.cia.gov/readingroom/docs/DOC_0001171647.pdf.
33. Pak, *Becoming Kim Jong Un*, 39–40.
34. The Constitution of the Republic of Korea, Seoul, July 17, 1948, last amended October 29, 1987.

35. Victor Cha, *The Impossible State: North Korea, Past and Future*, Updated Edition (Ecco Press, 2018); *Bruce Cumings, The Korean War: A History* (Random Publishing House, 2011).
36. Ramon Pacheco Pardo, *North Korea-US Relations from Kim Jong Il to Kim Jong Un* (Routledge, 2019).
37. Lara Jakes, "What Weapons Is North Korea Accused of Supplying to Russia?" *The New York Times*, June 17, 2024.
38. Kelly NG, "What We Know About North Korean Troops Fighting Russia's War," BBC, December 24, 2024.
39. Linus Hagstrom and Marie Soderberg, "Taking Japan-North Korea Relations Seriously: Rationale and Background," *Pacific Affairs* 79, no. 3 (2006), 373–85.
40. Pacheco Pardo, *North Korea-US Relations.*
41. Cumings, *The Korean War*, 156–57.
42. Pak, *Becoming Kim Jong Un.*
43. Cha, *The Impossible State;* Pacheco Pardo, *North Korea-US Relations.*
44. Don Oberdorfer and Robert Carlin, *The Two Koreas: A Contemporary History* (Basic Books, 2013).
45. IISS, *The Military Balance 2020* (Routledge, 2020).
46. Ministry of Unification, "Trust-Building Process on the Korean Peninsula," September 2013, https://www.ncnk.org/sites/default/files/content/resources/publications/trust_buidling_process.pdf (accessed January 14, 2021).
47. Pacheco Pardo, *North Korea-US Relations.*
48. Samuel S. Kim, *The Two Koreas and the Great Powers* (Cambridge University Press, 2006).
49. Pacheco Pardo, *North Korea-US Relations*, 29–30.
50. Pacheco Pardo, *North Korea-US Relations*, 39–30.
51. KOTRA, 2019년 북한의 대외무역 동향 (North Korea's Foreign Trade Trends) (KOTRA, 2020), 44.
52. Leif-Eric Eisley and In Young Park, "China's Norms in its Near Abroad: Understanding Beijing's North Korea Policy," *Journal of Contemporary China* 25, no.101 (2016), 651–68.
53. Elena Ponomareva and Georgij Rudov, "Russia-North Korea: State of Affairs and Trends," *Journal of Asian Public Policy* 9, no. 1 (2016), 45–56.
54. KOTRA, North Korea's Foreign Trade Trends, 43.
55. Ponomareva and Rudov, "Russia-North Korea."
56. Hagstrom and Soderberg, "Taking Japan-North Korea Relations Seriously."
57. Cha, *The Impossible State*; Cumings, *The Korean War*, 25.
58. Scott A. Snyder, *South Korea at the Crossroads: Autonomy and Alliance in an Era of Rival Powers* (Columbia University Press, 2018).
59. KCNA, "DPRK's Nuclear Deterrence Is Treasured Sword of Nation: Rodong Sinmun," KCNA, June 28, 2017.
60. The Socialist Constitution of the People's Republic of Korea.
61. Gi-Wook Shin, *Ethnic Nationalism in Korea: Genealogy, Politics, and Legacy* (Stanford University Press, 2006), 91–92.
62. Shin, *Ethnic Nationalism in Korea*, 85, 94.
63. Kongdan Oh and Ralph C. Hassig, *North Korea through the Looking Glass* (Brookings University Press, 2000), 133–34.
64. *Songun: All-Powerful Sword of the Present Times* (Foreign Languages Publishing House, 2008).

65. The Socialist Constitution of the People's Republic of Korea.
66. KCNA, "Report on Plenary of WPK Committee."
67. Kim Hakjoon, *Dynasty: The Hereditary Succession Politics of North Korea* (Shorenstein Asia-Pacific Research Center, 2015).
68. Hakjoon, *Dynasty*.
69. Thae Yong-ho, 3층 서기실의 암호 (*Password for the Third-Floor Secretariat*) (Gipa-rang, 2018).
70. Hakjoon, *Dynasty*.
71. The Socialist Constitution of the People's Republic of Korea.
72. The Socialist Constitution of the People's Republic of Korea.
73. The Socialist Constitution of the People's Republic of Korea.
74. IISS, *The Military Balance 2020*, 284–86.
75. IISS, *The Military Balance 2020*, 284–86.
76. IISS, *The Military Balance 2020*, 284–86.
77. Hyeong-wook Boo, "An Assessment of North Korean Cyber Threats," *The Journal of East Asian Affairs* 31, no. 1 (2017), 97–117.
78. IISS, *The Military Balance 2020*.
79. IMF, World Economic Outlook, October 2020: A Long and Difficult Ascent, 2020, https://www.imf.org/en/Publications/WEO/Issues/2020/09/30/world-economic-outlook-october-2020
80. Da-gyum Ji, "N. Korea Closes 7 Embassies, Now Down to 46, Says Seoul," *The Korea Herald*, https://www.koreaherald.com/view.php?ud=20231205000707
81. Jonathan D. Pollack, "Kim Jong-il's Clenched Fist," *The Washington Quarterly* 32, no. 4 (2009), 153–73.
82. Pak, *Becoming Kim Jong Un*, 72–85.
83. CSIS, North Korean Missile Launches & Nuclear Tests: 1984–Present, July 30, 2020, https://missilethreat.csis.org/north-korea-missile-launches-1984-present/
84. R.R. Krishnan, "North Korea and the Non-Aligned Movement," *International Studies* 20, no. 1–2 (1981), 299–313.
85. Pacheco Pardo, *North Korea-US Relations*.
86. Choe Sang-Hun, "Korean Leaders Meet in Pyongyang," *The New York Times*, October 3, 2007.
87. Jane Perlez, "Albright Greeted with a Fanfare by North Korea," *The New York Times*, October 24, 2000.
88. Lee Haye-ah, "DMZ Meeting Resets Nuclear Talks amid Lingering Skepticism," Yonhap News Agency, July 1, 2019.
89. Yonhap News Agency, "Moon Arrives in Pyongyang for Historic Summit with Kim," Yonhap News Agency, September 18, 2018.
90. Koh Byung-joon and Song Sang-ho, "Kim, Xi Hold Summit Talks in Pyongyang," Yonhap News Agency, June 20, 2019.
91. Kim Soo-yeon, "Putin Arrives in Pyongyang for Summit with Kim," Yonhap News Agency, June 19, 2024.
92. Keun-Sik Kim, "Inter-Korean Relations and the Future of the Sunshine Policy," *Journal of East Asian Affairs* 16, no.1 (2002), 103.
93. Howard W. French, "Japan and North Korea Reach Agreement on Relations," *The New York Times*, September 17, 2002.
94. Pacheco Pardo, *North Korea-US Relations*, 161.

CHAPTER 4

South Korea

Seong-Ho Sheen

The Republic of Korea (ROK; henceforth South Korea) was established on August 15, 1948. It was three years after the division of Korea in the aftermath of independence from 36 years of Japanese colonial rule in 1945. The Democratic People's Republic of Korea (henceforth North Korea) invaded South Korea in 1950. The Korean War ended with armistice, not a peace treaty, after three years of fierce battle between the Koreas killing more than a million soldiers and civilians from both sides. Surrounded by three great powers, China, Russia, and Japan, and facing lethal military threat from the North, South Korea's grand strategy has been largely shaped and driven by its trauma from the Korean War, division of the two Koreas, early twentieth-century Japanese colonial rule, and great power competition surrounding the Korean peninsula. Hence, South Korea's strategic priority has been deterring the North Korean military threat, survival of the nation against any foreign intervention, achieving economic prosperity out of ashes from the Korean War, and eventual unification of the Korean Peninsula under a democratic system. Such priorities have been influenced by both external and domestic factors. The external factors included North Korea's military threat and its policy toward South Korea, the US Asia and alliance policy, relations with regional neighbors, and most recently US-China strategic competition. In the meantime, domestic factors included economic development, evolution of domestic politics, and social and demographic changes.

STRATEGIC PRIORITIES

To achieve its strategic goals, South Korea adopted strategies of internal and external balancing, hedging, and active engaging. The operation of strategies has been evolved with its emphasis on a strong alliance partnership with the United States, strengthening its self-defense capability, strong economic development, managing diplomatic relations with neighboring powers, engaging Pyongyang with denuclearization efforts, and new global engagement.

Deterring the North Korean Threat

The North Korean army, armed with Russian T-34 tanks and artillery, launched a surprise attack on South Korea in the peaceful early hours of Sunday morning, June 25, 1950. The North Korean blitzkrieg was so successful that Seoul had fallen in three days, and in less than three months the invading army occupied almost 90 percent of the South Korean territory. The exiled South Korean government in the southern city of Busan was desperately looking for survival. Its only hope was United Nations coalition forces led by US Marshall General Douglas MacArthur and his American forces. More than seventy years after the outbreak of the Korean War, the two Koreas still remains technically at war with an armistice, not a peace treaty, after three years of fierce fighting between two Koreas, the US, and China.

Since the end of the Korean War, deterring the North Korean threat has been the number one priority of South Korea's national security policy. The two Koreas never had real peace. Vowing forceful unification under its constitution, North Korea remains as the de facto main enemy of South Korea. With totalitarian leadership devoted to the protection and survival of the Kim family, North Korea's military force poses an existential threat to South Korea. According to the ROK Ministry of Defense White Paper, North Korea maintains 1.28 million active military forces, more than twice the size of South Korea's half-million forces, as of 2020. The North has larger capacity in terms of field artillery and multiple rocket launchers, but the South exceeds in advancement as it continues to acquire and develop cutting-edge weapons.

Yet the most serious threat comes from North Korea's nuclear weapons development. In an ironic turn, the end of the Cold War in the early 1990s marked the beginning of the nuclear crisis on the Korean Peninsula. In fact, South Korea's rapprochement effort by President Roh Tae-woo's Nordpolitics led to the South-North Korean Joint Announcement of Denuclearization of the Peninsula after the withdrawal of US tactical nuclear weapons. Yet Pyongyang was caught with its secret nuclear program by the International Atomic Energy Agency (IAEA) inspection team in 1992. Soon the first nuclear crisis unfolded with Pyongyang announcing the withdrawal from the nuclear nonproliferation treaty (NPT). Since then rounds of nuclear negotiations and diplomacy have been tried by concerned parties, involving the US, China, South Korea, Japan, and Russia, for almost three decades without much success. Meanwhile, North Korea has conducted six nuclear tests between 2006 and 2017. At the same time, North Korea also tested various types of missiles, including intercontinental ballistic missiles (ICBMs), that may reach the US mainland. North Korea declared itself a nuclear power in 2012.[1]

Promoting Sustainable Economic Prosperity

Three years of the Korean War left South Korea one of the poorest countries in the world. Some seventy years later, South Korea has emerged as one of the most advanced economies today. With a population of fifty million, South Korea ranks number ten in terms of gross domestic product (GDP) according to the World Bank and International Monetary Fund (IMF) in 2021. South Korea's manufacturing sector ranks number five, following China, the US, Japan, and Germany. And its economy is led by a well-balanced combination of leading industrial sectors. South Korea has top global producers of steel, automobiles, shipbuilding, semiconductors, telecommunications, electric car batteries, and biosimilar. According to Bloomberg, South Korea ranks number one in terms of innovation, being equipped with the world's fastest nationwide internet service and aggressive investment in research and development (R&D). South Korea's economic success was largely driven by active engagement with global markets with an export-driven economy. Without much natural resources, international trade is critical to South Korea's economic survival and prosperity. Like most countries, providing economic prosperity to its people is the prime goal of South Korea. Adopting to the fourth industrial revolution with new technologies while navigating the challenges of increasing protectionism amid the global climate crisis will be the new mission of South Korea, which has written a great economic success story with the miracle of the Han River in the past century.

Independence and Self-Determination

The Korean Peninsula is located at the focal point of geopolitics of Northeast Asia. To the north, it is connected to the Eurasian continent while the peninsula is surrounded by three seas in the west, the south, and the east. To the west, it faces the Chinese mainland, while the east is facing the Japanese archipelago. The location has made Korea a subject of great power rivalry and foreign invasions by surrounding big powers. Hence there is an old saying among Koreans that "when there is a fight among whales, a shrimp's back is broken." Indeed, the Korean Peninsula experienced foreign invasions during the transition period of Chinese empires in ancient times. In modern times the rise of the Japanese empire did not bode well either as the last Joseon dynasty was annexed to become a Japanese colony in the early twentieth century. The brutal Japanese rule for almost forty years left a scar among Koreans with such a feeling of disgrace and indignity that Korea should never become a victim of foreign invasion. As such protecting its sovereign right from outside intervention has become the supreme mission of any government in South Korea.

Unification under Democracy

South Korea's constitution defines its territory to include the whole peninsula and its adjacent islands. This means South Korea does not recognize North Korea as a legitimate political entity. The reality is that the two Koreas exist as independent states as they are recognized as official members of the United Nations. However the history of the Korean nation that goes back more than thousands of years as one single nation makes Korean unification an ultimate national mission. As each of the two Koreas claims its legitimate mandate for unification, South Korea envisions the long-term goal of unifying Korea under a democratic system.

EXTERNAL FACTORS

South Korea's grand strategy has been largely influenced by its geostrategic factors. The division and ongoing hostility with North Korea have been the single most important factor in shaping its national security strategy since the Korean War of 1950. Additionally, South Korea's position at the crossroads of continental and maritime powers renders its strategy highly susceptible to its external relations with its much bigger neighbors like China, Japan and Russia as well as to its alliance partnership with the United States.

North Korea's Nuclear Development and Its Policy

Obviously North Korea's nuclear development and its policy are key factors for South Korea's grand strategy. North Korea's increasing nuclear and missile capability represents the most serious security threat to South Korea and will affect South Korea's defense strategy as well as its alliance policy. At the same time, North Korea's position on nuclear negotiation with the United States will be critical in South Korea's engagement strategy toward Pyongyang as well as policy coordination with Washington and Beijing. Meanwhile, Kim Jong Un's economic reform and position on inter-Korean relations will greatly affect South Korea's engagement strategy with North Korea.

The international community led by the United States has tried diplomacy with Pyongyang to give up its nuclear program for complete verifiable irreversible denuclearization (CVID) of the Korean Peninsula. Indeed, during various US administrations, some nuclear deals have been reached, such as the 1994 Agreed Framework by the Clinton administration and the 2005 2.13 Joint Agreement by the Bush administration.[2] Yet those agreements fell short of ultimate denuclearization and were soon followed by another nuclear crisis. Most recently the Trump administration tried to make a bid deal with North Korean leader Kim Jong Un with an unprecedented offer of a direct summit. Yet the much-anticipated second summit between Trump and Kim in Hanoi, Vietnam, in early 2019 ended with Trump walking away from the negotiation and refusing Kim's demand for the lifting of full economic sanctions for giving up North Korea's Yongbyon nuclear facility.

Since the collapse of the 2019 summit, the US and South Korean negotiators have urged North Korea to return to negotiations, assuring that they have no preconditions for the North's return. And the Biden administration came up with the same emphasis on diplomacy with a "pragmatic and calibrated approach" that is open to and will explore diplomacy with North Korea to eventually achieve the "complete denuclearization of the Korean Peninsula."[3] The problem is that the US has not shown willingness to grant the sanctions relief that Kim seeks.

As such Kim and his regime do not seem to be interested in another round of uncertain negotiations with the US. With the complete shutdown of the border in fear of the COVID-19 outbreak, Kim has emphasized self-help and protecting the homeland from outside enemies. Since its last test of nuclear weapons and ICBMs in 2017, Kim's regime has shifted its focus to building a wide range of short- to intermediate-range missiles that can strike US allies in the region and the US forces stationed there. Lately Pyongyang test fired longer ballistic missiles, showcasing its ability to hit the US mainland as well. In January 2021 Kim unveiled a five-year plan to expand his nuclear arsenal, including "preemptive" and "retaliatory" strike capabilities to allow North

Korean warheads to "accurately hit and extinguish" targets within 15,000 kilometers (9,320 miles), which would include Washington. His must-haves included the development of hypersonics, solid-fuel ICBMs that can be launched from land and sea, spy satellites, and reconnaissance drones.[4]

North Korea has intensified its military activities, conducting over fifty ballistic missile tests between 2022 and 2023, and continues to do so in 2024. If North Korea completes its ICBM capability, it could target major US cities as Kim has often vowed to do.[5] These tests underscore how Kim Jong Un's regime has been retreating inward—making apparent advances in its nuclear capabilities and ballistic weapons—while refusing to engage with US and South Korean negotiators seeking to restart denuclearization talks. In response the Biden administration announced fresh sanctions on North Korea. Pyongyang accused Washington of "intentionally escalating" tensions and said the move may trigger a "stronger" reaction. The new round of sanctions is likely to fuel North Korea's complaints that the United States has "hostile policies" toward Pyongyang. South Korea finds it more difficult to engage North Korea with no sign of talks between Pyongyang and Washington.

The United States and Its Alliance Policy

The US remains as the single most important player in shaping South Korea's defense policy and foreign relations with others. When it comes to defense policy, the US is the most important security provider with its alliance partnership forged by blood during the Korean War. Since the signing of the Mutual Defense Treaty in 1953, the US forces in Korea and US military power projection capability provide key deterrence against the North Korean threat and other potential adversaries. And the two militaries function as fully integrated forces with the Combined Forces Command (CFC) created in 1978. Currently the commander of US Forces Korea (USFK), an American four-star general, exercises the role of commanding officer of the ROK-US allied forces in case of war while a South Korean commander takes the vice commander's position. As such the US alliance policy has been a key factor to influence South Korea's defense strategy over the decades. In the past South Korea, a junior partner, has had perennial fear of US abandonment. And US decisions to reduce its military footprint and burden from the peninsula often drove South Korea's desire for building an autonomous defense capability. For example the Nixon doctrine[6] of reducing US military presence in Asia in the aftermath of the Vietnam War created such urgency for South Korea's Park Jung-hee administration to pursue a secret nuclear program of its own in the 1960s. At the same time, Nixon's surprising engagement with China led the Park government to initiate reconciliation with its arch enemy Kim Il-Sung, leading to the first ever South-North Joint Communique of July 4 in 1972.

Indeed, as South Korea becomes more prosperous, there has been increasing desire from the US to reduce its military responsibility on the peninsula with a decreasing military footprint. There were approximately 327,000 US service members in South Korea in June 1953, shortly before the signing of the Korean armistice. From 1953 to 2018 there have been three significant US troop withdrawals. In the second half of the 1950s the Eisenhower administration ordered major reductions in US forces down to the level of 55,000 by 1960. The Nixon administration withdrew the 7th Infantry Division from South Korea in 1971, reducing US troop strength to just above 40,000. The next major withdrawal came under President George W. Bush in 2004, as he ordered the dispatch of some 12,000 US troops in South Korea to Iraq. This withdrawal included major elements of the Second Infantry Division, the last remaining US Army combat division in South Korea. President Bush's order reduced US troop strength to about 28,000, where it stands today.[7]

Most recently, the America First policy by the Trump administration seriously damaged South Korea's confidence on US alliance commitment. President Trump demanded up to five times increase in South Korea's financial contribution to US military presence on the peninsula. Otherwise he threatened to pull US forces out of Korea, which raised serious concern on the future of the alliance from both Seoul and Washington. Meanwhile, increasing US-China rivalry creates a dilemma of entrapment for South Korea, which takes a strategy of hedging in between the two critical partners for Seoul. Likewise, South Korea's often fractured relations with Japan were the subject of mediation efforts from Washington, which wanted to build a strong trilateral partnership against North Korea and China.[8]

China and Its Policy toward the Korean Peninsula

Connected to China's northeastern provinces by land, Korea has shared a history of political, military, economic, and sociocultural ties with Chinese entities in mainland China for thousands of years. Until modern times, different Korean dynasties had become loyal allies of each Chinese empire under the China-centric tributary system. The alliance ties between the Joseon dynasty and Qing empire lasted almost three hundred years until the newly rising Japanese empire took control over the Korean peninsula after the Qings' humiliating defeat in the Sino-Japanese War of 1894–95.[9] With China itself fighting Japanese intrusion into the mainland, China has provided a sanctuary for Korean provisional governments and their independence fight throughout the Japanese occupation of Korea between 1910 and 1945. The division of Korea after the independence and establishment of communist China resulted in new dynamics in China-Korea relations. In the winter of 1950, China's People's Liberation Army crossed the Yalu River to assist the retreating North Korean army. Faced with surprising intervention by a massive Chinese force, the US-ROK alliance forces had to give up unifying Korea and signed an armistice treaty that was signed by Chinese as well as North Korean representatives. Since then China (officially the People's Republic of China, PRC) has become an arch enemy of South Korea until the two countries normalized relations in 1992.

After the normalization, however, China has become the single most important economic partner for South Korea. Soon China's growing influence on the peninsula's affairs was felt beyond the economic issues. Beijing played a key role in nuclear negotiations with North Korea as a host of the six-party talks in the 2000s. South Korea's Lee Myung-Bak government, well known for its pro-American stance, elevated its bilateral ties to a strategic cooperative partnership with Beijing in 2008.[10] And in recent years, China's political clout in Korean affairs has increased further. China holds a key in implementing international sanctions on North Korea as China provides more than 80 percent of its oil and food supply. While condemning North Korea's nuclear development, China has opposed a coercive approach by the US and emphasized peaceful diplomacy for denuclearization. President Xi met with Chairman Kim five times in 2018 and 2019, most among leaders of the region, including the US, South Korea, and Russia. And Beijing and Pyongyang celebrated the sixtieth anniversary of their mutual friendship and military partnership treaty in 2021. It is indisputable that China has keen interest and influence in security issues on the peninsula, including nuclear and peace talks with North Korea.

Meanwhile, increasing strategic competition with the US makes South Korea's alliance cooperation with the US more difficult as well. South Korea first learned of the danger of US-China competition when the US missile defense system was deployed in its soil. Triggered by North Korea's nuclear development, the terminal high altitude area defense (THAAD) missile defense system on the Korean Peninsula has caused lots of controversy. After North Korea's fourth nuclear test in January 2016 followed by months-long consultation with the US, the South Korean government officially announced in July that THAAD would be installed as a "defense measure to protect the people of South Korea and the armed forces of the South Korea-U.S. alliance." Seoul also tried to satisfy Beijing by stressing that the system "will focus only on the threats from North Korea and will not be used against a third party."[11]

In response, however, the Chinese government expressed "strong dissatisfaction and firm opposition" and took measures to sanction the South Korean economy. South Korea and the US have argued that THAAD is a purely defensive measure against the North Korean nuclear threat. Yet China's strong opposition reflects Beijing's concern about the strategic implications of THAAD on the US-China nuclear competition. The Chinese authority suspects that THAAD could damage China's minimum strategic nuclear deterrence against the United States. Furthermore, THAAD may implicate Seoul's de facto membership in the US missile defense system in Northeast Asia and offers the possibility of a closer military cooperation between Korea and Japan.

Indeed, China imposed various sanctions on South Korea as a protest against Seoul's decision to host the US missile defense system. The unofficial but effective sanctions included bans on Korean shows, movies, and celebrities in Chinese markets, shut down of Chinese tours bound for South Korea, and penalties on South Korean consumer goods companies. Since then South Korea tried to restore relations with Beijing. The newly elected Moon administration soon tried to mend the strained relations with Beijing by pledging "three no's"; Seoul had no intention to (1) install additional THAAD batteries, (2) participate in a regional missile defense system, or (3) form a trilateral alliance with the United States and Japan. In November 2018, President Xi and President Moon announced a joint statement on their rapprochement, which included high-level contacts and the renewal of the bilateral currency swap deal followed by gradual easing of economic sanctions imposed on Seoul.[12] Yet Seoul-Beijing ties are going through another difficult time as the new Yoon government prioritizes its relations with Washington and Tokyo. With its increasing influence on both Koreas as well as intensifying competition with the US, China will increasingly become an important factor for South Korea's grand strategy in the future.

Relations with Regional Neighbors: Japan and Russia

After its independence from Japanese colonialism in 1945, South Korea normalized its diplomatic relations with Japan in 1965 under the Park Junghee government. Since the Treaty on Basic Relations was signed, Japan subsequently recognized South Korea as the only legitimate government on the Korean Peninsula. As such, North Korea does not have official diplomatic ties with Japan. Meanwhile Japan provided $300 million to the Korean government as compensation for the grievance from the colonial period and extended an additional $200 million credit to South Korea. Along with economic aid, Japan has become an important source of capital investment and technology for South Korea's developing economy in the 1970s and 1980s. Yet since the 2000s, the rising voice of right-wing nationalism in Japanese politics met with increasing criticisms of history revisionism of Japan by Korean civil societies and political circles. In particular, an increasing number of Japan's ruling Liberal Democratic Party (LDP) politicians, led by former Prime Minister Abe Shinzo, tend to try to whitewash the history linked to Japanese military actions in World War II. Outstanding history issues intensified, including comfort women, forced labor, and territorial disputes between Japan and South Korea over the Dokdo islands (or Takeshima in Japan) in the East Sea (or the Sea of Japan, according to Tokyo).

The shaky bilateral relations further deteriorated in 2017 when President Moon, a former human rights lawyer questioned the legitimacy of the 2015 agreement on restitution for Korean women who were forced to serve in Imperial Japanese Army brothels during the Second World War, a deal negotiated with Abe by Moon's impeached predecessor, Park Geun-hye. Soon the Japanese government declared the Korean position unacceptable, saying it violates the basic norms of international treaties. Yet another blow came in 2019 when the Korean Supreme Court ordered Japanese companies to compensate former Korean employees in their civil lawsuit against the forced labor before the end of World War II. The Japanese government criticized the Korean government for breach of the 1965 Basic Treaty by which Tokyo claims all the outstanding colonial grievances were settled completely once and for all. And in the summer 2019, the Abe cabinet imposed an export control ban on key materials for South Korea's semiconductor industry, a critical component in the Korean economy. In retaliation South Korea threatened to withdraw from the General Security of Military Intelligence Agreement (GSOMIA), a military intelligence sharing agreement with Japan. The decision was postponed at the last minute only after a reported US intervention.[13]

The worsening bilateral relations have important security implications for South Korea. They create a challenge for US efforts to promote strong military cooperation between South Korea and Japan in dealing with security challenges like North Korea's nuclear development and China's aggressive behaviors. Over the past decades, their respective military alliances with Washington have cemented a series of steps to ensure deterrence and to signal to Pyongyang their unwavering support for the US military in case of a conflict. In fact the US military bases in Japan provide a critical supporting role for US military operations in the Korean contingency.

The troubled Seoul-Tokyo axis entered new phase when newly elected conservative president Yoon emphasized restoring the bilateral tie. His enthusiasm for building a new partnership with Japan was largely welcomed by both Washington and Tokyo. Yoon and Prime Minister Kishida resumed shuttle diplomacy in 2023. And the two leaders gathered at Camp David, along with US President Joe Biden, in August 2023 and celebrated a new trilateral partnership in enhancing regional stability and cooperation. In their joint statement the three leaders declared the inauguration of a new era of trilateral partnership to expand trilateral cooperation across domains and across the Indo-Pacific and beyond. In particular, the three countries will enhance strategic coordination between the US-Japan and US-ROK alliances and bring their trilateral security cooperation to new heights.[14]

Russia is another important regional power that affects South Korea's national security strategy. In the late nineteenth century and the early twentieth century, Russia emerged as a major geopolitical power vying for its hegemonic influence over Korea against Japan.[15] After the defeat in the Russo-Japanese War of 1904–05, Russian influence largely subsided as Moscow went through its domestic turmoil as well as two world wars in Europe. Yet the defeat of the Japanese Empire brought Russian interest and influence back to Northeast Asia as an occupying force north of the 38th parallel on the Korean Peninsula. The Korean War and the following Cold War had made Russia (then the Soviet Union) a critical player in Korean affairs as the key ally of North Korea. But the end of the Cold War in the 1990s and the rise of China in the twenty-first century rendered Russia's voice to be relatively minor compared to those of US and China. However, with its territory sharing a border with North Korea and vast Eurasian land with development potential, Russia may emerge as another prominent actor in the process of peace building on the Korean Peninsula. As such, South Korea's government pursued various northern policies to connect the South Korean economy with the Eurasian landmass and natural resources in Russian territory.[16] The Russian invasion of Ukraine strained Seoul's relations with Moscow as South Korea joined the West-led sanctions against Russia. Yet Seoul tried to strike a balance between the antiwar rhetoric and its various ties with Russia by limiting its support for Ukraine largely to defensive and humanitarian areas.

However, Russia's continuing war efforts in Ukraine put increasing pressure on South Korea as Moscow seeks diplomatic and military support from

Pyongyang. In June 2024 Russian President Vladimir Putin visited Pyongyang and signed a new treaty with North Korean leader Kim Jong Un. The treaty upgraded the countries' relationship to a "comprehensive strategic partnership." It specifies that if either side goes to war after being invaded, "the other side shall provide military and other assistance with all means in its possession without delay." There have been reports that North Korea is sending Russia munitions to use in its war in Ukraine in exchange for food, fuel, and military technology.[17] The South Korean government condemned the treaty and said it will reconsider its stance on arms supply to Ukraine. In light of deepening ties between Pyongyang and Moscow, Seoul vowed to further strengthen the extended deterrence of the South Korea-US alliance and the security cooperation among South Korea, the United States, and Japan to deter North Korea's nuclear and missile threats.[18]

DOMESTIC FACTORS

As South Korea has evolved from one of the poorest nations into an advanced economy with a vibrant democracy, domestic factors are playing an increasingly significant role in shaping its grand strategy.

Economic Growth

After more than four decades of continuing economic growth, South Korea today stands tall as one of the most advanced economy in the world. Its GDP ranks ninth, catching up to Italy in 2022. Average South Koreans are wealthier than their Japanese counterparts, whose economy has stagnated since the bubble burst in the 1990s. As the South Korean society is becoming more prosperous, their outlook for the world and foreign policy orientation went through some drastic changes. South Korea's growing confidence spilled into its major foreign policy areas. First, South Korea's economic wealth translated into a rapid increase in military spending, which makes it one of the strongest military powers in the world. South Korea dwarfs its northern rival in defense spending. In 2016, the last year for which estimates were available, North Korea reportedly spent an estimated $4 billion, or 23 percent of its GDP, on defense according to the US State Department's 2018 World Military Expenditures and Arms Transfers report.[19] Meanwhile South Korea's defense spending, currently at US $46 billion, is more than twenty times that of North Korea.[20] South Korea's military ranks number six in 2022 according to *Global Firepower*.[21]

With a widening economic gap over its impoverished northern neighbor, North Korea has become a subject of South Korean sympathy and aid rather than an arch enemy or rival. Such confidence was evident in South Korea's engagement policy toward North Korea under the liberal governments of Kim Dae-jung, Roh Mu-hyun, and Moon Jae-in. Despite criticisms from the conservatives of appeasing the North Korean authoritarian regime, increasing numbers of South Koreans see engagement with Pyongyang as more of a pragmatic solution over risky military confrontation and pressure campaigns. As such, growing numbers of South Koreans, especially among the younger generation, see unification as a long-term, if not unnecessary, goal for the two nations as they become more concerned about the cost of unification to absorb their much poorer northern neighbor. On the other hand, South Korea's ambivalent position on the US-China competition is largely due to its close economic ties with Beijing, which takes about one third of South Korea's total export, which is bigger than the combined trade with the US and Japan.[22]

Social and Demographic Changes

South Korea is experiencing the most radical demographic change in the world. It has recorded the lowest birth rate in the world for a decade. At the same time, it is becoming a super-aged society at record speed, with more than 20 percent of its populations older than 65.[23] The rapidly aging and decreasing population not only slowed down economic productivity and growth but also increased the demand for social welfare. The problem is South Korea is at the bottom of social welfare spending among Organisation for Economic Cooperation and Development (OECD) countries. The rapidly increasing demand for social welfare means strong pressure on other government spending such as defense.[24]

According to the OECD, public social welfare costs accounted for 12.2 percent of South Korea's $1.6 trillion GDP in 2019.[25] The country's 2019 healthcare costs amounted to 8 percent of GDP. While South Korea spent only about half what the average OECD member did on social welfare in 2018 (11.1 percent versus 20.1 percent), the country's Ministry of Health and Welfare stated, "with an aging population and low economic growth, social welfare spending is going to increase to about 20.1 percent of GDP by the late 2030s and, by 2060, it is expected to account for 28.6 percent of GDP."[26] South Korea allocated about $48 billion for its 2021 defense budget, or about 9.4 percent of government spending and roughly 2.9 percent of the country's GDP, a more than 7 percent increase from the previous year. However, South Korea's defense spending is highly unlikely to keep growing, given the country's sharp projected increases in social welfare and healthcare spending.[27]

Meanwhile, South Korea's 500,000-member standing army based on universal conscription is not sustainable given its rapidly shrinking young male population. In 2010 the number of South Korean males aged between zero and nineteen reached 6.13 million, according to the Ministry of Interior and Safety. After falling to 5.47 million in January 2015, the figure for male Koreans under twenty stayed at 4.68 million in 2020. The data indicates that the nation saw the population for future enlistment decline by 23.6 percent—or 1.45 million people—in ten years.[28] At the same time the volunteer military enlistment has come under the spotlight in the political debate, with each major party promising to reduce the burden of military service for young male populations. As a result the period of military service has continued to shorten since the Park Chung-hee military regime in the 1960s–70s. After peaking at 36 months in 1968, the service term in the army declined to 33 months in 1977 under Park and to 30 months in 1984 under the Chun Doo-hwan military regime. In the latest move, the term dropped to 18 months under the Moon Jae-in government starting from 2020. This means the military manpower will scale back from the current 500,000 to about 450,000 by 2025, and some 300,000 by 2050.

There is emerging debate how to compensate the manpower shortage in the military amid increasing uncertainty in the security environment. Advocates of the volunteer military system warn that the nation would have no choice but to increase the service term should it stick to the current obligatory draft, citing the so-called "demographic cliff." In contrast, opponents claim that volunteer enlistment could bring about social disparity in the national defense service. They say that the majority of those volunteering would be from low-income households—for the purpose of stable income. Irrespective of the pros and cons over the compulsory and volunteer enlistment, experts share the view that the Ministry of National Defense should map out mid- and long-term countermeasures against a sharp decline in the number of youth.

Evolution of Domestic Politics

South Korea is a dynamic and burgeoning democracy. Since the establishment of the Republic of Korea in 1948, the country has gone through tumultuous political processes under decades of authoritarian regimes by both civilian and military leaders like Seung-man Rhee, Park Jung-hee, and Chun Doo-whan until the 1980s. The first republic under Rhee ended with the

April 19 revolution, a mass protest led by young students from high schools and colleges against presidential election fraud in 1960. The second republic was short lived when the weak and chaotic civil government was overrun by the May 16 military coup led by Major General Park in 1961. After eighteen years of authoritarian rule, which saw some remarkable economic growth, President Park was assassinated by his own intelligence chief in 1979. And another military general, Chun, filled the power vacuum with his brutal suppression of civilian voices for freedom in Gwangju in 1980. The authoritarian rule could not ignore the ever-increasing demands for political freedom by civil society in the 1980s, and the Chun regime finally gave in to the angry protest of huge crowd in downtown Seoul demanding direct and fair elections in 1987. Due to rivalry between two prominent opposition leaders, Kim Young-sam and Kim Dae-jung, the 1987 presidential election gave a victory to the governing party candidate, Roh Tae-woo, former military general and classmate of Chun.

Yet Roh kept his promise to hand over his power peacefully in 1992 after five years of a one-term presidency to Kim Young-sam, who proclaimed his government the first civilian government in decades. Since then South Korea has elected six presidents, each serving five years in one term as designed by the 1987 Constitution. After thirty years of peaceful transfer of power by fair and direct election, South Korea is regarded as one of the most stable and successful democracies in Asia. As such its foreign policy and grand strategy embrace democratic values such as individual freedom, human rights, and the rule of law as important guiding principles along with other national interests. And the basic orientation of government policy is shaped by the interplay and balancing acts between different party ideologies like progressive liberals versus conservative hawks or left-wing versus right-wing voices. As such liberal governments tend to emphasize engaging North Korea diplomatically while conservative governments focus more on punishing North Korea's bad behaviors. Such differences translate into other areas like how to deal with human rights issues of North Korea or China, alliance management with the US, history disputes with Japan, and so forth.

OPERATIONALIZATION OF GRAND STRATEGY

To achieve its strategic priority of deterring the North Korean threat and dealing with North Korean problems of denuclearization and peace building, South Korea adopted strategies of internal and external balancing and hedging through various engagements.

External and Internal Balancing to Deter North Korean and Other Threats

Alliance with the US has been a backbone of South Korea's grand strategy as an external balance against threats from North Korea and other sources. Saved by US intervention against North Korea's full invasion during the Korean War, South Korea has faced existential threats posed by North Korea's overwhelming conventional forces throughout the Cold War, during which North Korea initiated various military provocations. The USFK has provided critical deterrence as well as assurance against North Korean invasion. With the North Korean nuclear development since the early 1990s, the US provides another key assurance of extended deterrence with its nuclear umbrella to nonnuclear South Korea. The alliance partnership also plays a similar external balancing against other outsides threats including China's rapidly growing military forces right next to the Korean peninsula. About 28,000 American troops are stationed in South Korea today. And South Korea provides about US $1 billion to compensate the cost of US troop deployment.

After serious concern and worries about US commitment to the alliance under the Trump administration, South Korea was much relieved to see the Biden administration come back with the traditional US emphasis on alliance partnership. Biden made it certain that he wanted to restore and strengthen the alliance partnership with South Korea. Immediately after Biden took office, the US and South Korea reached agreement on SMA (a military burden sharing agreement) that had been long overdue under the previous Trump administration. Washington accepted Seoul's offer of a 13 percent increase in burden sharing with a five-year term. The increase was modest compared to Trump's demand for a 500 percent increase with a one-year deal.[29]

Welcoming Biden's top security team, Secretary of State Antony Blinken and Defense Secretary Lloyd Austin at Blue House, President Moon said "having been a partner for seven decades, sharing values and philosophy on democracy and human rights, ROK and the US will continue to act together on shared challenges, including a thorough cooperation for a complete denuclearization and permanent peace in the Korean Peninsula."[30] In their joint statement after the summit in May 2021, Biden and Moon pledged their recommitment to "an ironclad alliance" and announced "a partnership that continues to provide peace and prosperity for our peoples, while serving as a linchpin for the regional and global order."[31] Such strong partnership was reiterated by Moon's successor. President Yoon went to elevate the alliance as a "global comprehensive strategic alliance" in his joint statement with Biden.[32]

Meanwhile, the ROK-US alliance, officially established as a treaty alliance signed in 1953, is going through a transformation suited for twenty-first-century security dynamics on the Korean Peninsula. And the two allies need to complete the transformation of the military partnership that has been going on since the end of the Cold War. One of the key issues is the wartime operational control (OPCON) that has been held by the US since the Korean War. Following the fall of the Soviet Union, Presidents Bill Clinton and Kim Young-sam agreed to return peacetime OPCON to South Korea in 1994. It took over a decade before President Roh Moo-hyun, in 2007, agreed with President George Bush on an initial timetable aiming for the completion of the transfer of wartime control by April 2012. Yet the transfer has been delayed due to North Korea nuclear tests as well as domestic politics under the conservative governments by Lee Myung-Bak and Park Geun-hye.

Coming to office following President Park's impeachment in 2017, Moon announced his new policy to expedite the OPCON transfer. Moon's announcement reflected South Korea's strategy of internal balancing that will enhance South Korea's autonomy backed by strong military buildup. The OPCON transfer, along with a bolstered ROK military, would deter North Korean aggression and make South Korea into a Northeast Asian security hub, Moon argued. The Moon administration has since initiated Defense Reform 2.0, aiming to complete the OPCON transfer by 2022. As part of these efforts, Moon, dubbed as a progressive liberal, has expanded the defense budget with an average annual increase of 7.5 percent, compared to 4–6 percent under the two previous conservative Lee and Park administrations. In this regard peace through strength and autonomous self-defense have been consistent themes in South Korean liberals' defense policy.[33] In particular Seoul and Washington have drawn up "customized deterrence strategies," as Pyongyang reinforces its asymmetric power with nuclear armed missiles. For this end the South Korean military is establishing strategically guided munitions and a domestically developed missile defense system for independent deterrence.

Engaging North Korea to Build Peace and Unification

While confronting the North Korean threat, various South Korean governments tried to engage Pyongyang to build peace on the peninsula. As mentioned earlier, the Park Chung-hee government initiated a secret diplomacy to come up with the 1972 July 4 Joint Statement on three unification principles of independence, peace, and national unity. In 1991 President Roh's aggressive

Nordpolitik led to the Agreement on Reconciliation, Non-Aggression, and Exchanges and Cooperation between South and North Korea, which set a comprehensive and detailed peace agenda.[34] A month later in 1992, the two Koreas signed a Joint Declaration of South and North Korea on the Denuclearization of the Korean Peninsula. The Joint Declaration was a treaty in which South and North Korea agreed not to possess, produce, or use nuclear weapons, and prohibited uranium enrichment and plutonium reprocessing.[35]

The peace initiative originating from the conservative governments was soon adopted under the liberal governments. President Kim Dae-Jung pursued the Sunshine Policy of engagement, which led to the first historic summit between leaders of the two Koreas in 2000. In a June 15 joint statement, President Kim and Chairman Kim Jong-il established the principle of peaceful reunification based on the common element of the parties' positions—confederation (South) and loose federalism (North). It also called for the normalization of relations through a humanitarian, economic, and social framework.[36] President Roh Moo-hyun, Kim's successor, continued engagement with Pyongyang, leading to the second inter-Korean summit in 2007. Again the two leaders issued a joint statement that laid out a more specific framework for building military trust and institutionalizing peace. With discussion on issues of military and peace, the two sides took a more proactive approach to formally ending the Korean War and settling peace on the peninsula.[37] The conservative governments that followed afterward under Lee Myung-bak and Park Geun-hey also tried to build mutual trust and peace. But uncertainty surrounding the succession in Pyongyang and new North Korean leader Kim Jong Un's determination to build nuclear capability with four nuclear tests and numerous missile provocations caused more tensions and crisis than dialogue between the two Koreas.

Coming into office while facing military crisis between Kim and Trump in 2017, President Moon announced peace on the peninsula as his top priority. He declared the three principles of his government policy to solve the peninsula conundrum: objection to any war, mutual security guarantees between the two Koreas, and common prosperity. His aggressive peace initiative led to the third inter-Korean summit and first meeting with Kim Jong Un in 2018. The meeting produced a much more detailed and comprehensive agenda for a peace process on the peninsula including denuclearization.[38] In their following summit in fall of the same year, the two governments signed a military agreement on specific confidence-building measures.[39] In order to build peace with North Korea, an official end of the Korean War was sought as a first major step. Especially given the stalemate of nuclear negotiation between Pyongyang and Washington since the failed Hanoi summit in 2019, the Moon government has sought the end of war declaration to revive the peninsula peace process. In his speech to the United Nations General Assembly in September 2021, President Moon reiterated a proposal to formally end the Korean War, calling for the support of the US and China. "Today, I once again urge the international community to mobilize its strengths for the end-of-war declaration on the Korean Peninsula and propose that three parties of the two Koreas and the U.S., or four parties of the two Koreas, the U.S. and China, come together and declare that the war on the Korean Peninsula is over," Moon said in his address to the 76th session of the U.N. General Assembly. "When the parties involved in the Korean War stand together and proclaim an end to the war, I believe we can make irreversible progress in denuclearization and usher in an era of complete peace."[40]

However, Moon's peace initiative ran out of time as his government was replaced by the conservative party candidate. Coming to office in 2022, the Yoon government's hawkish approach emphasizing deterrence by force against North Korea led to a complete stalemate between Seoul and Pyongyang in inter-Korean relations, with each side exchanging sharp criticisms. And the Korean War armistice remains intact seventy years after its signing in 1953. As of 2024 North Korea has declared that inter-Korean relations are in a state of war, denouncing the ROK-US joint military exercises as war drills and threatening to use maximum force, including nuclear weapons, in the event of conflict. Within South Korea, both the government and the public are increasingly pessimistic about the possibility of North Korea's denuclearization. Indeed, since the failed Hanoi summit in 2019, there has been little to no progress in inter-Korean or ROK-DPRK dialogue, let alone in denuclearization efforts. Instead, tensions between the two Koreas had escalated, what with the US Biden administration having made no serious efforts to engage with North Korea during its tenure. Incidents such as North Korea sending balloons filled with trash into Seoul and South Korea resuming loudspeaker broadcasts into the North have further exacerbated the situation, making the prospect of armed conflict between the Koreas seem more imminent. With the change of government in both Seoul and Washington in 2025, The situation on the Korean Peninsula remains precarious and fraught with danger.

Hedging to Manage the Dilemma of US-China Competition

Hedging has become a new feature of South Korea's grand strategy in managing the relationship with its two most important bilateral partners, the US and China, with their intensifying competition in the twenty-first century. THAAD was a hard lesson that Seoul could be suddenly involved in the dangerous dynamics of US-China strategic competition regardless of its original intention. Seoul never intended to provoke China, and the THAAD deployment was pursued purely against the North Korean threat. Yet it was Seoul that has become a target of Chinese economic sanctions, not Washington, by accepting the American offer of US missile defense deployment. In this context, South Korea would not want to seek further deployment of US missile defense systems. South Korea would be very cautious not to be caught between China and the US in their strategic competition.

There is a growing concern in Seoul about intensifying US-China strategic competition, which puts South Korea in the difficult position of making a choice between the two important partners. As much as Seoul appreciates the importance of alliance partnership with the US, it also perceives the growing influence of China in both economic and political issues on the Korean Peninsula. China has become by far the biggest trading partner for South Korea. Despite China's sanction on South Korea over the THAAD controversy, the overall trade with China remains central to South Korea. A US trade war against China created a strain on many South Korean companies for which China represents a major export market and business partner. South Korea's business community is worried about becoming a hostage to US-China strategic competition and exclusive supply chain policies. At the same time it is indisputable to see the Chinese interest and influence in security issues on the peninsula, including nuclear and peace talks with North Korea. President Xi met with Chairman Kim five times in 2018 and 2019, the most among leaders of the region, including the US, South Korea, and Russia. Beijing remains the single biggest supplier of food and energy to the much impoverished and isolated North Korean regime today. Both politically and economically, Washington's aggressive policy toward Beijing complicates Seoul's strategic choices in dealing with North Korea, trade with China, alliance management, and so forth

Indeed South Korea has been cautious of joining Washington's aggressive policy toward China in its Indo-Pacific strategy. The joint statement after the Moon-Biden summit in May 2021 did not explicitly mention China. Meanwhile, the US-Japan joint statement between Biden and Suga explicitly criticized Beijing on many issues.[41] Nevertheless the statement issued their opposition to "all activities that undermine, destabilize, or threaten the rules-based international order" and voiced their commitment to maintain peace and stability and defend international rules and norms in the South China Sea and Taiwan Strait. This was the first time a ROK-US joint statement has included reference to Taiwan.[42] Chinese authorities shortly responded with a certain concern. China's Ministry of Foreign Affairs spokesperson issued a statement noting that "the Taiwan question is China's internal affair" and warned both Washington and Seoul to "refrain from playing with fire."

The diplomatic tension with Beijing entered a new phase when Yoon mentioned Taiwan during an interview with a foreign correspondent. He said the tensions over Taiwan have been intensifying because of the attempts to change the status quo by force and that he stands by the international community opposing such a change. Yoon also said the Taiwan issue is much like the issue of North Korea and a global one. Beijing refuted Yoon's claim, insisted the Taiwan issue is a completely different matter, and warned that Beijing would not allow others to meddle by word.[43] Concerns are growing over China's possible economic retaliation against Korea after President Yoon Suk Yeol's remarks on Taiwan elicited angry responses from Beijing. Notwithstanding the new tone, it is unlikely that South Korea will embrace an overtly competitive approach to China in the long run.

CONCLUSION

From the ashes of the Korean War, South Korea has emerged as a comprehensive middle power in the twenty-first century. With a population of 50 million, its economy and military rank among the top ten in the world. And its economy is led by a well-balanced combination of leading industrial sectors in the age of the fourth industrial revolution. South Korea has top global producers of steel, automobiles, shipbuilding, semiconductors, telecommunications, electric car batteries, renewable energy, and biosimilar. At the same time, South Korea's soft power is well recognized by the world audience as K-pop, K-movies, K-dramas, K-web toons, and K-esports are making inroads into global markets. Yet it still faces the Cold War legacy of inter-Korean division with nuclear armed North Korea. Deterring North Korean threats remains its number one strategic priority. And Korea's geographic destiny makes South Korea a subject of great power rivalry in the age of US-China competition. In this context, achieving national unification while preserving peace on the peninsula remains a long and hard goal.

To achieve its strategic priority while meeting the challenges of the twenty-first century, South Korea has adopted a grand strategy of internal and external balancing and hedging while pursuing active engagement with all the concerned parties. Actively engaging the US for close alliance partnership is a backbone of its external balancing strategy against North Korean and other potential threats. Engaging North Korea for inter-Korean reconciliation is another strategy to achieve more urgent goals of denuclearization and peace building on the peninsula as well as a long-term goal of national unification. Engaging China with a hedging strategy in the US-China competition promotes its economic prosperity and induces a peninsula peace-building process along with North Korea and the United States. At the same time, for its independence and national self-determination, South Korea adopted an active internal balancing strategy of building strong defense capability and seeking more autonomy from the ROK-US alliance.

As a vibrant, prosperous democracy with a strong industrial and military base, South Korea has a new middle power role in regional and global issues. In his bilateral meeting with US president Biden, President Moon committed South Korea's opposition to "all activities that undermine, destabilize or threaten the rule-based international order" in order to "to [maintain] an inclusive, free, and open Indo-Pacific." His joint statement also talked about "maintaining lawful unimpeded commerce, and respect for international law, including freedom of navigation and overflight in the South China Sea and beyond."[44] And the newly elected Yoon government held the same stance in a joint statement with Biden a year later. At the same time South Korea is expanding its global role in tackling issues like climate change, public health, cybersecurity, and green recovery. As such the last Yoon-Biden summit pledged South Korea's contribution to combating climate change and advancing decarbonization, accelerating production and strengthening global public health institutions, while cooperating in global supply chains and the development of "critical and emerging technologies."[45]

The Afghanistan crisis showcased South Korea's new global activism. Right before the Taliban's evacuation deadline for August 31, 2021, South Korea dispatched three military airplanes to rescue 390 Afghans who supported South Korea in Afghanistan before the Taliban seized power. The evacuees include locals who worked at the South Korean embassy in Kabul, hospitals, vocational training centers, and provincial reconstruction teams. As South Korea's foreign ministry official cited the mission as the county's "moral responsibility," some South Korean lawmakers said that "Afghanistan needs the help of neighboring countries for getting immediate humanitarian aid; however, unfortunately, Europe and many surrounding nations are against accepting refugees from Afghanistan."[46] While domestic constraints make it unlikely that South Korea will pursue an overtly ambitious global role, Seoul may open a new chapter in its grand strategy by embracing a broader role in regional and global affairs in the twenty-first century.

NOTES

1. K.J. Kwon, "North Korea Proclaims Itself a Nuclear State in New Constitution," *CNN*, May 31, 2012.
2. "North Korean Nuclear Negotiations: 1985–2019," Council on Foreign Relations, https://www.cfr.org/timeline/north-korean-nuclear-negotiations
3. State Department, "Secretary Antony J. Blinken and UK Foreign Secretary Dominic Raab at a Joint Press Availability," May 3, 2021.
4. Michelle Ye Hee Lee, "North Korea Is Test-Firing Missiles Again. Here's What to Make of the Launches," *The Washington Post*, January 14, 2022.
5. Vann H. Van Diepen, "North Korea Emphasizes Theater Strike Missiles in the First Third of 2024," *38th North*, May 1, 2024.
6. The "Nixon Doctrine" emphasized that US troop commitments to allied countries would be reduced as those allies built up their own armed forces.
7. Larry Niksch, "Special Report: Potential Sources of Opposition to a U.S. Troop Withdrawal from South Korea," National Committee on North Korea, April 2019, https://www.ncnk.org/resources/briefing-papers/all-briefing-papers/special-report-us-troop-withdrawal (accessed on January 27, 2022)
8. Victor Cha, *Alignment Despite Antagonism: The United States-Korea-Japan Security Triangle* (Stanford University Press, 1999), xvii, 373.
9. S.C.M. Paine, *The Sino-Japanese War of 1894–1895: Perceptions, Power and Primacy* (Cambridge University Press); Jonathan Spence, *The Search for Modern China* (W.W Norton & Co, 2000), 194–262.
10. Scott Snyder, "Establishing a "Strategic Cooperative Partnership," *Comparative Connections Pacific Forum*, 10, no. 2 (July 2008), https://cc.pacforum.org/2008/07/establishing-strategic-cooperative-partnership/
11. "ROK-US, the Decision to Deploy THAAD to USFK Has been Reached," ROK, Ministry of National Defense, July 8, 2016, https://www.mnd.go.kr/user/newsInUserRecord.action?command=view&newsId=I_669&siteId=mnd&page=1&id=mnd_020400000000&newsSeq=I_9465
12. Jeongseok Lee, "Back to Normal? The End of the THAAD Dispute between China and South Korea," *China Brief* 17, no.15 (November 12, 2017), https://jamestown.org/program/back-normal-end-thaad-dispute-china-south-korea/
13. Kim Dong Hyung, "South Korea Will Keeps Its Military Intelligence Pact with Japan—For Now; Seoul Had Threatened to Withdraw from the Agreement amid Bilateral Tensions with Tokyo." *The Diplomat*, November 23, 2019.
14. The White House, "The Spirit of Camp David: Joint Statement of Japan, the Republic of Korea, and the United States," August 18, 2023, https://www.whitehouse.gov/briefing-room/statements-releases/2023/08/18/the-spirit-of-camp-david-joint-statement-of-japan-the-republic-of-korea-and-the-united-states/
15. Peter Duus, *The Abacus and the Sword: The Japanese Penetration of Korea, 1895–1910* (University of California Press, 1995), 169–244, 397–423; Raymond A. Esthus, *Theodore Roosevelt and Japan* (University of Washington Press, 1966), 3–127; Peter Duus, Ramon H. Myers, and Mark R. Peattie, *The Japanese Informal Empire in China, 1895–1937* (Princeton University Press, 1989), introduction, 101–57, 431–8.

16. Do Je-Hae, "Moon's New Northern Policy Gaining Spotlight," *The Korea Times*, February 21, 2020.
17. Anthony Kuhn, "Concerns Mount as Russia and North Korea Commit to a Mutual Defense Pact," *NPR*, June 20, 2024.
18. Kim Eun-jung, "S. Korea Slams N.K.-Russia Treaty; Hints at Potential Arms Supply to Ukraine," *Yonhop News Agency*, June 20, 2024.
19. Josh Smith, "Buying a Big Stick: South Korea's Military Spending Has North Korea Worried," *Reuters*, September 11, 2019.
20. Jon Grevatt and Andrew MacDonald, "South Korea Finalises USD46.32 Billion Defence Budget for 2022," *Janes*, December 3, 2021; Hiroyuki Akita, "Time for Japan to Concede South Korea Has Better Defense Strategy," *Nikkei Asia*, June 24, 2021.
21. "2022 South Korea Military Strength: Annual GFP Review," *Global FirePower*, January 12, 2022, https://www.globalfirepower.com/country-military-strength-detail.php?country_id=south-korea
22. Statista, "Main Export Partners for South Korea in 2020," https://www.statista.com/statistics/618514/south-korea-main-export-partners/; Seong Hyeon Choi, "Why Is South Korea Hesitant to Boycott the 2022 Beijing Winter Olympics? Heavy Economic Reliance Has Complicated Seoul's Relationship with Beijing," *The Diplomat*, January 20, 2022.
23. "South Korea Set to Be Superaged Society within 4 Years," *The Strait Times*, April 20, 2020.
24. Seongho Sheen, "Northeast Asia's Aging Population and Regional Security: Demographic Peace?" *Asian Survey* 53, no. 2 (March/April 2013), 292–318.
25. OECD, "Social Expenditure Database (SOCX)," https://www.oecd.org/social/expenditure.htm
26. Sang-Woo Heo, "South Korea Will Spend More than Average of OECD in Welfare in 20 Years," *The Chosun Daily*, June 24, 2020,https://www.chosun.com/site/data/html_dir/2020/06/24/2020062400237.html
27. Chung Min Lee, "South Korea's Military Needs Bold Reforms to Overcome a Shrinking Population," Carnegie Endowment for International Peace, June 29, 2021, https://carnegieendowment.org/2021/06/29/south-korea-s-military-needs-bold-reforms-to-overcome-shrinking-population-pub-84822
28. Kim Yon-se, "South Korea to Face Critical Shortage of Soldiers: Demographic Change, Short Service Term Threaten Military Power," *The Korea Herald*, February 11, 2020.
29. Under the 11th Special Measures Agreement, a six-year defense cost-sharing deal reached after eighteen months of negotiations, Seoul will pay 1.1833 trillion won ($1.059 billion) in 2021, a 13.9 percent increase from 2019, for the upkeep of some 28,500 US troops in Korea. Korea is expected to pay more from 2022 to 2025 at a rate that mirrors increases in its own defense spending compared to the previous year. Sarah Kim, "After 18 Months of Tough Talks, SMA Is Signed with U.S.," *Korea JoonAng Daily*, April 8, 2021; Mitch Shin, "South Korea and US Reach Agreement on Defense Cost Sharing," *The Diplomat*, March 8, 2021.
30. Jessie Yeung and Yoonjung Seo, "South Korea President Welcomes 'Return of Diplomacy' in First Meeting with Top US Diplomat," *CNN*, March 18, 2021.
31. The White House, "U.S.-ROK Leaders' Joint Statement," May 21, 2021, https://www.whitehouse.gov/briefing-room/statements-releases/2021/05/21/u-s-rok-leaders-joint-statement/

32. The White House, "U.S.-ROK Leaders' Joint Statement," May 21, 2022, https://www.whitehouse.gov/briefing-room/statements-releases/2022/05/21/united-states-republic-of-korea-leaders-joint-statement/
33. Nathan Park, "Why South Korea's Liberals Are Defense Hawks," *Foreign Policy*, Ooctober 22, 2021.
34. "Agreement on Reconciliation, Non-Aggression, and Exchanges and Cooperation between South and North Korea" *Peacemaker*, United Nations, https://peacemaker.un.org/korea-reconciliation-nonaggression91
35. "Joint Declaration of South and North Korea on the Denuclearization of the Korean Peninsula," *NTI*, https://www.nti.org/education-center/treaties-and-regimes/joint-declaration-south-and-north-korea-denuclearization-korean-peninsula/
36. "South-North Joint Declaration," *Peacemaker*, United Nations, https://peacemaker.un.org/koreadprk-southnorthdeclaration
37. "October 4 South-North Joint Declaration of 2007," *KBS World*, November 15, 2018. https://world.kbs.co.kr/service/contents_view.htm?lang=e&menu_cate=history&id=&board_seq=351287&page=1&board_code=
38. "Panmunjom Declaration for Peace, Prosperity and Unification of the Korean Peninsula (2018.4.27)," ROK Ministry of Foreign Affairs, https://www.mofa.go.kr/eng/brd/m_5478/view.do?seq=319130&srchFr=&srchTo=&srchWord=&srchTp=&multi_itm_seq=0&itm_seq_1=0&itm_seq_2=0&company_cd=&company_nm=&page=1&titleNm=
39. Both Koreas made notable concessions affecting their current combat readiness in all three battlespaces: land, sea, and air. They have committed to establishing so-called peace zones near the Northern Limit Line (NLL) at sea and the Military Demarcation Line (MDL) at land, without any military withdrawals or redeployment of troops from either side. Within these new buffer zones, live-fire artillery drills, major maneuvers, and new weapons will not be permitted; there will also be no-fly zones, including for unmanned aerial vehicles (UAVs), and joint fishing areas crossing the NLL. The existing Demilitarized Zone (DMZ) stretches for 2 kilometers on either side of the MDL; the new buffer zones will extend to 5 kilometers. Both sides agreed to withdraw a number of guard posts. Sukjoon Yoon, "North and South Korea's New Military Agreement," *The Diplomat*, October 2, 2018.
40. Chaewon Chung, "Moon Jae-in Again Calls for Formal End to Korean War in Speech at UN," *NK News*, September 21, 2021.
41. The White House, "U.S.-ROK Leaders' Joint Statement," May 21, 2021 https://www.whitehouse.gov/briefing-room/statements-releases/2021/05/21/u-s-rok-leaders-joint-statement/
42. Hwang Joon Bum, "S. Korea-US Joint Statement Mentions "Taiwan," Leaves China Out," *Hankyoreh*, May 24, 2021.
43. "South Korea, China Exchange Harsh Words over Yoon's Remarks on Taiwan," *Yonhap News*, April 20, 2023.
44. The White House, "U.S.-ROK Leaders' Joint Statement," May 21, 2021
45. The White House, "U.S.-ROK Leaders' Joint Statement," May 21, 2022.
46. David Choi and Yoo Kyong Chang, "'Moral Responsibility': South Korea Is Airlifting Hundreds of Afghans out of Kabul," *Stars and Stripes*, August 25, 2021.

CHAPTER 5

Taiwan

Chiung-Chiu Huang

The foreign policymaking of Taiwan, as one of the twelve highest military spenders among all East Asian nations,[1] has often been neglected in the literature on international relations (IR).

It goes without saying that Taiwan's grand strategy (GS) is profoundly shaped by power politics both in the region and across the globe.

Nevertheless, this does not necessarily mean that this island regime loses its agency and capability regarding GS design and practice, despite the policymakers of Taiwan having different perspectives and interpretations of GS implementation.

In addition to the external factors, the historical background of being a colony of Japan and continuing to be a divided nation also shape Taiwan's GS design and execution. Against the complicated historical background and crucial geopolitical conditions, Taiwan's GS more often than not appears less grand in terms of its goals and scope. Maintaining the perceived legitimacy of its statehood and the ruling status of the political elites has been at the core of Taiwan's GS-making.

Overall, the chief goal of Taiwan's GS-making is to defend the perceived legitimacy of the rule of the policymakers and control its domestic struggle among diverse political factions. Rather than achieving strategic goals internationally, the ruling elites' concerns about domestic power distribution are more influential on the process of Taiwan's GS design.

This is related to the country's history of being Japan's colony for 50 years and of the Kuomintang (KMT, or Nationalist Party) confronting the Chinese Communist Party (CCP) after 1949, so the GS design remains mainly focused on its perceived legitimacy within Taiwan. The KMT taking over the domain and the Republic of China (ROC)'s retreat to Taiwan forced the island and its people to enter the postcolonial era in a drastic way. Without Taiwan fully completing the process of struggling and redefining itself, the national identity building process has long been problematic and chaotic. These factors all contribute to the special style of Taiwan's GS design and practices.

The contemporary history of Taiwan is witnessing conflicts among diverse forces. Shortly after being returned to the ROC by Japan after World War II, Taiwan was placed under the Temporary Provisions of National Mobilization for the Suppression of the Communist Rebellion (*dongyuan kanluan linshi tiaokuan*) and martial law. During that period, the GS-making of the ROC had two major goals: strengthening and stabilizing the perceived legitimacy of the ruling status of the KMT domestically and completing the anticommunism mission internationally.

However, the gradual restoration of the bilateral relationship between Washington and Beijing in the 1970s had a dramatic impact on Taiwan and its GS design. The White House's decision to engage with the CCP hugely undermined the ROC's perceived legitimacy to represent "China" on international platforms. After the US officially recognized the People's Republic of China (PRC) and broke off diplomatic ties with the ROC in 1979, Taiwan lost most of its allies, withdrew from the major international organizations, and became isolated internationally.

The condition of being isolated in the international arena and loss of support from the US and the country's other traditional allies certainly damaged the perceived legitimacy of the KMT. The political reality pushed Taiwanese policymakers to reconsider their GS design. In addition, the democratization movement in Taiwanese society had never ceased to push the policymakers to readjust their political stance and yield to the calls of the masses. In 1986 the major opposition party, the Democratic Progress Party (DPP), was established. The competition between the KMT and DPP became the major factor shaping Taiwan's GS-making. Except for the struggles and competition among diverse political forces both domestically and internationally, the pursuit of economic development is also a crucial drive. Even after entering the new millennium, Taiwan seems to have lost some of its advantages, and the urge to maintain stable economic development has driven the policymakers' GS design.

This chapter introduces the strategic priorities of Taiwan's GS-making. It argues that maintaining and strengthening the perceived legitimacy to rule domestically have continually outweighed the pursuit of strategic goals internationally. Second, the Taiwanese political elites' logic when designing the GS is greatly shaped by the external environment, especially the US and PRC.

However, in terms of the interests and the expectations regarding GS achievement, the domestic factors within Taiwan are more critical. This chapter finally analyzes Taiwan's operationalization of its GS. The timeframe of the investigation and analyses mainly focuses on the period from 1980 to 2020.

STRATEGIC PRIORITIES

In this volume, the definition of GS is not only "a blueprint for action," but also a guideline for state's foreign policymaking. In addition, the GS of a state can be viewed as a pattern of foreign policy behavior that a state frequently repeats.[2] The GS of a state also provides for a long-term design that presents the state's top priorities; it includes military, diplomatic, and economic statecraft.[3] In Taiwan's case the top priority of the GS-making is to preserve the perceived legitimacy of the ruling party, so foreign policymaking and the management of the relationships with the great powers are subordinate to this prioritized goal. The utilization of military, diplomatic, and economic statecraft is aimed at legitimizing the ruling status of the party that controls the state. This has been more obviously the case since the 1980s, after the ROC lost the representation of China at the UN and broke off diplomatic relations with the US. After that Taiwan entered an era of uncertain international status, and the competitions between the two parties, namely the KMT and DPP, began to shape the country's GS-making.

Both the KMT and DPP have their own blueprint for the GS design. The core differences lie in their perceptions and expectations of the relationship between Taiwan and China and Taiwan's status in the international arena. Also, the degree of Washington's involvement in cross-Strait relations (i.e., the bilateral relations between Taiwan and China) differ slightly under different administrations' domains. Compared to the DPP, the KMT has a longer history of ruling the island; nevertheless, the history of being defeated by the CCP and leading the ROC government in the retreat to Taiwan has become the primary sin of the KMT.[4] Especially after ending martial law, the KMT has been trying hard to prove its compatibility with Taiwan, which the party leaders once defined as a temporary base before the recapture of mainland China. On the other hand, the DPP has emerged as a local political force without the same historical burden. However, its pursuit of true independence for Taiwan inevitably caused turbulence in the cross-Strait relations, which threatens Taiwan's national security. The DPP's radical move is to mold a desinicized Taiwanese identity; nevertheless, such an intention irritated Beijing greatly, and so the latter frequently created obstacles to Taiwan's economic and diplomatic development when the DPP was in charge.

Taiwan's GS Strategic Priority under KMT Rule

Being a party established in the late nineteenth century,[5] the KMT, after shifting its base to Taiwan, was for a long time labeled the ruling organ of "outsiders" or "mainlanders" in the eyes of the local Taiwanese people. This long-established party eventually failed in the domestic conflict with the CCP in 1949, and its meritorious past of overthrowing the ancient monarchical system in China did not win it the support of the majority of the people. This fact was strongly connected with the KMT's elitist style of managing personnel and ruling the country, which made it comparatively less skillful at communicating with the civilians. The KMT's preference for elitism continued even after the move to Taiwan; intellectuals and professionals of specific disciplines were largely recruited by the KMT after Taiwan was returned to the ROC by its previous colonist, Japan.[6]

The KMT's preference for elitism has been forced to change since the late 1970s. The rationale of readjusting its ruling style arose from an urgent need for localization and integration with the Taiwanese. This need emerged due to the ROC's loss of its position within the United Nations and the termination of diplomatic relations with Washington, while at the same time the birth of the opposition force domestically also threatened the perceived legitimacy of the KMT. To manage these issues, the former party leader and president of the ROC, Chiang Ching-kuo, determined that the KMT and ROC should begin the process of indigenization, including strengthening the connections with local Taiwanese people.[7] At the party congress held in February 1986, Chiang Ching-kuo nominated the very first local candidate for the upcoming vice-presidential election, Lee Teng-hui. Lee was chosen, according to the official documents, because of his extensive experience of interacting with Taiwanese people, especially the peasantry.[8] Lee later succeeded to the presidency after Chiang Ching-kuo passed away in 1988. Although President Chiang announced the termination of martial law, his successor, Lee Teng-hui, was honored as the first national leader who pushed the island toward democratization since the ROC has been based in Taiwan.[9]

However, the KMT kept being haunted by the reputation of external power (*wailai zhengguan*). This is not only because of its history, but also because the party's major mission has long been reuniting China (*tongyi zhongguo*) under the theory of the Three Principles of the People. Hence, a spiritual connection with China (not the PRC) has characterized the KMT and differentiated it from the locally born party, the DPP. After the first round of power transferring between the two parties and the gradual change in the orientation of Taiwanese identity, the KMT has been struggling between its original mission of reunification and the need to win back perceived ruling legitimacy.[10] Such a dilemma had a crucial impact on the KMT's design of the GS when it had a chance to rule the country again.

Overall, the KMT's GS design focuses on maintaining the status quo. This has included upholding a stable relationship with the external forces, namely China and the US. The KMT, through the process of indigenization and democratization, has developed a pragmatic style for managing foreign affairs, yet redefining and resetting the relationship with the PRC were its key missions. Hence, even President Lee focused on the preservation of the ROC and nurturing a stable relationship with the CCP, albeit personally preferring independence for Taiwan.[11] Under Lee's domain, the government of ROC established the National Unification Council in 1990, and the Guidelines for National Unification (*guo tong gangling*) were passed and implemented in 1991. These acts ensured temporary stability for the cross-Strait relations and eased Beijing's suspicion of Lee's pro-independence intention, albeit in 1996 this stability was destroyed by Lee's official visit to the US.[12] Nevertheless it was said that Lee decided to establish the National Unification Council for the purpose of reducing any disturbance arising from the bilateral relations with Beijing so that he could focus on pushing forward the democratization process in Taiwan.[13]

Another KMT party leader and ROC president who ruled after another rotation of power, Ma Ying-jeou, also adopted a pragmatic approach and focused on the preservation of a stable bilateral relationship with Beijing. President Ma has often been criticized by his political opponents for being too pro-China because of his relatively moderate attitude toward the PRC and his family background. (He is a second-generation mainlander and the son of a famous KMT party member.) Nevertheless, maintaining a balance between Beijing and Washington was the main theme of Ma's GS execution from 2008 to 2016. Ma insisted that the 1992 Consensus was the core principle of his China policy; the 1992 Consensus refers to the agreement between the ROC and PRC made before the two regimes agreed to meet semiofficially in Singapore in 1993. This consensus means that both sides agree that there is one China but with different interpretations, and they respect the fact that each side has its own perspective about the content of this "one China."[14] However, Ma's GS design and China policy eventually led the KMT to lose the presidential election in 2016. Despite the pragmatism Ma inherited from Lee, he remained partly elitist and failed to detect the radical change in the younger generation's perspectives and attitudes toward China; Ma and the KMT also failed to manage the emerging anti-China emotions domestically. This gave the DPP an opportunity to reshape the execution of Taiwan's GS by achieving another power transition in 2018.

The DPP's GS-Making and Strategic Priority

Unlike the KMT, the DPP was established from the grassroots movement, based on a strong desire to pursue independence for Taiwan (which was named the Tangwai movement, i.e., the outside the party movement). Having been established in 1986, the DPP later announced its party platform in 1991 and claimed that its major mission was to promote and achieve independence for Taiwan through a referendum. In contrast to the KMT, the DPP rarely needs to defend its identity, nor does it feel compelled to transform or readjust itself to suit the local Taiwanese. However this does not mean that the DDP leaders have no need to preserve their perceived ruling legitimacy; being a revolutionary party, the DDP tends to be less experienced in governance and foreign policymaking. The DPP's core funders and key members were either in exile abroad or in jail after being arrested during the martial law period; the party was unable to rule until the year 2000. Hence, compared with the KMT, the DPP relatively lacks facility for governing. Its governance of the country has often been criticized as split because of the conflicts of interest existing among the diverse party factions. Thus the DPP's concern about its perceived legitimacy is related not to the party's identity but to its ability to govern effectively.

The main pursuit of the DPP is the independence of Taiwan. For this reason, the party defines the CCP, PRC, and China as its enemy and the obstacles to its achievement of the final goal. This creates a huge difference between the DPP and KMT; for the KMT, the CCP and PRC are mainly opponents that compete to be the representative of China, and China remains a crucial part of their identity and final mission, albeit this characteristic of the KMT is gradually becoming controversial in the process of indigenization. The DPP perceives China and the PRC as the major external threat, and such perspective determines its foreign policy orientation. This is why the DPP policymakers adopt the strategy of balancing against China, while at the same time allying with and bandwagoning the US.

Hence when the DPP ruled the island for the first time from 2000 to 2008, President Chen Shui-bian initially claimed that China and Taiwan are "one country on each side" (*yi bian yi guo*) in 2002, which aimed to divorce Taiwan from China and all things Chinese. Later he announced that both the National Unification Council and Guidelines for National Unification had ceased to function, which caused a huge uproar in both Beijing and Washington. It was therefore predicable that, during Chen's presidency, the cross-Strait relations rapidly degenerated, and the fallout from this included Taiwan's swift loss of diplomatic allies.[15] Domestically Chen Shui-bian was able to be reelected in 2004; however in early fall 2006, Chen and the DPP regime faced a severe opposition movement initiated by a famous DPP funding member due to Chen and his cronies' corruption. More than one million people took to the streets to join the movement,[16] which certainly posed a serious threat to Chen's GS design.

President Chen's scandal eventually caused the DPP to lose the 2008 presidential election. Ma Ying-jeou inherited Chen's position, but Ma's relatively more pro-China GS design (while at the same time still allied with the US) provided the DPP and the pro-independence factions with an excuse to attack the KMT. The Sunflower student movement, which aimed at the PRC and KMT government's China policy, occurred in 2014. This event led to the collapse of the KMT's ruling legitimacy and gave the DPP another opportunity to rule the country.[17] President Tsai Ing-wen succeeded Ma and became the first female president of the ROC in 2016. Shortly after taking over the regime, she resumed the DPP's GS approach, which meant showing defiance to China and deepening the ties with the US. Tsai's execution of the GS included denying the 1992 Consensus, signing more arms procurement deals with the US (there were 12 deals in total by August 2021, amounting to over US$19 billion),[18] and searching for more international support by promoting the New Southbound Policy and increasing relations with Japan. These moves mean that Taiwan's GS direction now greatly leans toward the anti-China track and allows Washington more leverage to utilize Taiwan in its own GS, which aims to contain China and weaken Beijing's growing influence.

In 2024 Lai Ching-te led the DPP to win over the KMT in the presidential election again. President Lai succeeded his predecessor and adopted an even stronger stance on his China policy by enhancing cooperation and tightening the ties with Washington.[19] In addition Lai's strategy is more akin to further internationalizing the Taiwan issue and forcing Beijing to step back.[20]

EXTERNAL FACTORS

Taiwan's GS priorities shift in accordance with the ruling parties' need to gain or maintain their perceived legitimacy; yet in the process of their GS design and execution, the two major external actors, namely China (the PRC) and the US, more often than not wield greater influence than other regional actors. The trilateral relations among Taiwan, China, and the US are often analyzed through the framework of the theory of the Strategic Triangle created by Lowell Dittmer.[21] The original idea of the Strategic Triangle was applied to a case study of the trilateral relations among China, the US, and the Soviet Union. Such a Strategic Triangle was symmetrical and balanced, for the material capabilities of all of the players in the trilateral relations were relatively equal.[22] Several Taiwanese scholars followed this analytical approach and applied the framework to analyze Taiwan's role in the relations with Beijing and Washington; and Dittmer himself also extended the model to include a case study of Taiwan.[23]

Although the trilateral relationship among Taiwan and the other two great powers are the crucial factors shaping Taipei's GS design and execution, this strategic triangle is asymmetric and unbalanced. The main reason is the apparent discrepancy between the capability of Taiwan and the other two actors in the strategic triangle. The asymmetry embedded in such a triangle to a great extent limits Taiwan's ability to take leverage between Washington and Beijing. This is why Taipei could hardly make itself a "pivot," which is the most beneficial position in the strategic triangle according to Dittmer and other scholars. The pivot is embedded in what Dittmer named the "romantic triangle" and refers to the actor whose relations with the other two members of the triangle are positive in both cases, while the bilateral relations between the other two actors are negative.[24] In the case of Taiwan, the role of the pivot is more desirable (but barely achievable) when the KMT is the ruling party; when the DPP controls the regime, Taiwan's role in the triangle is more like that of a "partner" which is allied with Washington, thereby making Beijing the strong "outcast" in the "marriage triangle."

The KMT's relations with both Washington and Beijing are relatively positive compared with those of the DPP. The KMT has long been a faithful ally and follower of the US; without Washington's continuing support, Chiang Kai-shek (the KMT leader and former president of the ROC) and the KMT would not have survived the domestic war against the CCP and the turbulence across the Taiwan Strait. Nevertheless, exactly because of the support and protection provided by the US, the autonomy of the KMT and ROC regarding foreign policymaking was very limited; they had no choice but to be in the retinue of the US in the latter's strategic layout of the Asia Pacific region.

The restoration of diplomatic relationship between Washington and Beijing in 1979 forced the KMT to redesign its GS in order to restore its perceived legitimacy in Taiwan. Hence, the KMT leader Chiang Ching-kuo began the process of indigenization and ended martial law, while at the same time readjusting the relations with the CCP and all communist regimes on earth through ceasing the hostile attitude and confrontational policies. This "diplomacy for the general situation" (*daju waijiao*) began in the late 1980s, and the KMT's redirection of the GS design was designed to regain autonomy from Washington.[25] Following Chiang's path, President Lee Teng-hui defined the theme of his GS as "programmatic diplomacy" (*wushi waijiao*) and continued the democratization of Taiwan. Chiang's readjustment of the GS upset Washington but did not change Taiwan's role as the US's partner in East Asia. After all, no matter how the KMT redefines its relations with the CCP and PRC, Washington's impact remains crucial, especially regarding the KMT's strategic priority of maintaining its perceived legitimacy, for which US support is vital. This is why, even when the KMT rules, Taiwan could hardly give it the role of a pivot in the strategic triangle.

Compared with the KMT, the DPP adopts a more obvious attitude and strategy of confronting China and bandwagoning the US. Since the DPP's main GS design is combined with its goal of independence for Taiwan, China is defined as the major threat to Taiwan, and the US is the sole solution to conquering this threat and achieving the goal. Nevertheless the DPP's hope of gaining independence for Taiwan does not always fit with Washington's strategic interests. In addition, since this strategic triangle is asymmetric, with Taiwan as the weakest party to it, the DPP's GS practices more often than not resulted in highly unstable cross-Strait relations and a more hostile attitude and assertive response on the part of China. When DPP president Chen Shui-bian was in charge, the even more severe bilateral relations between Taiwan and China drove him to execute "all out diplomacy" (*quanmin waijiao*). Meanwhile, Chen proposed holding a referendum to determine Taiwan's application to join the World Health Organization and United Nations, regardless of the apparent and immediate opposition to this by Washington. This move on the part of the DPP irritated Washington and resulted in some American politicians viewing Chen as a troublemaker regarding the American GS execution in East Asia. Moreover, Chen failed to notify or negotiate with Washington before he abandoned the National

Unification Council and the Guidelines for National Unification; such an act certainly upset the US even more.[26]

Hence the bilateral relations between Taiwan and the US during the DPP's first administration were less stable and beneficial to Taiwan's GS-making; Taiwan not only had very little leverage in its confrontation of China, but the bilateral relations between Taiwan and the US eventually degenerated. In addition, during President Chen's administration, the ROC lost six traditional allies to the PRC in Africa, Caribbean, Oceania, and Europe.[27] Taiwan had become more isolated by the end of Chen's presidential term. Hence, when the DPP resumed power, its policymakers paid more attention to the maintenance of the bilateral relations with Washington. Since 2018 President Tsai Ing-wen has adopted a more pro-US, anti-China strategy while at the same time promoting the New Southbound policy. During her presidential term, the COVID-19 pandemic occurred and dramatically shaped and shocked the world. The pandemic further accelerated Tsai's pro-US, anti-China GS design and execution. The downside of such a GS layout not only caused Taiwan to lose leverage and autonomy in managing its foreign relations but also pushed the bilateral relations between Taipei and Beijing toward a breaking point. Under Tsai's administration, Taiwan increased its dependence on Washington politically as well as economically; even worse, the quickly soured cross-Strait relations greatly threatened Taiwan's national security and caused international public opinion to label Taiwan as the most dangerous place on earth in 2021.[28] Tsai's successor, President Lai Ching-te, further extended her GS design and not only made Taiwan a more intimate ally of the US but also strengthened the ties with Japan, which resulted in an even worse bilateral relationship between Taipei and Beijing.[29]

In sum, the most crucial external factors shaping Taiwan's GS-making are the two great powers and the trilateral relations among the three countries. Both the KMT and DPP adopt a strategy of inclining toward the US side; yet the KMT also tried to stabilize the relations with the PRC and reduce the antagonism over the Taiwan Strait, while the DPP defines China and the CCP as major threats and adopts a strategy of confronting Beijing. For the US, Taiwan occupies a crucial geographic position that is the linchpin in its GS layout of containing China. For China/the PRC, Taiwan is the last piece of lost territory, which represents the humiliation of the Chinese nation and indicates the most significant step to its national glory. Reunification with Taiwan means resuming China's glorious past and its status as the center of Asia, if not the world. In the strategic triangle consisting of Taiwan, the US, and China, the two political parties, namely the KMT and DPP, both have their own agendas and strategic priorities; their GS-making hardly matches the great powers' own respective wishes or needs. Moreover, this strategic triangle is asymmetric and unbalanced; it is difficult for Taiwan to play the role of a pivot in the trilateral relations. Without the advantages offered by the pivot role, Taiwan's GS designs will need to be constantly readjusted in accordance with the changing external environment and unstable bilateral relations between China and the US.

DOMESTIC FACTORS

Taiwan's GS-making is deeply entangled with the great power politics and competition between China and the US; however, in terms of the logic and rationale that dominated the Taiwanese ruling elites' GS thinking, the domestic factors are more crucial than the external ones. As mentioned previously, the history of being Japan's colony remains influential regarding the Taiwanese people's attitudes and perspectives toward national development and bilateral relations with China. In addition the history of antagonism against the CCP and the extended inner war between the two sides of the Taiwan Strait during the Cold War era still impact the formation of the Taiwanese identity and the related debate about the status of the nation. Since the termination of martial law, there has been an emerging awareness of subjectivity among the Taiwanese population, especially among the younger generation. Nevertheless, the complexity of the bilateral relations with the PRC and the economic dependency on the Chinese market remain the pull factor driving the ruling elites' GS implementation more often than not to be ambiguous and inconsistent.

The impact of the colonial legacy has caused the national values in Taiwanese society to become split and controversial. Having been colonized by Japan for more than 50 years and returned to the ROC soon after the Japanese empire was defeated in World War II, Taiwan, and the local population did not have an opportunity to complete the process of decolonization and form a comprehensive national identity.[30]

This means inevitable chaos and struggles in the process of searching for a consensus among diverse ethnic groups. Disputes and conflicts among different ideologies, belief systems, and plans for nation-building were inevitable and became even more apparent after the late 1980s. Diverse political factions continued to fight each other and struggle over the perceived legitimacy to rule. During the martial law era, the KMT represented oppressive China and the Chinese. The KMT's opponents often labeled the KMT as the oppressors and an eternal outside force that once dominated the island and the people illegally.[31] The split political agenda and propaganda provided by both political parties attracted different groups of people; the result of such divergence is the divided ideas regarding Taiwan's GS design and execution.

Taiwanese society as a postcolonial society is a divided one, which could only embrace a personal level of GS design; once the leadership ended, its successor tends to have other ideas about Taiwan's GS. This is because, in a divided society, different factions continue to fight each other. In Taiwan's case, the most significant cause of such fights is the perspective on the CCP and China, and either perspective leads to a specific agenda regarding national identity building. For the KMT the national identity should be cored with the statehood of the ROC; in contrast, the DPP only recognizes Taiwan as the essence of the national identity, and it is a desinicized Taiwan that opposes any oppression by China, the CCP, or the PRC.

According to a survey conducted by a credible research center in Taiwan, from 1992 to 2021, there remain three major divergences within Taiwanese identity: "Taiwanese," "Chinese," and "both Taiwanese and Chinese." Before 2005 the survey shows that the population identifying themselves as both Taiwanese and Chinese was larger than the other two groups. Moreover, since 1995, the number of people who chose to identify as Chinese began to fall and became less than the group choosing Taiwanese as their national identity. Since 2007 the most popular identity for the whole population has become Taiwanese, and the trend remains robust up till today.[32] Accordingly the political elites must accommodate the identity orientation of the majority in society and adjust their GS-making in order to ensure that their strategic priority is preserved, that is, the perceived legitimacy to rule.

The change in the national identity orientation in Taiwanese society occurred due to several complicated factors. First, the relationship with the CCP and increasing interaction between the societies of the two sides deeply influenced the populations' preferences regarding national identity since the late 1980s. After martial law ended, both the ROC and PRC governments agreed to lift the ban on family visits, and many Taiwanese people visited mainland China to see their relatives, while at the same time traveling to see famous tourist spots. From 2008 Chinese tourists were permitted to visit Taiwan for sightseeing, and Chinese students were allowed to attend universities and graduate schools in Taiwan. However, the travel ban on Chinese tourists visiting Taiwan was reinstated in August 2019 by the PRC government, and the number of Chinese students enrolled in Taiwan's higher education system has gradually declined since the DPP won the presidential election again. Neither the opportunity to travel in mainland China nor the frequent encounters with Chinese tourists and students in Taiwan enhance the Taiwanese people's perceptions about China and Chinese people; rather, the increasing number of interactions between the citizens of the two sides damaged the imagined communal identity, namely, the identification of being Chinese and being part of China.[33] This resulted in the birth of an awareness of Taiwanese subjectivity, which refers to the strong sense of being Taiwanese and apparent differentiation from Chinese and China, and the whole population's comprehensive disinclination regarding the political system of the PRC.

However, while the increased number of encounters with Chinese people failed to strengthen the sense of connection with China and the Chinese, the economic ties between Taiwanese enterprises and the Chinese market have been growing stronger since the late 1980s.[34] Due to the cheap labor and resources for production, there has been considerable Taiwanese foreign investment in China. Several Taiwanese businessmen have even migrated to the mainland; to secure their career and investment in China, they must show their agreement or even submission regarding Beijing's "One China" policy. Hence these groups of Taiwanese people are very wary of the negative impact of the political propaganda promoting the independence of Taiwan or the demarcation between Taiwan and China.[35] They have been the other force shaping the government's GS-making. Moreover, because these groups are mainly entrepreneurs and financial supporters of the government, regardless of which party is in charge, their influence tends to be relatively strong and apparent.

For the KMT and DPP, their GS-making is deeply rooted in how they have perceived and responded to the aforementioned issues occurring in domestic society. Due to the complexity of the local population's self-identification, the encounters with Chinese people from the mainland, and the high degree of economic dependency on the Chinese market, the policymakers in Taiwan must seek to balance these complicated factors. How they responded to these issues often turned to the materialization of projects that led to entirely diverse directions of national development, namely the blueprints for Taiwan's independence from or reunification with China; nevertheless, at the execution level, either the KMT or DPP is mainly working to maintain the status quo and maximize their perceived legitimacy to rule. To implement their GS designs, the policymakers of either political party utilize the split perspectives and self-identification among different groups of people to support their projects. Hence the debate and struggles regarding the national identity and future of the island continue and remain the major factors that lead to the further complexity of Taiwan's GS implementation.

OPERATIONALIZATION OF THE GRAND STRATEGY

At the operational level, Taiwan's GS execution is designed as a response to the changes in the external environment (especially the trilateral relations with China and the US) and the need to preserve their perceived legitimacy to rule. The major actors dominating the design of the GS, the KMT and DPP, often adopt different and even contradictory logics when executing the GS; nevertheless, their goal and expectation regarding the effect of the GS are quite similar, which is the maintenance of the de facto independence of Taiwan/the ROC and the prevention of the intrusion of the PRC.

Different administrations of Taiwan in diverse time periods have had their own themes for executing the GS. The administration led by President Lee Teng-hui executed the GS under the principles of "diplomacy for the general situation" and "programmatic diplomacy." These two themes of GS-making were a response to Taiwan's swift loss of allies due to the restoration of diplomatic relations between Washington and Beijing. Both principles aimed to preserve and expand Taiwan's international status as an independent regime through abandoning the dogma of political ideology. This was also the start of Taiwan's pursuit of de facto yet unofficial diplomatic relations with most states by establishing the Taipei Economic and Cultural (Representative) Office in the capitals or key cities of different nations. After Chen Shui-bian took over the presidency, "all out diplomacy" became the main theme of Taiwan's GS implementation, for this was the period when the bilateral relations across the Taiwan Strait degenerated severely and the PRC blocked Taiwan's efforts to expand in the international space by taking over many of Taipei's allied countries through economic inducements.[36]

The negatively developed external environment that the ROC faced in the early 2000s remained unchanged until the KMT leader, Ma Ying-jeou, became president. President Ma promoted a diplomatic truce (*waijiao xiu bing*) and "viable diplomacy" (*huolu waijiao*) as the major principle for executing Taiwan's GS. The premise of his "viable diplomacy" is the stability of the bilateral relations with mainland China and the minimal degree of mutual trust accumulated by the frequent interactions between the political elites of the KMT and CCP. Nevertheless, after President Tsai Ing-wen succeeded Ma, the diplomatic space for Taiwan once again shrank rapidly. Expecting the coming difficulty due to the DPP's rule of Taiwan and the pressure imposed by the PRC, President Tsai named the theme of the GS implementation as "steadfast diplomacy" (*tashi waijiao*), which aims to expand Taiwan's international space and enhance its national status through official, semiofficial, and nonofficial access, including inter-state interactions, trade and investment, and cooperation between civil societies.[37] The unfortunate fact is that the Tsai Ing-wen administration had lost nine officially allied states by early 2023, which forced Taiwan's GS execution further to bandwagon the US. Lai Ching-te, Tsai's successor, was inaugurated on May 20, 2024. He has not yet initiated a clear theme for implementing his own GS design but is mainly following the path Tsai set in her term. Nevertheless Lai also paid great attention to the maintenance of his ruling legitimacy, and such a mentality could be evidenced by his calling for solidarity of the Taiwanese people in his inauguration speech.[38]

Overall the Taiwanese political elites are operating the GS mainly to preserve their perceived legitimacy to rule and realize the political leaders' personal visions of national development. The following aspects are often considered when they design and implement Taiwan's GS and related tactics:

Focusing on the bilateral relations with China and maintaining the status quo: No matter which party is in power, the major concern when executing the GS and designing the related foreign policy is always China and the CCP. After the late 1980s, with China's apparent rise and the shrinking of Taiwan's international space, the political elites, regardless of party, had to make huge efforts to maintain the status quo of the nation, that is, to preserve the de facto independence and avoid being dominated by China and the PRC. Hence, the four presidents of the ROC and their designs of themes for executing the GS concerned the management of the relations with China. Both Lee Teng-hui and Ma Ying-jeou focused on pragmatically preserving and expanding Taiwan's international status while at the same time maintaining the active interaction with China and the CCP. Under Lee, two crucial semiofficial meetings were held between the ROC and PRC through the cooperation of two key characters, Koo Chen-fu and Wang Daohan, which were labeled a milestone in cross-Strait relations. Ma Ying-jeou built a channel for civilians on both sides to further encounter and interact with each other by accepting Chinese tourists and Chinese students in Taiwan. Ma even met Xi Jinping in person in Singapore before leaving office in November 2015, which was the very first meeting between the political leaders of the ROC and PRC. In contrast, the DDP leaders' GS operations were mainly designed to defend the nation's international status and respond to Beijing's antagonism through adopting a confrontational approach and even further allying with the other great power, namely the US.

Utilizing unofficial or semiofficial relations with third parties, including nongovernmental organizations and actors: Faced with the fact that the ROC is not officially recognized by most states on earth and that Taiwan's international space has been greatly compressed due to the PRC's insistence on the One China policy, Taiwanese policymakers have tried hard to utilize the ties with other political organizations, regardless of whether the relations are unofficial or semiofficial. The most crucial third party in Taiwan's GS-making is definitely the US; nevertheless, other regional actors—including Japan, South Korea, and many Southeast Asian nations—also play key roles in Taipei's implementation of the GS. Both the KMT and DPP leaders even tried to rely on third parties, in addition to the US, to reshape the relations with mainland China, such as Lee Teng-hui's promotion of the Southbound policy and Tsai Ing-wen's initiation of the New Southbound policy. Taking the New Southbound policy as example, this policy is in fact designed to promote cooperation in areas such as the economy, culture, and educational and public health care systems, between Taiwan and Southeast Asian countries.[39] The goal is to secure Taiwan's de facto independence by gaining support from the regional actors. Moreover, interactions in apolitical and less sensitive issue areas could also reduce the pressure that third parties might experience from China.

While it is important to understand *how* the Taiwanese ruling elites have operationalized their designs for a grand strategy, it is equally crucial to assess the logic and mentality behind their choices, that is, the *why* part of Taiwan's GS-making:

Small states' foreign policymaking is always limited due to structural factors: Taiwan is no exception. Although most small states in the twenty-first century are able to interact with their stronger counterparts through a multilateral platform and can lobby for a relatively equal status in the international arena,[40] Taiwan lacks this privilege due to its special status and unique relationship with China. Consequently, compared with other small states, Taiwan is far more likely to be framed by the asymmetric power structure when managing its foreign affairs. As Brantly Womack[41] points out, small states are more vulnerable to asymmetric relationships and tend to be more sensitive and anxious with regard to the great powers' intentions and behaviors. In Taiwan's case the asymmetric structure that it faces contains two sets of relations: the US-Taiwan relationship and the cross-Strait relationship. Along with the intensified competition and apparent rivalry between the US and China, these two sets of asymmetric relationships increasingly contradict each other and further restrict Taiwan's choices of GS-making.

To ease the stress embedded in asymmetric relations and secure autonomy while simultaneously reducing their exposure to a great power's influence, small states tend to adopt a strategy of strengthening their ties with both other states and the international institutions. Meanwhile, continuing to practice the diplomatic rituals is also a crucial tactic for the weaker player in an asymmetric relationship in order to stabilize the status quo and maximize its national interests.[42] Taiwan has adopted similar strategies too. In addition to utilizing their unofficial or semiofficial relations with third parties, Taiwan also continues to practice diplomatic rituals when managing their relations with Washington. The most crucial example of this is the Taiwanese politicians' visits to Washington immediately after claiming to have joined the presidential campaign. This ritual originated during the very first general presidential election held in 1996; before the election, the incumbent candidate, Lee Teng-hui, visited the US and delivered a speech at his alma mater (Cornell University).[43] After this, almost every candidate (especially the most promising ones) running for Taiwan's presidential elections have visited the US. Nevertheless the Taiwanese political elites do not practice similar rituals when managing their relationship with China. The major reason for this lies in the colonial history and the postcolonial mentality that is embedded in Taiwanese society.

The lack of decolonization experience contributes to Taiwan's complicated situation with regard to China: As mentioned previously, Taiwan was a colony of Japan for approximately fifty years and returned to China (the ROC) after Japan was defeated at the end of World War II. This meant that Taiwan and the Taiwanese were almost immediately handed over to another external dominator shortly after the former colonist retreated. Taiwan had never experienced a process of decolonialization, since its release from colonialism was not achieved by the indigenous population; rather, the so-called Chinese motherland replaced the colonial motherland, namely Japan.[44] The result of this lack of experience of decolonialization is a profound, enduring absence of a self-conscious dignity, which led to a short-sighted view and style of governance and GS-making subsequently.

On the other hand, before Japan retreated, the Taiwanese elites' perspective of China developed under the influence of Japanese colonialism, imbued with the concept of colonial modernity. Colonial modernity is defined as "achieving characteristics of modernization that make the colony useful to the colonizer." As argued by Chih-yu Shih,[45] "in Taiwan, though, the colonial modernity brought by Japan provides, to date, an intellectual foundation for those who strive for dignity before the disapproving KMT who, at the time of its arrival in Taiwan, lack a similar level of modernity." Today, a predisposition to view the KMT and China (represented by either the ROC or the PRC) as inferior with regard to modernization remains prevalent in Taiwanese society. In addition Taiwan's dependence on the US during the Cold War era has made Washington another alternative choice for Taiwan's "motherlands."[46] Consequently, facing the double asymmetric relationships that profoundly shape its GS-making, Taiwan opts to continue practicing diplomatic rituals with the US and looking to Washington for comprehensive support, while continuing to perceive China as the threatening, less civilized object that is meant to be detached.

The third facet of the Taiwanese postcolonial mentality is that the colonial motherland was immediately replaced by another external ruling regime, namely the KMT, and this had a twin effect. First, the KMT and Taiwanese society lacked a common memory of the colonial period; hence the former continues to strive to gain acceptance by the latter by proving its ruling legitimacy. Second, the lack of a common memory with the KMT and the frustration caused by the inability to overturn and replace the colonial motherland in themselves trigger the prevailing nostalgia in Taiwanese society. Such nostalgia leads to the perspective that Taiwan has inherited both the Japanese and American cultures and therefore is superior to the KMT and China (broadly defined). This is why, following the 2000 presidential election when the DPP came to power, its ruling elites did not feel the burden that the KMT has shouldered for decades, and the DPP's GS-making and execution focuses more on pleasing and accommodating Washington while adopting a more confrontational attitude toward the PRC.

CONCLUSION

Taiwan's GS-making and implementation are not like those of the great powers; it was rarely a grand project with a global scope. Rather, Taiwan's GS design is mainly intended to create and maintain the perceived legitimacy to rule of the party controlling the regime. This characteristic is a major strategic priority of the Taiwanese political elites, deeply rooted in Taiwan's past as a Japanese colony and the indigenous population's lack of experience of a decolonialization process. Nevertheless, being a small nation located in a crucial geographic spot allows Taiwan to utilize the pressure caused by the rise of China and the ensuing support of third parties in the international arena. Moreover, the development of bilateral relations between Washington and Beijing also gives Taiwan considerable leverage in terms of managing its

GS design and execution. In the current situation of escalating great power rivalry, Taiwan's strategic position appears even more crucial and critical. The domestic political factions are also debating the redirection of Taiwan's GS-making.

On the other hand, being a small nation allows Taiwan greater flexibility and creativity in expanding its international space and enhancing its global status. Developing soft power and increasing its connections with apolitical international organizations have also been key tactics for the Taiwanese political elites in implementing the GS. For instance, the promotion of the rights of LGBT groups and passing of the same-sex marriage law has given Taiwan a considerably more positive reputation in global public opinion. Some scholars are even encouraging Taipei to develop "Tongzhi diplomacy" or "queer diplomacy" to earn more friends and support in the international arena.[47] Nevertheless, GS-making and execution are still an issue in the field of high politics. Taiwan may continue to adopt less political and relatively indirect approaches to build a positive reputation and more nonofficial ties, but its GS execution still relies on how it manages its two sets of bilateral relations, respectively with China and the US. The key to the successful implementation of the GS for Taiwan remains the balance of its relations with both great powers.

NOTES

1. Taiwan ranked as eighth on the list of East Asian defense spenders in 2023. Lowy Institute, "Asia Power Index," https://power.lowyinstitute.org/
2. Introduction chapter of this book, 3.
3. Nina Silove, "Beyond the Buzzword: The Three Meanings of 'Grand Strategy,'" *Security Studies*, 27, no. 1 (2018), 31.
4. Banyan, "The KMT's Original Sin," *The Economist*, February 22, 2011, https://www.economist.com/banyan/2011/02/22/the-kmts-original-sin
5. Kuomintang Official Website, "Introduction of the Party," http://www1.kmt.org.tw/english/page.aspx?type=para&mnum=105
6. US Congress House Committee of Foreign Affairs, Subcommittee on Asian and Pacific Affairs, "Political Developments in Taiwan: Hearing and Markup before the Subcommittee on Asian and Pacific Affairs of the Committee on Foreign Affairs, House of Representatives, Ninety-eighth Congress, Second Session', *H. Con. Res. 129*, May 31, 1984, https://catalog.hathitrust.org/Record/007609172
7. Here the term "Taiwanese" is used in contrast with "mainlanders" (*wai sheng ren*), who migrated to Taiwan with the KMT and ROC government from mainland China around 1949.
8. Yang Xiaoping, "*Tonghe ningju zai chufa—ji Zhongguo Guomindang di shi er jie er zhong quanhui*" ["Integration, Cohesion, and Restart: Memorizing the Second Plenary Session of the 12th Central Committee of the Kuomintang"], *Taiwan Panorama*, March 1984,

https://www.taiwan-panorama.com/Articles/Details?Guid=17843e87-6172-416d-81dd-30ff5adebc80

9. James Baron, "The Glorious Contributions of Lee Teng-hui," *The Diplomat*, August 18, 2020, https://thediplomat.com/2020/08/the-glorious-contradictions-of-lee-teng-hui/
10. Huang Chiung-Chiu, *Jinchu quanqiuhua—dangqian Taiwan xianshen celue pingshu [In and Out Globalization: Analysis of Contemporary Taiwan's Strategies of Representation]* (Hanlu, 2005), 21–51.
11. Baron, "The Glorious Contributions of Lee Teng-hui."
12. Baron, "The Glorious Contributions of Lee Teng-hui."
13. Chen Meihua, "*Zhuanfang Li Denghui muliao: Li Denghui zhiding guotong gangling huajie tongdu zhengyi*" ["Exclusive Interview with Lee Teng-hui's Consultant: Lee Teng-hui Formulated the Guidelines for National Unification, Solving the Unification-Independence Divide"], *Radio Free Asia*, July 30, 2020, https://www.rfa.org/mandarin/yataibaodao/gangtai/cmh-07302020151807.html
14. Chou Hui-Ching, "How the '1992 Consensus' Colors Taiwan's Fate," *CommonWealth Magazine*, December 7, 2018, https://english.cw.com.tw/article/article.action?id=2214
15. Bonnie Glaser, "China's Taiwan Policy in the Wake of 'One Country on Each Side,'" *American Foreign Policy Interests*, 24, no. 6 (2002), 515–24.
16. Lu Chia-ying, "'Red-Shirt' Leader Calls for National Day Protest', *Taiwan News*, August 5, 2007, https://www.taiwannews.com.tw/en/news/497769
17. Hi Ming-sho and Lin Thung-hong, *The Power of Sunflower: The Origin and the Impact of Taiwan's Protest against Free Trade with China* (Cambridge University Press, 2020).
18. Tao Ben-he, "*Cai Yingwen rennei Meiguo wancheng 12 ci dui tai junshou 5300 yi maile shenme yi ci kan*" ["During Tsai Ing-wen's Tenure, the United States Has Completed 12 Batches of Arm Sales to Taiwan. Look at What Has Been Bought for 530 Billion TWD"], *ETtoday*, August 5, 2021, https://www.ettoday.net/news/20210805/2048566.htm
19. Lai Ching-te paid a visit to the US before the presidential election. His trip aimed at maintaining close ties with Washington and fulfilling his self-expectation of being capable of "walking into the White House" while at the same time being the "pragmatic worker for Taiwan's independence" once he is elected. Gang Lin and Weixu Wu, "External and Internal Factors Shaping the Outcomes of 2024 Elections in Taiwan," *China Review*, 24 (2023), 1–15.
20. Dene-Hern Chen and Amber Wang, "Taiwan's Incoming Leader Lai Ching-te to Bolster 'Porcupine' Defence against China Threat,' *Hong Kong Free Press*, May 17, 2024, https://hongkongfp.com/2024/05/17/taiwans-incoming-leader-lai-ching-te-to-bolster-porcupine-defence-against-china-threat/
21. Lowell Dittmer, "The Strategic Triangle: An Elementary Game-Theoretical Analysis," *World Politics*, 33, no. 4 (1981), 485–515.
22. Kim Ilpyong, *The Strategic Triangle: China, the United States and the Soviet Union* (Paragon House, 1987).
23. Lowell Dittmer, "Bush, China, Taiwan: A Triangular Analysis," *Journal of Chinese Political Science*, 10 (2005), 21–42.
24. Lowell Dittmer, "Taiwan, China, and the US Pivot," *East Asian Institute (EAI) Working Paper*, 164 (May 26, 2014), 1–12.
25. Lin Hsiao-ting, *Jiang Jingguo de Taiwan shidai: Zhonghua minguo yu lengzhan xia de Taiwan [The Chiang Ching-kuo Era: The Republic of China on Taiwan in the Cold War]* (Yuanzu Wenhua [Walkers Cultural Enterprise], 2021).

26. Liu Shih-chung, "*Lishi de jiujie—Tai Mei guanxi de zhanlve hezuo yu fenqi* (2000–2008)" [History Entangled: Strategic Convergence and Divergence of Taiwan-U.S. Relations: 2000 to 2008], *Taiwan International Studies Quarterly*, 6, no. 4 (2010), 180, 187–90.
27. Xu Hui-xin, "*Cong Li Denghui dao Cai Yingwen bangjiaoguo cong 31 ge jinsheng 15 ge*" [From Lee Teng-hui to Tsai Ing-wen: The Number of Countries with Diplomatic Ties with Taiwan Has Dropped from 31 to 15], *Up Media*, September 20, 2019, https://www.upmedia.mg/news_info.php?SerialNo=71752
28. Justin Metz, "The Most Dangerous Place on Earth," *The Economist*, May 1, 2021, https://www.economist.com/leaders/2021/05/01/the-most-dangerous-place-on-earth
29. Lin and Wu, "External and Internal Factors Shaping the Outcomes of 2024 Elections."
30. Shih Chih-yu, *Post-Chineseness: Culture Politics and International Relational Relations* (State University of New York Press, 2022), 127–35.
31. Chen Pei-jun, "*Wailai shili lun yinyi Lvying: minjian you gongshi Guomindang shi wailai zhengquan*" ["The Theory of External Powers Sparks Debates. Green Camp: There Is a Consensus among the People that the Kuomintang Is an External Power"], *New Talk*, August 18, 2021, https://newtalk.tw/news/view/2021-08-18/622482
32. More information could be gained from the survey, "Changes in the Taiwanese/Chinese Identity of Taiwanese," undertaken by the Election Study Center at National Chengchi University (NCCU), https://esc.nccu.edu.tw/upload/44/doc/6960/People202106.jpg
33. Kuan Hung-chang, "*Taiwan qingnian shidai tongdu yu liangan jingmao jiaoliu taidu zhi tansuo*" ["Exploring the Attitudes of Taiwan's Young Generation toward Unification-Independence and Cross-Strait Economic Exchanges"], *Prospect Quarterly*, 19, no. 2 (2018), 1–40.
34. Bonnie Glaser, "Taiwan and China Are Locked in Economic Co-Dependence," *Foreign Policy*, April 14, 2021, https://foreignpolicy.com/2021/04/14/taiwan-china-econonomic-codependence/
35. Lin Jin-Jie, "*Haijihui guwen: liangan guanxi jinzhang zaocheng Taishang beipo xuanbianzhan*" ["Straits Exchange Foundation's Consultant: Tensions in the cross-strait relations forced Taiwanese businessmen to pick sides"], *China Times*, December 9, 2021, https://www.chinatimes.com/realtimenews/20211209005922-260409?chdtv
36. John F. Copper, "Taiwan's Failed President," *Asian Affairs*, 34, no. 4 (2008), 179–92.
37. Office of the President ROC, "President Tsai Meets with Visiting Delegation of UN Ambassadors from Allied Nations," October 25, 2016, https://english.president.gov.tw/NEWS/5016
38. "Inaugural Address of ROC 16th-term President Lai Ching-te," Office of the President of the Republic of China, https://english.president.gov.tw/News/6726
39. See Taiwan's New Southbound Policy Portal, the official website of the Ministry of Foreign Affairs, ROC regarding the New Southbound Policy https://nspp.mofa.gov.tw/nsppe/
40. Andrew F. Cooper and Bessma Momani, "Qatar and Expanded Contours of Small State Diplomacy," *International Spectator*, 46, no. 3 (2011), 113–28.
41. Brantley Womack, *Asymmetry and International Relationships* (Cambridge University Press, 2006), 39–67.
42. Womack, *Asymmetry and International Relationships.*
43. David W. Chen, "Taiwan's President Tiptoes around Politics at Cornell," *The New York Times*, June 10, 1995, https://www.nytimes.com/1995/06/10/world/taiwan-s-president-tiptoes-around-politics-at-cornell.html

44. Shih Chih-yu, *Post-Chineseness: Cultural Politics and International Relations* (SUNY Press, 2022), 133.
45. Chih-yu, *Post-Chineseness*, 129.
46. Chih-yu, *Post-Chineseness*, 133.
47. Chen Nai-chia and Dafydd Fell, "Tongzhi Diplomacy and the Queer Case of Taiwan," in Mariah Thornton, Robert Ash, and Dafydd Fell (eds.), *Taiwan's Economic and Diplomatic Challenges and Opportunities* (Routledge, 2021), 194–214.

PART II

Southeast Asia

CHAPTER 6

Indonesia

Muhamad Haripin

Indonesia's grand strategy is influenced by the country's deep-seated anxiety over potential foreign infiltration and imminent territorial disintegration. The long trauma of living under different colonial powers still resonates in today's Indonesia. Since the dawn of independence in the mid-1940s, political elites and policymakers in Indonesia have, for the most part, maintained domestic-oriented strategic thinking and pursued an "independent and active" foreign policy whose main objective is to prevent the country falling into the sphere of influence of great powers. On the other hand, the threats of regional rebellions and secessionist movements, whose origins can be traced back to the early years of independence, have yet to be resolved. Different political regimes in Indonesia—from nationalist Sukarno (1945–66), to authoritarian Suharto (1966–98), to the present day of populist Joko Widodo (2014–24)—have sought to find peaceful resolution to conflicts in, for instance, West Papua, but to no avail. The strong intervention of the military during the authoritarian Suharto era, and the role of former high ranking military officers in the current democratic political system, has complicated the process of finding a sound and ethical conflict resolution policy.

Standing as the largest country in Southeast Asia, Indonesia has attempted different styles of foreign policy, even though in principle it has always pursued the "independent and active" values. Formerly employing a staunch nationalist approach under the Sukarno leadership, as demonstrated by Indonesia's *Konfrontasi* stance against the establishment of the Federation of Malaysia in the 1960s, Indonesia's grand strategy since the Suharto administration has gradually become more moderate. Since becoming one of founding members of the Association of Southeast Asian Nations (ASEAN) in 1967, Jakarta's diplomacy has been moving toward the goals of shared regional resilience, political stability, and economic prosperity. Indonesia could not risk a fragmented Southeast Asia, whether during the heights of the Cold War or in the time of strategic rivalry between the United States and China today. Thus, Jakarta has consistently nurtured a consensus-seeking and nonconflictual approach as part of its foreign policy. Indonesia has also sought beneficial reciprocal relationships and shared norms both with its immediate neighbor countries and the great powers in the region.

These past and present geopolitical challenges have continuously shaped the approaches undertaken by Indonesia in formulating and operationalizing its grand strategy. Indonesia thus promotes "national and regional resilience" to underscore its position as a global emerging power and natural leader of ASEAN.

This chapter describes Indonesia's grand strategy. The discussion is divided into three parts. First, we will explain Indonesia's strategic priorities. As mentioned previously, Jakarta prioritizes strategic autonomy at the national and regional levels, including territorial integration, economic development, and ASEAN unity and centrality. Indonesia's defense arrangements and foreign policy orientation are focused on deterring potential threats that could shatter territorial cohesion and on foreign powers meddling in domestic affairs. Next, we will continue with the examination of Indonesia's external relations. Particular importance is given to the country's relationship with the United States, China, Australia, Malaysia and Singapore, and ASEAN. We will see how Indonesia's independent and active foreign policy has unfolded in practice. After that, the discussion will move on to the domestic factors. Following the definition of domestic factors provided by Balzacq, Dombrowski, and Reich,[1] we are going to discuss a set of internal elements that inform us about the principles underpinning Indonesia's grand strategy, the applied decision-making process, and the material resources that Indonesia possesses to implement its grand strategy. The question is then, how does Indonesia's grand strategy operationalize in practice? We argue that diplomacy, total defense doctrine (*sishankamrata*), active and layered defense, peacekeeping, and defense diplomacy are the core aspects of Indonesia's operationalization of its grand strategy. The last section is the conclusion, which will summarize the findings and key elements of Indonesia's grand strategy.

STRATEGIC PRIORITIES

Indonesia prioritizes strategic autonomy—including territorial integrity, economic development, and ASEAN unity—through defense arrangements and foreign policy focused on deterring threats to territorial cohesion and foreign interference.

National Strategic Autonomy

Territorial integrity is a key priority. Indonesia experienced the devastating impacts of several secessionist movements in the early years after independence. In 1948 a communist rebellion broke out in Madiun city, East Java province. Disgruntled political elites and armed left-wing militias announced the formation of the Indonesia Soviet Republic to express their deep-seated grievances toward the Indonesian government led by the duumvirate of President Sukarno and Vice President Mohammad Hatta. Furthermore in 1949, dissatisfied with the way political elites in Jakarta negotiating with the Dutch government that sought to recolonize the archipelago, charismatic political and religious leader Kartosuwirjo declared and led the establishment of the *Darul Islam* movement (Islamic State) in West Java province.[2] Kahar Muzakar, a respected local military leader in the South Sulawesi province, decided to rebel against Jakarta as well. He took sides with Kartosuwiryo's Darul Islam after his guerrilla unit was excluded from the national armed forces. Fear of national disintegration continued to haunt the central government as the Free Papua Movement (*Organisasi Papua Merdeka* or OPM) in West Papua, also known as Irian Jaya, was created in 1965. OPM political and military leaders rejected the inclusion of West Papua into Indonesian territory. The movement refused to acknowledge any political settlement that denied West Papua's self-determination rights.[3]

Internal friction aside, Indonesia also considers external intervention as a potential threat that could jeopardize territorial integrity. The experience of colonialism under Dutch rule and the subsequent Japanese occupation taught Indonesia a bitter lesson of living under foreign rule. In spite of a changing global political landscape over the past century and the development of human rights norms, Indonesia's fear of foreign domination over its territory and natural resources remains unchanged. Therefore, Indonesia's defense posture is based on this goal of maintaining territorial integrity. Indonesia's geopolitical outlook envisions three interrelated concentric circles: the first encompasses the national territory, including the exclusive economic zone (EEZ); the second circle covers the area of Southeast Asia and Australia; and the third circle is the rest of the world.[4] In addition Indonesia also has been paying more attention to nontraditional security threats. In order to anticipate the escalation of terrorist threats, transnational crimes, and public health crises, the country relies not only on domestic resources but also on regional cooperation and global collaboration.

Economic development is another key priority. According to the World Bank, Indonesia is the tenth largest economy in the world in terms of purchasing power parity. Indonesia has done well in "cutting the poverty rate by more than half since 1999, to under 10 percent in 2019 just before the COVID-19 pandemic hit."[5] Based on 2018 estimates, income inequality in Indonesia as per its Gini coefficient is lower than other emerging economies (38.2 vs. 45.9) but higher than in most advanced economies (38.2 vs. 30.3).[6] Indonesia held the presidency of the G20 in 2022, focusing on three main pillars, namely the global health architecture, sustainable energy transition, and digital transformation.[7] Indonesia's economic progress slowed down due to the COVID-19 pandemic, but recent trends indicate that the economy should resume growth. The Asian Development Bank forecasts that Indonesia's GDP growth rate reached 5.0 percent by 2024, following minus 2.1 percent decline in 2020.[8] Indonesia aspires to accelerate its economic growth in the future. Major reforms have been implemented throughout post-Suharto governments, from fiscal to monetary policies, to maintain domestic growth as well as foreign investment. Indonesia has been seeking to recover from the Asian financial crisis of 1997 to become a high-income economy by 2045.[9]

Regional Strategic Autonomy

ASEAN unity and centrality are a core objective. To achieve its strategic objectives of maintaining territorial integrity and economic development, Indonesia is fully aware of the importance of regional peace and stability. The fact that Indonesia is one of the founding members of ASEAN speaks to the central position of this multilateral organization for Jakarta. ASEAN was originally designed to be a functional entity that could provide a level playing field for the member states to work together in achieving regional stability and common prosperity, regardless of their different domestic political systems, cultures, and economic achievements. In spite of its ups and downs, ASEAN has succeeded in settling disputes among the member states in accordance with the organization's principles and international laws. Indonesia, in particular, "has tried to ensure unity within ASEAN, including by mediating in bilateral conflicts between fellow ASEAN members," as was the case between Cambodia and Thailand in 2013.[10] Furthermore, facing growing strategic rivalry between the United States and China, it is in the best interests of ASEAN and Indonesia to uphold the organization's strategic autonomy and inclusive character.[11] In this regard, the core principle of Indonesia's vision of regional order will remain "ensuring ASEAN unity in order to safeguard Southeast Asia's strategic autonomy, founded on the member states' national and collective resilience."[12]

EXTERNAL FACTORS

This section examines Indonesia's threat perceptions and external relations, focusing on its ties with the United States, China, Australia, Malaysia, Singapore, and ASEAN, to illustrate the country's independent and active foreign policy in practice.

Third-Party Actors

The United States is a key external factor. After a short period of closer relations between Indonesia and China in the final years of the Sukarno era (early to mid-1960s), President Suharto took a drastic turn in Jakarta's foreign policy toward the Western world. As part of its no-holds-barred policy in eliminating communist influences domestically and a concerted attempt to attract foreign investment to support national development, Jakarta consciously sided with Washington and as a result obtained substantial amounts of economic aid, grants, and military supplies from the Western bloc. The United States also helped Indonesia, both politically and militarily, in the annexation of the former Portuguese colony of East Timor in 1975.

Nevertheless Washington started to recalibrate its relationship with Indonesia's Suharto in the aftermath of the so-called Santa Cruz massacre of early 1991. It was reported that the Indonesian military killed 271 civilians and hundreds more disappeared during a peaceful memorial ceremony in Dili city, the capital of East Timor province.[13] The United States imposed an arms embargo that crippled the capabilities of the Indonesian military, weakening force readiness, maintenance, and personnel training and education.

Following the resignation of Suharto in 1998, the United States and Indonesia entered a new phase in their bilateral relations. Shortly after the 9/11 terrorist attacks, the United States launched an all-out war against global terrorism, as exemplified by the Taliban and Osama bin Laden's Al-Qaeda, and waged two simultaneous wars in Afghanistan (Operation Enduring Freedom, initiated in 2001) and Iraq (Operation Iraqi Freedom, commenced in 2003). Washington expected Indonesia, home to the largest Muslim population in the world, to participate in this retaliation campaign. Nevertheless, Jakarta's initial response was lukewarm. Successive post-Suharto presidents—namely Abdurrahman Wahid (1999–2001), Megawati Sukarnoputri (2002–04), and Susilo Bambang Yudhoyono (2004–14)—had no interest in antagonizing the domestic Muslim population, which generally believed that the United States's war against terrorism was a veiled attempt to subjugate the Islamic world.[14] For most of the George W. Bush Jr. period in office, the United States seemed to be occupied with the Middle East, neglecting the gradually increasing yet profound preoccupation with China in the Asia Pacific region. China's charm offensive in the region ignited new enthusiasm in Indonesia and other Southeast Asian countries to accelerate their economic partnership with Beijing.[15]

Indonesia's interests, however, remain constant in upholding an independent and active foreign policy. Jakarta welcomed both the rise of China and the United States' rebalancing of its policy toward Asia (often dubbed the US pivot). In an attempt to better manage its great power relations, Indonesia signed the comprehensive partnership agreement with the United States in 2010. The agreement aims "to foster consistent high level engagement on democracy and civil society, education, security, resilience and mitigation, maritime, energy, and trade issues."[16] Jakarta and Washington then agreed to upgrade their bilateral relations to a strategic partnership in 2015, with both countries committing to enhance bilateral cooperation on the following areas: maritime, defense, economic growth and development, energy, global and regional affairs, and people-to-people contacts.[17] Indonesia and the United Stated further elevated the relations to a comprehensive strategic partnership in 2023. President Joko Widodo and President Joe Biden committed "to further expand cooperation on all issues of common concern, including good governance; pluralism; and respect for human rights, the rule of law, sovereignty, sustainable development, and territorial integrity."[18] To conclude, Indonesia is fully aware that the strategic rivalry between the United States and China could plunge Southeast Asia into instability and possibly disintegration. Jakarta will do its best to prevent this outcome.

China is another central factor. Throughout six decades of often complex relations, Indonesia and China have experienced numerous ups and downs. In the 1960s, Indonesia maintained close communication and solidarity with China under Sukarno's leadership.[19] The relationship deteriorated rapidly when Suharto, a former commander of the Indonesian army's largest forces, *Komando Cadangan Strategis* or Kostrad, took power and then ruled the archipelago for more than three decades. A staunched anticommunist, Suharto eliminated the Indonesian Communist Party (*Partai Komunis Indonesia* or PKI) and moved Jakarta away from China's sphere of communist influence in the wake of his coup in 1965. Diplomatic relations between Indonesia and China only started to recover and eventually normalized in 1990.[20]

After the resignation of Suharto in 1998, following student protests in Jakarta and other major cities, bilateral relations between Indonesia and China entered a new episode of cooperation. President Abdurrahman Wahid—a former leader of the largest Islamic organization in Indonesia, *Nahdlatul Ulama* (NU)—even suggested the establishment of an Asia Coalition, comprising Indonesia, China, and India (with the possibility of also including Singapore and Japan).[21] This notion reflected a more pragmatic and flexible post-authoritarian Indonesian foreign policy but to some extent also Indonesia's aspiration to forge better relations with fellow Asian countries. Similar positive gestures have been announced by Indonesian political leaders during the democratic era. In the course of the administration of President Susilo Bambang Yudhoyono, Indonesia signed a strategic partnership agreement with China in 2005, followed by the upgrading in bilateral cooperation on defense affairs in 2007. In 2013, Yudhoyono and President Xi Jinping agreed to elevate Indonesia-China relations to a comprehensive strategic partnership and to accelerate cooperation in trade and economic development, research and technology, and the defense industry.[22] China's economic power and consistent bilateral engagement have moderated Jakarta's previously hostile perceptions toward Beijing.[23]

China is now Indonesia's biggest trading partner. Jakarta's thirst for investment has made it seeks closer relations with Beijing. In return China has been willing to invest heavily in Indonesia, given the latter's expanding market and lucrative natural resources ready for exploitation. Therefore, China will continue to be a consequential external actor for Indonesia. The question is indeed how Indonesia and China will resolve the frequent incidents taking place in the South China Sea/North Natuna Sea. China's assertive policy in the so-called nine dashed lines that infringe Indonesia's territorial waters have escalated security as well as diplomatic tensions between Jakarta and Beijing and may weaken the various agreements that both countries have signed so far.[24]

Australia is another important factor. Indonesia-Australia relations have usually been depicted in negative terms, for instance "strange neighbors"[25] or "strangers next door."[26] The two countries differ in many respects, including culture, political structures, economic development, demographics, and military forces. In recent years bilateral relations between Jakarta and Canberra have also been marred by diplomatic tensions, suspicion, and distrust. "During the post-Suharto era, Indonesia has withdrawn its ambassador twice and Australia once, in disputes over sovereignty, espionage, and transnational crime."[27] At the same time, Indonesia and Australia have intensified their partnership in trade, investment, and security as well. In

2006 Indonesia and Australia agreed to conclude the Lombok Treaty that addressed both countries' interests in the strengthening of security cooperation, notably on maritime security, counterterrorism, humanitarian assistance and disaster relief, and defense cooperation. Recognizing each other's pivotal roles on the stability of the Asia-Pacific (or Indo-Pacific), Jakarta and Canberra agreed to upgrade their level of relations to a comprehensive strategic partnership in 2018. This "positioned Australia on the same level as China and the United States, the two countries Indonesia has had a comprehensive strategic partnership with since 2013 and 2015, respectively."[28] Another significant achievement is the Indonesia-Australia Comprehensive Economic Partnership (IA-CEPA), which was signed in 2019 and entered into force in 2020. Indonesia and Australia are also among the members of the informal middle-power group MIKTA, joining Mexico, South Korea, and Turkey.[29]

Australia's recent closer alignment with the United States and the United Kingdom, as demonstrated by the AUKUS trilateral security pact—signed in 2021—has made its bilateral relations with Indonesia more tense. By openly manifesting its willingness to acquire nuclear-powered submarines, Canberra has undermined the ASEAN Zone of Peace, Freedom and Neutrality (ZOPFAN), Treaty of Amity and Cooperation (TAC), and Southeast Asia Nuclear Weapon-Free Zone (SEANWFZ) and therefore is deemed to threaten regional security. Thus, the Indonesian Ministry of Foreign Affairs stated that:[30]

1. "Indonesia takes note cautiously of the Australian Government's decision to acquire nuclear-powered submarines;
2. Indonesia is deeply concerned over the continuing arms race and power projection in the region;
3. Indonesia stresses the importance of Australia's commitment to continue meeting all of its nuclear non-proliferation obligations;
4. Indonesia calls on Australia to maintain its commitment towards regional peace, stability and security in accordance with the Treaty of Amity and Cooperation;
5. Indonesia encourages Australia and other parties concerned to advance dialogue in settling any differences peacefully. In this regard, Indonesia underscores the respect for international law, including UNCLOS 1982, in maintaining peace and security in the region."

ASEAN is yet another important factor in Indonesia's grand strategy. Since its birth in 1967, ASEAN has been the cornerstone (*sokoguru*) of

Indonesia's foreign policy. Indonesia is one of ASEAN's founding members together with Malaysia, the Philippines, Singapore, and Thailand. Established during the tumultuous times of the Cold War between the United States and Soviet Union, ASEAN was the direct result of Indonesia's changing domestic priorities and external outlook.[31] Indonesia's Suharto left behind the previous anti-Western policy followed by Sukarno. Instead Jakarta strived for a multilateral platform where the influence of confronting great powers could be contained. Both during the past Cold War era and during the current era of strategic rivalry between the United States and China, it has been the interest of Jakarta to maintain the unity and neutrality of ASEAN.[32]

A recent ASEAN achievement, with strong support from Jakarta, has been the acceptance of the ASEAN Outlook on Indo-Pacific (AOIP) in 2019. AOIP was particularly formulated, first, to respond to the continuing strategic rivalry between the United States and China that may potentially jeopardize the peace and stability that the Southeast Asian region has enjoyed for decades and, second, to provide an alternative conception—and more suitable arrangement for ASEAN—on the security construct of the "Indo-Pacific" that in the past had been presented by, for instance, Japan, the United States, and Australia.[33] Indonesia is concerned that rivalry between the United States and China could create polarization within ASEAN, and therefore the future of ASEAN autonomy would be at risk.[34] In this case the objective of Indonesia is to preserve ASEAN's cohesiveness and to deter potential external influences or interventions.[35]

Malaysia and Singapore are important factors too. Indonesia's *Konfrontasi* (or Confrontation), circa 1963–66, during the Sukarno period was particularly traumatic for Malaysia and Singapore. Antagonism to the formation of the Federation of Malaysia, which included the Singaporean territory, as demonstrated by Jakarta's diplomatic condemnation as well as the actual threat of use of force, presented an existential threat to the two former British colonies. Ultimately the rise of Suharto in Indonesia put an end to this tense relationship, and Jakarta sought better relations with Kuala Lumpur and Singapore.[36] Using bilateral channels and ASEAN, Indonesia, Malaysia, and Singapore are said to have formed "the security core" of Southeast Asia.[37] In this regard, it is important to note that Malaysia and Singapore are also founding members of ASEAN. During the Cold War, their respective leaders—Suharto of Indonesia, Mahathir Mohamad of Malaysia, and Lee Kuan Yew of Singapore—developed strong personal bonds that in effect made Southeast Asia a politically stable and economically vibrant region. Despite frequent disagreements, particularly related to border disputes (Indonesia-Malaysia), the control of airspace (Indonesia-Singapore), and trans-border pollution generated from forest fires in Indonesia in recent years, their common security interests and shared goals of economic development will remain the dominant features of their relationships.[38]

Threats and Opportunities

As the largest archipelagic country in the world, Indonesia is fully aware of its strategic vulnerabilities. Located at the crossroads between the Indian and Pacific oceans, Indonesia must secure its vast land and water territories from a myriad of nontraditional security threats, such as sea piracy, particularly in the Malacca Strait and Sea of Sulu; flows of illegal drugs and smuggled arms; human trafficking; and illegal, unregulated, and unreported fishing. Though the scale and intensity of terrorist attacks have slowed down in recent years—the most devastating suicide bombing took place in Bali province in October 2002, killing hundreds of mostly foreign tourists—the government continues to confront underground radical Islamist networks with relations with international terrorist organizations. Following the rapid expansion of the cyber world, including the use of social media, e-commerce, and various online activities, Indonesia has become the subject of cyber attacks, cybercrimes, hacking, and data thefts. Some incidents include the defacing of governmental agencies' websites, such as the General Elections Commission (*Komisi Pemilihan Umum* or KPU) and National Intelligence Agency (*Badan Intelijen Negara* or BIN). Not to mention there have been personal data breaches of Indonesian users of digital commerce platforms, which have made the population at large question the state of cybersecurity governance in Indonesia. The COVID-19 pandemic has also increased Indonesia's concerns about health security. Marshal Hadi Tjahjanto, the *Tentara Nasional Indonesia* (TNI) commander-in-chief (2017–21), stated that the Indonesian military would strengthen both its organizational and technical capabilities in anticipating the spread of similar infectious viruses or diseases, as well as the possibility of biological and chemical warfare in the future.

Given the wealth of Indonesia's natural resources and strategic location within global trade routes, Jakarta also plans against the possibility of armed conflict with foreign hostile powers. Based on Indonesia's latest defense white paper published in 2015, this type of traditional threat still falls under the category of "not-yet-real threat" (see Table 6.1).[39] The combination of past experiences of revolutionary struggle against colonial powers and recent instances of foreign meddling in the Middle East and other regions have compelled Indonesia to pay attention to potential conventional warfare.

Table 6.1. Threats to Indonesia's National Security

Threats	
Real	**Not-Yet Real**
• Terrorism and radicalism • Separatism and regional rebellion • Natural disasters • National territorial violation • Piracy and natural resources theft • Virus/disease outbreak • Cyber-attack and espionage • Drugs smuggling	• Conventional warfare • Other forms of threats

Source: The Ministry of Defense of the Republic of Indonesia (2015)

Outside of formal settings, defense policymakers in Jakarta also often talk about ideological or cultural infiltration, targeted at Indonesia's sacrosanct national ideology of *Pancasila,* which consists of five pillars: belief in the one and only God, just and civilized humanity, national unity, deliberative democracy, and social justice. There is a belief that as modern warfare is being transformed into more subtle, indirect attacks, Indonesia needs to strongly shield its national values and cultures from allegedly foreign ideas, from "liberal democracy" to "LGBTQ," that, according to Jakarta's decision-makers, foreign actors deliberately promote with the support of domestic collaborators and that could polarize Indonesia's multicultural society and disintegrate national cohesion.[40] This sentiment finds its contemporary manifestation in the notion of "proxy war," popularly coined by several army generals, notably General Gatot Nurmantyo, a former Army chief of staff (2014–15), then TNI commander-in-chief (2015–17), and General Ryamizard Ryacudu, former Army chief of staff (2002–05) and Indonesia's defense minister during the first presidency of Joko Widodo (2014–19). Focusing on the potential effects of great power competition in the past and present, Indonesia's military elites have asserted that modern colonialism requires neither territorial occupation nor colony building but instead can be achieved via ideological, cultural, and economic control.[41] In this sense, the West's concern with the human rights situation in West Papua is perceived to fall under this category.

INTERNAL FACTORS

This section discusses domestic factors informing Indonesia's grand strategy, including its underlying principles, decision-making processes, and available resources for implementation.

National Values

Located between the Pacific and Indian oceans, Indonesia occupies 2,027,087 square kilometers of land area and 3,166,163 square kilometers of territorial waters; it has approximately 13,669 islands, and about 1,000 of them are inhabited.[42] Given this geographical condition, Indonesia stands as an archipelagic state (*negara kepulauan*). Since the early period of nation-state building from the 1940s onward, the discussion about Indonesia's strategic position within the world system has been focused on the central tenet of territorial integrity. In 1966 this idea culminated in the form of the "archipelagic outlook" (*wawasan nusantara*) doctrine that underpins Indonesia's geopolitical thinking.[43]

Wawasan nusantara embodies a perspective on national integration that aims to strengthen the political cohesion, economic sovereignty, social-cultural harmony, and security of the Indonesian polity. The doctrine, nevertheless, goes beyond the realm of ideas. During Suharto's New Order (1966–98), wawasan nusantara was adopted in practice as one of the main pillars in upholding *dwifungsi* (dual function), with active military personnel allowed be in charge of various civilian positions, such as provincial governors, heads of villages, and so on. The guidebook of dwifungsi implementation, published in 1982 by the Department of Defense and Security Affairs, further stipulated another important pillar: *ketahanan nasional* (national resilience).[44] Wawasan nusantara remains in place in the current post-authoritarian political setting, but dwifungsi has been effectively abandoned. Active TNI personnel are no longer allowed to receive appointments in nondefense sectors.

National resilience is essentially a self-defense mechanism relying on Indonesia's internal resources. It is a national doctrine formulated to ensure that all aspects of national development (*pembangunan nasional*) are well-protected and implemented smoothly, specifically political, economic, social-cultural, and security aspects. Consequently, national resilience requires domestic political stability and independent defense capabilities to deter any potential threats. The notion of national resilience reasserts Indonesia's aspiration for autonomy and no-strings-attached relations with its foreign counterparts.[45]

When it comes to its strategy to conduct international relations, Indonesia upholds an independent and active foreign policy (*bebas-aktif*). The doctrine emphasizes nonalignment and the nexus of national-regional resilience.[46] It was initially formulated by Vice President

Mohammad Hatta and then approved by the provisional parliament in September 1948. "Independent and active" means that Indonesia should pursue its own course at the international level without taking sides with any particular superpower.[47] This position helped Indonesia to gain the trust other postcolonial countries during the Cold War period. Thus Indonesia hosted the Bandung Conference in April 1955, which led to the establishment of the nonaligned movement in 1961, comprising Asian and African states.[48]

Institutional Process

In contrast with the authoritarian government of Suharto, today's democratic Indonesia provides an open and inclusive avenue for various stakeholders to participate in the decision-making process of strategic policies.[49] Political reform and electoral system changes undertaken in the early years of democratization, throughout 1999–2002, have placed the president and the legislature in a relatively equal position. The president holds wide-range authority to run the government, but nonetheless is now subject to oversight by the national legislature body and civil society in general. As reflected in Indonesia's extensive promotion of democratic values and human rights abroad, the post-authoritarian government has seriously taken into account the views and inputs of parliamentarians, nongovernmental organization representatives, and the domestic epistemic community in projecting Indonesia's democratic "independent and active foreign policy."[50] For instance, the legislature and the epistemic community have compelled the government to ensure the enforcement of the democracy and human rights principles laid out in the ASEAN Charter.[51] This open dialogue process, nevertheless, sometimes presents challenges. This is evident, for instance, in the changing—and inconsistent—positions of Indonesia on the resolution of the Iranian nuclear issue in the United Nations Security Council throughout 2007 and 2008, when the domestic legislature and civil society apparently were able to alter the government's position.[52] Also, the refusal of the Indonesian parliament, based on a strong public rejection, to ratify the Defense Cooperation Agreement (DCA) agreed by the Indonesian and Singaporean governments in 2007 is another example.[53] In January 2022 the Joko Widodo administration eventually took a bold move by signing the DCA with the Singaporean government without prior consultation with the legislature and no substantial revisions. Some members of the parliament expressed their disappointment.[54]

Material Resources

Indonesia's national armed forces (TNI) have approximately 404,500 active personnel, distributed in three different services: 300,400 in the army, 74,000 in the navy including marines and aviation, and 30,100 in the air force.[55] This makes TNI the biggest military force in Southeast Asia. Several recent acquisitions have substantially enhanced the TNI's inventory, including, inter alia, German-built Leopard main battle tanks (42 units of 2A4 type; 61 units of 2RI); Russian-built jet fighters comprised of Su-27SK Flanker, Su-27SKM Flanker, Su-30MK Flanker, and Su-30MK2 Flanker units; and submarines (one Cakra Type-209/1300 and three Nagapasa Type-209/1400).[56] In an effort to strengthen sea-denial capabilities, the government has procured several advanced technologies for the navy, such as Type 209/1400 submarines.[57]

According to the Organisation for Economic Co-operation and Development, Indonesia's GDP per capita increased from 19 per cent of the global average in 2001 to 29 per cent in 2019, and its share to ASEAN's GDP expanded from 27 per cent to 35 per cent. Indonesia's annual growth rate was the third highest among the G20.[58] Nevertheless, the COVID-19 pandemic then interrupted this steady and sustained growth, bringing down the country's annual growth rate from 5 percent in 2019 to minus 2.1 percent a year later in 2020.[59] Economic growth is expected to bounce back in the near future. Indonesia's demographic dividend, which means a high proportion of productive-working-age population, presents a big window of opportunity to move forward the national economy, not to mention the rise of middle class and strong macroeconomic management.[60]

In 2021 for the first time Indonesia was ranked among the group of middle powers, according to Lowy Institute's Asia Power Index.[61] Indonesia is in the ninth position, becoming one of the three Southeast Asian countries in the top ten, along with Singapore in eighth place and Thailand in tenth. Indonesia has ninety-six embassies around the world, making it the leading country in Southeast Asia in terms of its diplomatic network.[62] Based on the index's 2023 edition, Indonesia's position is basically the same.[63]

OPERATIONALIZATION OF GRAND STRATEGY

Indonesia's grand strategy is operationalized through diplomacy, the total defense doctrine (*sishankamrata*), active and layered defense, international peacekeeping operations, and defense diplomacy.

Diplomacy

Indonesia's grand strategy features a dual approach based on the "independent and active" (*bebas-aktif*) principles, as well intensive multilateralism for the purpose of protecting its strategic autonomy amid regional uncertainties. In theory Jakarta has also maintained a "middle way" approach to deal with the competing great powers of the United States and China. Jakarta has fostered constructive relations with these two great powers without alienating either of them. Standing as the most influential member of ASEAN, Indonesia has also successfully mitigated polarization within the association as well. Indonesia and other ASEAN member states can decide on their shared goals without foreign intervention.[64] As shown with some major regional initiatives such as the establishment of the East Asia Summit in 2005, the launch of the ASEAN Defense Ministers' Meeting (ADMM) and ADMM-Plus in 2006 and in 2010, respectively, and more recently in 2019 the promulgation of ASEAN Outlook on the Indo-Pacific, among others, Jakarta's game plan is to position ASEAN as not only the primary driver but also the key convener of existing as well as future regional initiatives.[65]

Indonesia aspires to expand its sphere of influence beyond Southeast Asia. Given its location at the center of the Indian and Pacific oceans, Jakarta's emerging global profile has brought with it the ambition to play a more salient role in the development of the future global order. As a regional power with global interests, Indonesia has continued to participate actively in various multilateral initiatives, most notably in the G20 and United Nations forums (e.g., via peacekeeping contributions). Indonesia has made its presence felt strongly in the region by pursuing an omnidirectional diplomacy, which was initially conceptualized by the Susilo Bambang Yudhoyono administration (2004–14) as "a million friends, zero enemies" foreign policy. Among others, this boosted Jakarta's South-to-South cooperation. For instance, Indonesia's growing relations with the Melanesian Spearhead Group (MSG) are a case in point. Jakarta believes that closer cooperation with Pacific countries such as Fiji, Papua New Guinea, Solomon Islands, Vanuatu, and others provides an opportunity to expand economic diplomacy. At the same time, Indonesia also needs to ensure that these Pacific countries remain committed to respecting the territorial integrity of Indonesia, which includes West Papua, in spite of the ongoing international campaign of pro-independence West Papuan groups. As a result of its policy, Indonesia succeeded in bolstering its status in the MSG from observer to associate membership in 2015.[66] President Joko Widodo's "global maritime fulcrum," which was first introduced in November 2014, reinforced the country's interests to shape the future of the Pacific and Indian oceans. In addition, Indonesia has been deepening its relations with fellow middle powers such as India, South Korea, and Turkey in recent years. Considering all of the foregoing, it is reasonable to suggest that Jakarta has paved the way to establish itself as a global powerhouse in the near future.

Defense

Indonesia's defense is arranged following a "total people's defense and security system" ("*sistem pertahanan dan keamanan rakyat semesta*" or "*sishankamrata*") that has been implemented since the genesis of the republic. Maximizing its large population, abundant natural resources, and large territory, Indonesia invests in its own peoples' intellectual, economic, and sociopolitical capital to protect the country from both domestic and foreign threats.

In strategic terms, sishankamrata requires unity between the armed forces and the general population. To cultivate such an arrangement, the army holds a pivotal role through its territorial command structure ("*komando teritorial*" or *koter*), which spans from the provincial to the rural levels. Koter has multiple functions, including to disperse the armed forces throughout the archipelago so that they can be mobilized swiftly to provide rapid response to various crisis situations, such as enemy infiltration, natural disasters, and virus outbreaks. During peace time, the army's territorial structure plays a salient role in intelligence gathering and maintaining lines of communication with local populations. Information and cooperation obtained from such seemingly trivial activities are in fact crucial to ensure that sishankamrata can become reality. The expected net effects are not only political stability and security in the different local and regional domains but also the development of a functional and decentralized "total people's defense."[67]

This approach is indeed not unique to Indonesia; other countries with relatively similar postcolonial experiences and security features apply this type of total people's defense and security as well. Nevertheless, Indonesia's defense and foreign policy stakeholders have begun to reconceptualize the strategy. Even though it remains heavily dependent on the tenets of "total warfare," former President Susilo Bambang Yudhoyono has argued that the current understanding of sishankamrata, in which the mobilization of all the nation's resources is prerequisite for its implementation, is no longer adequate. Instead, he has proposed the use of information communication technology and air power as the basis of Indonesia's modern sishankamrata.[68]

Active and Layered Defense

TNI, comprising the army, navy, and air force, stands as the core component of Indonesia's national defense (*komponen utama*). In 2019 the executive and the legislature agreed to ratify the Law on National Resources Management for Defense (*Undang-undang Pengelolaan Sumber Daya Nasional* or UU PSDN), providing an operational basis for the Ministry of Defense to establish civilian reserve components (*komponen cadangan* or *komcad*) and supporting components (*komponen pendukung* or *komduk*). In total Indonesia plans to recruit 25,000 komcad personnel.[69] This arrangement is designed to strengthen sishankamrata and to ensure the realization of national resilience (ketahanan nasional). All of these components are the building blocks of Indonesia's national forces.

In cases of armed conflict with hostile powers, Indonesia prefers to pursue a protracted war strategy (*perang berlarut*). Aside from military mobilization, the government would also rely on popular resistance in different areas across the whole country. According to the 2021 Indonesian National Defense Policy, each major island in the archipelago—Sumatra, Java, Borneo/Kalimantan, Sulawesi, Moluccas/Maluku, West Papua, Bali, and Nusa Tenggara—is designated a "defense area" (*wilayah pertahanan*) that could provide logistical and strategic resources autonomously without the need to wait for supplies from the central command in Jakarta.[70] Of particular importance is the deployment of a coastal missile defense system and a coastal surveillance system to monitor and control the situation in Indonesia's strategic straits and sea lanes.

Peacekeeping

As of July 31, 2024, Indonesia was ranked at the fifth largest troop contributor to the United Nations peacekeeping forces, with 2,741 peacekeepers (see Table 6.2).[71] Indonesia has a long history of involvement in UN peacekeeping. The first Indonesian contingent (*Kontingen Garuda* or *Konga*), was deployed in Egypt in 1957, becoming an important part of the UN's first peacekeeping forces, called United Nations Emerging Force (UNEF). Since then Indonesia's contribution has expanded to the dispatch of not only its military and police personnel but also several senior, experienced officers with proven leadership and command capacity.[72]

Indonesia restricts its participation in certain operations that fall into the category of Chapter VI of the United Nations Charter. Operations need to fulfill the following conditions: full consent of the parties involved in the UN mission, nonuse of force except in the case of self-defense, and the peacekeeping forces the Indonesian peacekeepers are part of should hold a strict neutral position.[73] In this regard, it was clear from the outset that Indonesia's peacekeeping contribution should be congruent with its independent and active foreign policy. In this sense, Indonesia also maintains respect for the host country's sovereignty and maintains a noninterference policy.

Indonesia has expressed its intention to increase the number of personnel it contributes to UN peacekeeping missions. Jakarta initially announced an ambitious plan to contribute 4,000 peacekeepers by 2019. In fact the Ministry of Foreign Affairs issued a specific regulation related to this plan in 2015, so that Indonesia had a clear roadmap and annual target to properly design and implement the policy.[74] Nevertheless, as shown in Table 6.2, Indonesia's contribution remains far below the target already set.

Defense Diplomacy

In recent years Indonesia has shown a keen interest in defense diplomacy. The activity, which "involves the peacetime cooperative use of armed forces and related infrastructure (primarily defense ministries) as a tool of foreign and security policy,"[75] has become a pivotal instrument for the country to project its expanding international activism. Defense diplomacy activity also provides Indonesia a valuable opportunity to enhance the technical capabilities and organizational network of its armed forces. Between 2003 and 2008 Indonesia undertook eighty-eight bilateral defense diplomacy interactions.[76] Throughout 2009 and 2013 Indonesia was involved in approximately 385 bilateral defense activities, not to mention a series of multilateral meetings that Indonesian military officials participated in under the umbrella of the ASEAN Regional Forum (ARF, established in 1994), ADMM, and ADMM-Plus, which consists of the ten ASEAN member states plus eight dialogue partners, namely Australia, China, India, Japan, New Zealand, Republic of Korea, Russia, and the United States.[77]

In 2018 the Ministry of Defense promulgated a regulation focusing specifically on defense diplomacy activities. Defined as "a part of state

Table 6.2. Indonesia's Contribution to the United Nations Peacekeeping Missions (report date July 31, 2024)

Mission	Personnel Types	Male	Female	Total
MINURSO	Experts on mission	2	1	3
	Individual police	0	1	1
	Total	**2**	**2**	**4**
MINUSCA	Experts on mission	4	1	5
	Formed police units	116	24	140
	Individual police	17	10	27
	Staff officers	9	1	10
	Troops	237	3	240
	Total	**383**	**39**	**422**
MONUSCO	Experts on mission	4	1	5
	Individual police	10	4	14
	Staff officers	3	4	7
	Troops	986	39	1025
	Total	**1003**	**48**	**1051**
UNFICYP	Individual police	2	0	2
	Total	**2**	**0**	**2**
UNIFIL	Staff officers	15	2	17
	Troops	1135	80	1215
	Total	**1150**	**82**	**1232**
UNISFA	Experts on mission	2	0	2
	Individual police	3	0	3
	Staff officers	1	1	2
	Total	**6**	**1**	**7**
UNMISS	Experts on mission	2	1	3
	Individual police	12	6	18
	Staff officers	1	0	1
	Total	**15**	**7**	**22**
UNSOM	Individual police	0	1	1
	Total	**0**	**1**	**1**
	TOTAL Indonesia	**2561**	**180**	**2741**

Source: United Nations, Department of Peace Operations[78]

diplomacy on defense realm, taking the form of international cooperation that aims to build mutual understanding, capacity building, and to participate in the making of world peace, as mandated by the policy of national government," Indonesia's defense diplomacy covers multiple activities, such as joint training, personnel exchanges, humanitarian assistance and disaster relief cooperation, and participation in United Nations peacekeeping operations.[79] Indonesia's enthusiasm for defense diplomacy reflects the archipelago's enduring grand strategy to manage regional instability in a peaceful way and to build trust among the armed forces in Southeast Asia and beyond.

CONCLUSION

Maintaining sovereignty and strategic autonomy while maintaining economic growth is the fundamental rationale of Indonesia's grand strategy. This requires Indonesia to find the balance between domestic stability and diplomatic activism. Hence Jakarta seeks to sustain territorial integrity and consolidate national resources for defense purposes while taking a pragmatic approach in its foreign policy to ensure regional and global stability via bilateral and multilateral channels.

Based on the foregoing discussion, we see that Indonesia's grand strategy is largely focusing on the strengthening of ketahanan nasional (national resilience). Jakarta's strategic concerns are territorial integrity, economic development, and the stability and strategic autonomy of ASEAN. To achieve these ends, Indonesia has been relying on the combination of its diplomacy and military power. A total defense doctrine (sishankamrata) as well as an active and layered defense are primarily assigned to mitigate territorial disintegration and to deter potential foreign infiltration. Indonesia's recent defense acquisitions and its current weapons arsenal suggest that military modernization is on its way. The geopolitical thinking based on wawasan nusantara (archipelagic outlook) also defines Indonesia's approach to handling contemporary nontraditional threats; it mandates the support and participation of the general population in grand strategy undertakings. Furthermore, Indonesia has used multiple channels, from bilateral to multilateral relations, to ease the strategic rivalry between the United States and China that has destabilized regional security for years. At the same time Indonesia also has consistently supported ASEAN to always be at the center and forefront of every possible regional initiative. Indonesia has thus made sustained efforts to maintain ASEAN unity and centrality. Jakarta cannot afford to let ASEAN disintegration and polarization happen. National resilience and regional resilience are essentially two sides of the same coin.

Following the ascendancy of Prabowo Subianto in 2024 as the eighth president of the Republic of Indonesia, we can expect that Indonesia will refer to the same defense and foreign policy playbook. Indonesia's grand strategy continues to focus on maintaining domestic and regional stability. Also, national territorial integrity and ASEAN unity and centrality remain key priorities.

The twist is, nonetheless, that to achieve these ends Prabowo is going to be more assertive and hyperbolic both in rhetoric and in practice rather than his predecessor, Joko Widodo. Several times, even going back to Prabowo's presidential race in 2014 and 2019—which he lost to Widodo—Prabowo has expressed his obsession to elevate the Indonesian position in the world stage. In the 2014 campaign, for instance, he once boasted that Indonesia should have become an "Asian tiger," a clear reference to the projection of Indonesia as a major geopolitical power. Now he gains momentum to make it happen. Unlike Widodo, it is also reasonable to anticipate that Prabowo will be more hands-on and take the lead on foreign affairs. As minister of defense, he has displayed keen interests and tangible achievements on defense diplomacy and cooperation. Under his leadership, Indonesia's Ministry of Defense has sealed several strategic agreements on weapons acquisition and defense industry partnership with multiple developed countries, such as the United States, France, Australia, Japan, South Korea, and China. We will likely see similar, if not intensified, proactive and omnidirectional Indonesian diplomacy at bilateral and multilateral levels, notably within ASEAN and the G20 frameworks.

NOTES

1. Thierry Balzacq, Peter Dombrowski, and Simon Reich, "Introduction: Comparing Grand Strategies in the Modern World," in Thierry Balzacq, Peter Dombrowski, and Simon Reich (eds.), *Comparative Grand Strategy: A Framework and Cases* (Oxford University Press, 2019), 16.
2. Chiara Formichi, *Islam and the Making of the Nation: Kartosuwiryo and Political Islam in 20th Century Indonesia* (KITLV Press, 2012).
3. Malcolm Gault-Williams, "Organisasi Papua Merdeka: The Free Papua Movement Lives," *Bulletin of Concerned Asian Scholars* 19, no. 4 (1987), 32–43.
4. Evan A. Laksmana, "The Enduring Strategic Trinity: Explaining Indonesia's Geopolitical Architecture," *Journal of the Indian Ocean Region* 7, no. 1 (2011), 103.
5. The World Bank, *Indonesia: Overview*, 2024, https://www.worldbank.org/en/country/indonesia/overview
6. OECD, *Indonesia Economic Snapshot*, 2022, https://www.oecd.org/economy/indonesia-economic-snapshot/
7. G20 Presidency of Indonesia, *Recover Together, Recover Stronger: Priority Issues*, 2022, https://g20.org/g20-presidency-of-indonesia/
8. Asian Development Bank, *Economic Indicators for Indonesia*, 2024, https://www.adb.org/countries/indonesia/economy

9. Asian Development Bank, *Asian Development Bank Member Fact Sheet: Indonesia*, 2023, https://www.adb.org/sites/default/files/publication/27769/ino-2023.pdf; Anwar Nasution, "Introduction," in Anwar Nasution (ed.), *Macroeconomic Policies in Indonesia: Indonesian Economy since the Asian Financial Crisis of 1997* (Routledge, 2015), 1:

> Indonesia was one of the main victims of the Asian Financial Crisis in 1997. The economy that had respectable growth at an average of 7 per cent per annum before the crisis between 1990 and 1996 sharply shrank to minus 13.1 per cent in 1998. During the same period, the inflation rate rose from 6 per cent to 60 per cent while the interest rate rose from 14 per cent to 63 per cent. The external value of the Rupiah devalued from Rp2,300 per US dollar before the crisis to Rp10,261 in 2001.

10. Dewi Fortuna Anwar, "Indonesia: Building Norms and Consensus on the World Stage," *Global Asia* 8, no. 4 (2013), 12.
11. Dewi Fortuna Anwar, *ASEAN Ensures Balance of Power in Asia*, 2018, https://www.asiaglobalonline.hku.hk/asean-southeast-asia-balance-power
12. Dewi Fortuna Anwar, "Indonesia's Vision of Regional Order in East Asia amid U.S.-China Rivalry: Continuity and Change," *Asia Policy* 13, no. 2 (2018), 62.
13. The Timor-Leste Commission for Reception, Truth and Reconciliation (CAVR), *Chega! The Final Report of the Timor-Leste Commission for Reception, Truth and Reconciliation (CAVR)*, (Gramedia, 2013), 256–68.
14. Muhamad Haripin, *Civil-Military Relations in Indonesia: The Politics of Military Operations Other War* (Routledge, 2020), 85.
15. Dewi Fortuna Anwar, "An Indonesian Perspective on the U.S. Rebalancing Effort toward Asia," *NBR Commentary*, February 26, 2013, 3.
16. US Department of State, Bureau of East Asian and Pacific Affairs, *U.S. Relations with Indonesia*, 2020, https://www.state.gov/u-s-relations-with-indonesia/>
17. The White House, Office of the Press Secretary, *Joint Statement by the United States of America and the Republic of Indonesia*, 2015, https://obamawhitehouse.archives.gov/the-press-office/2015/10/26/joint-statement-united-states-america-and-republic-indonesia
18. The White House, *Joint Statement from the Leaders of the United States and the Republic of Indonesia: Elevating Relations to A Comprehensive Strategic Partnership*, 2023, https://www.whitehouse.gov/briefing-room/statements-releases/2023/11/13/joint-statement-from-the-leaders-of-the-united-states-and-the-republic-of-indonesia-elevating-relations-to-a-comprehensive-strategic-partnership/
19. However, there is also an instance of bilateral tensions between the two countries. In 1959 President Sukarno annulled the trading licenses of Chinese merchants in Indonesia's rural areas. Moreover, the Indonesian army ordered the Chinese community to move out to major towns in West Java province. Responding to such a provocative ploy, Beijing dispatched ships to Indonesia to evacuate hundreds of thousands of local Chinese. See Michael Williams, "China and Indonesia Make Up: Reflections on a Troubled Relationship," *Indonesia*, Special Issue (1991), 148.
20. Rizal Sukma, *Indonesia and China: The Politics of a Troubled Relationship* (Routledge, 1999).
21. Rizal Sukma, "Indonesia's Perceptions of China: The Domestic Bases of Persistent Ambiguity," in Herbert Yee and Ian Storey (eds.), *The China Threat: Perceptions, Myths and Reality* (RoutledgeCurzon, 2002), 183–4.

22. Dewi Fortuna Anwar, "Indonesia-China Relations: Coming Full Circle?" in Daljit Singh and Malcolm Cook (eds.), *Southeast Asian Affairs 2019* (ISEAS, 2019), 153–4.
23. Muhamad Haripin, "Politik Persepsi Ancaman Kebangkitan Cina terhadap Keamanan Indonesia" ("The Politics of Indonesia's Threat Perception on the Rise of China and Its Impact on National Security Policy"), in Nur Rachmat Yuliantoro and Hikmatul Akbar (eds.), *Menghadapi Kebangkitan Cina* (*Facing the Rise of China*) (Graha Ilmu, 2018), 211–238.
24. Nanto Sriyanto, "Indonesia-China Relations: A Political-Security Perspective," in Lidya Christin Sinaga (ed.), *Six Decades of Indonesia-China Relations: An Indonesia Perspective* (Springer, 2018), 73–74.
25. See Desmond Ball and Helen Wilson (eds.), *Strange Neighbours: The Australia-Indonesia Relationship* (Allen & Unwin, 1991).
26. See Tim Lindsey and Dave McRae (eds.), *Strangers Next Door? Indonesia and Australia in the Asian Century* (Hart Publishing, 2020).
27. Jemma Purdey, Antje Missbach, and Dave McRae, *Indonesia: State and Society in Transition* (Lynne Rienner Publishers, 2020), 218–19.
28. Evan A. Laksmana, *Reinforcing Indonesia-Australia Defence Relations: The Case for Maritime Recalibration* (Lowy Institute, 2018), 3.
29. Purdey, Missbach, and McRae, *Indonesia*, 221.
30. The Ministry of Foreign Affairs of the Republic of Indonesia, *Statement on Australia's Nuclear-Powered Submarines Program*, 2021, https://kemlu.go.id/portal/en/read/2937/siaran_pers/statement-on-australias-nuclear-powered-submarines-program
31. Dewi Fortuna Anwar, "ASEAN as *Sokoguru* (Cornerstone) of Indonesia's Foreign Policy: Review of Indonesia's Leadership," in Policy Analysis and Development Agency of the Ministry of Foreign Affairs of the Republic of Indonesia in collaboration with the Centre of Indo-Pacific Studies, Universitas Negeri Padang (State University of Padang), *Proceedings of the International Seminar "Indo-Pacific Connectivity Outlook,"* March 11, 2019, xx.
32. See Seng Tan, "Indonesia among the Powers: Will ASEAN Still Matter to Indonesia?" in Christopher B. Roberts, Ahmad D. Habir, and Leonard C. Sebastian (eds.), *Indonesia's Ascent: Power, Leadership, and the Regional Order* (Palgrave Macmillan, 2015), 295.
33. Dewi Fortuna Anwar, "Indonesia and the ASEAN Outlook on the Indo-Pacific," *International Affairs* 96, no. 1 (2020), 111–29.
34. Dewi Fortuna Anwar, "Regional Security Outlook: More Continuity than Change in Indonesia's Security Posture," in Ron Huisken (ed.), *Regional Security Outlook 2020* (CSCAP, 2020), 40.
35. Anwar, "Regional Security Outlook," 37.
36. Natasha Hamilton-Hart, 'Indonesia and Singapore: Structure, Politics and Interests', *Contemporary Southeast Asia* 31:2 (2009), 250; Joseph Chinyong Liow, *The Politics of Indonesia-Malaysia Relations: One Kin, Two Nations* (Abingdon, Oxon: RoutledgeCurzon, 2005), 109–112.
37. Donald Emmerson, "Indonesia, Malaysia, Singapore: A Regional Security Core?" in Richard Ellings and Sheldon Simon (eds.), *Southeast Asian Security in the New Millennium* (M.E. Sharpe, 1996) as quoted in Liow, *The Politics of Indonesia-Malaysia Relations*, 1.
38. Purdey, Missbach, and McRae, *Indonesia*, 209–12.

39. The Ministry of Defense of the Republic of Indonesia, *Buku Putih Pertahanan Indonesia 2015* (Indonesia's Defense White Paper 2015) (The Ministry of Defense of the Republic of Indonesia, 2015), 23.
40. See Muhamad Haripin, Adhi Priamarizki, and Keoni Indrabayu Marzuki, *The Army and Ideology in Indonesia: From* Dwifungsi *to* Bela Negara (Routledge, 2021).
41. Muhamad Haripin, *Ryamizard's Proxy Wars*, 2016, https://www.newmandala.org/ryamizards-proxy-wars/
42. Robert Cribb and Audrey Kahin, *Historical Dictionary of Indonesia* (2nd Ed.), (Scarecrow Press, 2004), lxiii–lxiv.
43. Laksmana, "The Enduring Strategic Trinity," 100.
44. Jun Honna, *Military Politics and Democratization in Indonesia* (Routledge, 2003), 61.
45. Laksmana, The Enduring Strategic Trinity," 109.
46. Anwar, "Indonesia's Vision of Regional Order in East Asia," 57.
47. Dewi Fortuna Anwar, "Values in Indonesian Foreign Policy: Independent and Active Doctrine," in Krishnan Srinivasan, James Mayall, and Sanjay Pulipaka (eds.), *Values in Foreign Policy: Investigating Ideals and Interests* (Rowman & Littlefield International, 2019), 177–8.
48. Dewi Fortuna Anwar, "Indonesia and the Bandung Conference: Then and Now," in See Seng Tan and Amitav Acharya (eds.), *Bandung Revisited: The Legacy of the 1955 Asian-African Conference for International Order* (NUS Press, 2008), 180–97.
49. Dewi Fortuna Anwar, "The Impact of Domestic and Asian Regional Changes on Indonesian Foreign Policy," in Daljit Singh (ed.), *Southeast Asian Affairs 2010* (ISEAS, 2010), 128.
50. Leonard C. Sebastian and Christopher B. Roberts, "'Consensual' Regional Hegemony, Pluralist-Solidarist Visions, and Emerging Power Aspirations," in Christopher B. Roberts, Ahmad D. Habir, and Leonard C. Sebastian (eds.), *Indonesia's Ascent: Power, Leadership, and the Regional Order* (Palgrave Macmillan, 2015), 340.
51. The charter was collectively agreed by all ASEAN member states in 2007 and only ratified by the Indonesian parliament in late 2008. Jurgen Ruland, "Deepening ASEAN Cooperation through Democratization? The Indonesian Legislature and Foreign Policymaking," *International Relations of the Asia-Pacific* 9, no. 3 (2009), 383.
52. Iis Gindarsah, "Democracy and Foreign Policy-Making in Indonesia: A Case Study of the Iranian Nuclear Issue, 2007–08," *Contemporary Southeast Asia* 34, no. 3 (2012), 416–37; Anwar, "The Impact of Domestic and Asian Regional Changes on Indonesian Foreign Policy," 130–1.
53. Anwar, "The Impact of Domestic and Asian Regional Changes on Indonesian Foreign Policy," 129–30; Ruland, "Deepening ASEAN Cooperation through Democratization?" 394–5.
54. Friski Riana and Indri Maulidar, "Ultimatum DPR Tolak Ekstradisi Paketan" ("The Legislature's Ultimatum to Reject the Extradition Treaty"), *Koran Tempo*, January 27, 2022. The 2022 Indonesia-Singapore DCA is concluded concomitantly with two other agreements, namely an extradition treaty and flight information region agreement.
55. The International Institute for Strategic Studies, *The Military Balance 2024: The Annual Assessment of Global Military Capabilities and Defence Economics* (Routledge, 2024), 272.
56. International Institute for Strategic Studies, *The Military Balance 2024*, 273–5.
57. International Institute for Strategic Studies, *The Military Balance 2024*.

58. OECD, *OECD Economic Survey: Indonesia 2021* (OECD Publishing, 2021), 13, https://read.oecd-ilibrary.org/economics/oecd-economic-surveys-indonesia-2021_fd7e6249-en. This is the latest edition of OECD's Indonesian economic survey.
59. OECD, *OECD Economic Survey*, 9.
60. Anthony Reid, "Indonesia's New Prominence in the World," in Anthony Reid (ed.), *Indonesia Rising: The Repositioning of Asia's Third Giant* (ISEAS, 2012), 4–5.
61. Lowy Institute, *Asia Power Index 2021 Edition: Indonesia*, 2021 https://power.lowyinstitute.org/countries/indonesia/
62. Lowy Institute, *Asia Power Index 2021 Edition: Embassies (Global)*, 2021, https://power.lowyinstitute.org/data/diplomatic-influence/diplomatic-network/embassies-global/
63. Lowy Institute, *Asia Power Index 2023 Edition: Indonesia*, 2023, https://power.lowyinstitute.org/countries/indonesia/
64. Dewi Fortuna Anwar, "Indonesia's Wary Thinking on Foreign Policy," *Europe's World* (Summer 2013), 103.
65. Anwar, "Indonesia's Wary Thinking on Foreign Policy," 102–105.
66. David Scott, "Indonesia Grapples with the Indo-Pacific: Outreach, Strategic Discourse, and Diplomacy," *Journal of Current Southeast Asia* 38, no. 2 (2019), 197.
67. Laksmana, "The Enduring Strategic Trinity," 108; Sebastian, Leonard C., *Realpolitik Ideology: Indonesia's Use of Military Force* (ISEAS, 2006), 89.
68. Susilo Bambang Yudhoyono, "Perdamaian dan Keamanan dalam Dunia yang Berubah: Tantangan Penyusunan *Grand Strategy* bagi Indonesia" (Peace and Security in a Changing World: The Challenges to Indonesia's Grand Strategy Formulation), Inaugural Professorial Speech, Universitas Pertahanan Indonesia (Indonesian Defense University), June 12, 2014, 19–20.
69. Keputusan Menteri Pertahanan No. Kep/487/M/V/2020 Tentang Kebijakan Pertahanan Negara Tahun 2021 (Minister of Defense's Decree No. Kep/487/M/V/2020 on the 2021 National Defense Policy).
70. Keputusan Menteri Pertahanan No. Kep/487/M/V/2020.
71. United Nations Peacekeeping, *Contribution of Uniformed Personnel to UN by Country and Personnel Type*, 2024, https://peacekeeping.un.org/sites/default/files/01_contributions_to_un_peacekeeping_operations_by_country_and_post_76_july_2024.pdf
72. Major General Rais Abin was the Force Commander of UNEF II in Sinai, Egypt, from 1974 to 1978; Brigadier General Tamlicha Ali and Brigadier General Tuswadi were chief of staff and coordinator officer of United Nations Transitional Authority in Cambodia (UNTAC) in 1993; former president of the Republic of Indonesia Susilo Bambang Yudhoyono had served as chief of military observers of the United Nations Protection Force (UNPROFOR) in Bosnia-Herzegovina from 1995 to 1996; and Major General Zahari Siregar was the director of the Strategic Military Cell of the United Nations Interim Force in Lebanon (UNIFIL) and the UN Department of Peacekeeping Operation in New York, 2008–10. See L.C. Rachmadi, *Pola Pembinaan Karier Perwira dalam Penugasan Misi Pemeliharaan Perdamaian Dunia (The Pattern of Officer Career Management in Peacekeeping Assignment)* (Internal Report of Indonesian National Armed Forces, n.d.), 10, quoted in Haripin, *Civil-Military Relations in Indonesia: The Politics of Military Operations Other War*, 39.
73. Dewi Fortuna Anwar, "Indonesia's Peacekeeping Operations: History, Practice, and Future Trend," in Chiyuki Aoi and Yee-Kuang Heng (eds.), *Asia-Pacific Nations in International Peace Support and Stability Operations* (Palgrave Macmillan, 2014), 191.

74. Peraturan Menteri Luar Negeri No. 05 Tahun 2015 Tentang Peta Jalan Visi 4,000 Personel Pemelihara Perdamaian 2015–2019 (Minister of Foreign Affairs' Regulation No. 05 Year 2015 on the Roadmap Vision of 4,000 Peacekeepers in 2015–2019).
75. Andrew Cottey and Anthony Forster, *Reshaping Defence Diplomacy: New Roles for Military Cooperation and Assistance* (Routledge, 2004), 5–6.
76. Evan A. Laksmana, "Indonesia's Rising Regional and Global Profile: Does Size Really Matter?" *Contemporary Southeast Asia* 33, no. 2 (2011), 172.
77. Iis Gindarsah, "Strategic Hedging in Indonesia's Defence Diplomacy," *Defence & Security Analysis* 32, no. 4 (2016), 345.
78. United Nations Peacekeeping, *Contribution of Uniformed Personnel to UN by Country, Mission, and Personnel Type*, 2024, https://peacekeeping.un.org/sites/default/files/03_country_and_mission_76_july_2024.pdf
79. Peraturan Menteri Pertahanan No. 17 Tahun 2018 Tentang Mekanisme Pelaksanaan Diplomasi Pertahanan (Minister of Defense's Regulation No. 17 Year 2018 on the Implementation Mechanism of Defense Diplomacy).

CHAPTER 7

Malaysia

Yew Meng Lai

Malaysia's grand strategy (GS) reflects its status as a smaller state seeking to advance its myriad national interests in the context of an evolving East Asian order. Consistently informed by its geographical location and attributes and its power dynamics vis-à-vis big or great powers, these structural conditionalities have delineated the broad parameters of the country's GS and external behavior. Nonetheless, the intersubjective perceptions of the potential threats and/or opportunities rendered by the prevailing structural conditions have almost always been tempered by the Malaysian ruling elite's domestic political considerations, namely their quest to secure regime legitimacy via multiple legitimation pathways amid a socially and politically diverse domestic milieu.

This chapter describes Malaysia's GS by first identifying its strategic priorities, which include ensuring national security amid the challenging regional geopolitics, sustaining economic prosperity and well-being, and fostering national identity and nation-building in a diverse national demographic setting. This is followed by a discussion of the external factors, namely third-party actors that influence Malaysia's GS and foreign policy, insofar as the potential threats and/or opportunities and types of conflicts deriving from its interactions with these key actors are concerned. Understanding Malaysia's GS would also necessitate a scrutiny of the internal factors, including its elite-driven institutional process and patron–client political culture, juxtaposed against a domestic political landscape shaped by ethnoreligious dynamics, which have a bearing on elite legitimacy. These external -domestic sources have served to define its overarching foreign policy principles of nonalignment, neutrality, equidistance and peaceful coexistence. The final part describes Malaysia's operationalization of its GS, which encompasses the employment of astute statecraft geared toward economic pragmatism and strategic prudence as a means to hedge against the uncertainties of shifting power dynamics, relative power asymmetries, and great-power rivalries in East Asia.

STRATEGIC PRIORITIES

Malaysia's strategic priorities are informed by its national interests as a *smaller state* seeking for national survival and well-being in an anarchic international system. These interests are driven primarily by structural conditionalities defined in terms of the geopolitical dynamics of *proximity* (namely geographical location and distance) and *power* (namely *power asymmetry, power rivalries,* and *power uncertainties*) vis-à-vis other state-actors, which constitute the external environment informing its GS, as well as the broad parameters of Malaysia's foreign policy.[1]

Indeed, as a smaller state measured in terms of its modest material capabilities and relative power position vis-à-vis other more materially endowed East Asian neighbors, Malaysia has long been cognizant of the twin structural realities of its geographical and power attributes in limiting as much the scope and ambition of the country's foreign policy as the choices it has with regard to its GS. Elucidated in the following sections, Malaysia's location at the heart of maritime and continental Southeast Asia, as well as proximity vis-à-vis regional powers like China and Japan, imbues it with immense strategic value, generating both challenges and opportunities, which when prudently managed and leveraged together with other attributes of power have the propensity to not only ensure its survival and well-being as a smaller state but also allow Malaysia to potentially become a prominent actor in regional and global affairs. Similarly, Malaysia's pursuit of interests has always been constrained by geopolitical developments revolving around great-power politics and competition. Geopolitics fundamentally is about power, and like other smaller states, Malaysia is mindful of the power asymmetry or "capability gap" between itself and the competing big powers, which can both harm and help the country in multiple ways.[2] Putrajaya is, likewise, wary of big power rivalry, especially the extreme strategic competition between the US and China that is currently playing out and shaping the increasingly volatile, uncertain, complex, and ambiguous (VUCA) regional geopolitical milieu. From the Malaysian strategic perspective, the unpredictable power relations and actions-reactions between the rival powers and blocs are "structural risks" that smaller states like Malaysia have to deftly manage via their chosen GS and foreign policy approach.[3]

Nonetheless the manner in which Malaysia responds to the aforementioned structural conditions is saliently influenced by domestic imperatives, notably the country's ruling elites' domestic legitimation, which affect their threat-and-opportunities perceptions of the external -domestic milieus and ultimately delineate the specifics of Malaysia's GS and external behavior and preferences of action.[4] Malaysia's ruling elite coalitions, from the Alliance/ Barisan Nasional (BN) to the incumbent Pakatan Harapan (PH)-BN "unity" government, have largely depended on the pathways of *performance, procedural,* and *particularistic* legitimation[5] to secure their political legitimacy in a pluralistic, diverse, and multi-fault-line domestic political landscape. For a developing country like Malaysia, *performance*-based legitimacy refers predominantly to the ability of state elites in ensuring robust, sustained, and equitable economic growth. Conversely, procedural legitimacy hinges on successful institutional reforms and good governance in the context of Malaysia's maturing parliamentary democracy. Meanwhile, the expedient advocacy of identity politics affords *particularistic* legitimacy to political elites in Malaysia's ethnoreligiously diverse social setting. True to the "foreign policy as an extension of domestic policy" maxim, such domestic political considerations have more often than not affected how Malaysian ruling elites perceived through their opaque lens the threats and opportunities generated by the given structural-external conditions. Their intersubjective assessment of the perceived external environment, in turn, tended to delineate Malaysia's strategic priorities and the ensuing GS and external behavior and preferences of action.

Explicitly underlined in the 2019 Foreign Policy Framework of the New Malaysia, the country's national interests comprise three core elements, namely *security, economic well-being,* and *identity*.[6] These elements, which are also acknowledged in the currently evolving "*Malaysia Madani*"[7] narrative and international outlook, have by and large informed the following grand strategic priorities.

NATIONAL SECURITY

Notwithstanding its *smaller-state* status, Malaysia's delicate geographical attributes have unavoidably accentuated the significance of national security, defined in terms of defending and securing maritime territorial integrity and sovereignty as the primary strategic priority. As aforementioned, Malaysia is located strategically at the heart of Southeast Asia and between the Indian and Pacific oceans (serving as a bridge between the West and Far East). It also has one of its two landmasses conjoined to the Asian continent, making it quintessentially a "maritime nation with continental roots."[8] As such Malaysia, which by geographical default straddles one of the world's busiest sea lines of communication (SLOC) since time immemorial, namely the Straits of Melaka and South China Sea (SCS), has perennially attracted the attention of major powers. From the historical epochs of the Malacca Sultanate and Western colonialism to the Cold War and post–Cold War periods and beyond, Malaysia in both its past and present form has more often than not been at the epicenter of East Asian power competition involving both resident and nonresident powers due to its strategic location and proximity to regional powerhouses like China and Japan.

Additionally, the modern Malaysian federation comprises Peninsular and Bornean Malaysia (Sabah and Sarawak), which are physically separated by the SCS. The sheer distance between these two Malaysian landmasses undoubtedly brings with it multidimensional challenges that encompass issues from governance and national security to national cohesion and integration. Indeed, Noor concurs that this physical division "has several important and practical implications for the defence and integration of the nation."[9] From a national defense/security perspective, it means greater challenges for the Malaysian Armed Forces (MAF) in defending and securing Malaysia's vast but noncontiguous maritime-terrestrial borders from both traditional and nontraditional security threats.[10]

Exacerbating Malaysia's national security predicaments are its expansive maritime zones, long coastlines, and porous borders, parts of which are adjacent to some of the most volatile and contested locales in Southeast Asia. The most notable is the Malaysia-Indonesia-Philippines "tri-border" maritime region covering the Sulu and Celebes seas, infamous for its relative lawlessness and power vacuum that fuels a plethora of cross-border security issues ranging from terrorism and religious extremism-induced insurgencies to maritime piracy, contraband smuggling, and human trafficking. In this regard, Sabah in Bornean Malaysia is particularly vulnerable due to its proximity to the tri-border area, making it a de facto frontline state in confronting what is a hub for terrorism and cross-border criminal activities in Southeast Asia.[11] In fact Sabah, with its far-reaching coastline and maritime borders, is essentially vital to Malaysia's overall maritime-territorial security. Malaysia's continental shelf off Sabah covers the SCS and Sulu Sea to the north and the Celebes Sea to the east. Meanwhile Sabah's exclusive economic zones (EEZs) border Indonesia to the east, the Philippines to the northeast, and Vietnam to the north. Malaysia established these maritime boundaries based on its interpretation of the related

United Nations Convention on the Law of the Sea (UNCLOS) regimes, albeit unilaterally, following the 1979 publication of a two-sheet "Map Showing Territorial Waters and Continental Shelf Boundaries of Malaysia" (commonly known as "New Map" or *Peta Baru* in Malay). Unsurprisingly, parts of them are still subjected to ongoing sovereignty disputes with neighboring states.

Indeed, compounding Malaysia's geographically induced national security challenges are the numerous extant maritime-territorial disputes vis-à-vis almost, if not all of its neighbors, due to overlapping boundary claims. Besides being a claimant in the multination SCS disputes over parts of the Spratly archipelago and surrounding waters, Malaysia is also engaged in several other sovereignty contests. They include the Philippines' latent historical claims to Sabah,[12] the Celebes Sea/Ambalat maritime conflict vis-à-vis Indonesia, and the bilateral disputes involving Thailand and Singapore, respectively, over maritime borders and contiguous marine features.[13] The SCS imbroglio is by far the most contentious and challenging, as it involves not only multiple claimants including the regional power, China, but also nonclaimants and extraregional powers such as the United States (US), Australia, Great Britain, and others seeking to intervene under the pretext of safeguarding freedom of navigation in the contested waters. Although principally a maritime-territorial issue, the SCS has escalated into becoming a venue of great-power competition embroiling China and America, as well as allies of the latter, under the auspices of the Quadrilateral Security Dialogue (or "Quad"), and more recently, the Australia-United Kingdom-United States (AUKUS) pact. As a smaller-state-cum-SCS-claimant caught in this potential flashpoint in Sino-American strategic rivalry, the onus is upon Malaysia to deftly navigate these treacherous waters as much to ensure national survival as to safeguard its maritime-territorial interests.

Territorial nationalism notwithstanding, Malaysia's maritime zones are strategically as well as economically indispensable to its national security and well-being. From fisheries to hydrocarbon reserves, the Malaysian continental shelves and EEZs are a considerable source for its food, energy, and economic security. Likewise, the Melaka Strait and SCS, together with the Sulu and Celebes seas, are vital SLOCs for Malaysia and other trading nations. Hence, besides territorial integrity, the safeguarding of the nation's maritime sovereignty and interests is a key national security agenda. The primacy of this strategic priority has been unequivocally emphasized in both the New Foreign Policy Framework and the 2019 Defence White Paper (DWP), which pledges a renewed commitment to protecting Malaysia's land and maritime borders.[14]

Economic Prosperity and Well-Being

Malaysia is rich in natural resources and endowed with vast arable land and a conducive climate, and its economy has been traditionally anchored upon and driven by the likes of agriculture, mining, and resource-extraction activities. Although the primary sector remains an indispensable contributor to the nation's coffer, the gradual shift toward industrialization, and the emergent service and knowledge-based economy epitomizing Malaysia's economic transformation since the 1980s, have led to relatively high and sustained annual economic growth over the last few decades. Notwithstanding the cyclical economic downturns and recessions, Malaysia's admirable economic performance as one of the so-called Asian tiger economies has not only contributed to uplifting its overall national socioeconomic well-being but also saliently underpins the country's political stability. With an aspiration to achieve high-income nation status, both past and present Malaysian administrations have introduced numerous macroeconomic initiatives and blueprints, from Vision 2020 to the more recent Shared Prosperity Vision (SPV) 2030 and the Madani Economy Framework,[15] aimed at sustaining high growth while ensuring relatively egalitarian and inclusive socioeconomic development. Indeed, a recent World Bank outlook optimistically reckoned Malaysia's likely transition from an upper-middle income to a high-income nation between 2024 and 2028.[16]

However, the relatively fragile and uncertain global political economy since 2008 triggered by the long-standing ramifications of the American subprime crisis, the US-China trade war, and the unprecedented COVID-19 pandemic, among others, have dented such optimism. Compounding the global predicament has been Malaysia's apparent struggle to escape the so-called middle-income trap. A media commentary highlighted Malaysia's middle-income country dilemma since the mid-1990s, where slower productivity growth has emerged as its main challenge toward becoming a high-income nation. The conundrum is attributed to issues concerning the relocation of economic resources, limited indigenous/new knowledge creation, relatively low technology and innovation-driven impetus, skill gap, and structural issues in the labor market (e.g., skilled and highly skilled labor shortage, low female labor force participation rates, foreign labor dependency).[17]

Indeed, apart from sound macroeconomic policy planning, Malaysia's economic well-being is highly dependent on external forces due to the nature of its economy. Malaysia is a trading nation by default of its aforesaid strategic location, straddling the traditional East-West international trade routes. Yet, with a population of less than 35 million, it is constrained by its small domestic market and limited range of resources. It is therefore inevitable that the Malaysian economy is structurally and functionally geared toward export orientation and dependent on relatively free and unhindered access to global and regional markets to spur economic growth and development. It is likewise dependent on foreign direct investment (FDI) as much for knowledge and technology transfer as for generating employment opportunities in all economic sectors. By the same token, Malaysia is vulnerable to such external forces as fluctuations in commodity prices, cyclical downturns, and unfair practices in the global economy. Economic security thus serves as another strategic priority and major thrust driving Malaysia's grand strategic thinking and *pragmatic* external orientation. To this end, a principal thrust of Malaysia's economic-driven external pragmatism has accordingly been to embrace open trade and emphasize fair trade while developing both bilateral and multilateral economic partnerships that are as diverse and as productive as possible.[18]

To be sure, guaranteeing national economic well-being is vital to Malaysia's ruling elite, whose domestic political legitimacy is fundamentally tied to and dependent on the country's economic performance. Since independence, and ever more so in today's fluid and competitive domestic political landscape, Malaysia's ruling coalitions, from Alliance/BN and PH to Perikatan Nasional (PN) and now the PH-BN "Unity" government, have depended on *performance* legitimation as the primary pathway toward securing political legitimacy. The performance of any incumbent Malaysian administration irrespective of its ideological inclination is primarily gauged by its ability to ensure continuous economic prosperity. Notwithstanding a political economy ostensibly driven by patronage, clientelism, and rent-seeking practices,[19] where political power has been traditionally amassed, sustained, and loss, it is imperative for present-day ruling elites to not only preserve and grow their patron-client networks but equally to emphasize nonpartisan, inclusive, and egalitarian socioeconomic development to mobilize grassroots-level political support, where bread-and-butter issues are among the most salient in determining electoral outcomes. The primacy of *performance* legitimation over other pathways (*procedural* and *particularistic* legitimation)[20] thus necessitates a GS anchored on the centrality of economic development and one driven by an external *pragmatism* geared profoundly toward realizing such politically significant economic gains. Malaysia's continuous advocacy for global free trade institutions and regimes, apart from its multilayered external posturing anchored on ASEAN, East Asian, and global multilateralism,[21] is indicative of such a grand strategic priority, which has to be understood within the context of smaller-state pragmatism.

National Identity and Nation-Building

The Malaysian society is essentially multiethnic, multireligious, and highly pluralistic. Although the Malays, Chinese, and Indians are the largest ethnic groups forming more than three-quarters of the country's demography, there are hundreds of other ethnic and subethnic identities that make up Malaysia's diverse social fabric. Sabah alone comprises forty-two ethnic groups with over 200 subethnic groupings, each with their own linguistic and cultural traits, besides rituals and beliefs.[22] It is only natural that fostering nation-building and national integration against the backdrop of such a complex national social setting has become a nonnegotiable strategic priority that has major ramifications for Malaysia's internal stability and overall well-being. This is especially so since ethnoreligious dynamics and identity politics remain among the most persuasive in defining Malaysia's domestic political landscape, serving as a major fault-line that accentuates the challenges of fostering national unity and advancing the all-important nation-building agenda of making *Bangsa Malaysia* (Malaysian nation) a reality. Indeed, apart from the few that are genuinely multiethnic in composition and ideological stance, the majority of political parties in Malaysia are exclusively ethnic-based. Meanwhile, national political coalitions commonly manifest a politically expedient ensemble of potentially disparate ethnoreligious entities seeking political marriages of convenience to secure a broad-based electoral mandate from the country's diverse demography.

Further exacerbating the national identity fault-lines are the *Bumiputera*-versus-*non-Bumiputera* dichotomy, which divides the Malaysian citizenry into two large subnational groupings: the former comprising the indigenous peoples (including ethnic Malays and other indigenous groups), the latter mainly descendants of Malaysia's migrant community. Constitutionally enshrined special privileges are accorded to the Bumiputeras in various aspects of political, social, and economic life. This seemingly skewed arrangement is in return for the granting of automatic citizenship to the nonindigenous population based on the *jus soli* principle, a key element of the much-touted social contract that defines Malaysia's nationhood. Inevitably, such a consciously designed national identity chasm, and the introduction of corollary national policies of socioeconomic engineering epitomized by the New Economic Policy (NEP) and its offspring, have further amplified the challenges of national integration and nation-building.[23] It has also unwittingly elicited other divisively provocative and chauvinistic notions, such as the *ketuanan Melayu-Islam* (Malay-Islam supremacy) narrative that has purportedly gained popular traction[24] amid the countervailing official "unity-in-diversity" rhetoric.

Additionally, the issues of nation-building are compounded by the geographical divide between Peninsular and Bornean Malaysia, which has generated its fair share of challenges, insofar as interregional socioeconomic disparities and federal-state relations are concerned. According to Lai,[25] a macro view highlights glaring regional developmental disparities between Sabah/Sarawak and Peninsular Malaysia, with the underdevelopment of the former presumably resulting from imbalanced distribution and allocation of resources to the latter. Such regional imbalances have become a key impetus driving the Bornean states' agenda for the reinstatement of state autonomy in governing its share of revenues for economic development as originally envisaged by Malaysia's founding fathers. On the extreme, such parochial grievances have led to the occasional secessionist calls for unilateral independence (i.e., the *Sabah-Sarawak Keluar Malaysia* movement).[26]

As aforementioned, both past and present Malaysian administrations have been conscious of the necessity to foster national integration as the basis for harmonious and sustained national development. This is evident in all of Malaysia's overarching national agendas, despite the recalibration and rebranding to reflect the different periods of administration. From Vision 2020 and 1Malaysia to the SPV2030, *Keluarga Malaysia,* and now Malaysia Madani, these national visions-and-missions share the common overriding objective of promoting national unity and the potential end-goal of realizing the Malaysian nation. Taking lessons from the May 13, 1969 tragedy, no Malaysian government is prepared to risk another domestic ethnoreligious strife that could severely undo the country's progress during the last five decades. However, the contradiction between fostering national unity and Bangsa Malaysia based on the universal democratic principles of equality, inclusivity, and justice, on the one hand, and the simultaneous need to pander to the political realities of upholding the existing subnational identity divides, on the other, has made this grand strategic priority ever more elusive.

EXTERNAL FACTORS

As a small trading nation located at the epicenter of regional geopolitics and straddling vital SLOCs, Malaysia's GS is informed by external factors that determine the prevailing structural conditions within which the broad parameters of its external behavior and preferences of action are defined. The following section discusses the third-party actors, systemic threats and opportunities, and types of conflict affecting Malaysia's grand strategic calculations.

Third-Party Actors

Malaysia places great emphasis on its relations with ASEAN, both bilaterally vis-à-vis its member-states and multilaterally as a founding member of the regional organization. Geographical proximity as a structural condition inherently dictates that "Malaysia's most important relationships lie with its closest neighbours."[27] ASEAN's centrality in Malaysian GS calculations is explicitly identified in the aforesaid key documents underlining Malaysia's foreign and defense policies. Indeed, ASEAN has been the cornerstone of Malaysian foreign policy since 1967 and remains so despite the growing significance of Northeast Asian states like Japan, Korea, and China in Malaysia's external engagements.[28] As a smaller state within a geopolitically fluid and economically dynamic East Asian region, it is pertinent for Malaysia to leverage ASEAN and extra-ASEAN regionalism as much to preserve as to advance its multidomain national interests, especially within the wider Asia-/Indo-Pacific region. To this end, ASEAN-based multilateral frameworks such as the ASEAN-Plus-Three (APT), ASEAN Regional Forum (ARF), ASEAN Defence Minister Meeting-Plus (ADMM-Plus), and the strategically focused East Asia Summit (EAS) serve as crucial platforms for Malaysia to engage and address economic, security, and strategic issues with the related dialogue partners.[29] The prominence of ASEAN in Malaysia's GS and foreign policy has been further reinforced under the Anwar administration, with the Malaysian prime minister making it a priority to cultivate close relations with his ASEAN counterparts by visiting all ASEAN member-states except Myanmar during his first year at helm.[30]

Notwithstanding the primacy of structural conditionalities, ideational impetuses in the guise of culture and identity also influence Malaysia's external priorities. In this regard, favorable ties with members of the Muslim world under the auspices of the Organisation of Islamic Cooperation (OIC) are considered important, since Islam is a major tenet of Malaysian foreign policy. As a Muslim-majority nation in a post-9/11 world affected by the scourge of religious extremism and Islamophobia, Malaysia aspires to position and project itself "as an exemplary Islamic country, which is moderate, progressive, inclusive, and developed."[31] This aspiration is encapsulated in both the 2019 foreign policy framework's references to the *Maqasid Syari'ah* concept (higher objective of *Syari'ah*),[32] and the six pillars of the Malaysia Madani narrative. Domestically, Malaysia's leadership, advocacy, and proactivism in the Islamic world contribute to its ruling elites' political legitimacy.

In the broader regional context, Malaysia is cognizant of the effects that Northeast Asian states like Japan, South Korea, and China have on its national well-being due to the structural realities of geographical proximity and power dynamics vis-à-vis these relatively more powerful and affluent distant neighbors. Filtered by their domestic political considerations, Malaysia's ruling elites are also mindful of the perceived threats and opportunities emanating from these structural conditions, which may have a bearing on their performance-based political legitimacy. Such external-domestic calculations have resulted in what Kuik et al.[33] aptly call Malaysia's "dualistic" diplomacy toward Northeast Asia, embodied by its concurrent pursuit of economic pragmatism and strategic prudence to anchoring its Look East Policy (LEP) on Japan and Korea while expanding partnership with China, among others. Indeed, Malaysia has since the early 1980s redirected its traditionally Western-centric outlook and begun "looking east" as part of its GS to diversify its external engagements. While giving primacy to the immediate Southeast Asian neighborhood, Malaysia has steadily pivoted toward Japan, and to a lesser extent South Korea and Taiwan.[34] Besides the affinities in cultural identity and "Asian values," the success story of these Northeast Asian economies that inspired the World Bank's "East Asian miracle" narrative[35] has led Mahathir and his successors to replicate their developmental state models as a core component of Malaysia's own economic transformation agenda.

Nonetheless, China's unprecedented rise to regional geopolitical and economic prominence since 2008 has triggered a power shift in East Asia, correspondingly eliciting a recalibration of Malaysia's strategic priorities to reflect the structural realities of China's growing importance in its overall grand strategic calculus. On top of the burgeoning Chinese footprint in the Malaysian economy, where China has emerged as both Malaysia's largest trade partner and top foreign investor for consecutive years,[36] the uncertainties concerning Beijing's maritime-territorial ambitions and its related policy behavior have had ruling elites in Putrajaya perceiving the challenges and opportunities deriving from the People's Republic as among the most crucial in determining both the country's well-being and their domestic political authority.[37]

Beyond East Asia but within the wider Indo-Pacific region lies the US, another of Malaysia's key third-party actors and a traditionally important partner. Malaysia has generally enjoyed a longstanding, robust, and institutionalized relationship with the US. Despite not formally being an ally like that of Thailand and the Philippines, and irrespective of the occasionally acrimonious interactions during the Mahathir premierships, bilateral relations have largely remained comprehensive and resilient. America has been one of Malaysia's top trade, investment, and security partners for decades. This is in spite of the waxing and waning of Washington's Asia policy along with the change of US administrations, and despite China's increasing prominence in the Malaysian foreign policy calculus. Indeed, America's enduring significance in Malaysia's external affairs has seen both sides elevating their bilateral ties to the level of "comprehensive partnership" in 2014.[38] Amid the heightened geopolitical uncertainties concerning future Chinese ambitions especially in the SCS, the US's traditional role as a credible economic and security partner has become ever more pertinent in Malaysia's grand strategic considerations and its *hedging* policy approach. However, the escalating Sino-American strategic competition has also contributed to growing regional insecurity, where smaller states like Malaysia may find themself entrapped in the emerging great-power rivalry.

Threats and Opportunities

Real or perceived, the threats and opportunities imposed by the prevailing structural conditions are filtered by the intersubjective lens of Malaysian state elites, whose domestic political needs often affect the manner in which the external-structural challenges are interpreted and the ensuing preferences of action taken to address them. In Malaysia's case, the primacy of managing insecurity and defending national borders, set against the backdrop of unresolved maritime-territorial disputes and an increasingly assertive mutual claimant in China, has meant that the SCS conflict and the looming Chinese threat perception are among the most pressing.[39] Malaysia claims approximately a dozen insular features in the SCS's Spratly archipelago together with their respective maritime enclave. Effectively occupying five features including Pulau Layang-Layang (Swallow Reef), Malaysia's portion of the SCS overlaps either partially or *en masse* with those of the other five claimants, namely China, Taiwan, Vietnam, Brunei, and the Philippines. Beijing's expansive "historical rights" claim based on its contentious "nine-dash line" boundary encompasses almost 90 percent of this semienclosed sea, including that of Malaysia.[40] With the SCS being an area of core interest to both states, not to mention Beijing's proven belligerence in staking its claims, it is inevitable that Putrajaya views the SCS conundrum as an imminent security challenge, one in which Malaysia needs to tread cautiously, not only because of the glaring power asymmetry but also the economic costs and opportunities related to China's magnitude in its grand strategic equation.

The realities of the SCS threat to Malaysia are, likewise, accentuated by increased involvement of the US together with its allies under the pretext of protecting the freedom of navigation and securing the vital SLOCs, where a gargantuan volume of global trade traverses annually. Indeed, the SCS is emerging ominously as an arena of great-power competition between Washington and Beijing, with the former leveraging its alliance network of "like-minded" partners under the Quads, and the more recent tripartite AUKUS setup, to advance their free and open Indo-Pacific (FOIP) and possibly "Pax Pacifica" agenda.[41] Perceived as an American design to contain rather than compete with China's rise, the Sino-US great-power rivalry playing out in this "sea-of-conflict"[42] carries huge ramifications to Malaysia's national security, as previously highlighted.

Another element of Malaysia's national insecurity is the proliferation of nontraditional, cross-border security challenges. As highlighted, Malaysia's vulnerability to cross-border threats is due as much to its lengthy and porous borders as to its location in Southeast Asia's most volatile subregion. Apart from interstate disputes over unresolved national boundaries, Malaysia remains susceptible to security threats stemming from nonstate actors. Terrorism remains a major security concern, with the likes the Al-Qaeda and Islamic State or Daesh networks of terror cells, including their regional offspring (e.g., Jemaah Islamiyah and Abu Sayyaf) continuously raising the specter of potential terror attacks. Despite the fall of Daesh's self-proclaimed caliphates in Iraq, Syria, and southern Philippines, security observers like Elina Noor concurs that many countries including Malaysia presently have to contend with local sympathizers and supporters as well as returning fighters "who pose varying degrees of threat to the nation."[43] Besides terrorism and religious-driven militancy, Malaysia also encounters the threat of "foreign" intrusions by related militant-cum-secessionist groups from the southern Philippines seeking to reclaim Sabah. The 2013 intrusion of Sabah by the so-called Royal Sulu Forces, and the proliferation of kidnap-for-ransom incidents in the aftermath, serve as vivid reminders of such cross-border threats. In recent years an unsubstantiated regional media report regarding an alleged "secret plot" to invade Sabah by Sulu militias[44] that was eventually refuted as "fake news" by the Filipino Defence Secretary,[45] highlights this perennial and existential problem.

In the age of digital transformation and dependence on information communication technology in all domains of statehood, potential threats to national security are no longer confined to the traditional physical borders but instead have assumed a borderless disposition insofar as the cyberspace is concerned. In this regard, cybersecurity threats have become an obvious national security concern. The DWP has highlighted the MAF's urgent need to strengthen its cyber-defense capability to enable the achievement of "information superiority."[46] The emphasis on cybersecurity as another important national security domain has also manifested and been subsumed in various aspects of the national budget since 2022, as the Malaysian government strives to enhance the country's readiness for the Fourth Industrial Revolution (IR 4.0) and the challenges and opportunities related to it. The recent allocation of MYR60 million under the 2024 Malaysian budget for the implementation of the 5G Cyber Security Testing Framework as well as 5G technology local expertise (which includes the scope of hardware, equipment, applications, and advanced technology ecosystem) vividly highlights the Malaysian government's cognizance of this new and evolving frontier in managing national security threats and challenges.[47]

As a small trading nation and export-oriented economy, Malaysia is also susceptible to economic threats related to the external forces mentioned earlier. Apart from cyclical economic downturns, the Malaysian economy faces potential threats from protectionist and unfair economic practices including politically and economically induced trade restrictions and embargoes, such as the US's and EU's gradual ban as well as India's 2019 sanctions on Malaysian crude palm oil and related products. Similarly, unstable global commodity prices reminiscent of the 2014–16 plunge and the 2021 spike in global oil prices further expose Malaysia's economic vulnerability, a condition aggravated by structural attributes of its economy, where limited diversification has resulted in the concentration and dependency on selected economic sectors and products. Likewise, domestic political uncertainties following the infamous "Sheraton move" in February 2020 has done no favor in alleviating such national economic challenges. In fact, the political coup that brought down the then PH government has led to political power and the premiership changing hands three times in less than two years amid the economic ravages of the COVID-19 pandemic. Nonetheless, Anwar Ibrahim's installation as the tenth prime minister under the auspices of the historic PH-BN unity government following the fifteenth Malaysian general elections in November 2022 has since arguably restored some semblance of political stability and market confidence.

Types of Conflict

The types of conflict Malaysia faces are primarily determined by the prevailing international and regional strategic environment. During the nascent period of its establishment as a newly independent state, which coincided with the rigid bipolar Cold War order, the threat of communism influenced its grand strategic thinking and external orientation. Malaysia's pro-West foreign policy then placed it in direct conflict with socialist states, with the PRC arguably the major threat due to Beijing's overt support of the local communist insurgency. Malaysia was also involved in a limited conflict vis-à-vis Sukarno's Indonesia during the *Konfrontasi* (1963–66) following the apparently communist-influenced Indonesian president's nonrecognition of the new Malaysian federation and his call for the *Ganyang Malaysia* (Sweep Malaysia) campaign. Malaysia's GS was then focused on strengthening national defense via the "whole-of-nation" approach, which was subsequently conceptualized in the National Defence Policy (NDP 2010) as the "total defence" (HANRUH) doctrine, in the face of such conflicts of ideological persuasion.[48]

By the mid-1960s, the combination of regional geopolitical shift and the necessity of smaller-state pragmatism led Malaysia to recalibrate its grand strategic priorities, which manifested in a foreign policy of nonalignment, neutrality, equidistance, and peaceful coexistence that serve as the hallmark of its external engagements ever since. With the communist threat dissipating, especially following the normalization of diplomatic relations vis-à-vis China in May 1974, national priorities and resources have since been redirected principally toward economic development.

To be sure, the prospects of conventional interstate conflict have remained toward the end of the Cold War and beyond due to the reemergence of great-power competition and unresolved maritime-territorial-related issues with most of its neighbors. Indeed, the aforementioned multiclaimant SCS dispute, the Celebes Sea/Ambalat maritime contest vis-à-vis Indonesia, and Philippines's latent sovereignty claim over Sabah are among the potential conflicts in the traditional security realm that continue to inform Malaysia's contemporary strategic assessment. Meanwhile, terrorism, maritime piracy, and other forms of security threats emanating from nonstate actors also require Malaysia's national defense apparatus to be geared toward facing the possibility of such nontraditional security-oriented conflicts.

DOMESTIC FACTORS

Malaysia's GS is also informed by internal factors, namely its national values, institutional process, and material resources.

National Values

Consistent with its smaller-state pragmatism, Malaysia's national values that epitomize its grand strategic thinking and external behavior are *moderation, peace,* and *harmony*. These mutually contingent and reinforcing values are aligned with its core national interests. Externally, the need for a relatively stable and peaceful international and regional environment as prerequisite for advancing its national development agenda has ensured that Malaysia consistently adopts a moderate and pragmatic foreign policy based on the aforesaid principles of nonalignment, neutrality, equidistance, and peaceful coexistence. These overarching principles governing Malaysia's external behavior and hedging approach since the Abdul Razak administration have demonstrated *continuity* rather than *change* over the decades, despite the uncertain and evolving geopolitical milieu and in spite of the potential risk associated with such smaller-states' strategic ambiguity, especially in the context of an escalating Sino-American great-power rivalry.

Domestically, the diverse demographic characteristics forming Malaysia's rich yet politically divisive social fabric have meant that the same three core values serve as the basis underpinning its complex nation-building process and the related policies aimed at preserving/enhancing national unity and resilience. These fundamentally universal, national values have been consistently encapsulated in the aforesaid national vision and mission, despite its periodic rebranding. In fact, the *wasatiyyah* (moderation) concept promoted by the then Najib Razak administration as part of its domestic-centered 1Malaysia agenda had eventually led to Malaysia introducing the Global Movement of the Moderates (GMM), an initiative to reject all forms of extremism and promote moderation that was adopted by the ASEAN in its 2015 Langkawi Declaration.[49] Likewise, the six core values underlining the Malaysia Madani policy framework and government-of-the-day slogan (notably care and compassion, trust, and respect) are aligned and consistent with the Malaysian national values and ethos.

Institutional Process

Given Malaysia's parliamentary-democratic political system, decision-making pertaining to matters of the state is essentially bottom-up, pluralistic, and deliberative in both form and function. However, when it comes to GS and foreign policy, decision-making tends to assume a more top-down, elitist orientation, with the actors becoming more exclusive and process highly centralized. The conventional notion of GS and foreign policymaking being in the realm of high politics and thus in the preserve of state elites remains relevant, despite the gradual democratization under the then PH government, where engagement and consultation with various stakeholder-entities in matters pertaining to Malaysia's grand strategic and external priorities have become more institutionalized. Since the final arbiters of such decision-making remain at the highest levels, leadership personality and idiosyncrasies, especially those of the presiding prime minister, have traditionally left a heavy imprint in Malaysia's national strategic policies. This was especially so under Mahathir Mohamad's maiden premiership that spanned more than two decades, where "Mahathirism" saliently underpinned Malaysia's grand strategic design and external orientation.[50] Moreover, the elite-centric institutional process is expected since the ruling elite's domestic political survival is largely dependent on their performance in securing those core national interests.

To be sure, the previously highlighted successive leadership change following the "Sheraton move," which led to the Mahathir-led PH government's untimely demise, had somewhat lessened the policy imprint of the subsequent two prime ministers under the Perikatan Nasional-Plus administration. However, the arrival of Anwar Ibrahim is expected to regalvanize the elitist nature of Malaysian GS and foreign policymaking under the PH-BN government. This is especially since Anwar is a strong, vastly experienced, and visionary leader in his own right, not to mention an internationalist at heart, who is also renowned for his adroit statesmanship. The so-called Anwar Ibrahim factor is therefore likely to recalibrate Malaysia's grand strategic thinking, outlook, and external priorities under the new leadership's Malaysia Madani narrative.[51]

Material Resources

As a developmental state and one of Southeast Asia's tiger economies, Malaysia has enjoyed relatively robust economic growth since the late 1980s in both GDP and GDP per capita terms. Although external vulnerabilities and structural issues in the Malaysian economy have slowed down its economic performance in recent years, Malaysia still ranks highly among regional actors in most economic indicators. For instance, Malaysia's Human Development Index (HDI) has been trending progressively since the 1990s, with the country ranked 62 in 2019, based on a score of 0.810, which was above the East Asia Pacific average of 0.747.[52] Although its most recent HDI ranking (2022) has declined to sixty-third position with a score of 0.807, Malaysia remains in the "Very High Human Development" category. Notwithstanding favorable global conditions and sound macroeconomic policies, Malaysia's aforementioned geographical and natural resource-rich attributes are a critical material capability driving its economic dynamism.

Conversely, Malaysia is handicapped by its limited military capabilities, commensurate with its smaller-state identity. The MAF doctrine and force structure is primarily designed and equipped for limited deterrence, with the tri-services operating predominantly as a self-defense force with restricted power-projection capabilities.[53] Despite the plethora of security challenges detailed earlier and the DWP's emphasis on the urgent need to modernize and strengthen the nation's military capabilities, Malaysia's defense apparatuses are still underfunded.[54] Indeed, its shoestring defense budget has seen negligible year-on-year increase, with the 2022 allocation of MYR16.14 billion representing merely a 1.8 percent hike from the previous year,[55] while the MYR17.74 billion allocated for 2023 saw a nominal 10 percent increase over last year's funding.[56] Even more concerning is the fact that the bulk of the annual allocation goes to operational rather than development expenditures.[57] Over the years, the Royal Malaysian Navy (RMN)'s limited budget for the procurement of new combat ships has somewhat encumbered its "15-to-5" naval transformation and modernization program.[58] Meanwhile, the long overdue replacement of the RMAF's ageing multirole combat aircraft (MRCA) squadrons with newer fourth- to fifth-generation fighters, which has been hampered by the country's recent fiscal woes, is a vivid example of what defense experts deemed as the "demand-and-supply asymmetry dilemma" that the Malaysian defense ministry faces in its quest to transform itself.[59]

To compensate for its limited military capabilities, Malaysia has saliently depended on its diplomatic resources to effectively implement its GS. In this regard, its commendable diplomatic corps together with the employment of deft diplomacy, astute statecraft, and adroit statesmanship have thus far enabled Malaysia to proverbially "punch above its weight" in the international arena.[60]

OPERATIONALIZATION OF GRAND STRATEGY

Given the resources at its disposal and the interplay between external-structural and domestic imperatives in defining its grand strategic priorities, Malaysia operationalizes its GS via a combination of legislative, administrative, diplomatic, legal, defense, and economic instruments. This multipronged statecraft is rooted as much in geopolitical and economic as normative and ideational considerations.

Externally, Malaysia has consistently adopted a pragmatic foreign policy approach based on hedging, or more specifically *light-hedging,* to advance its national interests as a smaller state in an evolving international/regional strategic environment characterized by growing power asymmetries, rivalries, and uncertainties.[61] According to Lai and Kuik, hedging is defined as "insurance-seeking behaviour under high-stakes and high uncertainty conditions," which commonly entails three operational attributes: (1) an insistence on not taking sides; (2) attempts to pursue opposing measures (i.e., concurrent adoption of defiance and deference vis-à-vis big powers)[62]; and (3) diversification to cultivate a fallback position. This middle-ground, low-profile, and nonconfrontational approach comprising multidomain engagements with multiple partners, and the adoption of myriad measures, sometimes counterintuitive and contradictory, is meant to provide smaller states like Malaysia with strategic options to offset *multiple risks* stemming from high-uncertainty scenarios.[63] Likewise, hedging requires the effective conduct of diplomacy, a key determinant in the success and failure of smaller states with limited wherewithal in advancing their GS and external goals. Observers have used different terms to describe Malaysia's hedging approach, from "playing-it-safe"[64] and "selective alignment and strategic ambiguity"[65] to "mousedeer diplomacy" and "smart-accommodation,"[66] among others. This pragmatic policy approach has been evidently displayed in Malaysia's interactions with the region's powerhouses, notably China, Japan, and the US, including Putrajaya's handling of the various episodes of the SCS dispute.[67]

Effective hedging requires the Malaysian government to strategically employ the aforementioned multipronged statecraft. To this end, Malaysia has been pragmatically optimizing legislative and administrative as well as diplomatic and legal instruments, which serve as the principal statecraft to advance its core interests in the international realm. In the case of the SCS imbroglio, Malaysia has appropriated legislative-administrative means, including the passing of various domestic legislations to assert its sovereign rights over the SCS portion claimed [e.g., the 1966 Continental Shelf Act (revised in 1972 and 2009); Petroleum Mining Act (1966) and Petroleum Development Act (1974); Exclusive Economic Zones Act (1984); and Baselines of Maritime Zones Act (2007)], with the most important being the introduction of the "New Map" on December 21, 1979.[68]

Lai and Kuik concur that diplomacy via both bilateral (e.g., "quiet" diplomacy vis-à-vis China) and multilateral channels (e.g., ASEAN frameworks, including the Code of Conduct [CoC] for the SCS) and "selective deference" is "central to preserving sovereignty and keeping bilateral ties," while "indirect defiance" via selective legal means or *lawfare* (i.e., lodging unpublicized diplomatic notes of protest as record of official actions to assert claims; adoption of relevant UNCLOS regimes for maritime boundary delimitation; joint and unilateral submissions to the CLCS for continental shelf extension) have served to safeguard Malaysia's enduring interests in the disputed waters.[69] Undeniably, the use of diplomatic and legal hedges are the most practical and feasible approach for smaller states with limited military capabilities like Malaysia to manage maritime-territorial disputes, especially those involving big powers like China.[70] Besides the SCS, Malaysia had also sought legal redress via the International Court of Justice (ICJ), albeit with mixed results over the Sipadan/Ligitan islands and Batu Puteh/Pedra Branca disputes with Indonesia and Singapore, respectively. With its persistent emphasis on the importance of rule-based international order, regimes, and institutions, Malaysia is expected to continue leveraging legal means to protect as much as advance its competing maritime-territorial interests vis-à-vis other disputants.

That said, Malaysian state elites remain acutely aware of the limitations of legal instruments and the efficacy of rules and norms in what is still fundamentally an anarchic international system governed by the dictates of power dynamics. This enduring sense of realism is the reason behind its simultaneous employment of diplomatic and defense tools, which widen Malaysia's strategic options when dealing with asymmetric power relations, rivalries, and uncertainties in the external realm. In this regard, Malaysia has forged both bilateral and multilateral defense-security cooperation with multiple partners as a vital component of its *military* hedge to complement its ongoing efforts to augment and transform the MAF as an instrument of foreign policy to accomplish its GS. Besides modernizing and better equipping the tri-services via strategic procurement and maintenance of military assets (e.g., Royal Malaysian Air Force (RMAF)'s planned acquisitions of newer generation of MRCAs, light combat aircraft, and unmanned aerial vehicles; RMN's commissioning of Scorpene-class submarines, littoral-mission ships, and off-shore patrol vessels and the construction of frigates; establishment of additional land/maritime border outposts), Malaysia has maintained robust and institutionalized defense partnership with the likes of the US and Five-Power Defence Arrangements (FPDA) members while forging new ones, including with China, arguably the major source of its security concerns. The upgrading of Sino-Malaysian ties to comprehensive strategic partnership in 2013, which entails the enhancement of their previously underdeveloped defense/security cooperation, while concurrently cultivating robust military partnerships with the US and Australia, is a classic manifestation of the counterintuitive and seemingly opposing measures associated with Malaysia's hedging approach to offset multiple risks stemming from the uncertainty of Chinese intentions and US commitment, entrapment in a potential Sino-American conflict, and the risk associated with domestic legitimacy erosion.[71]

Additionally, Malaysia continues to leverage the aforesaid security-related ASEAN-driven multilateralism and institutions (e.g., Southeast Asia Regional Center for Counter-Terrorism), apart from bilateral and trilateral arrangements (e.g., Malindo CORPAT/Malacca Straits Patrol [MSP]; Malaysia-Indonesia-Philippines coordinated patrol in the Sulu Sea) to effectively manage its national security challenges. Malaysia's international activism within the UN system is another striking element of its defense diplomacy that contributes to its overall security. The long-held notion of "paying it forward" for its national security has seen Malaysia actively participating in numerous UN peacekeeping operations since the early 1960s, earning it a nonpermanent seat in the UN Security Council during four separate terms while increasing its international visibility and security guarantee. In 2019 Malaysia had approximately 800 peacekeepers abroad, with the DWP targeting an increase to 8,000 personnel as part of the country's call to boost its national resilience through international activism.[72]

Meanwhile, the need to manage its vulnerability to external forces has driven Malaysia to leverage expanded bilateralism and multilateralism as the cornerstone of its economic pragmatism to sustain economic prosperity. Bilaterally, Malaysia has willfully fostered all-round progressive ties with most countries, especially with key economic partners like China, Japan, South Korea, the US, and its ASEAN neighbors, to maximize market access, investments, and technology transfer. Putrajaya has also pragmatically opted to downplay problematic bilateral issues in favor of protecting mutually beneficial economic interactions when managing potentially challenging bilateral relationships. For instance, Malaysian state elites have been delicately handling the SCS dispute vis-à-vis China due to the reality of their increasing dependence on Chinese economic largess, as much to facilitate Malaysia's grand strategic agenda as to continuously legitimize their performance-based domestic authority. This has led to Malaysia's "quiet diplomacy" and selective deference toward China, including buying in to the latter's Belt-and-Road Initiative (BRI) to safeguard its overall economic interests in their bilateral relations, while conversely seeking to diversify its economic dependence by revitalizing ties with Japan via the LEP 2.0.[73] Multilaterally,

Malaysia remains a staunch advocate of regional and extraregional economic partnership schemes, where the likes of the ASEAN-driven ASEAN Free Trade Area (AFTA) and APT, together with the more expansive Regional Comprehensive Economic Partnership (RCEP) and Comprehensive and Progressive Agreement on Trans-Pacific Partnership (CPTPP), as well as Washington's "partnership-with-liked-minded-countries"-driven Indo-Pacific Economic Framework (IPEF) and the purportedly Sino-Russian-galvanized BRICS (Brazil, Russia, India, China, South Africa)[74] will receive continuous emphasis as key GS enablers.

Domestically, the efficacious operationalization of its GS has a bearing on the third strategic priority of nation-building, as far as the domestic political legitimacy of Malaysia's ruling elites and their ability to ensure the overall well-being of the nation are concerned. This is especially so since national unity and integration can be effectively fostered through the sustenance of economic prosperity, together with the earnest implementation of inclusive national development policies that ensure the equitable distribution of wealth and opportunities across Malaysia's demographic and geographical divides. Safeguarding national sovereignty and economic security would also allow *performance* legitimation to supersede *particularistic* legitimation as the ruling elites' dominant domestic legitimation pathway, which in turn reduces their inclination toward seeking divisive, primordially and/or parochially related political expediencies while increasing their political will to genuinely drive the nation-building agenda.

CONCLUSION

In conclusion, Malaysia's GS is a means-end construct meant to facilitate a smaller state's attainment of its strategic priorities amid a fluid external-structural environment characterized by growing power asymmetries, rivalries, and uncertainties. It is also designed to concurrently facilitate the multiple legitimation pathways of Malaysian ruling elites in their quest to secure political authority in a competitive domestic political landscape. The grand strategic priorities of safeguarding national sovereignty and maritime-territorial integrity, ensuring economic well-being, and fostering nation-building are informed by both external and domestic imperatives. Externally, Malaysia's interactions with major third-party actors, like ASEAN, China, and the US, are largely determined by *proximity* and *power,* two fundamental structural conditionalities that define the potential threats and opportunities as well as the probable types of conflict and avenues of cooperation that Malaysia encounters. Yet the threat-opportunity perceptions emanating from asymmetrical power relations vis-à-vis China, unresolved sovereignty disputes with neighboring ASEAN states, and the uncertainties concerning China's rise, as well as the intensification of Sino-US geopolitical competition, are filtered by state elites' domestic political considerations and other internal factors, which affect the manner in which Malaysia operationalizes its GS and responds to the prevailing external conditions. To this end, Malaysia's hedging policy, which employs a multipronged statecraft geared toward economic dynamism and strategic prudence, reflects its smaller-state pragmatism, as this Southeast Asian nation strives to navigate and optimize its national interests in an uncertain and evolving East Asia.

NOTES

The author gratefully acknowledges support from Universiti Malaysia Sabah's grant number SDK0126-2020, *Crouching Tiger, Ascending Dragon: Malaysia's China Policy Transition in the Post-Barisan Nasional Era,* and the varsity's Indo-Pacific Security Research Group. The usual caveats apply.

1. Yew Meng Lai and Cheng-Chwee Kuik, "Structural Sources of Malaysia's South China Sea Policy: Power Uncertainties and Small-State Hedging," *Australian Journal of International Affairs* 75, no. 3 (2021), pp: 277–304; Yew Meng Lai, Maureen De Silva, and Yunqi Wang, "Crouching Tiger, Ascending Dragon: The Trends and Dynamics of Malaysia-China Relations," *Kajian Malaysia: Journal of Malaysian Studies* 41, no. 1 (2023): 85–108.
2. Lai, De Silva, and Wang, "Crouching Tiger, Ascending Dragon."
3. Lai, De Silva, and Wang, "Crouching Tiger, Ascending Dragon."
4. Lai, De Silva, and Wang, "Crouching Tiger, Ascending Dragon"; Yew Meng Lai and Ravichandran Moorthy, "Emerging Dynamics in Malaysia-Japan Relations under the Second Mahathir Administration," *Issues and Studies* 58, no. 2 (June 2022), https://doi.org/2240002-5-6; Cheng-Chwee Kuik, Abdul Razak Ahmad, and Ayman Rashdan Wong, "Malaysia and Northeast Asia: What Drives Small-State Forward Diplomacy?" *Issues and Studies* 58, no. 3 (September 2022), 2240003.
5. Kuik, Ahmad, and Wong, "Malaysia and Northeast Asia."
6. Elina Noor, *Foreign and Security Policy in the New Malaysia* (Lowy Institute, 2019).
7. "Malaysia Madani," https://malaysiamadani.gov.my/
8. Ministry of Defence (MINDEF), Malaysia, *Defence White Paper: A Secure, Sovereign and Prosperous Malaysia* (Percetakan Nasional Malaysia Berhad, 2019).
9. Ministry of Defence (MINDEF), Malaysia, *Defence White Paper*, 20.
10. Yew Meng Lai, "Malaysia's Security Concerns: A Contemporary Assessment," in *The Routledge Handbook of Contemporary Malaysia*, ed. Meredith L. Weiss (Routledge, 2015), 391–402.
11. Lai, "Malaysia's Security Concerns," 398; Angel Rabasa and Peter Chalk, *Non-Traditional Threats and Maritime Domain Awareness in the Tri-Border Area of Southeast Asia: The Coastal Watch System of the Philippines* (RAND Corporation, 2012).

12. The Republic of Philippines's latent claim was recently reignited on June 15, 2024, following Manila's "opportunistically-timed" UN filing to extend its continental shelf from Sabah's baselines, drawing a categorical rejection and reassertion of Malaysia's "indisputable sovereignty" from Putrajaya. Raissa Robles, "'Indisputable Sovereignty': Philippines' UN filing reignites Sabah dispute with Malaysia," *The South China Morning Post,* July 4, 2024, https://www.scmp.com/week-asia/politics/article/3269063/indisputable-sovereignty-philippines-un-filing-reignites-sabah-dispute-malaysia
13. Lai, "Malaysia's Security Concerns," 394–6.
14. MINDEF, *Defence White Paper.*
15. Prime Minister's Office of Malaysia Official Website, "Madani Economy Has Comprehensive Implementation Framework, unlike SPV 2030—PM Anwar," October 9, 2023, https://www.pmo.gov.my/2023/10/madani-economy-has-comprehensive-implementation-framework-unlike-spv-2030-pm-anwar/
16. Manokaran Mottain, "Malaysia on Track to Achieve High-Income Nation Status," *The Star,* May 22, 2021, https://www.thestar.com.my/business/business-news/2021/05/22/malaysia-on-track-to-achieve-high-income-nation-status
17. Mottain, "Malaysia on Track to Achieve High-Income Nation Status."
18. Kuik, Ahmad, and Wong, "Malaysia and Northeast Asia."
19. Edmund Terence Gomez and Jomo Kwame Sundaram, *Malaysia's Political Economy: Politics, Patronage and Profits* (Cambridge University Press, 1997).
20. Kuik, Ahmad, and Wong, "Malaysia and Northeast Asia."; Lai, De Silva, and Wang, "Crouching Tiger, Ascending Dragon."
21. Johan Saravanamuttu, *Malaysia's Foreign Policy: The First Fifty Years: Alignment, Neutralism, Islamism* (ISEAS Publishing, 2010).
22. "Sabah Lists 42 Ethnic Groups to Replace 'Lain-Lain' Race Column', *The Star,* February 13, 2015, https://www.malaymail.com/news/malaysia/2015/02/13/sabah-lists-42-ethnic-groups-to-replace-lain-lain-race-column/840691
23. "PM Launches Bumiputera Development Action 2030," *New Straits Times,* December 6, 2021, https://www.nst.com.my/news/nation/2021/12/751688/pm-launches-bumiputera-development-action-2030
24. B.A. Hamzah, "Ketuanan Melayu' Will Erode Malaysia's Meritocracy', *Asia Sentinel,* November 10, 2021, https://www.asiasentinel.com/p/ketuanan-melayu-erode-malaysia-meritocracy
25. Yew Meng Lai, "Sabah: Autonomy and Integration within the Malaysian Federation," in *Routledge Handbook of Comparative Territorial Autonomies,* eds. Brian C.H. Fong and Ichijo Atsuko (Routledge, 2022), 273–83.
26. Lai, "Sabah."
27. Noor, *Foreign and Security Policy in the New Malaysia,* 9.
28. Saravanamuttu, *Malaysia's Foreign Policy.*
29. Noor, *Foreign and Security Policy in the New Malaysia,* 14.
30. Angeline Tan, "Recapping the First Year of Malaysia's Foreign Policy under Anwar Ibrahim," *The Diplomat,* December 18, 2023, https://thediplomat.com/2023/12/recapping-the-first-year-of-malaysias-foreign-policy-under-anwar-ibrahim/
31. Tan, "Recapping the First Year of Malaysia's Foreign Policy under Anwar Ibrahim," 15.
32. Tan, "Recapping the First Year of Malaysia's Foreign Policy under Anwar Ibrahim," 15.
33. Kuik, Ahmad, and Wong, "Malaysia and Northeast Asia."

34. Kuik, Ahmad, and Wong, "Malaysia and Northeast Asia."; Saravanamuttu, *Malaysia's Foreign Policy*, 186–93.
35. World Bank, *The East Asian Miracle: Economic Growth and Public Policy* (The World Bank, 1993).
36. MalaysiaKini, "China Glad of Investment Growth, M'sia Export in H1-Ambassador," *MalaysiaKini*, October 1, 2020, https://www.malaysiakini.com/news/544777; Hooi Hooi Lean and Russell Smyth, "The Malaysia-China Economic Relationship at 40: Broadening Ties and Meeting the Challenges for Future Success," in *Chinese Global Production*, ed. Kim Young-Chan (Springer, 2016), 39–52.
37. Lai, De Silva, and Wang, "Crouching Tiger, Ascending Dragon," 85–108; Cheng-Chwee Kuik and Yew Meng Lai, "Deference and Defiance in Malaysia's China Policy: Determinants of a Dualistic Diplomacy," *International Journal of Asian Studies* (first view), 2023, 1–20. https://doi.org/10.1017/S1479591423000104
38. Noor, *Foreign and Security Policy in the New Malaysia*, 12.
39. Lai and Kuik, "Structural Sources of Malaysia's South China Sea Policy."
40. Lai and Kuik, "Structural Sources of Malaysia's South China Sea Policy."; Yew Meng Lai, Cheng-Chwee Kuik, and Amy Azuan Abdullah, "Pulau Layang-Layang in Malaysia's South China Sea Policy: Sovereignty Meets Geopolitical Reality amid China–U.S. Rivalry," *International Journal of China Studies* 12, no. 2 (2021), 189–222.
41. Henry Sokolski, "Building on AUKUS to Forge a Pax Pacifica," *Pacific Forum International* PacNet#57 (December 10, 2021), https://mailchi.mp/pacforum/pacnet-57-building-on-aukus-to-forge-a-pax-pacifica-1172586?e=165e4c0f37
42. Yew Meng Lai, "'Sea of Cooperation' or 'Sea of Conflict'?: The South China Sea in the Context of China-ASEAN Maritime Cooperation," *International Journal of China Studies* 8, no. 3 (2017), 319–43.
43. Noor, *Foreign and Security Policy in the New Malaysia*, p. 15.
44. "Esscom Investigating Alleged Secret Plot to Invade Sabah," *The Star*, December 9, 2021, https://www.thestar.com.my/news/nation/2021/12/09/esscom-investigating-alleged-secret-plot-to-invade-sabah
45. "Report on Plan to Invade Sabah Fake News—Manila,' *Borneo Post Online*, December 11, 2021, https://www.theborneopost.com/2021/12/11/report-on-plan-to-invade-sabah-fake-news-manila/
46. Ivy Kwek, "Malaysia's Defence White Paper at Two: Progress and Challenges," *IDSS Paper* No.019/2021 (November 29, 2021), https://www.rsis.edu.sg/wp-content/uploads/2021/11/IP21019-Kwek-masthead-final.pdf
47. "Budget 2024: CyberSecurity Malaysia to Use RM60m Allocation to Strengthen National Cyber Security Ecosystem," *Malay Mail*, October 14, 2023, https://www.malaymail.com/news/malaysia/2023/10/14/budget-2024-cybersecurity-malaysia-to-use-rm60m-allocation-to-strengthen-national-cyber-security-ecosystem/96256
48. Lai, "Malaysia's Security Concerns."
49. "The Asean Declaration on the Global Movement of Moderates Is Excellent Framework–Razali Ismail," *Malay Mail*, May 5, 2015, https://www.malaymail.com/news/what-you-think/2015/05/05/the-asean-declaration-on-the-global-movement-of-moderates-is-excellent-fram/890641
50. John Hilley, *Malaysia: Mahathirism, Hegemony and the New Opposition* (Zed Books, 2001).

51. Yew Meng Lai, "Boosting the Potential of Malaysia's Soft Power," paper presented at the Wisma Putra Retreat, Ministry of Foreign Affairs, Malaysia, March 6–7, 2023.
52. United Nations Development Programme (UNDP), "Human Development Reports 2020—Malaysia," http://hdr.undp.org/sites/default/files/Country-Profiles/MYS.pdf
53. Lai, "Malaysia's Security Concerns," 399.
54. "Underfunded Military Unlikely to Get More Money, Says Expert," *Free Malaysia Today*, October 24, 2021, https://www.freemalaysiatoday.com/category/nation/2021/10/24/underfunded-military-unlikely-to-get-more-money-says-expert/
55. "2022 National Security Budget," *Malaysiandefence.com*, October 29, 2021, https://www.malaysiandefence.com/2022-national-security-budget/
56. Jon Grevatt and Andrew MacDonald, "Malaysia Proposes Strong Budget Increase with Eye on Military Procurement," *Janes*, February 28, 2023, https://www.janes.com/defence-news/news-detail/malaysia-proposes-strong-budget-increase-with-eye-on-military-procurement
57. B.A. Hamzah, Yew Meng Lai, and Cheng-Chwee Kuik, "Crucial to Increase Defence Spending," *New Straits Times*, October 14, 2024, https://www.nst.com.my/opinion/columnists/2022/10/840364/crucial-increase-defence-spending
58. Hamzah, Lai, and Kuik, "Crucial to Increase Defence Spending."
59. *Free Malaysia Today*, "Underfunded Military Unlikely to Get More Money, Says Expert"; B.A. Hamzah, Yew Meng Lai, and Cheng-Chwee Kuik, "Royal Malaysian Navy Faces Tipping Point," *The Sun*, October 15, 2024, https://thesun.my/opinion-news/royal-malaysian-navy-faces-tipping-point-FF9979337; Malaysian Defence, "RMN New 15-to-5 Plan," *Malaysian Defence*, May 3, 2024, https://www.malaysiandefence.com/rmn-new-15-to-5-plan/
60. Noor, *Foreign and Security Policy in the New Malaysia*, 4.
61. Lai and Kuik, "Structural Sources of Malaysia's South China Sea Policy."
62. Cheng-Chwee Kuik and Yew Meng Lai, "Deference and Defiance in Malaysia's China Policy: Determinants of a Dualistic Diplomacy," *International Journal of Asian Studies* (2023).
63. Kuik and Lai, "Deference and Defiance," 280.
64. Prashanth Parameswaran, "Playing It Safe: Malaysia's Approach to the South China Sea and Its Implications for the United States," *CNAS Maritime Strategy Series* (February 2015), 4.
65. Adam Kok Wey Leong, "A Small State's Foreign Affairs Strategy: Making Sense of Malaysia's Strategic Response to the South China Sea Debacle," *Comparative Strategy* 36, no. 5 (2017), 392–9; Adam Kok Wey Leong, "The Strategic Logic of Malaysia's Muted Response to the South China Sea Standoff," *RUSI Newsbrief* 40, no. 4 (2020).
66. Anthony Milner, "Sovereignty and Normative Integration in the South China Sea: Some Malaysian and Malay Perspectives," in *Southeast Asia and China: A Contest in Mutual Socialization*, eds. Lowell Dittmer and Chow Bing Ngeow (World Scientific Publishing, 2017), 229–46; Anthony Milner, "Long-Term Themes in Malaysian Foreign Policy: Hierarchy Diplomacy, Non-interference and Moral Balance," *Asian Studies Review* 44, no. 1 (2020), 117–35.
67. Lai and Kuik, "Structural Sources of Malaysia's South China Sea Policy."
68. Yew Meng Lai, Cheng-Chwee Kuik, and Abdullah Amy Azuan, "Pulau Layang-Layang in Malaysia's South China Sea Policy: Sovereignty Meets Geopolitical Reality amid China-U.S. Rivalry," *International Journal of China Studies* 12, no.2 (2021), 201–202.

69. Lai and Kuik, "Structural Sources of Malaysia's South China Sea Policy," 290.
70. Lai and Kuik, "Structural Sources of Malaysia's South China Sea Policy," 293.
71. Cheng-Chwee Kuik, "The Twin Chessboards of US-China Rivalry: Impact on the Geostrategic Supply and Demand in Post-Pandenic Asia," *Asian Perspective* 45, no.1, 157–176; Lai and Kuik, "Structural Sources of Malaysia's South China Sea Policy," 277–304.
72. Fauziah Mohd Taib, "Call to Boost National Resilience," *New Straits Times*, December 14, 2019, https://www.nst.com.my/opinion/columnists/2019/12/547639/call-boost-national-resilience
73. Lai and Moorthy, "Emerging Dynamics in Malaysia-Japan Relations under the Second Mahathir Administration."
74. Bernama, "Malaysia Has Applied to Join BRICS-Anwar," *Bernama.com*, July 28, 2024, https://www.bernama.com/en/news.php?id=2322706

CHAPTER 8

Myanmar

Maung Aung Myoe

It is a standard narrative and common understanding among political and security elites in Myanmar that the Union of Myanmar is constantly in danger of disintegration due to internal disunity and external interference. Elites are acutely aware that Myanmar is affected by chronic insurgencies, making its survival highly uncertain and undermining its security.

From a broader view on the subject, grand strategy refers to a state procuring security for itself.[1] For Myanmar as a weak state, the "survival of Myanmar as a modern nation-state" has been at the core of its grand strategy ever since its independence in 1948.[2] In this regard, "Our Three Main National Causes (OTMNC)"—nondisintegration of the Union, nondisintegration of national solidarity, and perpetuation of sovereignty—enshrined and legalized in the 2008 constitution—serve as the cornerstone of Myanmar's grand strategy of survival. Although the concept of OMTNC officially entered into Myanmar's security lexicon only in late 1988, the reality is that it has always been at the core of Myanmar's grand strategy ever since the country regained its independence. In fact, the Declaration of Independence, the First Presidential Address to the Constituent Assembly on the Day of Independence, and the prime minister's address at the ceremony for laying the foundation for the Independence Landmark Pillar on January 4, 1948 all highlighted the importance of national unity, sovereign equality, and territorial integrity.

This chapter studies Myanmar's grand strategy by looking at the country's strategic priorities as well as both internal and external factors that influence its content. Officially known as the Union of Myanmar, the country is home to eight major races, which could be subcategorized into more than one hundred ethnic minorities; it is one of the most heterogeneous societies in Southeast Asia. On the one hand, the country's grand strategy is influenced and shaped by its geography, history, strategic culture, and political elites' worldview. On the other hand, the country's geopolitical and geostrategic realities are instrumental.

STRATEGIC PRIORITIES

By all accounts, successive administrations in Myanmar have considered the survival of the Union of Myanmar as a modern nation-state in the international community of nations as the fundamental objective, which entails territorial integrity, national unity, political independence, and sovereign equality as the centerpiece of Myanmar's grand strategy. This core objective is occasionally further supplemented by other objectives such as "building a socialist democratic system," "building a democratic federal system," and so on. However, the political reality is that Myanmar has never meaningfully been a nation-state; the nationhood is constantly contested, and the statehood is persistently challenged from within and without. It is in this context that Myanmar's strategic priority is essentially the "enhancement of national resilience and state security" through nation-building and state-building, the development of military capabilities, and pursuing a nonaligned foreign policy—via political, military, and diplomatic means.

Nation-Building and State-Building

Even 75 years after its independence, Myanmar has yet to become a nation; there is little evidence to suggest that there is a sense of "imagined political community" among the citizens of the country.[3] The Panglong Agreement signed on February 12, 1947 among the representatives of the Executive Council of the Governor of Burma, the Federated Shan States, the Kachin Hills, and the Chin Hills did not produce lasting national unity among the citizens of the Union of Myanmar. Besides the notion of nationhood being minimal, the postcolonial state in Myanmar was equally weak. Not long after independence, as correctly argued by Robert H. Taylor, the Myanmar state was displaced as the creator of political order and economic direction and functionally lost its hegemonic position. Moreover, as Taylor pointed out, "the state was not only no longer able to determine many of the conditions of social and economic life, but also became a rival object for control by groups possessing different perceptions of what kind of society Burma (Myanmar) should be."[4] The state was challenged by various societal and political forces both at the center and the periphery. Moreover, the legacy of the colonial policy of divide and rule, which created a division between "administrative Burma" and "scheduled or frontier areas" in terms of governmental institutions, suggested that frontier areas had never been properly under the central state apparatus and authority. The colonial government in British Burma had hardly facilitated the process of nation-building and state-building, consequently generating general misperception and misconception among ethnic nationalities and subsequently leading to the breakdown in communication, trust, and confidence among them. The combination of all these factors complicated the national unity and triggered internal armed conflicts.

With a devastated war-torn economy, a lack of nationhood with a weak state and governmental institutions, a tendency for separatism, and the growing impact of regional great powers rivalries, postcolonial Myanmar was ripe for internal armed conflicts. Therefore, the Myanmar government faced a pressing task of nation-building and state-building that is far from over yet. Even after more than seven decades, the Myanmar state remains weak, feeble, and fragile in many respects, and it is nonexistent in many different parts of the country. The lack of peace, security, stability, and law and order is still persistent and prevalent in the country. Even as of 2023, there are over 100,000 antistate armed ethnic fighters in Myanmar. Challenges to nation-building and state-building are insurmountable, and it will take years, if not decades, to resolve internal armed conflicts that have lasted over seven decades.

At the time of the country's independence, to make the Union of Myanmar a modern nation-state, political elites envisioned that the state would implement democratic socialism and adopt a socialist model of national development in the process of nation-building and state-building. The 1947 Constitution, the Declaration of Independence, the Presidential Address to the Constituent Assembly (Parliament) on the day of Independence, and the prime minister's address at the ceremony for laying the foundation for the Independence Landmark Pillar on January 4, 1948, indicated that Myanmar would be a democratic socialist nation. President Sao Shwe Thaik, in his address to the assembly known as "The Goals of Independent Burma," stated that "our primary objective that is always looking forward and aspire to is to abolish capitalism in the Union and to establish a socialist state that has a guarantee for all citizens to own the nation's production of good and services."[5] Likewise, Prime Minister Thakin Nu promised to build a new republic where there would be no more exploitation of man by man or the exploitative class.[6] The 1947 Constitution and the Declaration of Independence guaranteed liberty, equality, fraternity, and justice for all nationalities living in the Union.[7]

However, despite all these policies and promises, not long after the historic moment of national independence, fissures appeared along ideological lines and ethnic dimensions. The Burma Communist Party (BCP) commenced an armed revolution in March 1948 and the Karen National Defence Organization (KNDO) rebelled in February 1949, triggering a series of insurrections and insurgencies in Myanmar, and fundamentally weakened the state. The truth is that the prolonged insurgency, factional struggle within the ruling party, electoral politics, and external security challenges, such as Kuomintang (KMT) aggression, had derailed the initial aspiration of building Myanmar as a democratic socialist nation from the onset.

Meanwhile, the Tatmadaw (Myanmar military) started to work on a political ideology that could guide its officers and rank soldiers. In October 1952, the Tatmadaw published *Sit-Hna-Lone* Bulletin No. (1), titled "Our Future Direction," and questioned the goals of the Union while positing that "the independence that we gained after the anti-imperialist struggle is not yet our goal but building a paradise on earth (*Lawka Neikban*) for the people—emancipation, meaning democratic socialism, by making use of independence or sovereign authority, while avoiding the bloodshed as much as possible, is our goal and the State's future direction."[8] By 1958 the Tatmadaw had firmly developed its guiding political ideology and philosophy, based primarily on its own version of socialism, nationalism, and Buddhism.

Soon after the military takeover of the state on March 2, 1962, in the name of the Revolutionary Council (RC) and projecting a self-image as the vanguard of revolution in Myanmar, the Tatmadaw declared "the Burmese Way to Socialism (BWS)" in April 1962 and "the System of Correlation of Man and His Environment" in January 1963. This time, rather than democratic socialism, the new leaders announced that they would build a socialist democracy in Myanmar, emphasizing the "socialist" element. The BWS would go on to serve as the guiding principle for nation-building and state-building in Myanmar for next two and a half decades. Blaming a multiparty democracy as the culprit behind the failure to realize a socialist society (*Socialit Lubaung*) in Myanmar, the RC introduced a law in July 1964 banning all political parties except the Burma Socialist Programme Party (BSPP) that it helped establish on July 4, 1962. The BWS addressed the question of nationalities by declaring that it was "only when the solidarity of all the indigenous racial groups has been established that socialist economy which can guarantee the welfare if every racial group can be achieved."[9] At the same time the RC announced its policy on nationalities. Nevertheless, despite its best effort to promote fairness among nationalities and sociopolitical mobilization within the framework of a socialist democracy under a single-party leadership, the BWS failed to satisfy the political aspirations of various ethnic minorities and failed to end insurgencies while it managed to co-opt aboveground left-wing political forces. The state-building program made limited progress as it focused on countering insurgencies in the central and delta areas of the country. Meanwhile, border areas were firmly under the control of various insurgent groups. The state remained weak and the nation feeble.

Following twenty-six years of the Burmese Way to Socialism, the Myanmar state remained weak and still had to confront more than a dozen insurgent groups. National unity thus remained unattainable. The nation-building and state-building project was far behind expectations. There were mass protests against BSPP rule and demands for political changes—such as a multiparty democracy—that resulted in the fall of the BSPP, ushering into a new era of military rule for nearly twenty-two years. On the day of the military takeover of the state, September 18, 1988, the Tatmadaw declared what was known as "Our Three Main National Causes" (OTMNC). This was done under the name of the State Law and Order Restoration Council (SLORC), later renamed as the State Peace and Development Council (SPDC) on November 15, 1997. Building national unity was at the top of the new rulers' political agenda. Starting from early 1989, the SLORC government entered a series of ceasefire agreements, more commonly known as peace settlements, with various insurgent groups. By 2000 the government claimed that there were seventeen groups covered by the arrangement. Having realized the reality of national disunity, the military regime called for a "national reconsolidation" as one of its political objectives when it announced the "Twelve Objectives" in July 1995. The government explained that "national reconsolidation" was a step higher than "national reconciliation." Meanwhile, starting from the early 1990s, the military regime had been working on a concept of "Union Spirit" and eventually came up with a monograph on the subject by the end of that decade. The monograph, entitled "Union Spirit," published in 2000, defined the concept as follows:

> The Union Spirit is the established notion of regarding the entire Union as a family or a household. It is based on patriotism, the sense of safeguarding the race and promoting the welfare of the race with attachment to the bloodline and land. The sense of mutual help among the people of the Union, the will to solve problems upon being encountered with them, the sense of cooperation on a mutually

> beneficial basis, mutual sympathy and understanding, forgiveness and patience are the fundamental virtuous attributes of Union Spirit. The most important aspect is to have good nature, honesty and straightforwardness. The seed of Union Spirit can thrive well on the land of honesty, simplicity and good nature.[10]

Prior to the release of the monograph, Senior General Than Shwe, chairman of the SPDC, also explained on April 7, 1999, that

> Union Spirit is the spirit that binds all citizens in unity no matter in which section, which region they may reside. Union Spirit is built on the spirit of nationalism that engenders nationals to love, cherish and value a single motherland, our mother nation, and work for its prosperity. In a way, Union Spirit is that of oneness and unity of nationals who have lived together with affection, in weal or woe on the same land drinking the same water for a very long time.[11]

Throughout the 2000s, the OTMNC, the Twelve Objectives, and the Union Spirit were regularly featured in mass media and highlighted at important political occasions. In reality, the ceasefire agreements were nothing but armed peace, and there was little progress on national reconsolidation. The Union Spirit appeared rhetorical. Despite a big expansion in the number and scope of governmental institutions, the state remained weak.

In accordance with the 2008 constitution, general elections were held across the country in 2010, leading to the transfer of power from the military regime to a constitutional government headed by a pro-military party, the Union Solidarity and Development Party (USDP), in March 2011. The constitution itself incorporated the OTMNC as basic principles and called for a "genuine, disciplined multi-party democratic system" in Myanmar. The USDP administration carried over the banner of national reconsolidation and initiated a process of peace negotiation, resulting in the signing of the Nationwide Ceasefire Agreement (NCA) between the government and eight ethnic armed organizations (EAOs) in October 2015. By then, it was agreed that the future of Myanmar should be to build on a "democratic federal union" where the OTMNC and the Union Spirit are instrumental.

After the general elections of November 2015, the National League for Democracy (NLD) came to power in March 2016. The NLD administration continued to use the Union Spirit, with a slight modification: to engage in national reconciliation and nation-building. In his message on the seventieth anniversary of Union Day on February 12, 2017, the first such occasion to be held under the NLD administration, President Htin Kyaw stated that "Union Spirit is the source of building a democratic federal union. Union Spirit means the strong determination of all the national people to live in unity, having negotiation in building a union. We are sure that there will never be a democratic federal union without strong and genuine union spirit." In other words, "building a democratic federal union," which is considered as "the solution to end up the long-lasting armed conflicts and to get national reconciliation" is based on the Union Spirit, and the message called for the development of the Union Spirit and the strengthening of the national unity. Likewise, the NLD administration continued to uphold the OTMNC. During the seventy-third anniversary of Union Day, President Win Myint, following the national objectives of said occasion, again urged all citizens "to strive for non-disintegration of the Union, non-disintegration of the national solidarity, and perpetuation of sovereignty with the united effort of all national brethren, and to continue to carry out the successful implementation of the peace process with the union spirits." Therefore, the OTMNC and the Union Spirit firmly remain in Myanmar's political discourse and security lexicon.[12] At the same time, the NLD administration initiated a series of peace conferences, known as the 21st Century Panglong. As a result, after four such occasions, a total of seventy-one points were agreed upon as part of the "Union Accord."[13] The process has been temporarily suspended since February 2021. The military coup in February 2021 has triggered a widespread armed resistance, even in the areas traditionally considered as Bamar's heartland, and undermined the NCA, further weakening the state-building and nation-building in Myanmar. As a result, by late 2024, the state is so weak that it has lost control over much of its territorial reach in Northern Shan State, the Sagaing Region, and Rakhine State.

Development of Domestic Military Capabilities

While the nation-building and state-building programs are sociopolitical means to enhance national resilience and state security as well as to forge national unity, developing military capabilities is instrumental in safeguarding the OTMNC. As the most serious threat to national survival was internal, the Tatmadaw devoted its resources to developing counterinsurgency capabilities. After nearly four years of security operations following independence in 1948, the central government regained control over major cities across the country and managed to keep the Union intact. When it was about to end the darkest days of its postcolonial existence, however, the Union encountered a foreign aggression by the KMT. With its limited capacity to engage in conventional regular combat, the Tatmadaw launched several operations to drive the KMT aggressors out of the Union's territory. Generally, for nearly forty years following independence, the Tatmadaw maintained armed forces only capable of counter-insurgency operations. The doctrine, structure, armament, and training of the Tatmadaw reflected the need to confront insurgent warfare. It was insurgency forces, both ideological and secessionist, that undermined the OTMNC and the survival of the Union. In 1964 the Tatmadaw introduced a "People's War" doctrine to deal with external and internal security challenges. After the breakdown of peace discussions in 1963, the government resorted to military means to deal with insurgencies, to safeguard the OTMNC, and to enhance security.

In 1988 it was estimated that the Tatmadaw had about 186,000 soldiers, mostly infantry, with a small number of warships, aircrafts, tanks, and artilleries dating back to World War II or similarly outdated. There were indeed limited or no capabilities that could withstand any sizable external aggression. However, external security challenges to the grand strategy of national survival—territorial integrity and national sovereignty—were managed through strict adherence to a nonaligned foreign policy by staying away from Cold War great power rivalry. Arms procurement was diversified to make sure that Myanmar did not lean toward any superpower. At the same time a domestic small arms industry was developed to equip the country's troops. In this way the Myanmar government defended the national sovereignty and territorial integrity and prevented the Union from disintegration. It had managed to hold the Union territory together. In fact, the BCP's attempt to establish a liberated zone that could have resulted in a separate political entity, breaking up the Union, had failed due mainly to the Tatmadaw's military operations.

Since the early 1990s the Myanmar government has viewed externally sponsored proxy wars and/or military interventions seeking regime change as a significant security challenge to the survival of the Union. The military doctrine was accordingly modified to meet the new challenges. By the early 1990s the Tatmadaw started a large-scale force modernization program. Not only did it expand the size of the army and establish new battalions across the country, it also bought advanced weaponries including tanks, aircrafts, artilleries, and air defense missiles. For a decade China was a major arms supplier and a source of military training since Myanmar was under sanctions imposed by Europe and the United States. At the same time, the military regime was increasingly concerned with the US's forceful military interventions seeking regime change in different parts of the world during the post-Cold War era. In order to address these security challenges, the military regime relied on a doctrine known as "People's War [under Modern Conditions]," a defensive strategy of nationwide asymmetric guerrilla warfare should the standing conventional force fail to defeat an invading force on the beachheads or landing zones. These state actors could either employ proxies or directly intervene to undermine the national sovereignty and territorial integrity.[14] The success of this doctrine depends on the Tatmadaw's capacity to mobilize public support for its security operations.

Force modernization was carried out with a view toward building a standard army capable of fighting a conventional, regular war either sponsored or initiated by an external power. In other words, this was conventional deterrence to guarantee the security and survival of the Union. However, during the early phase of the force modernization, the newly acquired military capabilities were limited. The armed clashes with the Thai military throughout 2001 exposed the weakness of the Tatmadaw. As a result the Tatmadaw shifted its sources of arms procurement from China to other countries, most importantly Russia, and bought more advanced weaponry, including multirole fighters, modern frigates, advanced air defense systems, and so on. Since the early 2000s the Tatmadaw improved the quality of its military capabilities for the purposes of conventional deterrence and fighting a conventional regular war. Joint services and combined arms exercises were then eventually regularized since the 2010s.

In his address at the Seventy-Fourth Anniversary of Tatmadaw, the commander-in-chief said that "the best guarantee for the perpetuation of State sovereignty is the possession of powerful defence force."[15] The Tatmadaw paid attention to modernization of the navy, air force, and air defenses. Within two decades, by the end of 2021, the Tatmadaw commissioned two submarines—although they are only good enough for training—five frigates, three corvettes, two offshore patrol vessels and several smaller warships. Credible reports indicated that a total of ninety-four various types of vessels, built by naval shipyards, were commissioned between 2011 and 2021.[16] The navy started to plan the acquisition of a sea-denial capability, and it is reportedly being developed into a "Three-Dimensional Combat Ready Navy" in the first phase of modernization. With regards to the Air Force, the Tatmadaw purchased thirty-two MiG-29B/UB, fifty K-8 Trainers, twelve YaK-30 fighter aircrafts, sixteen JF-17 fighter aircrafts, ten Mil Mi-24P/35P gunships, and six Su-30 fighter aircraft between 2001 and 2021. In the view of the Myanmar security elites, these military capabilities and the territorial expansion of military units across the country could provide sufficient power to safeguard the OTMNC and thus the survival of the Union of Myanmar as a nation-state.

Pursuance of a Nonaligned Foreign Policy

In the early days following the country's independence, Myanmar's foreign cum security policy was based on the twin pillars of collective security centered on the United Nations and the collective defense provided by alliances with likeminded states, particularly a great power.[17] On the day of independence, the president mentioned that Myanmar was to maintain friendly relations with other countries while forming alliances with likeminded states.[18] At the peak of the post-independence insurgency period, the then deputy prime minister and foreign minister advocated the idea of joining a Western alliance.[19] When it realized that such an alliance was not forthcoming and that the United States was siding with the KMT aggressors, Myanmar decided to follow a nonaligned foreign policy. Throughout the 1950s Myanmar maintained an active foreign policy, yet its activism became less pronounced during the RC/BSPP era. Rather than pursuing multilateralism, Myanmar's foreign relations were based on bilateralism. Throughout the Cold War period, Myanmar strictly followed a nonaligned foreign policy. By the early 1970s Myanmar adopted an independent and active nonaligned foreign policy. The purpose of such policy was to steer away from great power rivalry and to maintain good relations with all of the great powers. In this way the Union's political independence could be preserved and national sovereignty respected. There should be no reason for any external power to interfere in Myanmar's internal affairs, and the foreign policy served to minimize the impact of great power politics on the Union. At one stage this went to such an extent that Myanmar followed an isolationist foreign policy.

Under the broad umbrella of nonaligned foreign policy, bilateral relationships were adjusted to serve the best interests of the Union. Among them, perhaps, Myanmar's relations with China were the most important. Despite the fact that China could be a source of security threats, Myanmar dealt with its neighbor in a delicate manner focused on neither balancing nor bandwagoning. In 1954 Prime Minister U Nu explained the fear of China's invasion or intervention in Myanmar among the country's people, thus "destroying Myanmar's independence."[20] The Myanmar government was fully aware of China's geopolitical and geostrategic interests in the country. In reality the Myanmar government has been dealing with the fundamental question of how to deal with China in order to preserve the country's political independence, national sovereignty, and territorial integrity since its independence.

Being aware of this geopolitical reality, Myanmar was the first noncommunist country to recognize the People's Republic of China (PRC) in December 1949.

As Myanmar faced its own communist insurgency, the government was keenly aware and suspicious that China would support the BCP. Myanmar maintained a "One China" policy and assiduously supported the PRC's bid for UN membership. China's support for the BCP insurgency remained covert until 1968, even if the Myanmar government was aware that China had trained BCP cadres.[21] Meanwhile, as the KMT maintained its forces on Myanmar soil, the country's government was afraid that the PRC might use this as a reason to militarily intervene in Myanmar's affairs. Moreover, there was a territorial dispute along the bilateral border between Myanmar and China, with Beijing claiming a significant portion of the Union's territory. These are key concerns for Myanmar as they undermine the country's sovereignty and territorial integrity. Eventually, the peaceful and successful demarcation of the boundary between Myanmar and China in 1960 partially alleviated the security concerns of the government. At the same time that the boundary treaty was agreed, the Myanmar government signed a treaty of friendship and mutual nonaggression. According to this treaty, Myanmar and China were to recognize and respect the independence, sovereign rights, and territorial integrity of each other.

Having said that, China's leverage over EAOs along the border area was and remains another matter that influences Myanmar's China strategy. As a case in point, China pressured some EAOs not to sign the National Ceasefire Accord of 2015.[22] At the same time Beijing strongly "encouraged" EAOs to join the Union Peace Conferences held by the Myanmar government.[23] While China's influence over EAOs is complex and complicated, it is undeniable that Beijing's role in any Myanmar peace process is important. It is thus Myanmar's nonaligned policy that has helped the country to steer away from being drawn into China's strategic orbit.

Another important aspect in Myanmar's grand strategy is its relations with regional neighbors. Among them, Myanmar has always paid close attention to its relations with Thailand, which is a close ally of the United States and the broader West. Thailand's policy of maintaining a buffer zone along the bilateral border with Myanmar is an important factor informing the government's views. For historical reasons, Thailand seems to view Myanmar as a potential security threat. Thai nationhood was partially based on anti-Myanmar sentiment, and Thai political elites had from time to time seemed to have tried to use this to their advantage.[24] Also, Thailand has supported anti-Naypyidaw insurgent groups in border areas. Moreover, the Myanmar-Thailand border is yet to be demarcated, and there are several disputed areas. During the SLORC/SPDC administration, the military regime believed that Thailand could serve as a springboard for a Western military intervention. On several occasions, skirmishes between military forces of Myanmar and Thailand took place. Since 2011 and thanks to defense diplomacy, the two militaries have maintained a good relationship, and bilateral issues are discussed at several levels on a regular basis. Also, there are multiple bilateral exchanges among delegations from the two countries to promote mutual understanding.

Differently, Myanmar's relations with India, Laos, and Bangladesh have been historically stable and relatively free from trouble. Myanmar also maintains good relations with other regional countries and joined the Association of Southeast Asian Nations (ASEAN) in 1997. Myanmar's decision to join ASEAN could have been motivated by the military regime's desire to enhance its security as it faced growing Western pressure and sanctions. In other words, the Myanmar government appeared to expect that ASEAN would serve as a collective diplomatic shield to limit Western interference in Myanmar's internal affairs while enhancing state and regime security.

EXTERNAL FACTORS

Being a weak state located in a region of great power rivalries, Myanmar's grand strategy is strongly impacted by external factors. The fact that Myanmar is at the junction of Northeast Asia, Southeast Asia, and South Asia means it could be in a geopolitically favorable position to play an important role in regional affairs. However, this has never been the case in any meaningful way. Instead the country is vulnerable to external interference in its domestic affairs. This section discusses the type of actors that Myanmar security elites need to address, the nature of threats the country encounters, and the kinds of conflicts it is prepared to deal with.

The Defence White Paper published and released in 2015 outlined these factors as security challenges in the following terms:

> The main challenges to the Union are military build-up of neighboring countries, provision of equipment, financial assistances and encouragement by external elements to internal armed groups and unsettled boundary issues. In the field of international relations where eternal interest is consistently pursued, certain powerful countries are launching multi-dimensional warfare on smaller countries for their own national interests.[25]

Moreover, for many years and under the banner of "People's Desires" the military regimes—SLORC/SPDC—identified the threats to Myanmar and called for people to "Oppose those relying on external elements, acting as stooges, holding negative views; Oppose those trying to jeopardize stability of the State and progress of the nation; Oppose foreign nations interfering in internal affairs of the State; and Crush all internal and external destructive elements as the common enemy."

In the view of foreign policy and security elites in Myanmar, major sources of security challenges come from both state actors and nonstate actors, including insurgent groups and terrorists. In terms of state actors, Myanmar is concerned with either outright external aggression or proxy war supported by external powers, such as China or the United States. These state actors could either employ proxies or directly intervene to undermine the country's national sovereignty and territorial integrity. As mentioned earlier, Prime Minister U Nu explained the fear of China's invasion or intervention in Myanmar and "destroying Myanmar's independence." In fact, in the mid-1950s, several PLA troops were deployed in border areas claimed by China as its own.

Being next to China, Myanmar is aware of Beijing's strategic interest in the country and also that it could undermine Naypyidaw's sovereignty and territorial integrity. China could use its proxies, particularly insurgent groups, to destabilize the regime, to undermine the state, and to threaten the country's territorial integrity and national sovereignty without the need of a military intervention. Historically, China supported insurgent groups in the border areas and exercised a degree of influence over them.[26] Some security analysts in Myanmar believe that China maintains some EAOs or insurgent groups as its proxies.

Another state actor that could undermine the OTMNC and threaten Myanmar's security, particularly the regime's security, is the United States. The threat perception was particularly high in the 1990s and 2000s, when the nature of the perceived threat was either a military intervention or proxy war to achieve regime change. Two officers who are close to Myanmar security elites explain:

> In the 1990s, after the collapse of the "Eastern Bloc," under the slogan of "New World Order," the West led by the United States had interfered in Myanmar internal affairs. Myanmar was a soft target for the West in their pursuit of their agenda of global domination. Through economic sanctions, diplomatic pressure, tacit military support for insurgents, and various forms of support for and control of anti-government organizations, the West had pursued a multidimensional warfare on Myanmar.[27]

Some observers noted that even the relocation of the national capital from Yangon to Naypyidaw in central Myanmar was partially influenced by a possible scenario of invasion or proxy war by the United States and its allies.

This would have included a land-based invasion from the east and amphibious operation from the west.[28]

Perhaps nonstate actors, among them insurgencies, are the most serious security challenge to the Union and have strongly impacted Myanmar's grand strategy. The Defence White Paper of 2015 outlined that the "diversity of ethnic groups and existence of armed groups and their chance to take refuge along boundaries became challenges to national security." Myanmar is home to long-running insurgencies, and they are not only threats to national security and territorial integrity but also detrimental to the grand strategy of survival as a modern nation-state.

In his message on the third anniversary of Independence Day, on January 4, 1951, after three years of insurgencies, President Sao Shwe Thaik stated: "If the Union of Burma is to retain her independence and if she is to develop, there is a grimmer and sturdier struggle lying ahead of her... In the greatest task that lies before the Union of Burma we need men who are Union-conscious, Union-minded, for with unity of aim and singleness of purpose, we can, while working for our own welfare, become an asset to the comity of nations which is out to make the world a better place to live in."[29] Even seventy years after this presidential message, the Union of Myanmar is still plagued with insurgencies and rebellions, and these nonstate actors are primary threats to the Union and the Myanmar state.

With regard to non-state actors, the military regime viewed terrorist organizations, such as the Arakan Rohingya Salvation Army (ARSA), as major threats with a tendency to challenge the territorial integrity of the Union. Others include political parties and non-governmental organizations that are considered as hostile toward the military regime and anti-state, serving the interests of the "external elements."

In terms of the nature of this threat, Myanmar security elites believe that the county is facing multidimensional warfare via political, economic, social, ideological propaganda, diplomatic, and military means. By using antistate organizations and ethnic armed groups, in the view of the security elites, external powers can politically and militarily intervene in Myanmar affairs and undermine the OTMNC. These challenges are to be dealt with by building national resilience and enhancing state security.

DOMESTIC FACTORS

Before discussing the impact of factors endogenous to Myanmar's grand strategy, it is important to start with an explanation about security elites in Myanmar. Due to the almost uninterrupted dominance of the military in both the political process and national-level policymaking, it is safe to argue that the Tatmadaw—which considers itself as the guardian of the state, or even perhaps as the embodiment of the state—is the most important institution in shaping Myanmar's security policy and grand strategy. The security elites are essentially senior military commanders, and their security perception and worldview prevails in the country's grand strategy. For all practical purposes, this near monopoly on the conceptualization and prioritization of national security by the military-dominated security elites has effectively insulated the existing security discourse from any other perceptions, and it remains essentially state-centric. The concept of "National Unity is essential; State Capacity is primary; Internal Strength is forever" forms the cornerstone of national security policy and, as a result, Myanmar's grand strategy. There is little information publicly available on how the security elites discusses, debates and deliberates grand strategy. However, the National Defence College (NDC) that almost all senior commanders are required to attend since the late 1990s is the most likely venue for such matter. The yearlong master's degree program at the NDC includes seminars on the political, economic, and security affairs of Myanmar, studies focusing on Myanmar's security and, finally, an exercise focusing on drafting a security policy and grand strategy for Myanmar. According to the 2008 Constitution, the National Defence and Security Council (NDSC), composed of eleven members—at least six of which represent the Tatmadaw—is where senior military commanders and elected officials will meet to discuss matters related to national security. Yet it is not a place to debate and discuss the details. This body, in any case, has been dysfunctional since 2016 as the NLD administration has never convened a meeting.

At the core of Myanmar's grand strategy of survival, as explained earlier, is the OTMNC, which could be considered as the most important core national values. Myanmar has consistently encountered challenges to core national values as both external and internal destructive elements that have persistently undermined the national unity and territorial integrity of the Union. The Union Spirit, as discussed before, is fundamental in safeguarding the OTMNC. The country's geography, history, and strategic culture are factors that inform the core values of Myanmar's grand strategy.

As for its geography, Myanmar is located at the junction of South, Southeast, and Northeast Asia. With a total land area of 261,228 square miles (676,578 km^2), bounded by 3,906 miles of land border shared with five neighboring countries and 1,385 miles of coastline, populated by more than a hundred different national races that together comprise about 55 million people, located strategically on the Indochina Peninsula that bridges the

Indian Ocean and the Pacific Ocean, and situated between the two most populous nations—India and China, also centuries-old great civilizations—Myanmar has a long history of maintaining and retaining its political entity and cultural identity and shaping its destiny. Historically speaking, its physiographic features and demographic characteristics made precolonial Myanmar essentially a (dry) land-based power, with little interest in its maritime borders. Consequently, until recently, Myanmar's grand strategy and security policy were informed by an inward-looking perception.

Historical memories of precolonial and colonial Myanmar cast a strong influence on Myanmar's grand strategy. For many centuries, under different dynasties, Myanmar remained an independent polity located more or less on the same stretch of land. Ancient Myanmar kingdoms withstood external aggressions, particularly against Yuan troops in the thirteenth century and Qing forces in the eighteenth century. At the same time, they extended their influence or suzerainty over several polities located on mainland Southeast Asia. However, in the nineteenth century Myanmar lost three wars against British troops and became a colony. With a proud history behind it, this was the most humiliating moment for the people of Myanmar. Therefore, the collective memory of anticolonial struggle and the national liberation movement has been an epitome of Myanmar historiography, framing a mainstream nationalist discourse and shaping its postcolonial political-security outlook.

If the strategic culture, as defined by Ken Booth, is "a nation's traditions, values, attitudes, patterns of behavior, habits, symbols, achievements, and particular ways of adapting to the environment and solving problems with respect to the threat or use of force,"[30] Myanmar has its distinctive strategic culture. When encountering external security challenges, traditionally, Myanmar fiercely fought even against much more powerful forces. Diplomacy was thus not necessarily the first choice for dealing with security threats. Besides, Myanmar's political culture is also weak in seeking compromise and consensus. In essence, the country's geography, history, and strategic culture are reinforcing each other and together shape the country's grand strategy.

As a weak developing state, Myanmar has limited resources and capacity to deal with various threats and challenges to its security and national survival at the same time. Most of the time, therefore, the priority is to deal with internal security threats. When security elites believe that the threat to national survival is more closely related to external intervention or externally sponsored proxies rather than internal forces, they prioritize the capabilities to deter, deny, and degrade the ability of these external elements to act on this perceived threat.

CONCLUSION

As a weak state, the Union of Myanmar's survival and security as a modern nation-state has been at the core of the country's grand strategy. This essentially encompasses maintaining and attaining long-lasting national sovereignty, territorial integrity, and national unity. The Myanmar government has persistently pursued its grand strategy through political, military, and diplomatic means. The content and context of Myanmar's grand strategy is defined and characterized by a persistent domestic political and security necessity, and it is remarkably consistent. Myanmar is plagued with a chronic problem of national disunity resulting in feeble nationhood and a weak state, and it is still a union without unity. National disunity is the vulnerability that could be exploited by others to undermine territorial integrity and national sovereignty.

The issue of national unity has always been at the top of the political and security agenda for successive administrations in postcolonial Myanmar. The national unity ceremonially forged at Panglong in February 1947 had never been solid or consolidated; it remains frail and fragile. The traditional asymmetric tributary pattern of center-periphery relations in the precolonial era, the effects of the British divide-and-rule policy with the ascendency of ethnic consciousness among ethnic minorities in colonial times, and the inability and insufficiency of successive administrations in postcolonial Myanmar polity, largely dominated by majority ethnic Bamars, to meet the political inspiration of ethnic minorities have resulted in long-lasting armed conflicts. Myanmar is thus unable to resolve the issue of long-lasting insurgencies. This is further compounded by external interference in Myanmar's affairs. The pomp and magnificent celebration of the Union Day on February 12 is a major event in Myanmar; however, it remains symbolic rather than having real substance. The threat to Myanmar's grand strategy is therefore largely internal, with the possibility that it could be exploited by external elements. While deterrence and diplomacy will alleviate the threats and challenges to Myanmar's security or grand strategy of national survival coming from state actors, unless the issue of national disunity is resolved, the effectiveness of these instruments is certainly questionable.

Some may wonder why Myanmar has opted for such strategic priorities in its grand strategy. Apart from historical and geographical factors, the political reality of a weak state, feeble nation, and regional great powers rivalry in the early years of the country's postcolonial existence defines the context and content of Myanmar's grand strategy. For all practical purposes, the state has been the referent object facing this existential threat—both territorial and institutional; therefore, the survival (and security) of the state has been at the core of Myanmar's grand strategy, and that is where the OTMNC is instrumental. While the OTMNC is the primary political goal, it has been further supplemented by other political agendas, such as building Myanmar as a socialist nation-state. The powerful role of socialism as an ideological instrument in the national liberation struggle has deeply impacted and dictated the course of Myanmar's politics, and some could even argue that it was a historical necessity. While it was not a political aspiration nor an imagined community among many non-Bamar nationalities, for most Bamar nationalists socialist Burma was indeed the postcolonial state/nation-building project, not without further implications on national unity. In order to deal with both internal armed challenges, as a result of national disunity, and external aggression against the state, when it appeared that no meaningful political accommodation and diplomatic solutions were feasible, the Myanmar government has prepared to deal with them by building up the military capabilities while preventing external interference through a nonaligned foreign policy.

The geopolitical and geostrategic reality of Myanmar in the context of growing rivalry among regional and extraregional great powers has influenced Myanmar's grand strategy. Assessing the opportunities and challenges that result from the shift in the global distribution of power has been an important part of grand strategy formulation and adjustment among political elites and the security establishment of Myanmar. Any possibility of spill-over effects coming from regional armed conflicts or resulting from fighting a proxy war has constantly informed Myanmar's grand strategy. In terms of domestic factors, the country's demographic characteristics, historical and collective memory of anticolonial struggle or nationalist movement, strategic culture of dealing with external security challenges in both the precolonial and contemporary eras, and preoccupation with internal armed challenges to the state as Myanmar's security predicament are critically shaping the country's grand strategy. For all practical purposes, Myanmar's military establishment has exercised hegemony over the conceptualization, strategizing, and operationalization of the country's grand strategy.

If Myanmar's grand strategy is just simply to safeguard and fulfil the OTMNC, then holding the country together could be a testimony of serving its objectives. However, if it is eventually to overcome the challenges to the OTMNC and move forward to be a modern nation-state in the international family of nations, then it does not meet its expectations. Although Myanmar may aspire to be a dynamic regional player in Southeast Asia, the reality is that it is too much preoccupied with saving the state from being disintegrated.

NOTES

1. Thierry Balzacq, Peter Dombrowski, and Simon Reich (eds.), *Comparative Grand Strategy: A Framework and Cases* (Oxford University Press, 2019); Barry R. Posen, *Restraint: A New Foundation for U.S. Grand Strategy* (Cornell University Press, 2014), 1.
2. In Myanmar, it is not unusual to see the conflated use of regime security, state security, and national security. National security could simply mean regime security, particularly during the military regime.
3. This idea is borrowed from Benedict Anderson's classic work titled *Imagined Community: Reflections on the Origin and Spread of Nationalism* (Verso, 1983).
4. Robert H. Taylor, *The State in Myanmar* (Hurst & Company, 2009), 219.
5. *Presidential Address at the Constituent Assembly on January 4, 1948* (author's private collection).
6. "Prime Minister Thakin Nu's Address at the Ceremony for Laying Foundation for Independence Landmark Pillar y on January 4, 1948" in *Pyidaungsu Pantaing [Union's Goal]*, in Myanmar language (Sarpay Beikman Press, 1955), 20–24.
7. *Preamble to the 1947 Constitution; the Declaration of Independence* (author's private collection).
8. Education Section (War Office), *NgaDoet ShaeShuChet [Our Future Direction]*, in Myanmar language (War Office, October 1952), 24.
9. *The Burmese Way to Socialism* (Information Department of the Revolutionary Council, 1962), 7.
10. *The Union Spirit* (News and Periodicals Enterprise, 2000), 5.
11. *The New Light of Myanmar* (April 8, 1999).
12. On the other hand, some EAOs and public intellectuals came up with an alternative discourse framed as the "Panglong Spirit," yet the term never entered into official lexicons, with an exception in the presidential messages on the Shan State Day and Union Day on February 7 and 12, 2014, respectively.
13. The first Peace Conference (or Twenty-First Century Panglong Conference) was held in August–September 2016. It was followed by the second, third, and fourth in May 2017, July 2018, and August 2020, respectively. Part I of the Union Accord was signed on May 29, 2017, followed by Part II on July 17, 2018, and Part III on August 21, 2020.
14. Maung Aung Myoe, *Building the Tatmadaw: Myanmar Armed Forces since 1948* (ISEAS Press, 2009), 36.
15. *Myawady Newspaper* (December 25, 2021), 18.
16. *Myawady Newspaper* (December 25, 2021), 19.
17. Maung Aung Myoe, "Myanmar Foreign Policy: Principles and Practice" in Takashi Inoguchi (ed.) *The SAGE Handbook of Asian Foreign Policy*, Vol. II, 768–9.
18. President Sao Shwe Thaik's Address at the Constituent Assembly on January 4, 1948 (author's private collection).

19. In February 1950, Chief of Staff Lieutenant General Ne Win asked his close friend, Bo Setkya, to contact the US embassy in Yangon to find out the possibility of joining a Pacific pact.
20. Prime Minister U Nu et al., *Gandalarit Hmut-Tan (Record on China)*, in Myanmar language (Burma Translation Society, 1955), 3–4.
21. In fact, during the internal peace talks in 1963, many of these China-trained BCP cadres came back to Myanmar and later joined their party's HQ in Bago Yoma.
22. "Myanmar Official Accuses China of Meddling in peace Talks with Rebels," *The Guardian* (October 9, 2015), https://www.theguardian.com/world/2015/oct/09/myanmar-official-accuses-china-of-meddling-in-peace-talks-with-rebels.
23. Lawi Weng, "Chinese Envoy Encourages UWSA, Mongla Group to Participate in Peace Conference," *The Irrawady Online*, https://www.irrawaddy.com/news/burma/chinese-envoy-encourages-uwsa-mongla-group-to-participate-in-peace-conference.html
24. Pavin Chachavalpongpun, *Plastic Nation: The Curse of Thainess in Thai-Burmese Relations* (Rowman & Littlefield, 2010).
25. Ministry of Defence, *The Defence of Myanmar–White Paper* (Ministry of Defence, 2015), 5.
26. For instance, according to Myanmar intelligence sources, between 1968 and 1978, the PRC supplied the BCP with about 30,000 rifles, millions of rounds of ammunition, an unknown quantity of mines and hand grenades, a few hundred heavy artillery pieces, about Yuan 20 million for general expenditure, over sixty trucks, various military equipment, and several thousand sets of uniforms. Moreover, the PRC provided intercepted combat intelligence for the BCP troops and sent military advisors. [Maung Aung Myoe, *In the Name of Pauk-Phaw: Myanmar's China Policy since 1948* (ISEAS Press, 2011), 81–82.]
27. Sithu Aung and Maung Hmet, *ShwePyiTaw Hmyaw Mawae PiMoet [Golden Land Is No Longer in Distance]*, in Myanmar language, updated edition (Myawady Press, 2020), 544.
28. Maung Aung Myoe, *The Road to Naypyitaw: Making Sense of the Myanmar Government's Decision to Move its Capital*, ARI Working Paper No. 73 (Asia Research Institute, National University of Singapore, 2006).
29. Sao Shwe Thaik, "President's Message to the Nation," *Burma: The Third Anniversary* (Director of Information, 1951), 5.
30. Ken Booth, "The Concept of Strategic Culture Affirmed," in Carl G. Jacobsen (ed.), *Strategic Power: USA/USSR* (Palgrave Macmillan, 1990), 121.

CHAPTER 9

The Philippines

Renato Cruz De Castro

Since the Philippines became an independent republic in 1946, it had never formulated and publicly released a grand strategy until May 16, 2018, when President Rodrigo Duterte signed the country's first National Security Strategy (NSS). This was because, for more than sixty-five years, the Philippines focused its security attention and efforts on containing social unrest generated by economic inequality and the lack of national cohesion. However, this pervasive preoccupation with internal security was disturbed in 2011 when President Benigno Aquino III implemented a strategy of balancing or challenging China's expansive maritime claim in the West Philippine Sea/South China Sea. In late 2016, however, Duterte unraveled his predecessor's strategy of balancing China's expansive claim in the South China Sea by adopting a policy of appeasement. Applying this policy, he extended two key diplomatic concessions to China—downgrading the Philippine-US alliance and putting aside the July 12, 2016, arbitral ruling.

This chapter examines the Philippines' changing grand strategy in the face of China's maritime expansion in the South China Sea. It raises the following central question: What is the Philippine grand strategy in a changing Indo-Pacific region? It also addresses the following corollary questions: What are the domestic and external factors that influenced the Philippines' efforts to develop a grand strategy in the twenty-first century? What are the security challenges confronting the Philippines? What are the roles of external actors in formulating the Philippine grand strategy? What domestic factors affect the development of the Philippine grand strategy? What is the Archipelagic Defense Concept (CADC)? And what is the future of Philippine grand strategy in the face of a rapidly changing Indo-Pacific region?

STRATEGIC PRIORITIES

In 2018 President Duterte signed the first NSS since the Philippines became independent in 1946. It paints a realistic picture of the country's external environment.[1] It indicates that the Philippines has not been confronted by any direct foreign threat since the end of the Second World War. Nevertheless, it warns that the current regional security environment has become increasingly uncertain and dangerous for the country. The 2018 NSS did not mention any specific country that threatens the Philippines. Instead, it raised three important issues concerning the Philippines' external security environment.[2]

1. The perils of traditional geostrategic threats as the competing interests of the great powers and other countries converge, requiring the Philippines to chart its role in an increasingly multipolar system.
2. The need for the Philippines to be fully equipped not only to deter potential aggressors but also to protect the archipelago from international terrorists, pandemics, transnational crimes, and natural disasters.
3. The Philippines must develop a credible defense capability and strengthen its comprehensive strategic alliances or cooperation with its friends and security partners in the international community.

The release of the 2018 NSS coincided with a shift in Philippine policy toward China from appeasement to limited hard balancing. This strategy of limited hard balancing toward China stemmed from the administration's realization that a policy of appeasement requires the weaker party (the Philippines) to put its strategic stakes in the hands of a more powerful state (China), which is harboring hostile intention of maritime expansion in the West Philippine Sea and is bent on exploiting the country's military weakness.

The administration's adoption of this strategy was also partly triggered by Chinese coercive actions against Armed Forces of the Philippines (AFP) units deployed in the West Philippine Sea and the Philippine military's stance against China's expansion into the South China Sea. The distrust of China runs deep in the Philippines society, where Beijing's motives are often seen in the context of the two countries' chronic, long-running dispute over territory in the South China Sea.[3] Public sentiment against the administration's appeasement policy forced the government away from bandwagoning toward China. Instead, it adopted a two-pronged policy. Since 2016 the

Philippines has actively promoted economic cooperation with China and sought a peaceful resolution to the South China Sea dispute. Concurrently, it pursued efforts to counter Chinese maritime expansion by effectively applying the rule of international law.[4]

The Duterte administration's July 12, 2020, decision acknowledging the 2016 United Nations Convention on the Law of the Sea (UNCLOS) ruling on the South China Sea dispute indicates that there are limits to the Philippines' appeasement policy toward China. On the fourth anniversary of the UNCLOS arbitral ruling, Foreign Affairs Secretary Teodoro Locsin declared that the arbitration case initiated and won by the Philippines versus China is a contribution "of great significance and consequence to the peaceful settlement of disputes in the South China Sea and to the peace and stability of the region at large."[5] He said that the tribunal "authoritatively ruled that China's claim of historic rights to resources within the sea areas falling within the nine-dash line has no basis in law." He then mentioned that the tribunal also ruled that "certain actions within the Philippines' EEZ violated the Philippines' sovereign rights and were thus unlawful."[6] He cited that the large-scale reclamation and construction of artificial islands and harvesting endangered marine species had aggravated the disputes in the South China Sea. More significantly, the administration pursued several measures to boost its limited-hard balancing policy toward China.

Limited Hard Balancing Policy

The Duterte administration's pondering on a policy of limited balancing toward China is best manifested by its decision to proceed with the long-term AFP modernization program. In June 2019 Duterte agreed to bankroll the second phase of the AFP's 15-year modernization program. The first phase of the program, running from 2013 to 2017, entailed the acquisition of military equipment mainly for internal defense. The second phase or horizon, from 2018 to 2022, is an ambitious and expensive transition period where the Philippine military will concentrate on arms purchases for territorial defense. Under the updated Horizon 2 of the AFP modernization program, the Philippine military has identified these essential items that had to be acquired from 2018 to 2022: multirole fighters, helicopters, and long-range patrol aircraft for the Philippine Air Force (PAF); frigates, corvettes, and submarines for the Philippine Navy (PN); and multiple launch rocket systems, weaponry, and night fighting equipment for the Philippine Army (PA).[7]

Duterte also decided to maintain the Philippine-US alliance and implement the 2014 Enhanced Defence Cooperation Agreement (EDCA). He also saw that managing the US-Philippine alliance depended on two critical security issues—the South China Sea dispute and the growing ISIS threat in Mindanao. He also decided to bolster the Philippine-Japan security partnership and stabilize Philippine-Australia bilateral relations, suggesting that he saw the need for equibalance among the major powers.

The Duterte administration's efforts are all directed against a specific Chinese policy related to maritime expansion rather than China's emergence as a great power in the Indo-Pacific region. Limited hard balancing involves the Philippines' effective coordination of military and diplomatic efforts to obtain outcomes contrary to China's preference for controlling a large portion of the West Philippine Sea and the waters of the First Island Chain. Limited hard balancing seeks to constrain China's ability to unilaterally impose its preferences on the littoral states of First Island China through limited arms build-up and reliance on a diplomatic coalition of states that will defend their interests.

The Duterte administration's policy of limited hard balancing was aimed at constraining China's expansionist agenda in the South China Sea. It resulted from the defense, military, and foreign affairs establishments challenging former President Duterte's appeasement policy and his administration's belated realization that it needed an impromptu strategy to constrain China's revisionist agenda in the South China Sea. This, in turn, created an impasse within the Duterte administration as it was caught in a bind on whether it would continue its appeasement policy or adopt an approach of limited balancing against China's maritime expansion into the West Philippine Sea in the last few months of its six-year term. At the start of his six-year term, President Ferdinand Marcos Jr. was confronted by his predecessor's unplanned and makeshift strategy of limited hard balancing, which forced him to initiate a well-thought, comprehensive, and formal archipelagic defense doctrine that would guide the Philippines in the next six years.

From Limited Hard Balancing to the Archipelagic Defense Concept

Two and a half years into his term, President Marcos discovered a new and heightened sense of urgency in developing the armed forces' naval capabilities to enhance maritime security in the face of relentless and aggressive Chinese maritime expansion. He adopted a renewed balancing policy toward China that was more vigorous, strategic, and ambitious than his predecessors'. Specifically, his administration's renewed balancing policy entails building up the Philippine military's external defense capabilities, enhancing its alliance with the US by increasing American strategic presence in the Philippines and fostering security arrangements with other American allies like South Korea, Japan, and Australia, and more recently, adopting a Comprehensive Archipelagic Defense Concept (CADC).

CADC aspires to project the country's military power to the country's 200-nautical-mile exclusive economic zone (EEZ). These moves are designed to strengthen the Philippines' diplomatic and strategic posture vis-à-vis Chinese maritime expansion in the South China Sea. However, it is becoming apparent that the Philippines is preparing for another potential flashpoint in its immediate northern neighborhood: Taiwan. In this major undertaking to develop the county's overall resources and capabilities in assuming a comprehensive archipelagic defense approach, the Marcos administration comprehends the urgency to leverage its alliance with the US and strategic partnerships with other US allies like Japan, Australia, South Korea, and India. The *2023–2028 Philippines National Security Policy* empathically states that the Philippines must integrate all the military domains (land, air, maritime, cyber, and space) and nonmilitary spectrums with allies and partners.[8]The CADC represents the Marcos administration's efforts to formulate a formal and comprehensive grand strategy based on the country's archipelagic characteristics in the face of China's maritime expansion in the South China Sea.

EXTERNAL FACTORS

The idea that Chinese maritime expansion is the quintessential threat to Philippine national security began in early 1995 when the PN confirmed the presence of Chinese wooden structures on the Mischief Reef, also known as Panganiban Reef, which is 150 nautical miles from the Philippine westernmost island of Palawa and 620 miles southeast of the southernmost Chinese province of Hainan. This incident was seen then as a form of Chinese incursion that arose from the power vacuum in the regional strategic environment after the end of the Cold War when the US pursued a policy of disengagement from Southeast Asia marked by the withdrawal of its military bases from the Philippines.[9] On February 15, 1995, President Fidel Ramos ordered the strengthening of Filipino military forces near the disputed reef, while the PN implemented Operational Plan *Bantayan* (Guard) to boost naval patrols in the disputed areas as well as to integrate its available ships for joint operations with the PAF.[10]

Eventually, since the beginning of the twenty-first century, the relationship between the Philippines and China has undergone ups and downs. The relationship experienced a golden age during President Gloria Macapagal Arroyo's term when her administration established vibrant economic and diplomatic relations. Then it became highly problematic during Aquino's presidency when the Philippines challenged China's expansive claims in the South China Sea. Philippine-China relations underwent another golden age when Duterte pursued an appeasement policy toward Beijing. This policy is embodied by his and his foreign affairs and defense officials' concerted efforts to foster closer relations with China, coupled with calculated moves to distance the Philippines from the United States and its allies (Japan and Australia) over the South China Sea disputes in particular and in other international issues in general.

Threats and Opportunities

Despite the Duterte administration's efforts to appease China, there is still no evidence that it aligned Philippine foreign policy with China's revisionist goal of maritime expansion in the South China Sea. In other words, the Philippines has not yet bandwagoned toward China. Bandwagoning behavior is confined to weak and isolated states with no choice but to accept greater vulnerability, hoping that the emerging power's appetites for expansion are satisfied or directed elsewhere. The Philippines is not a weak and isolated Southeast Asian state. It is a middle power with a formal treaty alliance with the US and security partnerships with other middle powers such as Japan, Australia, and South Korea. This allows the Philippines to challenge Chinese maritime expansion in the South China Sea despite its limited military capabilities.

China's Maritime Expansion

China's expansion into the South China Sea is the primary security conundrum confronting the Philippines since the second decade of the twenty-first century. This body of water is a semienclosed sea surrounded by China and several small and militarily weak Southeast Asian powers such as the Philippines, Vietnam, Malaysia, and Brunei. These littoral states have been in a chronic competition to extend their jurisdictional claims over a hundred islets, reefs, rocks, and surrounding waters for almost three decades. The dispute became dormant in the late 1990s and the early twenty-first century after China and the Association of Southeast Asian Nations (ASEAN) signed the 2002 Declaration on the Conduct of Parties (DOC) in the South China Sea.

Tension arose again in 2009 when China discarded its tactic of delaying the dispute's resolution and asserted its sovereignty over the contested waters instead. In an assertive posture, China consolidated its jurisdictional claims in the South China Sea by expanding its military reach and pursuing coercive diplomacy against the other claimant states. For instance, it increased its naval patrols using submarines, survey ships, and surface combatants in Vietnam's and the Philippines' EEZs and territorial waters. It intimidated foreign oil companies that tried to operate in the South China Sea.

China's assertiveness in pushing its claims in the South China Sea and East China Sea has increased with the expansion of its navy and maritime services.[11] The Chinese navy backs the official claim of Beijing that the South China Sea is its territorial waters. Hence Vietnamese and Philippine vessels are harassed, detained, or even fired upon by Chinese patrol craft. These are Chinese bullying tactics to pressure these claimant states to back away from the disputed area.[12]

China's naval prowess generates regional tension by challenging the claims of small littoral states over parts of the South China Sea and by changing the strategic pattern in the maritime commons of East Asia and the West Pacific, where the US Navy is still dominant. In August 2010, two months after Benigno Aquino III assumed office, China sent a belligerent signal to the other claimant states—specifically to Vietnam and the Philippines—and the US that its claim of sovereignty over the sea and its islands is "indisputable." The People's Liberation Army Navy (PLAN) three major fleets deployed surface combatants, fighter plane strikes, and missile launches against hypothetical long-range targets when it conducted a live-fire exercise in the South China Sea.[13] Altogether, this show of force demonstrated that China has indisputable sovereignty over the South China Sea and is proof of its rapidly developing capacity to sustain more extensive naval deployment deep into this maritime territory. By the end of the first decade of the twenty-first century, China's nationalism, growing naval prowess, and unilateral actions are overtly directed against a militarily weak Southeast Asian country—the Philippines. Consequently, since 2011, the Philippines has adopted three forms of grand strategy—balancing, appeasement, and limited hard balancing—against China's maritime expansion in the South China Sea.

Balancing China's Maritime Expansion: The Role of the Philippine-US Alliance

The Philippines and the US have maintained close historical ties that started with the American colonization of the archipelago and stemmed from a history of extensive military cooperation during and after the Second World War, common strategic and economic interests, shared democratic values, enduring cultural affinities, and close people-to-people relations.[14] Philippine-US security relations can be traced back to when the archipelago became an American territory at the start of the 1900s. During this period, political and military leaders in Washington anticipated the need for a US naval presence and forward bases in the Pacific Ocean.[15] After the Second World War, American defense strategists retained the Philippine bases. They linked them with other US bases in South Korea, Japan, the Ryukyu Islands, and Taiwan, all located along the sea lines of communication in the Western Pacific. The US included the Philippines in its defense perimeter as part of its containment policy and preserved the islands as a bulwark of US security.[16] Consequently, the Philippines and the US signed a Mutual Defence Treaty (MDT) on August 30, 1951.

During the Cold War, the US maintained two large military bases in the country. It extended military assistance and training to the AFP to neutralize internal security threats against the Philippine state. The American bases loomed large in the host country's security from 1947 to 1991. During the Cold War, the US Seventh Fleet and the Thirteenth Air Force stationed substantial naval and air assets in Subic Bay/Cubi Point naval complex and Clark Air Base—located in Luzon, the main island in the Philippine archipelago. These two US military facilities lent to American strategic posture in East Asia and could respond to any Southeast Asian crisis.[17] They were also committed to the defense of the host country, the Philippines, and of the western Pacific in the event of an armed conflict with either China or the Soviet Union during the Cold War. The American forces operating from the Philippine bases secured sea and air lanes in the Philippines, balanced the Soviet military presence in Cam Ranh Bay, and provided security and defense for the Southeast Asian region.[18] In 1992, however, the US withdrew its military forces and facilities from the country after the Philippine Senate rejected a new agreement extending the lease and use of American-built air force and naval bases on Philippine territory.

Since the withdrawal of American forces from the Philippines in 1992, the Philippine-US alliance has been institutionalized and operationalized by several cooperative arrangements between the two countries' defense departments. The two allies signed the Visiting Forces Agreement (VFA) in 1999 to extend legal guarantees for American servicemen and women conducting joint military exercises with the AFP units in Philippine territory.[19] These exercises have allowed the AFP to develop its readiness to respond to various contingencies and promote cooperation with the US armed forces.[20] They have also developed interoperability in terms of equipment, intelligence, navigation, and communications and, more importantly, military doctrines and common strategic outlook and mindset. These military capabilities have proven invaluable in safeguarding Philippine sovereignty and sovereign rights over parts of the South China Sea.

In mid-June 2011, in the face of China's maritime expansion in the South China Sea, the Aquino administration publicly acknowledged the urgency of US diplomatic and military support. Aware of its military inadequacies, Manila asked for an unequivocal US commitment to Philippine defense and security as provided in the 1951 MDT, specifically American naval/air support in the Spratlys. On April 28, 2014, Defence Secretary Voltaire Gazmin and US Ambassador to the Philippines Philip Goldberg signed the EDCA shortly before US President Obama arrived in Manila for his first state visit. The Aquino administration used the Philippine-US alliance to bolster US military presence in the South China Sea and Southeast Asia. With EDCA as the core of the alliance, the American military footprint in the Philippines was assured.[21]

Balancing China's Maritime Expansion: The Role of the Philippine-Japan Security Partnership

Before 2012 Tokyo and Manila did not find the need to sign or even consider a formal agreement on defense cooperation. Both countries feared that Beijing might misconstrue security cooperation as an anti-Chinese alliance. This thinking, however, changed when the two countries were confronted by China's heavy-handed behavior in the South and East China Seas in the second decade of the twenty-first century. A month after the Scarborough Shoal stand-off, Japanese Defense Minister Satoshi Morimoto and his Filipino counterpart, Gazmin, inked a bilateral agreement on maritime security. A few days later, Foreign Affairs Secretary Albert del Rosario announced that Tokyo would likely provide the Philippine Coast Guard (PCG) with ten 40-meter boats as part of Japan's Official Development Assistance (ODA) to the Philippines by the end of the year.

In his state visit to Japan in early June 2015, Aquino and Prime Minister Abe Shinzo issued a joint declaration on "A Strengthened Strategic Partnership for Advancing the Shared Principles and Goals for Peace, Security, and Growth in the Region and Beyond." The communique encapsulated the Filipino and Japanese commitment to ensure maritime safety and security in the South China Sea and severe opposition to unilateral actions to change the status quo in the contested territory, including China's construction of artificial islands and military outposts on the land features. It also listed Japan's commitments as follows: (1) enhancing the capacity of the PCG; (2) cooperating with the Philippines on maritime security and domain awareness; and (3) exploring the possibility of transferring Japanese defense equipment and technology to the Philippines.

Japan solidified its security relations with the Duterte administration by fostering periodic consultations between the two countries and buttressing the PN's and PCG's maritime domain awareness capabilities. Keeping the partnership intact for the Philippines is necessary because Japan remains the country's most important trading partner, its largest investor, and the home of several thousands of overseas Filipino workers (OFWs) whose regular remittances boost the local economy.[22]

In September 2017, Abe met Duterte for their first summit meeting. Both leaders agreed to enhance maritime security through Japan's provision of two large patrol vessels to the Philippines.[23] During his working visit to Japan from October 25 to 27, Duterte witnessed the signing of the lease of five Japanese Self-Defense Force (JSDF) TC-90 maritime reconnaissance planes to monitor Chinese activities in the South China Sea.[24] Leasing the five TC-90 planes was one of the Duterte administration's important decisions regarding territorial defense, as the AFP lacks valuable assets for maritime domain awareness.[25] Duterte also raised the prospects of the Philippines and Japan holding military exercises in the future.[26]

In March 2018, Japan completed its delivery of five TC-90s to the PN. The five donated reconnaissance aircraft augmented the PN's six 40-year-old Britten-Norman Islanders used in maritime patrol, surveillance, humanitarian assistance and disaster relief (HADR), and rapid assessment missions. The PN plans to purchase more advanced maritime patrol aircraft under its long-range patrol aircraft acquisition program, particularly two long-range reconnaissance aircraft.[27] Along with Abe's pledges for more grants and investment, donating the five TC-90 reconnaissance aircraft to the PN was part of Tokyo's efforts to assist the Philippines economically and militarily.

Japan completed the delivery of ten multirole response vessels (MRRVs) to the PCG in 2018. The PCG stressed that these vessels would be used for routine search and rescue and law-enforcement operations. However, Philippine defense officials have also indicated that the PN could deploy these MRRVs to fight piracy or provide the PN greater capacity to patrol the country's extensive EEZ in the South China Sea.[28] The Philippines' acceptance of this security hardware suggests that the Duterte administration considers Japan a balancer between the US and China in its diplomatic gambit to diversify its foreign relations, including its ties with Japan, China, and Russia.[29]

DOMESTIC FACTORS

The Philippines is an archipelagic state currently threatened by China's expansion into its maritime domain in the South China Sea. As mentioned, bilateral tension between the two countries flared in the mid-1990s when Chinese forces seized Mischief Reef, which was inside the country's continental shelf. The government must address its national security concerns regarding protecting its maritime domains. Yet, it did not have any grand strategy until recently, and its navy is considered the weakest in Southeast Asia. This could be attributed to domestic factors such as its challenging geography as an archipelagic state, a political elite indifferent to matters related to national security, the state and military's single-minded focus on internal security, and a weak and flawed democratic system of governance.

The Philippines as an Archipelagic State

The Philippines occupies the most interior position among the littoral countries of the maritime regions of East Asia. It is bounded north by the South China Sea and Taiwan, east by the Pacific Ocean, south by Indonesia, and west again by the South China Sea. The Philippines sits squarely in the geographic heart of Southeast and Northeast Asia.[30] It is an archipelagic state comprising 7,199 islands and occupies a wide maritime area stretching 1,850 kilometers from about the fifth to the twentieth parallel north latitude. Of these sprawling 7,100 islands, only 1,000 are inhabited. The Philippine archipelago is volcanic in origin, and its land surface is 114,839 square statute miles crisscrossed with mountains and drained by small rivers.[31]

Topographically, the country is fragmented by inland waters, which also gives the Philippines one of the longest coastlines of any country in the world.[32] The country's long coastline and fragmented features make it difficult for the Philippines islands to defend against a naval power dominating the archipelago's maritime surroundings. The Philippine coast is primarily irregular, with indentions along the shorelines of the various islands that provide several harbors. Most of the country's ports and harbors are easily defended and can accommodate large naval and merchant marine ships.[33] Given its natural maritime geography, foreign powers' discovery, conquest, colonization, and occupation of the Philippines has been possible thanks to large-scale, determined, and well-equipped naval operations.[34]

The country's limited resources and challenging topography have created a view among the Philippine elite that no amount of funds will enable the government to defend itself against external threats. This view is further bolstered by the Philippines' geographic isolation from the rest of Asia, which nurtured a widespread belief that its maritime borders provide an impenetrable moat against any external threat emanating from the continent.

The Political Elite's Reluctance to Allocate Resources for National Defense

The Philippine political elite comprises coalitions of powerful families that control the country's political parties.[35] Before the Philippines became independent in 1946, the elite families captured control over land and labor in the Philippines' most productive countryside. Using their control over the most fertile and productive agricultural lands, these political families often apportion candidates for provincial or municipal officers among their heirs, generating intense conflicts over this tangible political legacy. In turn, these political families sought rents in the form of state revenues to ensure their survival in Philippine politics.[36] For the Filipino political elite, the Philippine state is not an abstract set of anonymous and autonomous functionaries but a loose alliance of individuals who have gained office by political favoritism and have their own individual interests, allies, and enemies.[37]

For these political families, self-help and political negotiation are the only reliable sources of security and assistance.[38] Consequently, the elite has shown little interest in strategic matters, affecting the reallocation of the state's limited resources from defense spending to their sociopolitical priorities.[39] Their control over the country's legislative institutions and local government units enabled the elite to limit the defense budget and establish essential checks on the military even before the country became independent in the mid-1940s.

In the aftermath of the Second World War, the elite families formed alliances with new local strongmen.[40] These alliances of the old political elite and strongmen ensured that the Philippine Congress was on an equal footing with the presidency. This weakened the executive branch as it retained the legislative power to approve the national budget and kept the military on a tight leash via congressional appointment and promotion.[41]

The Philippine elite influenced defense policies by controlling the bicameral Philippine Congress. Through their power and influence over appropriation and budgetary matters, these legislators were able to affect the country's defense programs. Regarding defense spending, the legislators generally concentrate on acquiring the requirements for their electoral success—public works projects and patronage—while remaining suspicious of the military by subjecting defense budgets to minute scrutiny.[42] Consequently, an American academic observed that while the Philippine civil-military record bears considerable similarity to its Southeast Asian neighbors, the AFP did not have the influence or actual clout of the militaries in Indonesia, Thailand, and Burma.[43]

Currently, the Philippine elites' control of the Philippine Congress has enabled them to exercise an essential check on the military through the creation of a separate Philippine National Police (PNP) under a separate civilian agency; the institutionalization of a ban on active military personnel holding civilian government positions; insulating the military from partisan politics; subjecting top-ranking AFP officers, including the chief of staff, to the concurrence of the powerful Commission on Appointments; subjecting the defense budget to the minutest scrutiny; and controlling and limiting the country's defense budget.

A Single-Minded Focus on Internal Security

In the past four decades the Philippine government and its military have focused their attention, efforts, and resources on containing rebel movements in the local scene, such as the communist-led *Hukbong Magpapalaya ang Bayan* (People's Liberation Army) in the 1950s and later the New People's Army (NPA), the secessionist Moro National Liberation Front (MNLF), and later the Moro Islamic Liberation Front (MILF) and the bandit/terrorist group Abu Sayaff. During the Cold War, the Philippine military focused on these insurgent movements because the country was under the US security umbrella. Before the withdrawal of the American military facilities in 1992, the presence of US forces was deemed an effective deterrence against any external attack (primarily conventional) on the country. The Philippines also received base-related economic and security assistance packages under the Military Assistance Program (MAP) of 1947, Economic Support Fund (ESF), and Foreign Military Sales (FMS) credit. Consequently the Philippine government saved many resources that would have been allocated for defense expenditures if the US bases were not in the country.[44] During this period the Philippine military veered from developing any external defense capability and instead focused on counterinsurgency.[45]

Well into the first decade of the twenty-first century, the Philippines was faced with a perennial security challenge—its long wars against various insurgent groups. Focused on internal security, the AFP's territorial defense development efforts were relegated to the sidelines. Resources intended for territorial defense were used for internal security purposes. Furthermore, scarce financial resources for the AFP modernization were diverted to personnel costs and combat operations against insurgent groups. The September 2007 AFP Capability Assessment gave a thorough and candid observation of the AFP's deteriorating materiel and combat capabilities. The report stated that the poor condition of the equipment severely affected the military's effectiveness and efficiency in counterinsurgency operations and that the emphasis on low-intensity conflicts (LICs) diverted the AFP's attention and resources away from external defense-related modernization projects.[46]

A Flawed System of Democratic Governance

In 2013, the Economist Intelligence Unit (EIU) ranked the Philippines 69th out of 167 countries in terms of its level of democracy, putting the country in the category of "flawed democracy."[47] Philippine democracy, a legacy of the American colonial rule of the country, has to struggle deeply within Philippine society to take root among the ordinary Filipino people. The government has a robust civil society and a free, dynamic, and independent press, and citizens enjoy their constitutionally mandated political and civil rights, with limited restrictions, by publicly criticizing their national leaders and participating in the periodic electoral processes. However, cultural factors such as strong familial ties, the colonial legacy of the powerful and entrenched land-owning political elite, socioeconomic conditions such as pervasive poverty and gross inequality, persistent patterns of political patronage and economic cronyism, and rarely ending Muslim and communist insurgencies have undermined the effectiveness and accountability of democratic political institutions.

The Philippines is a unitary state with a winner-take-all electoral system in which the presidency exercises enormous power over budgets and appointments and congenitally fragmented political parties. Every Philippine president's ability to implement policies effectively and decisively is often frustrated by the Philippine Congress, which acts as a watchdog against the executive branch. However, historically, Congress has had difficulty articulating and carrying out broad policy objectives and governance and national security programs.[48] The political parties and other groupings, such as the bureaucracy and the military, also find it challenging to carry out policies effectively because they tend to be tenuous and shifting, driven primarily by individual personalities and interests rather than overarching ideologies, coherent policy platforms, and clear goals.[49] What remains constant in Philippine politics is the traditional political elite, which has longevity and adaptability. Consequently, they exert a powerful clout over policymaking and the distribution of resources.

OPERATIONALIZATION OF THE GRAND STRATEGY

The president of the Philippines plays a central role in determining policy outcomes and the norms and behavior that shape politics, governance, and national security. However, the president is limited to a single six-year term, so the power and influence of every Philippine executive is transitory.[50] In the realm of national security and foreign policy, the president plays a significant role in influencing the direction of security and foreign policies, with their personal opinions and priorities powerfully shaping these policies. Consequently, when a new president assumes office, there is no systemic and legal guarantee of continuity from one administration or from one presidential term to the next, so foreign and national security policies can change significantly when the president changes. This is reflected in the changes in Philippine grand strategies from 2011 to 2021.

The Aquino Administration's Balancing Strategy

Aquino pursued a balancing strategy, although it could never develop a formal NSS. This was because, during his early months in office, Aquino showed little interest in foreign relations and strategic matters. In his inaugural speech in late June 2010, his administration's foreign policy agenda was glossed over.[51] He said that "he wants to settle pressing domestic problems before he leaves the country."[52] Unfortunately Aquino was overtaken by unexpected developments that forced him to pay more attention to foreign policy and defense matters than he initially anticipated in mid-2010.

On March 2, 2011, two Chinese patrol boats harassed a survey ship commissioned by the Philippine Department of Energy (DOE) to conduct natural gas exploration in the Reed Bank (also called Recto Bank). The Reed Bank lies 150 kilometers east of the Spratly Islands and 250 kilometers west of the Philippine Island of Palawan. Stunned by this maritime encounter within the Philippines' EEZ, the Aquino administration filed a protest before the Chinese embassy in Manila. A Department of Foreign Affairs (DFA) spokesperson commented that "the Philippines is (simply) seeking an explanation for the incident." Brushing aside the Philippine complaint, a Chinese embassy official insisted that China has indisputable sovereignty over the Nansha (Spratly) Islands and their adjacent territory.

With these incidents, the Aquino administration hastened to develop the AFP's territorial defense capabilities. The Philippines' territorial defense goal has been establishing a modest but "comprehensive border protection program." This task is anchored on the surveillance, deterrence, and border patrol capabilities of the PAF, the PN, and the PCG that extend from the country's territorial waters to its EEZ.[53] This objective required enhancing the AFP's capabilities, prioritizing its needs, and gradually restructuring its forces for territorial defense. According to the 2011 AFP's Strategic Intent, the long-term goal was to maintain a "credible deterrent posture against foreign intrusion or external aggression, and other illegal activities while allowing free navigation to prosper."[54] The Philippines' territorial defense goal is very modest—to develop a credible posture for territorial defense and maritime security through building a competent force capable of defending the country's interests and the land features it occupies in the South China Sea.[55]

Cognizant of its limited military capabilities, the Philippines enhanced its security ties with the United States—its long-time strategic ally—and fostered a security partnership with Japan. The aftermath of the Scarborough Shoal Stand-off further pushed the Philippines closer to Tokyo. The Philippines and Japan conducted several high-level meetings and consultations to solidify their security cooperation and counter China's assertiveness. In June 2015 Aquino discussed with Abe the strengthening of their countries' strategic partnership in the face of China's aggressive behavior.[56]

In January 2013 the Philippines directly confronted the Chinese expansive claim in the South China Sea by filing a statement of claim against Beijing in the Arbitral Tribunal of the United Nations Convention on the Law of the Sea. Del Rosario presented Manila's case against China's expansive maritime claim in the disputed waters before the five-member tribunal hearing. He also argued that the 1982 UN Convention on the Law of the Sea does not recognize or permit the exercise of so-called historic rights in areas beyond the limits of maritime zones recognized or established by UNCLOS.[57] China did not participate in the proceedings, citing its policy of resolving territorial and maritime rights disputes only through direct consultation and negotiation with the countries directly involved.[58]

The Duterte Administration's Appeasement Strategy

The unexpected election of Duterte as the Philippines' sixteenth president in May 2016 was seen as an adverse consequence of the country's long and often troubled experience with liberal democratic governance and an example of the widespread global disillusion toward the political and economic elite.[59] He surprised many of his countrymen as he downgraded the Philippines' long-standing alliance with the US, alienated Australia and the European Union, and announced his plan to move closer to China and Russia.[60] He doubts the Philippines' reliance on the US, questioning its willingness to defend the Philippines in any armed engagement over its territorial dispute with China in the South China Sea.

Duterte announced that he was seeking to improve relations with China. He was candid about his intention to change Manila's hardline policy toward Beijing; this was manifested when he reacted with sobriety and extreme caution when the UNCLOS Arbitral Tribunal came out with the July 12, 2016, awards to the Philippines that ruled that China's extensive maritime claim and expansionary moves in the South China Sea have no legal basis. Then, a few months later, he announced he was ready to set aside the arbitral ruling as he sought trade, economic, and diplomatic concessions from China. Indeed, his open contempt for the Philippines' alliance with the US, his optimistic pronouncements on China, and his willingness to accept Beijing's preferred means of managing the South China Sea dispute, such as direct bilateral negotiations and joint development, are diametrically at odds with the conventional design and trajectory of twenty-first-century Philippine foreign policy on these critical issues.[61]

The Duterte administration accepted China's core procedural norms for dealing with the South China Sea dispute—shelving the sovereignty issue, discussing the conflict in bilateral forums, and agreeing on bilateral engagements such as joint development, strengthening of bilateral trade, and increased trade—in exchange for Chinese support for Philippine development.[62] The Philippines' 180-degree shift in its South China Sea policy should be understood in the context of China's growing political influence over ASEAN member states through its massive involvement in infrastructure development.[63]

Five years into his six-year term, however, the Duterte administration found it imperative to adopt a strategy of limited hard balancing toward China. This policy change is a result of two developments in the Philippine-China rapprochement: (1) China's failure to deliver the promised loans and direct investments to finance the Philippine government's Build, Build, Build program and (2) increasing Chinese naval presence and coercive actions near the artificial islands in the South China Sea. This policy aims to develop the Philippines' external defense capabilities due to the dangerous great powers competition in the Indo-Pacific region. The Philippines resorted to this strategy by continuing some of Aquino's policies, such as (1) building up the AFP's territorial defense capabilities, (2) maintaining its alliance with the US, and (3) fostering the security partnership with Japan.

The Return to Hard Balancing

The Duterte administration deliberated on a grand strategy of limited hard balancing to constrain the hegemon's revisionist agenda. This policy resulted from the defense, military, and foreign affairs establishments questioning Duterte's appeasement policy and his administration's belated realization that it needed an impromptu strategy to constrain China's revisionist agenda in the South China Sea. Initially, the newly elected President Ferdinand Marcos Jr. seemed to follow in his predecessor's footsteps of pursuing a policy of limited hard balancing toward China. This strategy requires Manila to foster closer ties with Beijing to manage the dispute while making attempts to counter Chinese aggressive efforts by applying lawfare and leveraging on its alliance and security partnerships with the US and other American allies such as Japan and Australia, and limited arms building.

Marcos considered that the most urgent agenda for his administration was economic recovery after the COVID-19 pandemic. To speed up the country's economic recovery, Marcos negotiated with China to revive three rail projects under the Belt and Road Initiative that had lapsed during the Duterte administration because of a lack of funding.[64] Marcos emphasized the urgency for closer economic ties with China during his first meeting with Chinese President Xi Jinping on the side of the Asia-Pacific Economic

Community (APEC) Summit in Bangkok, Thailand. He also agreed with Xi that the maritime dispute between the two countries should not define the relationship.[65]

Marcos also prioritized fostering a healthy and vibrant security relationship with the US, which marks a significant break from his predecessor, Duterte, who initially tried to unravel the Philippine-US alliance, lessen Manila's dependence on Washington, and diversify the country's security relations to include revisionist states such as China and Russia.[66] In August 2022, he warmly welcomed US Secretary of State Anthony Blinken. During the meeting, Marcos told Blinken: "We cannot, we can no longer isolate one part of our relationship from the other. We are too closely tied because of the special relationship between the United States and the Philippines and our shared history."[67]

However, China's uncompromising position regarding the West Philippine Sea/South China Sea dispute undermined Marcos' efforts to pursue a balancing policy between Washington and Beijing. Chinese maritime strategy requires the PLAN, the CCG, and the maritime militia to pressure foreign vessels in disputed waters and have the initiative to escalate moves to force littoral countries to abide by its jurisdiction and privileges in the South China Sea.[68] Under the Marcos administration, China applied this strategy against the newly elected president as CCG patrols in the South China Sea became more frequent.

This led to two maritime incidents in the South China Sea at the onset of the Marcos administration, namely (1) a CCG ship blocking and harassing a PN supply ship on its way to resupply a small AFP garrison on Ayungin Shoal and (2) swarming by fishing boats manned by suspected Chinese Maritime Militia to establish control over disputed South China Sea features.[69] Then, in February 2023, a CCG vessel directed a military-grade laser at a PCG ship that was escorting a resupply mission to the Philippine garrison onboard the BRP *Sierra Madre* on Ayungin Shoal. China's zero-sum game against the Philippines has pushed it to file several *note verbales* against what it perceives as a provocation. This also led Marcos to pursue a policy of hard balancing toward China. This policy was reflected by:

1. *Continuing the AFP's modernization program*: On December 21, 2022, Marcos assured the Philippine military of his administration's commitment to acquiring more equipment for external defense. He declared, "We will be partners towards your vision of a strong, credible, world-class armed force that is a source of national pride or national security."[70]

2. *Fostering closer security partnerships with Japan and South Korea*: The Philippines is fostering closer security partnerships with Japan and South Korea. In early October 2022, the Philippines hosted a ten-day live fire training exercise involving Filipino and American marines, South Korean marines, and JSDF troops. About 3,000 ground troops from Japan, South Korea, the Philippines, and the US participated in the live-fire exercises north of the Philippine capital.[71]
3. *Strengthening its alliance with the US*: Marcos considered a robust alliance with the US necessary considering the Duterte administration's experience; there is no guarantee that closer economic relations with China would mitigate its coercive behavior. As a formal treaty ally and one of the few Southeast Asian states with robust defense relations with other US allies such as Japan and Australia, a significant conflict over Taiwan would likely drag the Philippines into the fray. The US no longer maintains substantial military bases in the country. Nevertheless, US forces have access arrangements with the Philippines through regular military exercises and access to the joint locations inside five common areas.[72]

The Comprehensive Archipelagic Defense Concept

The Philippines engages in arms build-up and, more significantly, in alliance formation and coalition to constrain Chinese maritime expansion in the South China Sea. Enhancing the Philippines' alliance and security partnerships with the US and other American regional allies is part of the Marcos administration's hard balancing policy toward China. Consequently, it relies on a superpower ally and several security partners that can match China's growing power, which the current modernization of the Philippine military cannot possibly check. Thus, the Marcos administration facilitated greater American strategic access to its territory and, in the process, linked its force modernization program with its alliance and security partnerships. The Marcos administration, however, deemed that it should formulate and adopt a grand strategy based on the Philippines' archipelagic characteristics and, in light of the threat it faces in the country's western seaboard, China's maritime expansion in the South China Sea.

In January 2024, Secretary of the National Defense Department Gilberto Teodoro revealed a new defense concept called the Comprehensive Archipelagic Defense Concept (CADC).[73] CADC is based on the assumption that as an archipelagic state, the Philippines' land mass is limited while the population is increasing, causing the need for resources to expand exponentially.[74] Since the early twenty-first century, Manila has planned to survey and eventually exploit the natural gas and oil deposits on Reed or Recto Bank, which is inside the country's EEZ.

Unfortunately, Secretary Teodoro observed that "The country's resources in its maritime territory are illegally and unilaterally encroached upon by a country using a distorted nine-ten-dash line, which nobody in the world accepts or recognizes since this would open up a rewriting of international law."[75] This is because China claims almost 90 percent of the South China Sea. Consequently, the Philippines' efforts to explore the area have been hampered by the long-running dispute with China, leading the Aquino administration to suspend exploration at Reed Bank in 2014 due to the growing maritime tension with Beijing.[76] Lately, China has intensified its harassment of Philippine public vessels and ordinary fisherfolk's boats in the West Philippine Sea/South China Sea.

CADC admonishes the AFP to project its capabilities into areas where the Philippines must protect and preserve its natural resources in its EZZ based on its constitutional fiat and duty.[77] This means the Philippine military must abandon its passive defense strategy. This defense strategy required the Philippine military to use force only once the threat had already arrived on the Philippines' shores or if the territory was already subjected to armed attacks.[78] Instead CADC requires the AFP to develop capabilities for awareness, access, and control of its maritime territory, including its EEZ, through the joint forces to be able to engage and neutralize approach kinetic and nonkinetic threats as far out as possible to prevent the same from executing hostile actions that are inimical to country's national security interests. Furthermore, this also compels the AFP to develop capabilities to ensure that the Filipino nation benefits from the natural resources in its EEZ.

CADC aims to project the AFP's capabilities up to the Philippines' EEZ and, in the process, expand the country's strategic depth to enhance the defense of its entire archipelagic territory. According to Secretary Teodoro, "We are evolving into a defense concept which projects our (military) power into our areas (maritime) where we must protect and preserve resources."[79] This requires the Philippines to build up its surface combatants; improve its intelligence, surveillance, and reconnaissance capacities; and construct more military facilities in strategic maritime border areas adjacent to the vital lines of trade and communications in the West Philippines/South China Sea.[80] This entailed serious and expensive capabilities-based planning as part of the Philippines' defense strategy. As a case in point, the Philippine Marines

Corps (PMC) has established strategic locations in Luzon, facing the South China Sea and Luzon Straits, for its new coastal defense regiments, which are now equipped with Brahmos missiles. Clearly, from a capability standpoint, it is a matter of time until ranged land-based missiles are positioned along the Philippine coastal area that could threaten CCG and PLAN ships operating within the Philippines EEZ. This implied a more vigorous form of archipelagic defense that aimed to deny China the ability to achieve its expansionist goals in the South China Sea through aggression or coercion.[81]

In January 2024, AFP Chairman of the Joint-Chiefs-of-Staff Lieutenant General Romeo Brawner announced the Marcos administration's decision to fund the Horizon or Stage Three of the 18-year Revised AFP Modernization Program.[82] General Brawner noted that the final stage of the modernization program focuses on the concept of archipelagic defense; thus, the military plans to acquire more ships, aircraft, and radar systems. It will also involve upgrading the Philippine military's facilities and deploying personnel to secure the country's archipelagic waters and 200-nautical-mile EEZ.[83] It will require the AFP to rehabilitate all the military facilities on Philippine-held islands and land features in the West Philippine Sea to make them more habitable to the troops manning them.[84] Secretary Teodoro's announcement of the CADC as the country's new defense strategy and the AFP's decision to reconfigure the Horizon Three of the AFP modernization program based on the CADC's requirements are the most apparent indications of the development of a robust Philippine military strategy—one that is geared more toward defending the country from external threats than addressing the internal insurgencies that have plagued the country since its independence in 1946.[85] CADC's long-term goal is to guarantee the unimpeded and peaceful exploration and exploitation of all the natural resources with the country's EEZ for Philippine nationals, corporations, and others authorized by the Philippine government. This inferred a more comprehensive and defiant grand strategy against Chinese maritime expansion in the South China Sea.

CONCLUSION

The Philippines is a militarily weak archipelagic state confronted by Chinese maritime expansion in the South China Sea since 2010. From 2010 to 2016 the Philippines, under the Aquino administration, adopted a grand strategy of challenging China's goal in the disputed waters. In 2016, the Duterte administration pursued a policy of appeasement toward China. However, in 2018, the Philippines shifted from appeasement to a limited hard balancing policy because of (1) China's slow infusion of public capital to the Philippine government's ambitious infrastructure-building program and (2) continuing coercive actions against the units of the AFP in the South China Sea.

This strategy is an immediate result of the Duterte administration's realization that a strategy of appeasement requires the weaker party, the Philippines, to put its strategic stakes in the hands of an emergent and assertive power, China, which is harboring hostile intentions of maritime expansion in the disputed waters. The goal is to build up the country's territorial defense capabilities in the face of continuing Chinese expansion in the South China Sea and the growing danger of great powers competition in the Indo-Pacific region. The Duterte administration pursues this strategy by continuing some of its predecessor's efforts, such as (1) building up the AFP's territorial defense capabilities, (2) maintaining its alliance with the US, and (3) fostering security partnership with Japan.

Several external factors influence this grand strategy. The first is China's determination to pursue its maritime expansion in the South China Sea. Fortunately for the Philippines, its treaty ally, the US, also shares its interests in constraining China's efforts. In 2011 the US and the Philippines redirected their alliance from counterterrorism to maritime security. In 2014 the two allies signed the 2014 EDCA. In 2019, despite Duterte's skepticism about the reliability of the US, the Biden administration extended American security guarantees to Philippine forces operating in the South China Sea. Japan also shares the Philippines' interest in constraining Chinese maritime expansion.

Internal factors that account for this strategy of limited hard balancing include the country's archipelagic nature, its political elite's reluctance to allocate enormous resources for military build-up, its historical preoccupation with internal security matters, its flawed democratic system of governance, and finally the president's decisive role in determining the country's grand strategy. The Philippines' grand strategy of limited hard balancing involves the effective coordination of military and diplomatic efforts to obtain outcomes contrary to China's preference for controlling a large portion of the West Philippine Sea and the waters of the first island chain. It is directed against a specific policy related to China's maritime expansion. The Philippines seeks to constrain China's ability to unilaterally impose its preferences on the littoral states of the first island chain through limited arms build-up and reliance on a diplomatic coalition of states that will defend their shared interests.

President Marcos moved beyond former President Duterte's limited balancing policy as he revived the late President Aquino's hard balancing policy toward China. This is shown as he continued the Philippine military's modernization program, fostered security partnerships with Japan and South Korea, and, more significantly, revived the country's alliance with the US. Under the administration of President Marcos Jr., however, the Philippines found a new sense of exigency in developing the armed forces' naval capabilities to enhance its maritime security in the face of Chinese expansion in the South China Sea. President Marcos's renewed balancing policy toward China is more vigorous, strategic, and ambitious than that of the Aquino administration. Specifically, his administration's renewed balancing policy entails building up the Philippine military's external defense capabilities; enhancing its alliance with the US by increasing American strategic presence in the Philippines and fostering security arrangements with other American allies like South Korea, Japan, and Australia; and more recently, adopting the CADC. The Marcos administration's adoption of the CADC is an indication of the Philippines' pursuit of a more defiant, robust, and long-term grand strategy geared primarily toward defending the country's vast archipelagic domain from external threats rather than addressing the internal insurgencies that have plagued the country since its independence in 1946. Its long-term goal is to safeguard the total, unimpeded, and secure exploration and exploitation of all the natural resources with the country's EEZ for Philippine nationals, corporations, and others authorized by the Philippine government. This inferred a more comprehensive and defiant grand strategy against Chinese maritime expansion in the twenty-first century.

NOTES

1. National Security Council, *National Security Strategy: Security and Development for Transformational Change and Well-Being of the Filipino People* (National Security Council, 2018), 5.
2. National Security Council, *National Security Strategy.*
3. Cliff Venzon, "Philippine President Struggles to Sell his China Pivot at Home," *Financial Times* (October 2019), 1.
4. National Institute for Defence Studies, *East Asian Strategic Review 2021* (Interbooks, 2021), 128.
5. Teodoro Locsin, "Statement of the Secretary of Foreign Affairs on the 4th Anniversary of the Issuance of the Award in the South China Arbitration," Department of Foreign Affairs (July 12, 2020), 1.
6. Locsin, "Statement of the Secretary of Foreign Affairs."
7. Interview with a ranking senior Philippine Army officer, National Defense College of the Philippines (NDCP), August 9, 2021.
8. National Security Council, *National Security Policy, 2023–2028* (National Security Policy, August 2023), 28.

9. National Institute for Defense Studies, *NIDS China Security Report 2019: China's Strategy for Reshaping the Asian Order and Its Ramifications* (National Institute for Defense Studies, 2019), 26.
10. Office of the Assistant Chief of Naval Staff for Operations, N-3, *Learning Lesson from Naval Battles and Operations in the Philippines for PN Doctrines Development* (Philippine Navy Headquarters, date unknown), 200.
11. Peter Dutton, "Three Disputes and Three Objectives: China and the South China Sea," *Naval War College Review*), 54, no. 4 (Autumn 2011), 47.
12. Robert Sutter and Chin-Hao Huang, "Managing Rising Tension in the South China Sea," *Comparative Connections: A Triannual E-Journal on East Asian Bilateral Relations,* September 2011, 1. http://csis.org/files/publication/1102qchina_seasia.pdf
13. Barry Wain, "Chinese Diplomacy Off Course," *Wall Street Journal,* August 5, 2010, 13.
14. Thomas Lum and Ben Dolven, *The Republic of the Philippines and U.S. Interests—2014, Congressional Research Service Publication, No. 43498, April 23, 2014* (Congressional Research Service, 2014), 179.
15. A. James Gregor, *In the Shadow of the Giants: The Major Powers and the Security of Southeast Asia* (Stanford University Press, 1989), 126.
16. Andrew Yeo, *Asia's Regional Architecture: Alliances and Institutions in the Pacific Century* (Stanford University Press, 2019), 33.
17. Gregor, "*In the Shadow of the Giants,*" 110.
18. Gregor, "*In the Shadow of the Giants,*" 110.
19. The 1999 VFA is a Status of Forces Agreement that provided the legal regulatory mechanism for the treatment of American military and civilian personnel visiting the Philippines for joint military exercises and for other matters. See Eduardo Malaya and Maria Antonina Mendoza-Oblena, *Forging Partnerships: Defense Cooperation under Constitutional and International Law* (Foreign Service Institute, 2016), 53.
20. Luisito F. Angeles, "Assessment of the Impact of U.S. Security Assistance Programs on the AFP Capability Upgrade" (M.A. Thesis, National Defense College of the Philippines, 2017), 79–80.
21. National Institute of Defense Analysis, *East Asian Strategic Review 2016* (The Japan Times, 2016), 159.
22. Anthony Rivera, "Simply by Design," *Business Mirror,* June 28, 2016, 1.
23. The National Institute for Defense Studies, *East Asian Strategic Review 2017* (The Japan Times, March 2017), 136.
24. Ministry of Foreign Affairs, "Japan-Philippines Joint Statement," Tokyo, October 26, 2016.
25. Rene Acosta, "Duterte Pushes for Contracts to Modernize Armed Forces," *New Nations,* October 27, 2016, 1.
26. Anonymous, "Duterte Says Open to Idea of Military Exercises with Japan," *Kyodo News,* October 27, 2016, 1.
27. Mike Yeo, "Japan to Bolster Philippine Maritime Security with TC-90 Aircraft," *Defense News,* October 30, 2017, 1. https://www.defensenews.com/global/asia-pacific/2017/10/30/japan-to-bolster-philippine-maritime-security-with-tc-90-aircraft/
28. Prashanth Paramesaran, "A Big Week for Japan-Philippines Defence Ties," *The Diplomat,* March 29, 2018, 2, https://thediplomat.com/2018/03/a-big-week-for-japan-philippines-defense-ties/
29. The National Institute for Defense Studies, "East Asian Strategic Review 2017," 136.

30. The National Institute for Defense Studies, "East Asian Strategic Review 2017," 4.
31. Teodoro A. Agoncillo, *History of the Filipino People* (C &E Publishing, 2012), 3.
32. Agoncillo, *History of the Filipino People,* 4.
33. Office of the Assistant Chief of Naval Staff for Operations "*Lesson from Naval Battles and Operations in the Philippines for PN Doctrines Development,*" 4.
34. Office of the Assistant Chief of Naval Staff for Operations "*Lesson from Naval Battles and Operations in the Philippines for PN Doctrines Development,*" 4.
35. Alfredo W. McCoy, "An Anarchy of Families: The Historiography of State and Family in the Philippines," in *An Anarchy of Families: States and Family in the Philippines* (Ateneo De Manila University Press, 1996), 8.
36. McCoy, "An Anarchy of Families," 22.
37. Brian Fegan, "Entrepreneurs in Votes and Violence: Three Generations of a Peasant Political Family," in Alfred W. McCoy (Ed.), *An Anarchy of Families: State and Family in the Philippines* (Ateneo De Manila University Press, 1994), 50.
38. Fegan, "Entrepreneurs in Votes and Violence."
39. Timberman, *A Changeless Land: Continuity and Change in Philippine Politics* (Institute of Southeast Asian Studies, 1992), 45.
40. Patricio Abenales and Donna J. Amoroso, *State and Society in the Philippines* (Quezon City: Ateneo De Manila Press, 2017), 168.
41. Abenales and Amoroso, *State and Society in the Philippines.*
42. Abenales and Amoroso, *State and Society in the Philippines.*, 45.
43. Donald J. Berlin, *Before Gringo: History of the Philippine Military: 1830–1972* (Anvil Press, 2008), 145.
44. Kathline Anne S. Tolosa, "Owning Sovereignty," in *Digest: A Forum for Security and Defense Issues* (4th Quarter 2008), 6.
45. AFP Modernization Board, *Annual Accomplishment Report 2006* (General Headquarters Armed Forces of the Philippines, 2007), 1.
46. Office of Plans and Program, *AFP's Capability Assessment,* presented during the National Defense and Security Review Module Priming Session (National Defense College of the Philippines, September 3–6, 2007), 25.
47. Lum and Dolven, "The Republic of the Philippines and U.S. Interests—2014," 182.
48. Lum and Dolven, "The Republic of the Philippines and U.S. Interests—2014," 182.
49. Lum and Dolven, "The Republic of the Philippines and U.S. Interests—2014," 182.
50. Timberman, "Philippine Politics under Duterte," 2.
51. Xinhua News Agency, "Aquino to Consider Foreign Trips When Domestic Issues Settled," *Xinhua New Agency* (July 5, 2010), 1.
52. Xinhua News Agency, "Aquino to Consider Foreign Trips When Domestic Issues Settled."
53. National Security Council, *National Security Policy 2011–2016* (National Security Council, April 2011), 39.
54. Office of the Deputy Chief-of-Staff, *Armed Forces of the Philippines: Strategic Intent* (Camp Aguinaldo, 2011), 27.
55. Secretary of National Defense Voltaire T. Gazmin, *Defense Planning Guidance, 2013–2018* (Department of National Defense, October 11, 2011), 4.
56. The Philippines News Agency (PNA), "Japan Shares Philippines Serious Concern over China's Reclamation Activities in West Philippines Sea," *The Philippines News Agency* (June 5, 2015), 1.

57. Michaela Callar, "China's Historical Claim over South China Sea Invalid under UNCLOS," The Philippines News Agency (July 8, 2015), 1
58. BBC Monitoring Asia-Pacific, "China Not to Accept Third Party Decision over Sea Dispute with Philippines," *BBC Monitoring Asia-Pacific* (July 14, 2015), 5.
59. Timberman, "Philippine Politics Under Duterte," 7.
60. Carolina G. Hernandez, "The Philippines in 2016," *Asian Survey* 57, no. 1 (January/February 2017), 117.
61. Lowell Bautista, "The Philippines and the Arbitral Tribunal's Award: A Sombre Victory and Uncertain Times Ahead," *Contemporary Southeast Asia* 38, no. 3 (December 2016), 353.
62. Peter Kreuzer, "Duterte Seizing the Right Moment," *Dealing with South China Sea: Duterte Changing Course* (Peace Research Institute Frankfurt, 2018), 16.
63. National Institute of Defense Studies, *NIDS China Security Report 2019,* 41.
64. Catharin Dalpino, "External Order, Inner Turmoil," *Comparative Connections: A Triannual E-Journal of Bilateral Relations in the Indo-Pacific,* 24, no. 3 (January 2023), 74. https://cc.pacforum.org/wp-content/uploads/2023/01/06-US-SEA-Relations-2.pdf
65. Robert Sutter and Chin-Hao Huang, "Xi Moderates to U.S. and Others amid Continued Competition," *Comparative Connections: A Triannual E-Journal of Bilateral Relations in the Indo-Pacific,* 24, no. 3 (January 2023), 86. https://cc.pacforum.org/wp-content/uploads/2023/01/07-China-SEA-Relations.pdf
66. Derek Grossman, "The Philippines Is the New Star Ally: Manila's Geopolitical Shift Is More than the Biden Administration Could Have Hoped For," *Foreign Affairs* (February 21, 2023), 1. https://foreignpolicy.com/2023/02/21/philippines-marcos-bongbong-china-japan-us-alliance-indo-pacific-geopolitics/
67. "U.S. Philippines Flex Alliance in the Heat of Taiwan Crisis," *Yerepouni Daily News* (August 8, 2022), 1.
68. NIDS China Security Report 2023, *China's Quest for Control of the Cognitive Domanin and Gray Zone Operations* (Interbooks, 2023), 78.
69. Sutter, Robert, and Chin-Hao Huang. "Xi Moderates to U.S. and Others amid Continued Competition." *Comparative Connections: A Triannual E-Jounral of Bilateral Relations in the Indo-Pacific* (January 24, 2023), 3, 81–90. https://cc.pacforum.org/wp-content/uploads/2023/01/07-China-SEA-Relations.pdf
70. "Philippines: Marcos to AFP: Stayed Committed to Sustaining Peace." *Asia News Monitor* (December 21, 2022).
71. Richard Heydarian, "Relations Reshaped: Richard Heydarian Says the U.S. and the Philippines Have Been Brought Closer Together by the Issue of Taiwan," *South China Morning Post* (October 11, 2022), 1–2.
72. Ryo Nakamura and Yuchi Shiga, "Philippines May Allow U.S. Military Access during Taiwan Crisis," *Nikkei Asia* (September 5, 2022), 1.
73. "Philippines Defense Chief: Military to Be Used for Safeguarding Philippine Access to Sea Resources." *Asia News Monitor* (January 29, 2024), 1.
74. "Philippines Defense Chief," *Asia News Monitor.*
75. "Philippines Defense Chief," *Asia News Monitor.*
76. Strangio Sebastian, "Philippine Military to Provide Unimpeded Acess to Sea Resources," *The Diplomat* (January 25, 2024), 1–3.
77. Sebastian, "Philippine Military to Provide Unimpeded Acess to Sea Resources," 2.

78. Armed Forces of the Philippines, *Armed Forces of the Philippines National Military Strategy 2019* (Armed Forces of the Philippines, 2018), 14.
79. Priam Nepomoceno, "AFP Shrugs Off China's Warning versus Hiked Military Presence in Batanes," *Philippine News Agency* (February 13, 2024), 1–2.
80. Justin Baquisal, "More Purposes, Fewer Platitudes: The Philippines' Defense Diplomacy under Marcos," *The Diplomat* (August 11, 2023), 1–7.
81. Andrew F. Krepinevich, "How to Deter China: The Case for Archipelagic Defense," *Foreign Affairs* 94, no. 2 (2015), 78–86.
82. Philippines News Agency, "AFP Modernization's Horizon 3 to Focus on Archipelagic Defense," *Philippine News Agency* (January 15, 2024), 1–3.
83. Nepomoceno, "AFP Shrugs Off China's Warning versus Hiked Military Presence in Batanes," 1–2.
84. Nepomoceno, "AFP Shrugs Off China's Warning."
85. Sebastian, "Philippine Military to Provide Unimpeded Acess to Sea Resources," 2.

CHAPTER 10

Singapore

Ang Cheng Guan

To understand Singapore's grand strategy, it is essential to revisit its experience when it separated from Malaysia, which it was a part of since 1963, and when it became independent in August 1965. While it was a bloodless independence, it was swift if not sudden in the eyes of most people. The national narrative is that independence was "thrust" upon Singapore.[1] As an "unexpected nation,"[2] to borrow the words of one historian, policies had to be made on the run and the fundamentals of a grand strategy were shaped, informed, and forged during the aftermath of August 9, 1965. As this essay will show, Singapore's grand strategy has been remarkably consistent since the country came into being in 1965.

The term "grand strategy" is never used in the context of Singapore. Indeed, Bilahari Kausikan, a former permanent secretary in the Ministry of Foreign Affairs of Singapore, wrote that he had "never understood the obsession of some academics with the so-called 'grand strategy,'" which he described as a "meaningless term." He agreed that "one must set goals," "but having done so, all one can do is to keep a distant star in sight even as one tacks hither and thither to void treacherous reefs and shoals to scoop up opportunities that might drift within reach."[3] While that be may true, leaders still "draw on some set of notions about how the world works as they respond to new situations"[4] even when they at times have to react at short notice and with limited information. As Hal Brands, quoting Eisenhower, reminds us, "Grand Strategy" is not "some immutable blueprint from which policy must never deviate." It "requires purpose and a willingness to look ahead" and at the same time, it "demands significant tactical flexibility as well."[5] It is more common to talk or read about Singapore's foreign policy or defense policy, or occasionally

Singapore's national strategy or national security strategy. Essentially, they refer to the same set of deliberations and concerns as grand strategy.[6]

There are a multitude of useful definitions of "grand strategy." While there are differences in emphasis, focus, and nomenclature, there are also considerable overlaps and a fair amount of consensus among scholars who study the concept. For this paper, I have chosen that of Peter Feaver, who defined grand strategy as "the collection of plans and policies that comprise the state's deliberate effort to harness political, military, diplomatic and economic tools together to advance that state's national interest"[7] for its simplicity and clarity, substituting the word "state" in this case with "Singapore."

The study of grand strategy would require analyzing principles, strategic planning, and behavior. This chapter will provide an interpretative analysis of the etiology of Singapore's grand strategy, ideology, and praxis of three cabinets and two leadership transitions—Lee Kuan Yew (1965–90), Goh Chok Tong (1990–2004), and Lee Hsien Loong (2004–present), which span the Cold War and post-Cold War periods.

STRATEGIC PRIORITIES

Singapore has a singular and crystal-clear strategic priority or goal since 1965, and that is to ensure its survival and independence as a nation-state. As its founding prime minister Lee Kuan Yew said, Singapore "cannot be a satellite of any nation" for unless it is able "to retain its own point of view," "it would lose all effectiveness in the new world order."[8] In the words of its present prime minister Lee Hsien Loong, "How to be masters of our own destiny?"[9]

This strategic priority is derived from the belief that small states cannot survive for long, or, as the senior Lee once said, "in the context of the second half of the 20th century, Southeast Asian island nations are a political joke."[10] Overnight, the narrative that an independent Singapore was not viable, and therefore a part of Malaysia (the main argument proffered in the late 1950s and early 1960s in support of a merger to form Malaysia in 1963) was an existential necessity that had to abruptly be revised. The hope that Singapore would become the "New York" of Malaysia also evaporated.

On August 8, 1965, the new country was 581.5 square kilometers in size with a population of just 1.887 million people, a trading port without a hinterland and unable to defend itself. Everything that was done in the domains of foreign policy, defense, and economics (specifically the importance of free trade and, related to that, sea lines of communication [SLOC]) in the last sixty years (which will be elaborated subsequently) was to address this strategic priority of ensuring that Singapore will and can survive and prosper. This is based on the premise that Singapore, unlike its larger neighbors, is "of no intrinsic interest to any developed country." Small states have little if any power to alter the region, not to mention the world. Thus, to survive, Singapore needs to be relevant, useful, and successful—"Singapore has to continually reconstruct itself and keep its relevance to the world and create political and economic space." Because Singapore is successful, the world pays attention to it as nobody would take a failed state seriously.[11] This has remained the mantra.

EXTERNAL FACTORS

As Richard Fontaine and Kristin M. Lord noted, "Grand Strategy starts with an assessment of the international and domestic environments."[12] This and the following section will focus on the external and internal factors that determine the formulation and implementation of Singapore's grand strategy.

When one unpacks Singapore's strategic priority, two sets of relationships are most important to Singapore—the Singapore-Malaysia-Indonesia relationship, and the Singapore-United States-China relationship. Singapore's relations with its immediate neighbors, Malaysia and Indonesia, is the country's "most intense" and "complex" relationships.[13] Once part of Malaysia and separated by just a one-kilometer long causeway, its first Foreign Minister S. Rajaratnam, in his first foreign policy speech in Parliament after Singapore's independence, said he found it "difficult to keep a straight face in talking about a foreign policy towards Malaysia" and that "there was something unreal and odd about lumping relations with Malaysia under foreign relations." But given that the separation had taken place, the relationship between the two countries by default "comes under the category of foreign relations."[14] As for Indonesia, it is best summed up by Benny Moerdani, who pointed out that "the distance from Jakarta to Singapore is nearer than Jakarta to the extremes portion of Indonesia. So, what happens in Singapore would have a greater impact on Jakarta than what happens in some other parts of Indonesia."[15] The opposite is naturally true as well.

Singapore's relationship with these two strategic neighbors went through ups and downs in the last half a century and more. Relations from the start were poor, if not bad. Singapore-Malaysia relations remained acrimonious after separation for several years. Jakarta (under the pro-communist Sukarno) was still in a state of war, commonly referred to as the Confrontation, with Kuala Lumpur in 1965 because of the merger of Singapore (as well as Sabah and Sarawak) to form the Federation of Malaysia in 1963, which the Indonesians view as a neo-imperial/colonialist plot. Singapore and Indonesia eventually established formal diplomatic relations in September 1967, two years after Singapore's independence.

Much have been written of the trials and tribulations of Singapore-Malaysia-Indonesia relations, and space does not allow us to go into the details here. What is relevant to note in the context of Singapore's grand strategy is its approach to its two neighbors spelled out by two of its founding leaders in 1966 and 1971, respectively, which had stood the test of time:

First, however difficult the relationship may have between Singapore and its immediate neighbors at times and regardless of how much its relation with neighbors improved, Singapore's mindset was conditioned by the view that in foreign relations, "your best friends are never your immediate neighbors," a point that Lee Kuan Yew reiterated on several occasions. "Your neighbors are not your best friends, wherever you are," Lee declared in a speech on the subject of international relations. This is because "it gets too close and your neighbor's hedge grows and infringes on your part of the garden and the branch of his fruit tree covers your grass, and your roses do not get enough sunshine and so many things happen."[16] Thus, he felt that with Malaysia, both sides should forget about sentiments and just do business with each other because "if we go into sentiments, emotions, feeling, there is going to be a great deal of antipathy . . . you can go into real orgies of bitterness and hate."[17] And, as Lee Hsien Loong said forty-seven years later, when problems arise, which is bound to happen from time to time, "we aim to resolve them dispassionately without affecting our wiser relationship or raising the temperature."[18]

Second, as Goh Keng Swee (Singapore's first minister of defense) noted, many people were inclined to draw similarities between Singapore and Israel, and indeed there were some points of resemblance, such as standard of living and the level of technology as compared to Singapore's neighbors. But it would be "dangerous to read too much into the similarities" between the two countries. There were at least four fundamental differences that remain true today: (1) while Singapore's neighbors might dislike and envy Singapore, they "do not hate" Singapore in the way the Arabs hate Israel; (2) the superpowers were not competing like in the Middle East with the Russian supporting the Arab cause and the Americans supporting Israel; (3) the Singapore economy, unlike Israel's, is extremely vulnerable to economic blockade. The imposition of a naval blockade would be considered by Singapore as sufficient *casus belli*; and (4) unlike Israel, which was established as a Jewish state, Singapore is multiracial despite its Chinese majority population. Every attempt to turn Singapore into another China is strenuously resisted. In Goh's prognosis, he did not think that there is "any realistic danger of war" between Singapore and her neighbors unless a "madcap regime" is established in either or both countries. But since Singapore cannot be certain that this would not happen, "it is necessary for us to continue to develop our military strength."[19] (We will discuss defense in a later section).

Beyond the immediate vicinity and region, Singapore's management of relationships with both the United States and China is the most important. In Singapore's view, "the US-China relationship will remain the most important bilateral relationship for the world in the years to come."[20] This is not a recent assessment. In 2009, Lee Kuan Yew noted how "the relationship between the US and China had already become the most important geopolitical issue of this century" and predicted that "in the latter 21st century, US-China relations will become the most important bilateral relationship in the world, like the US-USSR relationship during the Cold War."[21] (It happened sooner than Lee had anticipated).

Singapore had since its early political history realized the strategic significance of the United States and China for the island-state. Relations with both, however, did not begin well. In August 1965, the Singapore leadership were unfamiliar with the United States. As the American Consul General noted, all the senior Singapore officials spoke Anglo-English and were schooled under British rule; "their direct knowledge of the United States is practically nil."[22] Both George Thomson (director of Political Study Centre, Singapore) and Devan Nair (secretary general, National Trade Union Congress) then believed that Lee had a distorted view of US foreign policy.[23] Similarly, the Americans were also unfamiliar with Singapore and did not know Lee Kuan Yew well, if at all. Henry Thayer (US ambassador to Singapore, 1980–84) recalled that before 1980, the United States knew little of Singapore and had very limited access to the Singapore leadership. In fact, the relationship was surely and gradually changing to the positive in 1966 when the Americans concluded that Lee was not procommunist and supported US efforts in Vietnam. Lee, at the same time, saw the US as a potential and eventual replacement power for the British.

As for the People's Republic of China (PRC), in his inaugural parliamentary speech on December 16, 1965, Foreign Minister S. Rajaratnam pointed out that while Singapore, "generally speaking" was "sincere in our wish to be friendly with all countries which want to be friends with us, in the hard world of international realities, there are bound to be degrees of friendship between countries." Those closest were naturally the countries "whose foreign policy principles and deeds coincide with our national interests and our basic aspiration."[24] The PRC, being communist, during this period certainly did not belong to this category of countries. But Rajaratnam went on to say that things could change; thus "in international politics, it is not wise to formulate foreign policies on the basis of permanent enemies."[25]

Singapore from very early had recognized the strategic importance of the PRC. "The whole world has got to live with 'Mainland China' as you call it . . . The countries in Southeast Asia are not big enough to come to terms with China on their own. It will have to be up to the major powers to come to some accommodation . . . Then the countries of Southeast Asia can find accommodation with China within the framework of the United Nations, I hope," Lee said.[26] In Lee's analysis, one big power that would never lose interest in Southeast Asia was China, and we could not "afford to forget that."[27] Almost a year after Singapore became independent, Beijing had still not recognized Singapore. But it also did not condemn the country. The Chinese had expressed their wish to trade with Singapore, to which Lee did not object.[28] Being a trading nation, Singapore had always been interested in any country that wanted to trade with it, be it Taiwan or China.

If 1966 marked the beginning of Singapore's relations with the US, Deng Xiaoping's visit to Singapore in November 1978 is often hailed as the beginning of Singapore's relations with the PRC, although both countries only established formal diplomatic relations in October 1990, making China the last Southeast Asian country to do so after Indonesia. As in the case with the United States, apart from some episodic hiccups, relationship has generally been smooth. As Lee Kuan Yew said, the world's small nations could survive only by finding a "coincidence of interests with the big Powers."[29]

DOMESTIC FACTORS

Christopher Layne defined grand strategy as "the meeting point where the international system's geopolitical constraints intersect with a state's domestic political culture and its sense of identity."[30]

Through a process of firsthand experience and osmosis, four generation of decision-makers in Singapore shared a common strategic culture "which influence[s] their strategic choices at the highest political level (in terms of relating means to political ends) and military options at the operational or tactical level."[31] "Strategic culture" here refers to "the body of attitudes and beliefs that guides and circumscribes thought on strategic questions, influences the way strategic issues are formulated, and sets the vocabulary and perceptual parameters of strategic debate."[32] This "body of attitudes and beliefs" take reference from Singapore's "traditions, values, attitudes, patterns of behavior, habits, symbols, achievements and particular way of adapting to the environment and solving problems with respect to the threat and use of force."[33]

That Singapore had so far been able to maintain a cohesive multiracial society, despite its ethnic Chinese majority, helps. This as well as the fact that the ruling government has been in power since 1965 gives Singapore's grand strategy coherence and continuity, which in turn allowed for an effective all-of-government approach to operationalizing its grand strategy. The need "to work effectively as a seamless whole" is, according to then-Senior Minister and Co-ordinating Minister for National Security S. Jayakumar, "increasingly vital" in dealing with "multifaceted challenges to ensure Singapore's continued economic success and relevance on the international stage."[34] As Lee Hsien Loong noted, political stability is important "to maintain a clear understanding of our national interests, and to pursue that consistently over a long period." Political stability could "compensate" for Singapore's "lack of heft."[35] The notion that politics should "stop at the water's edge" remains an unwritten maxim of Singapore politics since 1965.

Finally, it is to the makers and shapers of Singapore's grand strategy we now turn before we continue to recount how the strategy that the leadership spelled out previously was implemented and operationalized. According to S. Rajaratnam, the first and longest serving foreign minister of Singapore, Singapore's foreign policy was shaped principally by him and Lee Kuan Yew, with inputs from Goh Keng Swee when there were economic implications.[36] Chin Kin Wah noted that Singapore does not have a tradition of public debate on matter of national defense.[37] Kishore Mahbubani described the three men as "Singapore's three exceptional geopolitical masters."[38] Indeed, historians who had perused the archival documents, both in Singapore and abroad, would agree that it is not possible at all to reconstruct Singapore's foreign policy without reference to Lee Kuan Yew. Michael Leifer noted that by the time Rajaratnam stepped down as foreign minister in 1980, the pattern of Singapore's foreign policy had been well established, and subsequent foreign ministers "had little to do by way of radical innovation although foreign policy had become more proactive." His successors had, in the main, continued to implement "Lee Kuan Yew's and Rajaratnam's design."[39] Indeed, one cannot miss the echoes of Lee's thinking in every single foreign policy speech and interview given by the second, third, and even fourth generation of Singapore leadership. Among his other portfolios, Goh Keng Swee was twice the minister of defense.

Readers will find Lee (1923–2015), Rajaratnam (1915–2006), and Goh (1918–2010) frequently mentioned in this chapter, especially Lee, who remained influential up to his death (and some may say even after his death).[40] An understanding of their beliefs and premises is imperative for anyone interested in understanding and analyzing Singapore's grand strategy because they serve as "a prism" that shapes their "perceptions and diagnoses" of international politics as well as "provide norms, standards and guidelines" that influences Singapore's choice of "strategy and tactics, structuring and weighing of alternative courses of action."[41]

Rajaratnam and Goh both retired from political office in 1986 and 1988, respectively. They gradually faded out in the 1990s due to poor health. After Lee stepped down as prime minister in 1990, he assumed the title of senior minister from 1990 till 2004,[42] and then minister mentor from 2004 to 2011. He remained a member of Parliament till his death in 2015. Thus, unlike his other two colleagues, Lee was a key maker and shaper of Singapore's grand strategy during the Cold War as well as the post-Cold War periods. Goh Chok Tong, Lee's successor and the second prime minister of Singapore, said that he "learnt to swim in the swirling ocean of foreign affairs from Rajaratnam, Mr Lee Kuan Yew." He recalled that he "read their speeches . . . taken by them to many meetings, and observed how they engaged other leaders," and "benefited from their advice." Goh noted that "together, they laid down the fundamental tenets of Singapore's foreign policy—to safeguard our sovereignty and freedom of action, stay relevant, make maximum number of friends and—if possible—no enemies, and respect international laws and norms in our dealings with other countries. These tenets continue to be salient today."[43]

OPERATIONALIZATION OF GRAND STRATEGY

Security studies scholars devote considerable attention to the development and content of strategy. While appropriate, it is incomplete because the implementation of strategy is as important. Singapore's grand strategy is operationalized or manifested in the following ways: One, through the promotion and support for multilateralism, both for economics and security. Lee Kuan Yew was already calling for "multilateral cooperation" (although the multilateral security arrangement idea was ahead of its time and did not take off) as early as 1966. To Lee, "the self-contained national unit, national self-sufficiency, is old-fashioned and out-of-date. It does not work unless you are a really big land mass like the United States of America or the USSR."

Thus, with regional cooperation, "you lump together 300 million people, and everybody stands to gain." He envisaged Singapore "could be the catalyst that could speed up the course of economic development" and act as "a spark plug" for economic progress and development in the region. But first, all the countries had to agree that "nobody can swallow up the whole and we have to cooperate."[44] Geographical proximity is a necessary but not sufficient condition for "if blind persons get together you are unlikely to get anywhere," Lee quipped.

Singapore supported the formation of ASEAN and "gave it an overt economic focus."[45] ASEAN has often been variously described as "the cornerstone," "keystone," as well as "linchpin" of Singapore's foreign policy.[46] The view is that with globalization, countries are becoming "more interconnected and interdependent," and thus what happens in the region affects Singapore—if the region prospers, Singapore will prosper. Conversely, if the region has problems, Singapore would also be negatively impacted.[47] Thus Goh Chok Tong (Singapore's second prime minister) said it is not in Singapore's interest to let ASEAN be divided.[48] By land area, Singapore, the smallest member of ASEAN, knows that it cannot be the leader of ASEAN but hopes "to be at best an honest broker."[49]

Twenty years later, in 1987, Lee again proposed multilateral cooperation—"In one inter-dependent inter-related world, the decline in the relative dominance of the leaders of the two blocs increases the likelihood of a multi-polar world, and with it the difficulties of multilateral cooperation." Multilateral cooperation was the "key to development"—"Hopes for a better life for our peoples depend on peace, stability and economic development in the world. We need to avoid or resolve regional wars and conflicts and to have international and regional economic cooperation . . . Of course, each can survive without the other (referring to the developed and developing countries). But to grow, to thrive, and to flourish, we need to work with each other."[50]

Lee repeated the foregoing two ideas or themes two years later in 1989 when it was much clearer that the confrontation between the communist and noncommunist blocs since World War II was over. Going forward, the competition between nations was likely to concentrate on economics.[51] In his October 1989 Commonwealth Heads of Government Meeting (CHOGM) speech, one month before the fall of the Berlin Wall, he observed that "as the balance between the major powers changes, other states in the world have little choice but to adjust. But not all these developments are adverse. There is a strong desire in the East and West, in the North and South, to concentrate energies and resources on economic development, and to restrain expenditure on arms. This could usher in an era of worldwide international cooperation through multilateral institutions."[52]

In December 1989, Goh (then first deputy prime minister) mooted the idea of the Singapore-Johore-Riau (SIJORI) Growth Triangle with the aim of strengthening "the regional links and to optimize the complementarity" of the three adjacent areas by combining "Singapore's management expertise, capital, technology and infrastructure with the abundant labour, land and natural resources of Johore and the Riau province."[53] The Riau Islands are the closest Indonesian province to Singapore. Singapore and Johore have, in the word of historian Kwa Chong Guan, a "deeply connected history."[54] With more Malaysian and Indonesian states joining, SIJORI was renamed and formalized as the Indonesia-Malaysia-Singapore Growth Triangle (IMS-GT) in December 1994.[55]

Singapore also supported the establishment of Asia-Pacific Economic Cooperation (APEC) first broached by Australian Prime Minister Bob Hawke in January 1989, initially as an informal ministerial-level dialogue group of twelve countries in November 1989, was a major expression of the increasing interdependence of regional economies at the cusp of the end of the Cold War. APEC as an institution was formalized in 1993. Singapore was "Australia's strongest backer within ASEAN."[56]

In a speech on January 8, 1993, Lee Kuan Yew (now senior minister) spoke about Singapore's need to develop an external economy—a "second wing" to give its economy an "external boost" just like other successful mature economies.[57] Since the speech, Arun Mahizhnan noted, "the development of the external economy has become a major preoccupation in Singapore."[58] Lee's speech echoed and gave his imprimatur to the report entitled *The Strategic Economic Plan: Towards a Developed Nation* issued by the Singapore government in 1991, which called upon "Singaporeans, who lacked a hinterland, to think of the whole world as their hinterland . . . Singapore needed to go global." The report envisaged going global as a series of concentric circles—"Singapore as a country, the region, the outer world, and finally the global economy in the outer ring."[59]

The Goh administration thus oversaw the development of Singapore's "second wing" (aka the "external economy"). Singapore became "a leader in negotiating free trade agreements to the rest of the world."[60] In the wake of the Asian financial crisis (1997), Singapore saw free trade agreements as the antidote or solution to ensure Singapore's economic survival. Its first bilateral free trade agreement was with New Zealand. As Manu Bhaskaran explained, "the web of bilateral agreements" would enhance Singapore's "regional hub status by expanding" the country's connectivity and access to many large economies." Given that Singapore is one of the most trade-dependent countries in the world, such agreements would also offer "some insurance" against a possible collapse of the multilateral trade order.[61]

By the end of Goh's tenure as prime minister in August 2004, Singapore had signed free trade agreements (FTAs) with Japan, Australia, the European Free Trade Area, Jordan (the first with a Middle Eastern country) and most importantly, the United States. Singapore is also one of the four founding members of the Trans-Pacific Partnership. The number of FTAs continue to grow.

There is another aspect of FTAs besides business and economics. An FTA is more than just "an economic integration that eliminates tariffs (and quantitative restrictions) between participating countries."[62] FTAs can also serve as "a tool that for addressing security issues, namely: cooperative diplomacy, security alliance, competitive bilateralism and isolation avoidance."[63] In Singapore's case, the leadership has "grafted the country's security requirements into its FTA agendas in the hope of effectively containing potential threats to its survival as a sovereign nation-state."[64] One example is that signed with the United States which is "the product of crisscrossing interests between the two states attempting to implant security elements within their trade relations."[65] It may be worth briefly noting that Singapore's "linkage attempts" to overcome its multidimensional security complex brought about by geographical constraints, Michael Magcamit warned, could result in for example, "its failure to strategically balance conflicting American, Chinese and Japanese interests in the region" as linkages can be a "double-edged sword" as "for every additional security that a linkage provides a specific referent, corresponding insecurity is reflected in other referents."[66]

Multilateral cooperation or multilateralism, which Singapore strongly advocated and continues to advocate, is not confined to the economic realm. One early example is the formation of the ASEAN Regional Forum (ARF). The ARF was inaugurated in Singapore in 1993. It was formally launched in Bangkok in July 1994. Although it was a Japanese idea, ASEAN was the driving force from the outset. ASEAN played a leading role in establishing the ARF with the objective of fostering "multilateral dialogue on security matters."[67] Singapore played a "quietly nudging" role by providing the first drafts of two key papers on the structure, role, and membership of the ARF that were later adopted at the ARF meetings in 1995 and 1996.[68]

It is common knowledge that ASEAN's twin objectives for the ARF (though not mentioned so explicitly) were, first, to "envelop" a rising China in this multilateral organization[69] and, second, to keep the unipolar power of the United States (absorbed by developments in Eastern Europe and elsewhere) engaged in the region within a multilateral framework. As the former Singapore diplomat Kishore Mahbubani observed, "the task of both restraining" the United States and China "while preserving at the same time their enthusiasm for the ARF is an inherently difficult task" even during the "propitious and relatively benign security environment" in the Asia-Pacific of the early 1990s. Then-Singapore Prime Minister Goh Chok Tong cautioned that if the Sino-US relation fail to stabilize, it would start a second Cold War affecting the whole region.[70] Singapore's support for the objectives of the ARF is consistent with Singapore and Lee Kuan Yew's views.

Another example is the creation of the Forum of Small States (FOSS) at the United Nations, another idea mooted by Lee Kuan Yew. It was launched in 1992 as an informal grouping of like-minded countries with populations of 10 million or thereabouts. In line with Singapore's policy of making as many friends as possible "who would be friends with us"[71] and be relevant and useful to the world, it has been, to cite some examples, helping developing countries build up their human resource capacity to address climate change threats, and more recently, helping small states with digital transformation and Covid-19 recovery, under an initiative called "Foss for Good."[72]

Singapore has also made itself relevant and useful to the United States and China at critical times while remaining nonaligned. For example, when the Philippine Congress in 1991 voted to shut down the American bases there, Singapore offered to upgrade its naval base to service the US fleet and serve as a transit point for US naval operations in the region. Singapore also played a positive role in assisting China's economic development when Deng Xiaoping was embarking on his open door and economic modernization policy in the 1980s, even when China was ostracized by the West in the immediate years after the Tiananmen Square incident. In return, Singapore is a beneficiary of security cooperation with the US and of China's economic success.

The next two demonstrations of Singapore's grand strategy are in the areas of defense and international law. Singapore takes the rule of law very seriously as it believes that "small states cannot survive, if interaction is governed by relative power."[73] Singapore has on occasions been criticized as being too legalistic in its interactions, but as Professor S. Jayakumar (who had held various ministerial appointments, including foreign minister, law minister, and coordinating minister for national security) said, "we should not be put off by such criticism of being legalistic."[74] Singapore had always advocated the settlement of disputes through international law, for example its territorial disputes with Malaysia. Similarly with the issue of the South China Sea dispute, while Singapore is not a claimant, as a trading nation, the security of the SLOC is critical. Singapore's consistent position is that it does not take sides on the merits or otherwise of the various disputes in the South China Sea and advocates for disputes to be resolved peacefully in accordance with international law. In the 2014 case of Russia's annexation of Crimea, the Singapore Foreign Ministry declared that "Singapore opposes the annexation of any country or territory as it contravenes international law. Singapore also objects to any unprovoked invasion of a sovereign country under any pretext."[75] This was the same attitude Singapore adopted with regard to the Vietnamese invasion of Kampuchea in December 1978. Singapore thus adopts a very consistent position. In response to Russia's invasion of Ukraine launched in February 2022, Singapore stood out among the Southeast Asian countries by imposing financial measures on Russian entities to restrict Moscow's ability to finance its war with Ukraine. As Singapore's chief justice put it, "For Singapore, the rule of law for Singapore is not so much an aspirational ideal as it is an existential necessity."[76]

Lee Hsien Loong quoted a Finnish diplomat who said that "as a small country, our only weapons are words and treaties." Singapore takes international norms and agreements seriously, "but ultimately, words have to be carried out and realized in actions and outcomes, consequences. Therefore, it is important for us to have a strong defence, to be able to protect Singapore when all else fails."[77] The primary role of the Singapore Armed Forces (SAF) is to be "the final guarantor of Singapore's sovereignty."[78] Singapore has certainly come a long way since 1965. The Yang Di-Pertuan Negara, in his address at the opening of the first Singapore Parliament, acknowledged that in 1965, Singapore had to "accept British bases for some time to come" because it was then unable to defend itself.[79] The goal was to "to be as independent of foreign defence assistance as possible."

Goh Keng Swee, Singapore's first minister of defense, recalled that on independence, Singapore had "two battalions, three quarters of them were Malaysians and British."[80] Goh elaborated during the second reading of the Singapore Army Bill on December 23, 1965, that the army is meant to defend Singapore and its people against external aggression but "today we are unable to do this task by ourselves" and "there is no use pretending that without the British military forces in Singapore today, the island cannot be easily overrun within a matter of hours by any neighboring country within a radius of 1,000 miles, if any of these countries care to do so." But Singapore cannot always depend on Britain. As early as December 1965, Goh was already laying plans for an eventual British withdrawal (which the British did earlier than expected). Fifty years later, Singapore's armed forces are generally considered one of the most powerful in the region, particularly its air force and navy.[81] The principle behind the transformation of Singapore's defense capability is distilled in Goh Keng Swee's 1971 speech, "What Kind of War?"[82] In this speech, Goh addressed the question of the options "open to Singapore in the prosecution of war against much larger countries." Singapore's physical size "makes it even more imperative to fight defensive battles outside the country." This meant that the sea "must be regarded as a vital means of movement of troops." In addition, "air supremacy must be achieved over a sustained period." In Goh's view, if Singapore could achieve "air supremacy and have the means of sea transport," the "geography of the archipelago" would confer "a decisive advantage upon Singapore." Given Singapore's population size, it should avoid at all costs avoid "a rifleman's war" because Singapore would not be able to bear the attrition of manpower compared to countries with large populations. Therefore, keeping abreast with, if not ahead of, technological developments has always been important to Singapore. In keeping with the times, "Digital Defence" (cyber-security) had been added as the new sixth pillar of Singapore's "Total Defence" strategy "in view of the increasing pace of global digitalization."[83]

CONCLUSION

In conclusion, this chapter, through describing a combination of Singaporean texts, institutions, and behaviors,[84] has shown that Singapore's grand strategy has been remarkedly consistent since the country came into being in 1965. This is principally because of two reasons—political stability through three cabinets (Singapore has been led by the same political party for the last half a century or more) and the fact that the fundamental realities that frame Singapore's existence, concerns, and interests have not changed: Singapore is still a very small state with no natural resources "except human beings in a small, strategic location,"[85] even if its land size has grown to 728.3 square kilometers and its population to 5.69 million.[86]

For the first time in twenty years, in May 2024, Singapore has a new prime minister. Lawrence Wong now leads what is described as the 4-G (fourth generation) government. The crafting of grand strategy has and still is concentrated in the topmost ranks of government. This is unlikely to change in the foreseeable future even though it has been observed that "foreign policy features more prominently in Singapore's domestic discourse."[87]

This being said, it is worth remembering that "grand strategy changes when the international system changes."[88] In the last fifty-odd years, despite having straddled the Cold War period and after, Singapore saw little need to change its grand strategy. Jennifer Mitzen reminds us that "no state's grand strategy can succeed in isolation; each requires a supportive international environment,"[89] and so far, it would appear the US, China, Malaysia, and Indonesia with their mixed motives have implicitly been cooperative.

Whether the current strategic rivalry between the US and China would lead to, or compel a change in Singapore's grand strategy, which has so far been successful, remains to be seen. As Singapore's prime minister Lee Hsien Loong (now senior minister) said in 2017, "as a friend to both America and China, Singapore can be put in a difficult situation if there is a friction between the two giants."[90]

NOTES

1. See for example, S. R. Nathan, "Singapore's Foreign Policy: Beginnings and Future," The Inaugural S. Rajaratnam Lecture, March 10, 2008 (MFA Diplomatic Academy, 2008); Lee Kuan Yew, "The Fundamentals of Singapore's Foreign Policy: Then & Now," S. Rajaratnam Lecture, April 9, 2009 (MFA Academy, 2009).
2. Edwin Lee, *Singapore: The Unexpected Nation* (ISEAS, 2008).
3. Bilahari Kausikan, "Pragmatic Adaptation, Not Grand Strategy, Shaped Singapore's Foreign Policy," in Barry Desker and Ang Cheng Guan (eds.), *Perspectives on the Security of Singapore: The First Fifty Years* (World Scientific & Imperial College Press, 2016), 295.
4. Paul C. Avery, Jonathan N. Markowitz, and Robert J. Reardon, "Disentangling Grand Strategy: International Relations Theory and US Grand Strategy," in *Texas National Security Review*, 3, no. 1, November 2018, 30.
5. Hal Brands, "Getting Grand Strategy Right: Clearing Away Common Fallacies in the Grand Strategy Debate," in Elizabeth Borgwardt, Christopher McKnight Nichols, and Andrew Preston (eds.), *Rethinking American Grand Strategy* (Oxford University Press, 2021), 32–34.
6. See for example Andrew Preston, "National Security as Grand Strategy: Edward Mead Earle and the Burdens of World Power," in Elizabeth Borgwardt, Christopher McKnight Nichols, and Andrew Preston (eds.), *Rethinking American Grand Strategy* (Oxford University Press, 2021), Chapter 11.
7. Peter Feaver, "What Is Grand Strategy and Why Do We Need It?" in *Foreign Policy*, April 8, 2009, https://foreignpolicy.com/2009/04/08/what-is-grand-strategy-and-why-do-we-need-it/
8. "MM Lee: We Cannot Be a Satellite of Any Nation" in *The Straits Times*, December 30, 2009.
9. Lee Hsien Loong, "Choice and Conviction—The Foreign Policy of a Little Red Dot," S. Rajaratnam Lecture, November 27, 2015 (MFA Academy, 2015).
10. Lee Kuan Yew speaking at the Singapore Legislative Assembly on March 5, 1957, quoted in Bilahari Kausikan, "A 'Happy Mistake': Bilahari Kausikan on Singapore's Biggest Foreign Policy Blunder" in *The Straits Times*, January 21, 2020.

11. Lee Kuan Yew, "The Fundamentals of Singapore's Foreign Policy: Then & Now," S. Rajaratnam Lecture, April 9, 2009 (MFA Academy, 2009); Lee Hsien Loong, "Choice and Conviction—The Foreign Policy of a Little Red Dot," S. Rajaratnam Lecture, November 27, 2015 (MFA Academy, 2015).
12. Richard Fontaine and Kristin M. Lord (eds.), *America's Path: Grand Strategy for the Next Administration*, May 31, 2012, https://www.cnas.org/publications/reports/americas-path-grand-strategy-for-the-next-administration
13. Loong, "Choice and Conviction."
14. Speech by the Minister of Foreign Affairs (Mr. S. Rajaratnam), December 17, 1965, *Singapore Parliament Reports* (Hansard).
15. Loke Hoe Yeong, *Speaking Truth to Power* (World Scientific, 2020), 275. General Benny Moerdani was commander-in-chief of the Indonesian National Armed Forces from 1983 to 1988 before becoming minister of defense and security of Indonesia.
16. Broadcast excerpts from an address given by the Prime Minister, Mr. Lee Kuan Yew, on "Changing Values in a Shrinking World" at the Political Study Centre; also see transcript of a speech by the Prime Minister Mr. Lee Kuan Yew at a seminar on "International Relations," held at the University of Singapore, October 9, 1966.
17. Transcript of a television interview with Prime Minister Lee Kuan Yew by three foreign press correspondents, Mr. Creighton Burns of the *Melbourne Age*, Mr. Nihal Singh of the *Statesman of India*, and Mr. Dennis Bloodworth of the *London Observer*, recorded at the studios of Television Singapura, July 28, 1966; transcript of a speech by Prime Minister Lee Kuan Yew at a seminar on "International Relations" held at the University of Singapore, October 9, 1966.
18. Lee Hsien Loong, "Choice and Conviction."
19. Closing address by Dr. Goh Keng Swee, minister of defense, at the 3rd SCSC course, November 19, 1971. This is one of the most important speeches to read for an understanding of the thinking behind the military dimension of Singapore's grand strategy. See also Lee Kuan Yew, *Hard Truths to Keep Singapore Going* (Straits Times Press, 2011), 322–3.
20. "Not Too Late for US, China to Rest Ties and Avert Clash; PM," in *The Straits Times*, January 30, 2021.
21. Lee Kuan Yew, "The Fundamentals of Singapore's Foreign Policy."
22. From American consulate in Singapore to Department of State, "Singapore Government Officialdom and Attitudes towards the United States," December 21, 1964, RG 59, Box 2452, POL 15-1 Malaysia.
23. From American Consulate in Singapore to Department of State, May 21, 1964, RG 59, Box 2452, POL 15-1 Malaysia.
24. Speech by the Minister of Foreign Affairs (Mr. S. Rajaratnam), December 16, 1965.
25. Speech by the Minister of Foreign Affairs (Mr. S. Rajaratnam), December 16, 1965.
26. Interview (Hugh D.S. Greenway, *Time/Life* bureau chief, Southeast Asia) with the prime minister, Mr. Lee Kuan Yew, Tuesday, June 10, 1969.
27. Interview (Hugh D.S. Greenway, *Time/Life* bureau chief, Southeast Asia) with the prime minister, Mr. Lee Kuan Yew, Tuesday, June 10, 1969.
28. Transcript of a press conference given by the prime minister, Mr. Lee Kuan Yew, at City Hall to local and foreign correspondents, June 2, 1966.
29. "'Pawns' in Conflict," *Wellington Dominion*, March 12, 1965.

30. Christopher Layne quoted in Elizabeth Borgwardt et al., (ed.), *Rethinking American Grand Strategy* (Oxford University Press, 2021), 220.
31. Chin Kin Wah, "Reflections on the Shaping of Strategic Cultures in Southeast Asia," in Derek de Cunha (ed.), *Southeast Asian Perspectives on Security* (ISEAS, 2000), 5.
32. Elizabeth Borgwardt et al. (ed.), *Rethinking American Grand Strategy* (Oxford University Press, 2021), 11.
33. Ken Booth, "The Concept of Strategic Cultures Affirmed," in Carl G. Jacobsen (ed.), *Strategic Power: USA/USSR* (Macmillan, 1990), 121.
34. S. Jayakumar, "Reflections on Diplomacy of a Small State," S. Rajaratnam Lecture, 2010, May 19, 2010; Goh Chok Tong, "The Practice of Foreign Policy for Sustained Growth—the Singapore Experience," S. Rajaratnam Lecture, October 17, 2014 (MFA Academy, 2009). For the "whole of society approach to cyber security," see Shashi Jaykumar (ed.), *State, Society and National Security: Challenges and Opportunities in the 21st Century* (World Scientific, 2016), Chapter 15.
35. Lee Hsien Loong, "Choice and Conviction."
36. Chan Heng Chee and Obaid ul Haq (eds.), *The Prophetic and the Political: Selected Speeches and Writings of S. Rajaratnam* (Graham Brash, 1987), 485–6.
37. Chin Kin Wah (ed.), *Defence Spending in Southeast Asia* (ISEAS, 1987), 203.
38. Kishore Mahbubani, *Has China Won?* (Public Affairs, 2020), 3.
39. Michael Leifer, *Singapore's Foreign Policy: Coping with Vulnerability* (Routledge, 2000), 7. See also Ang Cheng Guan, *Lee Kuan Yew's Strategic Thought* (Routledge, 2013), Introduction.
40. See Wilairat Kawin, *Singapore's Foreign Policy: A Study of the Foreign Policy System of a City-State*, unpublished PhD dissertation, Georgetown University, 1975, Chapter 4.
41. Alexander L. George, "The 'Operational Code': A Neglected Approach to the Study of Political Leaders and Decision-Making," in *International Studies Quarterly*, 13, No. 2 (June 1969), 190–222.
42. S. Rajaratnam was senior minister from 1985, the first time the title was introduced to 1988.
43. Goh Chok Tong, "The Practice of Foreign Policy for Sustained Growth—the Singapore Experience," S. Rajaratnam Lecture, October 17, 2014 (MFA Academy, 2009).
44. Transcript of a talk given by the prime minister, Mr. Lee Kuan Yew, on the subject "Big and Small Fishes in Asian Waters" at a meeting of the University of Singapore Democratic Socialist Club, June 15, 1966: Interview (Hugh D.S. Greenway, *Time/Life* bureau chief, Southeast Asia) with the prime minister, Mr. Lee Kuan Yew, Tuesday, June 10, 1969.
45. S. R. Nathan, Singapore's Foreign Policy: Beginnings and Future," Inaugural S. Rajaratnam Lecture, March 10, 2008 (MFA Diplomatic Academy, 2008).
46. Loong, "Choice and Conviction"; "ASEAN to Remain Linchpin of S'pore Foreign Policy," *The Straits Times*, November 8, 2016; Dr. Tony Tan, "The Domestic Context of Singapore's Foreign Policy," S. Rajaratnam Lecture, November 28, 2017 (MFA Academy, 2017).
47. "ASEAN to Remain Linchpin of S'pore Foreign Policy," *The Straits Times*, November 8, 2016.
48. Tong, "The Practice of Foreign Policy for Sustained Growth—the Singapore Experience."
49. "Vivian Balakrishnan: S'pore Will Never Be Leader of ASEAN, Can at Best Be Honest Broker," https://mothership.sg/2017/12/singapore-asean-chair-vivian-balakrishnan-small-states/

50. Speech by Mr. Lee Kuan Yew, prime minister of Singapore, opening the discussion on "World Political Scene: Global Trends and Prospects," Commonwealth Heads of Government meeting, Vancouver, Canada, October 13, 1987.
51. Lecture by the prime minister of Singapore to the Thai National Defence College, Oriental Hotel, Bangkok, September 19, 1989.
52. Toast by the prime minister at a dinner for Commonwealth Heads of Government, Shangri-La Hotel, October 25, 1989.
53. "Growth Triangle," https://eresources.nlb.gov.sg/infopedia/articles/SIP_58_2005-01-06.html
54. I wish to thank Mr. Kwa Chong Guan for sharing his draft essay, "Singapore and Johor: A Connected History."
55. "Growth Triangle"; see also Ooi Giok Ling, "The Indonesia-Malaysia-Singapore Growth Triangle: Sub-Regional Economic Cooperation and Integration," *GeoJournal*, 36, no.4, August 1995, 337–44.
56. Grame Dobell, "Lee Kuan Yew and Oz," March 24, 2015, https://www.aspistrategist.org.au/lee-kuan-yew-and-oz/
57. Lee Kuan Yew, "Efforts to Overcome the Dearth of Entrepreneurs in Singapore," speech at the Business Awards Ceremony at the Shangri-La Hotel, Singapore, January 8, 1993. See also Arun Mahizhnan, "Developing Singapore's External Economy," *Southeast Asian Affairs 1994* (ISEAS, 1994), 285–301.
58. Mahizhnan, "Developing Singapore's External Economy," 285.
59. Mahizhnan, "Developing Singapore's External Economy," 285–6. An earlier 1986 report, produced in the wake of Singapore's first post-independence recession in 1985, entitled *The Singapore Economy: New Directions,* cited offshore activities as a key factor for future growth.
60. Bridget Welsh, James Chin, Arun Mahizhnan, and Tan Tarn How (eds.), *Impressions of the Goh Chok Tong Years in Singapore* (NUS Press, 2009), 211.
61. Bridget Welsh, James Chin, Arun Mahizhnan, and Tan Tarn How (eds.), *Impressions of the Goh Chok Tong Years in Singapore* (NUS Press, 2009), 211–2.
62. Koichi Ishikawa, "The ASEAN Economic Community and ASEAN Economic Integration," *Journal of Contemporary East Asian Studies*, 10, no.1, 2021, 32.
63. Michael Intal Magcamit, *Small Powers and Trading Security: Contexts, Motives and Outcomes* (Palgrave Macmillan, 2016), 49–50.
64. Magcamit, "Trading in Paranoia: Exploring Singapore's Security-Trade Linkages in the Twenty-first Century," *Asian Journal of Political Science*, 23, No. 2, 2015, 186.
65. See discussion of the United States-Singapore Free Trade Agreement in Magcamit, "Trading in Paranoia," 194–7.
66. Magcamit, *Small Powers and Trading Security*, 223.
67. Carlyle A. Thayer, *Multilateral Institutions in Asia: The ASEAN Regional Forum* (The Asia-Pacific Center for Security Studies, December 2000), 5.
68. Presentation by Kishore Mahbubani, permanent secretary (Singapore Ministry of Foreign Affairs) at the Policy Forum organized by the Institute of Policy Development, September 20, 1996.
69. See Rosemary Foot, "China in the ASEAN Regional Forum: Organisational Processes and Domestic Modes of Thought," *Asian Survey*, 38, no. 5, May 1998, 425–40.
70. Presentation by Kishore Mahbubani, permanent secretary (Singapore Ministry of Foreign Affairs) at the Policy Forum organized by the Institute of Policy Development, September 20, 1996.

71. See Teo Chee Hean, "New Challenges and Strategies for a More Secure World," S. Rajaratnam Lecture, November 30, 2012 (MFA Diplomatic Academy, 2012).
72. "S'pore Prioritises and Structures Its Foreign Aid" in *The Straits Times*, November 9, 2004; "S'pore Quietly Helping Developing Nations, Says Envoy," *Today*, November 27, 2015; "Urgent Global Action Needed to Tackle Digital Divide: Vivian" *The Straits Times*, September 27, 2021.
73. Professor S Jayakumar, "Reflections on Diplomacy of a Small State," S. Rajaratnam Lecture, May 19, 2010 (MFA Diplomatic Academy, 2010).
74. Professor S Jayakumar, "Reflections on Diplomacy of a Small State."
75. http://www.mfa.gov.sg/content/mfa/media_centre/press_room/pr/2014/201403/press_20130321.html
76. The Honorable Chief Justice Sundaresh Menon, "The Rule of Law, the International Legal Order, and the Foreign Policy of Small States," S. Rajaratnam Lecture, October 15, 2019 (MFA Diplomatic Academy, 2019).
77. Loong, "Choice and Conviction."
78. Hean, "New Challenges and Strategies for a More Secure World."
79. Yang Di-Pertuan Negara's policy speech on the opening of Parliament on December 14, 1965, Singapore Parliament Reports (Hansard).
80. Melanie Chew, *Leaders of Singapore* (Resource Press Pte. Limited, 1996), 147.
81. "Taking a Closer Look at Singapore's 'Poison Shrimp' Defence Doctrine," *Defence Connect*, February 11, 2020, https://www.defenceconnect.com.au/key-enablers/5555-taking-a-closer-look-at-singapore-s-poison-shrimp-defence-doctrine; "How a Tiny City-State Became a Military Powerhouse with the Best Air Force and Navy in Southeast Asia," April 8, 2018, https://www.businessinsider.com/singapore-military-best-air-force-navy-southeast-asia-2018-4
82. Closing address by Dr. Goh Keng Swee, Minister of Defence, at the 3rd SCSC course, November 19, 1971.
83. "Digital Defence as the New Sixth Pillar of Total Defence," https://www.mindef.gov.sg/web/portal/mindef/news-and-events/latest-releases/article-detail/2019/February/15feb19_fs
84. Rush Doshi proposed that grand strategy can be deduced from a country's texts, behavior, and also national security institutions. See Rush Doshi, *The Long Game: China's Grand Strategy to Displace American Order* (Oxford University Press, 2021), 9–10, 16–18.
85. "Singapore Is a Nation in the Making," *The Straits Times*, January 5, 2010.
86. These are 2020 figures. See also Professor S Jayakumar, "Reflections on Diplomacy of a Small State"; and ST Graphics in *The Straits Times*, August 9, 2015, Microfilm Reel NL 33598.

    Loong, "Choice and Conviction."
87. Tan, "The Domestic Context of Singapore's Foreign Policy."
88. Michael Clarke, *American Grand Strategy and National Security* (Palgrave Macmillan, 2021), 27.
89. Jennifer Mitzen, "Illusion or Intention? Talking Grand Strategy into Existence," *Security Studies*, 24, no. 1, March 2015, 65.
90. "PM: S'pore's Position Will Be Become Tougher if US-China Tensions Rise," *The Straits Times*, March 2, 2017.

CHAPTER 11

Thailand

Pongphisoot Busbarat

Unlike major powers, Thailand's grand strategy is not officially stated as such in any particular document. Rationalist theorists, both within realism and liberalism, assume that only great powers may possess enough resources and institutions to build such a grand strategy that aims for a long-term goal.[1] However, as the second-largest economy in Southeast Asia and the most advanced nation in the mainland subcontinent with an active role in the region, Thailand's grand strategy is present if we look at the continuing pattern of its foreign policy behavior. The author argues that Thailand's grand strategy exists, though sometimes unconsciously. It is in the form of self-designation as a pivotal state in mainland Southeast Asia. This unwritten and discursive grand strategy was shaped through Thailand's nation-building process whereby Bangkok elites attempted to consolidate its political control domestically and legitimacy regionally.

In this case, history matters and helps us understand and predict the course of Thailand's grand strategy to respond to various facing issues. The first core feature influencing the construction of Thailand's grand strategy lies in the transformation of Siam (the former name of Thailand) from a traditional kingdom to a modern state in the late nineteenth century. Faced with pressure and encroachment from the European powers, Siamese elites responded by gradually modernizing their kingdom. This is somewhat different from its neighboring polities, some of which opposed changes or resisted militarily if they perceived they were strong enough. Other weaker kingdoms mostly sought protection from Western powers and eventually fell into their colonization.

In the case of Siam, responses to the European powers resulted in many outcomes. First, the Bangkok modernizer elites led by King Mongkut attempted to consolidate their power by utilizing the West as their tool vis-à-vis other conservative forces. However, the king's power was relatively weak and still needed to rely on the support of great noble families, who controlled Siam's purse and military forces in practice.[2] It was not until his son, King Chulalongkorn, that the palace could slowly mobilize support from various groups of elites and centralize power. The centralization project under King Chulalongkorn importantly expanded Bangkok's control not only over local elites but also over other traditional vassal states. Siam initially sent its own officials to give consultation to them and eventually convinced or forced them to be under its sovereignty.[3] The centralization process not only transformed Siam into a modern absolutist state but also gradually transferred local people's loyalty to a new ruler in Bangkok.

Siam's subsequent modernization aimed to demonstrate to the West that Siam was civilized, hence not subject to colonization. The modernization mostly modeled Western ideas and state-building, including a bureaucratic system, modern military, legal system, transportation, and Western-styled architecture and urban planning. It also included adjusting, adopting, or abandoning Siamese traditional practices and mannerisms that were regarded by Westerners as barbaric acts—crawling, sitting on the floor, using hands to eat, including refining Buddhism to be compatible with scientific rationality.[4] In turn, the making of a civilized Siam shaped the Bangkok elite's perception of foreign countries. It can be said that while the Thai elites did not trust the West's intention, they look at the West as a source of civilization and advancement. In turn, civilizing Siam distinguished itself from its adjacent neighbors as less civilized, weaker, and more threatening to its country's security.[5]

Therefore, this process of modern state-building created a mindset of Thai policymakers that survival amid great power politics was essential to the nation. It also shaped Thai elites' perception that Thailand was superior and in a leading position in the region and needed to secure such a position in the region. This author argues that this ontological security consciously and unconsciously shapes Thailand's grand strategy throughout history until today.

This chapter is divided into four sections to explain how Thailand's grand strategy can be viewed. The following section discusses Thailand's strategic priorities and how these are connected to the aforementioned ontological security construct. The next section focuses on Thailand's key strategic actors that it cares about most in formulating foreign policy and strategy. The subsequent part looks into how domestic factors, in the case of Thailand, are relevant in building its grand strategy. This will mainly touch upon

Thailand's "holy trinity"—nation, religion, and monarchy—that constitute the frame within which its grand strategy may be shaped. Finally, the chapter delves into how this grand strategy reveals medium- and short-term operationalization, as we can observe from Thailand's foreign policy and security strategies.

STRATEGIC PRIORITIES

Informed by its history of modern state-building, Thailand's strategic priorities are thus built around two primary goals: first, strengthening the authority of Bangkok as the center of modern Thai politics; and second, elites' desire to maintain Thailand's leading position vis-à-vis other neighboring countries. Therefore, Thailand's grand strategy will explicitly or implicitly reflect these two goals in its official policies and practice.

National Integrity

Thailand is always proud of its independence amid the power scramble for Southeast Asia among European powers. This pride is credited mainly to the adroit diplomacy of the Thai kings and elites. However, although Siam or Thailand has never been colonized and a modern Thailand has relatively clear boundaries, its struggle with the colonial powers during the late nineteenth century to protect its territories helps shape the significance of the priority over national integrity.

The Thai policy elite and a large segment of the population have been struck with a historical legacy of "unequal treaties" in which Siam had conceded its claims over its old controls.[6] The major narrative maintains that Siam was forced to let go of some vast land areas to preserve its core area that appears on a modern map. Similar to China's century of humiliation, Thailand's national narrative also centers around Siam as a victim of colonization that lost its territories encompassing the whole of modern Laos and Cambodia, part of the Shan State and Tenasserim State in Myanmar, and a few northern Malay states.[7] This narrative is well integrated into Thai official history and is still taught in Thai schools from the primary level today.

From this perspective, territorial integrity is unequivocally the first priority in Thailand's grand strategy. The recent National Security Policy and Plan (2023–27) demonstrates the importance of this element. It says:

> The ultimate goal of the National Security Policy and Plan (2023–2027) attaches priority to preserving the national interests stipulated in the National Strategy (2018–2037), including independence, sovereignty, and the stability of the major national institutions from any forms of threats . . ."[8]

In the document, many issues related to the protection of national integrity are listed. These include aims to strengthen Thailand's capabilities in intelligence, national preparedness, defense capability, protection of Thailand's southernmost provinces, border security, and maritime security. The list corresponds to preceding national security policy documents in the past. Therefore, it can be said that national integrity in the physical sense ranks as the top priority of Thailand's grand strategy.

Regime Security

As part of the national integrity, the regime's security is deemed significant and became an integral part of Thai politics. During King Chulalongkorn's reign, Bangkok's centralization projects helped strengthen the palace's power. Bangkok's administrative controls, such as abolishing slavery and building a modern military and bureaucracy, all empowered the king to control the new modern state apparatuses. These tactics gradually stripped the power of other rival princes and noble families.

King Vajiravudh also encountered internal and external challenges to his legitimacy. Faced with less respect compared to his father, Vajiravudh promoted an official nationalism to boost his legitimacy, which centered around loyalty to the king and the Thai race. Externally, Siam also feared the spread of China's republican ideas among overseas Chinese communities. This development could challenge the Thai monarchy's political and economic stability due to the large Chinese ethnic population who controlled significant parts of the economy. In response, Vajiravudh raised an anti-Chinese sentiment that strongly criticized them as a parasite of Thai society. A similar attitude against the Chinese also reemerged during the interwar period under the nationalist government of Marshall Plaek Phibunsongkhram or Phibun. Phibun also utilized this strategy to consolidate his power amid his decision to align with Japan in December 1941 and join the Axis allies in World War II a month later. Phibun justified his alignment with Japan to preserve Thailand's national integrity. On the other hand, siding with Japan also helped strengthen his political power vis-à-vis other political cliques.

In the postwar context, communism was viewed as a vital threat to Thailand's national security and integrity. The Thai elites viewed communism as incompatible with Thai values and institutions. In particular, the communist ideas promoted the overthrow of religious beliefs and the monarchy. All of these were against Thainess and harmful to Thailand's "holy trinity": the nation, religion, and monarchy.[9] Therefore Thailand's grand strategy during the Cold War was set to guard against communist expansion both within and from outside the country. Aligning with the US-led free world was an obvious strategic choice. Apart from forming a security alliance with Washington, Bangkok also launched economic development projects that aimed to minimize the root causes for the Thai people to support communism against the Thai state.

Therefore, guided by the preceding strategy, Thailand supported the United States against the communist expansion in the region in the two major wars in East Asia, the Korean War and the Indochina Wars. Notably, during the Vietnam War, Bangkok saw the expansion of communist influence in Indochina as a great danger. Bangkok supported the royalist Lao government and sent a secret operation to help the American Central Intelligence Agency (CIA) fight against the leftist movement in Laos.[10] Bangkok also sought Washington to reconfirm its security commitment to Thailand's national integrity by signing the Rusk-Thanat Joint Communiqué in March 1962.[11] This security syndrome was intensified when South Vietnam, Cambodia, and Laos fell into communism within the same year in 1975. With the changing international and regional environment following the rapprochement between China and the United States and the Vietnamization, Bangkok adjusted its foreign policy strategy to restore official relations with communist countries so that it could neutralize their support for internal communist insurgencies. However, the attempt to coexist with communist neighbors failed when Vietnam invaded Cambodia on Christmas Day, 1978.

The Vietnamese invasion once again shook Thailand's national integrity. The fear of communist neighbors resurged within the Thai elites and the public. Internationally, Thailand sought omnidirectional support from different countries to pressure Vietnam, not only from the United States and the West but also China. Thailand was active within ASEAN to build an international coalition. It can be seen that, in retrospect, Thailand's active role in ASEAN during the course of this event was meant to secure its regime stability and the holy trinity of the Thai nation.

Regime stability also played an important role in shaping Thailand's grand strategy in the post-Cold War era. Although the political legitimacy during the democratization period in the early 1990s was relatively stable, economic shock in the late 1990s put pressure on post-crisis governments. Despite being a US security treaty ally, the Thai elites experienced not only minimal

American assistance but more pressure from the IMF backed by Washington. This disillusion was exacerbated by Washington not supporting the Thai candidate for the World Trade Organization director-general post in 1999. Thai policymakers started to cast doubt on American ill intention.[12] This series of late 1990s events prompted Thailand to reconsider adjusting its grand strategy. While having bitter experiences with America, other Asian powers rendered more significant help, especially China and Japan. As a result, Thai policymakers in the early 2000s started to divert their economic orientation toward Asia, especially China. Under Prime Minister Thaksin Shinawatra, Thailand's turn to China aimed to tap its market potential for Thai exports. More than other prime ministers before him, Thaksin visited China to discuss expanding bilateral trade and seeking its support for Thailand's regional initiative (which will be detailed in a later section). At this turn of the century, Thailand's grand strategy started to swing away from the United States and focus more on Asia.

The focus on regime stability was strong after the military coup in 2014. The coup government aimed at securing its standing and recognition in the international community. The coup leaders were cornered by Western sanctions and criticism, especially from Washington. This resulted in Bangkok turning to Beijing for political support to boost its legitimacy and recognition. Since 2014 Thailand's external strategy stepped closer to China in every realm.[13] Bilateral political, economic, and security cooperation were expanded. The military leadership also want to emulate the China model to consolidate its power at home. The new constitution built a complex mechanism to empower the Senate, all members appointed by the coup leaders. In contrast, the lower house faced barriers to challenging the power of the executive and the upper house.[14] In terms of security relations, Thailand relied more on China as an alternative source of arms supplies. More arms sales were agreed upon during the military government to modernize the Thai arms forces, such as purchasing submarines and tanks, including the establishment of military maintenance, repair, and overhaul (MRO) facility for Chinese weaponry.[15] All of these developments in the post-2014 coup point to the change in Thailand's strategy to secure the regime in power.

Economic Development

Economic development is also an essential part of Thailand's grand strategy planning. Like many countries in East Asia, economic performance is indispensable for regime legitimacy. During the Cold War, economic development was viewed as a way to reduce poverty in rural areas, hence delegitimizing communist ideology. After Marshall Sarit Thanarat seized power in 1957 and pledged full support to US-led anticommunism, Thailand kicked off its five-year economic development planning in 1961. Allying with the United States not only secured Sarit's regime for almost another decade but also came with enormous US economic assistance. Many infrastructure projects were supported by the United States, such as a new highway from Bangkok to the rural area in the northeast. Ports and airports were built and partly used for American operations in Indochina for military purposes. Investment and trade from the United States and its allies, especially Japan, also flourished.[16] Admittedly, American troops in Thailand during the Vietnam War also stimulated and diversified the Thai economy despite its social consequences such as urban migration, sex tourism, environmental impacts, and so on.

In the latter half of the 1980s, after the Plaza Accord, Thailand experienced the relocation of Japanese investment, and later from other Northeast Asian economies. It helped boost the Thai economy from 1985 onward when gross domestic product (GDP) growth was around 8 percent on average, with a peak of 13 percent in 1988.[17] During the decade of the economic miracle, Thai policy elites also aimed to use the justification of economic development to improve Thailand's national integrity. The government of semiauthoritarian General Prem Tinsulanonda issued executive order No. 66/2523 to reconcile with the leftist movement in Thailand. The order focused on addressing political grievances' social and economic causes, including promoting more open space for political participation.[18] This helped lessen pressures from communist insurgencies that had challenged the Thai state. Coupled with economic growth in the 1980s, Thailand experienced further political stability. The size of the middle class grew steadily and became an important force for democratization from the late 1980s through the 1990s.[19]

The democratization bore fruits in 1988 when Prem stepped down and opened for a general election, which brought the first elected civilian prime minister since 1979 under former General Chatichai Choonahavan. Chatichai's grand strategy is reflected in his famous policy, *turning the battlefields into marketplaces.* It had economic development as a core by pushing to end the Cambodian conflict and aiming to integrate Indochina into the market economy. This helped alleviate Thailand's security threat while ensuring its continued economic growth. Although the military attempted to reassert its role in politics through the 1991 coup, it was strongly resisted by the growing middle class and businesses that benefited from economic expansion for a decade.[20]

The Asian financial crisis (AFC) in 1997 also deepened economic issues into a core grand strategy of successive Thai governments for economic rehabilitation and reform. Importantly, the AFC saw a gradual gearing of Thailand's grand strategy toward Asia and China's economic centrality. The bitterness from the AFC influenced the elites' perception that the West was unreliable and may even threaten the kingdom. From the late 1990s onward, Thailand joined other Asian countries, especially within a broader East Asia, to promote East Asian cooperation.[21] The ASEAN Plus Three process gained momentum as part of a regional effort to seek regional solutions to various problems many countries were facing from globalization, including economic security, transnational crimes, piracy, and even terrorism.

Thailand and the region enjoyed relative economic stability due partly to relying more on China's economic power. Compared to America and other Western nations, East Asia and Thailand recovered faster from the global economic recession between 2007 and 2010. Although Thailand's GDP plummeted in 2008 and 2009, it bounced back to 7.5 percent in 2010.[22] In the 2000s East Asia also witnessed complex arrangements of free trade agreements (FTAs) both bilaterally and regionally. Thailand was also within this trend and entered bilateral FTAs with, for example, Australia, Chile, China, Laos, New Zealand, Japan, Peru, and India. Thailand was also part of ASEAN's effort to expand its FTAs with major trade partners. FTA talks were concluded between ASEAN and Australia, New Zealand, China, India, Japan, and Korea. Recently, ASEAN also successfully led the establishment of a broader FTA under the Regional Comprehensive Economic Partnership (RCEP) between ten ASEAN countries, Australia, China, India, Korea, Japan, and New Zealand,[23] forming the largest free trade group and accounting for one-third of the world GDP. This post-AFC development points to Thailand's economic growth and development as one of the primary goals of the grand strategy.

In recent decades Thailand has faced challenges to its political stability. The country experienced two military coups, in 2006 and 2014, which deepened the political divide between conservative and progressive forces. Despite this ongoing political turmoil, the government in power consistently prioritized economic development as a means of maintaining regime stability and showcasing its performance. After the 2014 coup, General Prayut Chan-o-cha ruled under military governance for six years before transitioning to a civilian government through a democratic election in 2019, extending his leadership for another four years. During his nine years in power, significant economic development projects were launched, including the completion of the nearly 900-kilometer-long Thai-Chinese high-speed railway, the transformation of the eastern seaboard economic zone into the Eastern Economic Corridor (EEC), and the high-speed railway project connecting U-Tapao Airport in the EEC with Bangkok's two major airports, Suvarnabhumi and Don Mueang. The long-envisioned Kra Canal project, aimed at boosting the economy by creating a seafaring route between the Indian Ocean and the Gulf of Thailand, was also revived. Despite its potential to enhance regional connectivity and trade, the project ultimately failed to gain parliamentary approval.

Following the May 2023 election, economic policies remain a central focus for the new governments under Prime Minister Srettha Thavisin of the Pheu Thai Party, and subsequently Ms. Paetongtarn Shinawatra. The proposed Land Bridge project, which replaces the Kra Canal initiative, continues to receive political backing. While both projects share the goal of enhancing connectivity between the Indian Ocean and the Gulf of Thailand, the Land Bridge envisions road and railway links between seaports on Thailand's east and west coasts.[24] In addition to infrastructure development, the government actively promotes Thailand's "soft power" through initiatives aimed at showcasing Thai culture, tourism, and products on the global stage.[25]

Various economic stimulus packages have also been introduced and are gradually being implemented, most notably the "digital wallet" initiative that provides THB 10,000 to low-income individuals.[26] These economic policies reflect the consistent prioritization of economic development as the foundation of political stability in Thailand, regardless of the governing regime. Importantly, these efforts aim to revitalize the Thai economy to maintain its influential role in the region.

EXTERNAL FACTORS

Third-Party Actors

Due to the disappearance of ideological barriers, Thailand's strategy became more pragmatic by diversifying its interaction with different powers. In the security area, while the Thai-US security alliance remains the core of strategic planning, China is among the significant actors asserting more roles in Thailand's defense. Due partly to US sanctions following the military coup in 2014, Bangkok turned to seek more cooperation with China especially in arms procurement and joint exercise. For example, Thailand decided to buy three Chinese submarines in 2015. In 2019 the Thai army also made other arms deals with China to replace its 150 outdated American tanks and armored vehicles. There were also other arms procurements from other arms forces, such as antiship missiles, amphibious ships, and air missiles. Moreover, Thailand also seeks China's military technology transfer. A high-level discussion on this issue led to the establishment of a military MRO facility in Khon Kaen province for repairing certain Chinese tanks (VT-4 and VT-1) and for future domestic production of similar equipment.[27]

Security cooperation with China is not merely instrumental but also reflects Thailand's negative perception of the United States. The negative image may have stemmed from two decades ago when the American response to Thailand's financial crisis was minimal. However, this memory is retained by the Thai policy elites. The coup in 2014 was merely the tip of the iceberg that deteriorated the changing dynamic in Thai-US relations in the twentieth century.

Economic diversification with different partners would be ideal in terms of economic strategy. Certainly, traditional trade partners remain important. For instance, the US market remains a top destination for Thai exports, and Japan is still one of the top investors and trade partners with the kingdom and has been for decades. However, Thailand's foreign economic strategy has gradually geared toward China since the early 2000s. Chinese trade and inbound investment have increased as a result. China surpassed Japan as Thailand's number-one trade partner in 2014.[28] Thailand exported to the United States and China equally, accounting for approximately 12 percent of its total export in 2019.[29] Although export to the US market increased in 2022 to approximately 17 percent, mainly due to the diversion of trade during the US imposition of higher tariff on China, Thailand's export to China remained around the same figure.[30] While Japan invests in Thailand more than other investors, China fiercely competes with Japan, and its annual inward foreign direct investment (FDI) far exceeded Japan's in 2019.[31] Although Japan, the United States, and Singapore remain the major three biggest investors in Thailand, China's role is speedily catching up. Therefore, closer ties with China benefit Thailand in many ways and affect Thailand's ability to exercise its balancing strategy within the fierce power competition between Washington and Beijing in the recent decade.

However, since experiencing friction with Washington during the AFC and under military regimes, Thailand has viewed deepening economic interaction with China as a strategy to sustain its economic and political stability. This has shaped the perception among Thai policy elites that Beijing is more reliable than its American counterpart. Therefore, despite the Thai-US alliance, in practice, Thai-Chinese relations are relatively more vibrant, with regular contacts between leaders, including members of the Thai royal family and policymakers. This perception was evident when Thailand reopened its borders to welcome foreign tourists after the pandemic. While in the earlier phase of reopening, Thailand experienced a surge of tourists from other parts of the world—especially Russia, the Middle East, and South Asia—the arrival of the first group of Chinese tourists after China lifted its zero-COVID policy was marked by special attention. Deputy Prime Minister and Minister of Public Health Anutin Charnvirakul, Minister of Transport Saksayam Chidchob, and Minister of Tourism and Sports Phiphat Ratchakitprakarn personally greeted them at the gate of Bangkok airport.[32] This gesture underscored the importance of China's place in Thailand's policymakers' minds.

Threats and Opportunities

The Thai-US relationship is still a cornerstone in Thailand's security policy based on its Cold War security treaties. The majority of arms and equipment in the Thai armed forces are from American suppliers. Most of the Thai military are US-trained, and Thailand's military doctrine is still aligning with the Americans. Every year, Thailand and the United States continue to hold Exercise Cobra Gold—the largest joint military exercise in the Asia-Pacific region, which later expanded to incorporate other Thai and US strategic partners.

Therefore, close ties with the United States are an opportunity for Thailand to utilize as a balancing tool against increasing Chinese influence in the country and the region. Thai policy elites understand this leverage and try to keep the relationship as normal as possible. Certainly, bitter experiences throughout the post-Cold War period have affected the ties from time to time. However, it is unimaginable that Bangkok would abandon Washington. Closer ties in recent years with China could have an advantage on Thailand's grand strategy to a certain degree. As the United States is a global power with various priorities, Thai policymakers are concerned that Thailand's strategic value within US foreign policy strategy is reduced. Playing a China card by showing that Thailand is increasingly comfortable with China could, in a way, also attract Washington's attention.

This opportunity can be seen from President George W. Bush onward when US administrations tried to reassure their Thai counterpart of US interests. The strengthening of counterterrorism between the two countries prompted Washington to designate Thailand as a major non-NATO ally in 2003. During the Obama administration, Thailand was expected to be a key ally in the Pivot to Asia. Unfortunately, this goal failed due to Thai domestic politics once the military staged a coup in 2014. During the Trump administration, there was a brief attempt in 2017 when the White House offered an olive branch to the junta leader, which practically normalized the cold relations since the 2014 coup. During a series of Asia trips by US high-level officials in 2021, the Biden administration also dispatched some of them to Thailand, including Secretary of State Anthony Blinken. Unfortunately, his trip had to cut Thailand at the last minute because a reporter traveling with the delegation was detected with COVID-19 before heading to Bangkok.[33]

China is also an opportunity for Thailand's grand strategy to maintain its effective hedge. As mentioned earlier, Thailand's economic bandwagon with China helps sustain its economic growth, contributing to the elites' political legitimacy and stability. Courting China also benefits Thailand's attempt to assert its regional leadership, as seen in the case of the Asia Cooperative Dialogue (ACD). China also backed the military leaders since the 2014 coup against Western criticism and sanction. Notably, strengthening Thai-Chinese relations has enabled the military-led government to implement a grand economic development project to upgrade the Thai economy under Thailand 4.0. The EEC project on the eastern seaboard is a spearhead of this grand plan. The EEC aims to attract a new round of foreign investment focusing on automation and robotics, aviation and logistics, biofuel and biochemicals, and digital and green economy.[34]

In this connection, Thailand has sought cooperation with its Chinese counterparts to support the EEC's strategic plan for investment and trade, especially the Chinese Ministry of Commerce. The Hong Kong Trade Development Council and the Industrial and Commercial Bank of China also assist in cooperation in business opportunities promotion. The EEC also partners with the Beijing Genomics Institute to promote medical industry cooperation, with Alibaba Group for e-commerce and logistic business, and with China's Jiulong Automobile for the electronic automobile industry. At the same time, the Thai government's plan to develop the EEC into Thailand's aerotropolis is modeled on the Zhengzhou Airport Economic Zone in Henan Province.[35] In mid-2021, as a result, China (including Hong Kong) invested the most in this economic zone.[36]

In turn, the opportunities from hedging between Washington and Beijing pose a challenge to Thailand's grand strategy. As Thai-US ties soured from time to time since the AFC and deteriorated deeply during the recent coup, Thai-Chinese relations have gained strength in an disproportionate manner. Economic dependence on China has started to limit Thailand's ability to maneuver its hedging strategy. Thai policy elites often take China factors into account when dealing with the United States to avoid offending the former. Although this is not a vital threat to Thai national integrity, it challenges Thailand's policy autonomy and choice. In fact, in the early years after the Cold War, Thai policymakers assessed that China would potentially become a challenge in manipulating Thailand's political and economic policy due to its close relationship with Thai political and business elites.

Moreover, as a major country in ASEAN, Bangkok's positioning closer to Beijing widens ASEAN's differences in terms of the group's attitude toward China and the United States. ASEAN's disunity would affect its ability to manage external powers' relations, some of which may directly impact ASEAN member states' national interests. Examples can be seen in ASEAN's dividing position toward China's assertive stance in the South China Sea disputes or China's influence in the lower Mekong subregion.

Types of Conflicts

Besides its border disputes with neighboring countries, Thailand has no immediate severe conflicts with other countries. Although most of the border disputes with all the neighbors except Malaysia are not settled, they do not pose any serious challenge to Thailand's grand strategy. The problems have several bilateral demarcation mechanisms to facilitate negotiation on a regular basis.

However, Thailand's grand strategy in the long term is more about intense power competition between the United States and China, as mentioned earlier. The ability of Thailand to maintain a balanced position amid this tension mainly relies on its internal factors. A decade of domestic conflicts since the mid-2000s that brought military power back into politics has caused foreign policy imbalance and disarray. The polarization of Thai politics between the conservative and progressive forces, in turn, influences how each perceives the United States and China. A simple evaluation may suggest that the former sees China more positively as an economic and political opportunity. The latter is warier of Chinese influence in Thailand, especially as a challenge to Thailand's democracy and human rights.

Therefore, as long as the military remains strong and holds a tight grip on Thai politics, we may expect warm ties between China and Thailand. As a result, China's good relationship with the regime may act as an opposing force against the pro-democracy movement. China's image and soft power will seriously deteriorate, especially among the younger generation who share more democratic values with liberal democracy. In the future, therefore, generational change in political leadership and public opinion toward progressive values may strain Thai-China relations. This logic also applies to the case of American influence and image in Thailand. Although Thai-US relations will likely continue, clashes in political values between Bangkok establishments and Washington can reemerge from time to time, particularly on democracy and human rights. This is reflected in the survey among Thai military officials in 2017 indicating that, instead of China, the United States was viewed more as a threat to Thailand's security.[37] It is apparent that this survey demonstrates Thai elites' frustration over the American pressure during the coup government.

This difference will augment the long-standing suspicion of American intentions toward Thailand accumulated since the AFC. The possible leadership change toward the progressive political front in the future will likely help upgrade Thai-US relations while putting stress on Thai-Chinese relations. In short, domestic conflict in Thailand is closely linked to Thailand's balancing and hedging strategy between external powers. In the context of US-China competition, Thailand's grand strategy to keep both powers to its advantage may not be fully effective.

In this situation, countries around the region are also gradually adjusting their strategy toward each pole, though implicitly. While China is still an economic opportunity, many countries also try to reduce their reliance on the Chinese market. For instance, in the past five years, South Korea, Taiwan, and Japan have refocused their investment sites and markets to Southeast Asia. Their security policies also align with Washington, such as on Taiwan issues, the South China Sea, and the management of the Mekong basin. In recent years, Singapore, Vietnam, and the Philippines have also increasingly supported Washington's policy in Southeast Asia. Again, this could widen the policy gap among East Asian nations, especially within ASEAN, which will exacerbate ASEAN's ineffectiveness in dealing with great power tension.

Thailand's Fundamental Values

Thailand's grand strategy is shaped by certain fundamental values embedded within Thai identity, which were constructed during the country's modern state-building processes. The worldview behind this identity has profoundly influenced Thailand's elite policymakers, serving as a cognitive framework that guides them in shaping institutions and processes. As a result, this perspective functions as a heuristic tool in formulating strategies and in addressing national security and other foreign policy concerns.

DOMESTIC FACTORS

Underlying national integrity as a core of the grand strategy, there is an overarching value that Thai policymakers maintain constructed around its holy trinity mantra: the nation, religion, and the monarchy. The Thai policy elites also emphasize that the Thai people must uphold and protect these institutions, which are also crystallized as core elements of Thai nationalism. Throughout Bangkok's centralization project over its vassal states in the late nineteenth century, Bangkok attempted to mobilize loyalty from these peripheral areas not only from their rulers but from their people, both by persuasion and coercion.[38] Bangkok gradually replaced local authorities and power with Bangkok officials. Not only did Siamese elites impose their power over traditional local administrations, but they also promoted a new identity for the new nation.

An essential tool for propagating Thai nationalism was mass education throughout the newly demarcated territory under Siamese control using standard Thai language rather than spoken vernacular and local scripts. Public education was, therefore, rolled out in the late nineteenth century.[39] By 1921 the Thai state enacted a compulsory education law requiring everyone from the age of seven to fourteen to be schooled. Practically, this helped expand the number of schools around the country, both those run by the state administrations at different levels and private schools.[40] Within compulsory education, official Thai nationalism was used as the state's tool to imbue the imagined Thai community and identity. Thai school textbooks reinforced both physical and ideational elements of national integrity. They told the story of the Thai race that upheld peace but was forced to move to present-day Thailand. They repeated the national heroes, both past kings and commoners, who fought against neighboring enemies and helped build and protect the kingdom. They also portrayed the loss of parts of the original territories to Britain and France and praised the skillfulness of the Thai kings who preserved Thai independence.[41]

In fact, since the end of the Cold War, Thailand's physical sovereignty faced less pressure apart from sporadic small-scale skirmishes over some areas along the border. The historical temple of the Preah Vihear area from time to time reemerged as a border conflict between Thailand and Cambodia. Generally, the tension arose due to domestic struggles in each country that mobilized nationalism to strengthen their ruling party's political power. The most recent eruption of tension over this ancient temple was between 2008 and 2011. It was a combination of Thai and Cambodian politics. The

Thai nationalist front opposing the then-incumbent government of the time highjacked the issue to discredit the government. In Cambodia the issue also touched upon Cambodian nationalism and benefited Hun Sen's public support in the incoming election in 2013.[42]

The separatist movement in the three southernmost Muslim-majority provinces is perhaps the most pressing issue for Thailand's national integrity. The insurgency reemerged in 2001 after waning in the 1990s due to political liberalization. Structural causes, including history, ethnic and religious differences, socioeconomic marginalization, the government's hawkish approaches to the problem, and the Islamization of the Muslim identity in Thailand enabled the insurgency to expand.[43] Although the Muslim world showed sympathy to the insurgents and provided moral support and humanitarian assistance to those taking refuge in their countries, none officially recognized or aided the group. Most Muslim countries maintain good relations with Thailand, especially within ASEAN, in which noninterference is a paramount intramural principle. The Organisation of Islamic Cooperation (OIC) also showed its concern and sometimes played a good office role in mediating the conflict; however, it did not support the separation of the provinces from Thailand.[44] It cannot be denied that the insurgency has challenged Thailand's national integrity; nevertheless, it has not achieved its goal so far.

Institutional Process

The military and conservative establishment have more control over the decision-making of Thailand's grand strategy. This current institutional process resulted from the recent military coup in 2014 when the coup leaders promulgated the new constitution in 2017. This constitution empowers the executive power and the Senate against the House of Representatives. The Senate is headed by the coup makers, so it becomes a reassurance that the military will remain influential in Thailand's policymaking and law-making process. The constitution even put more restraints on the charter's amendments as most of the changes will require the Senate's votes for approval.

The military government also enforced its social and economic development plan, the so-called Twenty-Year National Strategy, in the constitution, effective until 2036. This strategy aims to upgrade Thailand's economy and stimulate future growth. However, the process of making the strategy was far from involving broader public participation. It was drafted among a close group of experts handpicked by the junta. Imposing the strategy within the constitution could suggest that the succeeding governments will have to observe it in planning their policies. Violation of the plan could risk a political attack in the parliament, especially with the Senate still under the control of the military. Although the provisional clause allowing the military junta to select members of the Senate expired in 2024, the new Senate remains controlled by a significant conservative faction with close ties to military elites.[45] Therefore, without a constitutional overhaul, Thailand's policymaking will continue to be predominantly influenced by conservative forces, including major political parties closely connected to the military and, to some extent, the palace.[46]

Material Resources

The linkage between regime legitimacy and economic performance requires the Thai state to direct its grand strategy to secure growth and improve the standard of living. Thai policymakers realize that Thailand's economy is more advanced than those of other mainland Southeast Asian countries. Its GDP is the second largest in ASEAN and is relatively diversified. With this consideration, Thailand could potentially take the lead in promoting economic development in this geographical area. For this reason, Thailand's material resources stem from its decades of economic expansion, which helped build more advanced industrialization, more diversified industries and markets, and skilled labor. These elements enable the country to push for this grand strategy. This leverage helps maximize Thailand's material gains from economic connectivity within the region and the broader world. This means that connecting to the world through trade is one of Thailand's national interests. This can roughly be seen from its trade ratio to GDP reaching around 140 percent around the 2010s.[47] Therefore, it is not a surprise that Thailand has actively participated in regional projects that aim to expand the transportation network across mainland Southeast Asia, especially within the Greater Mekong Subregion (GMS) project under the Asian Development Bank (ADB).

OPERATIONALIZATION OF GRAND STRATEGY

As mentioned earlier, maintaining a balance between great powers has been a core operationalization of Thailand's grand strategy. As a small or middle power in the region, Thailand adopts every possible means to reduce the impacts of great power politics. At the same time, Thailand also utilizes its political and economic potential to push for a more active role. Therefore, we may observe two major operationalizations of Thailand's grand strategy. On the one hand, Thailand is hedging against possible risks in regional politics. On the other, Thailand also attempts to exercise its leadership in various areas in the region.

Hedging

Scholars agree that Southeast Asian nations individually engage in hedging strategies to manage their relations with external powers. As a result, collectively, this common strategy helps maintain regional order, stability, and prosperity. Although hedging may be seen simply as having a middle position between rival powers,[48] it is more complicated than that. According to Kuik's analysis, a country may hedge by simultaneously adopting different policies, some of which contradict each other. So, the risks from the failures of one policy can be offset by the other successful ones. The combination of policies aiming for hedging also depends on the convergence of interest between the hedging state and the countries targeted for hedging.[49] Kuik proposes five broad hedging policy categories: indirect balancing, dominance denial, economic pragmatism, binding engagement, and limited bandwagoning.[50] We can see that Thailand, similar to other Southeast Asian countries though to a different degree, exhibits a combination of these strategies to operationalize its grand strategy.

In the context of uncertainties in the region, especially amid the US-China competition, Thailand seems to prefer *indirect balancing* based on the US-Thai security alliance. Despite being a treaty ally, Thailand does not explicitly use it against China. While bilateral security cooperation continues, Thailand has been more reluctant to deepen it to the degree that it might offend China. Without being pressured by Washington, Bangkok would refuse to engage in US policy proposals such as by denying US troops access to the U-Tapao naval airfield for military and scientific purposes or its earlier stance on the US war on terror.[51] Therefore, the United States cannot dominate the Thai security direction. This reluctance can exhibit the *dominance denial* intention as the flip side of the coin. For example, Thailand has diversified its arms procurements from more than twenty countries. Apart from the United States, the top ten list includes Sweden, Ukraine, China, South Korea, Germany, Italy, Singapore, the United Kingdom, and France.[52]

Another strategy is expanding security cooperation with other partners. There are different joint military exercises and patrols between Thai armed forces and their foreign counterparts. For example, although the Thai-US joint military exercise, Cobra Gold, remains the largest, Thailand and China strengthened their various joint exercises even before the 2014 coup. For example, all the Thai armed forces established joint military exercises with China: Strike between the armies, Blue Strike between the navies, and Falcon Strike between the air forces.[53]

Economic pragmatism is also an undeniable means to pursue Thailand's grand strategy. This can be seen from the aforementioned trade ratio. Thailand's high level of trade dependence has resulted from its export-led industrialization strategy since the 1980s. The World Bank data in 2019 suggests that Thailand trades with 226 economies.[54] Recently, Thailand has submitted applications to join both the OECD and the BRICS+.[55] BRICS, an organization led by Brazil, Russia, India, China, and South Africa, is often seen as an alternative to the G7. While the intent to join BRICS+ amid the current geopolitical tensions may risk Thailand's balanced position between the US-led coalition and the China-Russia axis, it reflects the country's pragmatic foreign policy. By diversifying its economic partnerships with various international groups, Thailand aims to expand its economic opportunities.

At the same time, Thailand also joined other Southeast Asian neighbors in a *binding engagement* strategy by persuading other external powers to be part of the institutionalization of bilateral and regional arrangements. This can be seen, as mentioned earlier, in Thailand's attempt to engage Asian countries in its ACD initiative in the early 2000s. Under the Ayeyarwady-Chao Phraya-Mekong Economic Cooperation Strategy (ACMECS), Thailand also invited external stakeholders to be ACMECS development partners.[56] Thailand joined ASEAN to persuade regional powers to institutionalize their engagement with ASEAN-led mechanisms at the broader level. These can be seen from the pushes from the early post-Cold War period, such as the ASEAN Regional Forum (ARF), ASEAN Plus Three processes, East Asia Summit, ASEAN free trade agreements with major trade partners, as well as the recent conclusion of the RCEP.

Last but not least, Thailand also engages in *limited bandwagoning*, especially with China. As mentioned earlier, Thailand has strengthened its economic ties with China since the AFC in the late 1990s. Its economic strategy in the early 2000s was explicitly courting China to improve Thailand's economic performance.[57] The Thailand-China FTA was concluded in 2003 to take advantage of Thailand's agricultural sector and China's big consumer market. Trade and tourism relations with China increased dramatically since the latter half of the

2000s, while Chinese FDI has gradually increased. However, under the current promotion of the EEC project as a spearhead in attracting a new round of FDI, China's investment presence in the EEC is second to none. The short-lived Srettha government after the election in 2023 continued to see China as the priority. Srettha's first official overseas visit was China during the Belt & Road Initiative (BRI) summit in Beijing in October 2023, where he also held a bilateral talk with President Xi Jinping. This was to promote his Land Bridge idea while encouraging Chinese investment in Thailand.[58]

While economic bandwagoning with China is quite noticeable, Thailand does not abandon other economic partners. As mentioned in the second section, bilateral and regional FTAs with other counterparts are expected to lessen economic dependence on China. In addition, accumulative FDI stock from the United States is still far more extensive. In 2019 US FDI stock accounted for 6.7 percent compared to 2.8 percent from China[59] The foregoing examination shows that hedging is an essential operationalization of Thailand's grand strategy. This strategy helps reduce the risk of uncertainties in global politics and improves Thailand's stability and prosperity. At the same time, Thailand also joins the US-led Indo-Pacific Economic Framework (IPEF) aiming at promoting trade facilitation and economic resilience in the Indo-Pacific region.[60] Although IPEF does not negotiate the issue of market access, geopolitically it is meant to offer an alternative channel for upgrading Thailand's economy and economic standards and practices.

Promoting Thailand-Led Regional Initiatives

Linked to Thailand's attempt to sustain its economic development, Thailand has promoted regional arrangements as another way to operationalize its grand strategy. The most striking way to do so is, notably, through Thailand-led initiatives. Bangkok has attempted to designate itself as a prime mover into the broader region. In the post-Cold War era, this can trace back to Chatichai's "turning the battlefields into marketplaces" strategy. Thailand played a leading role in ending the regional conflict and integrating Indochina into ASEAN's economic dynamic. Thailand, together with Singapore, also firmly pushed for the ASEAN Free Trade Area (AFTA) in 1992. The success of AFTA reflected Thailand's benefit from the Japanese production network in Southeast Asia. The reduction of trade barriers facilitated the movement of components and parts across the region.

During the AFC, Thailand also tried to assert its regional role in proposing "flexible engagement"—an amendment of ASEAN's intramural principle of noninterference. Thai policymakers viewed that in the interconnected world, problems in one country could spill over to other countries. Therefore, ASEAN members should be able to warn or criticize each other on policy mismanagement to prevent possible negative ramification. The flexible engagement proposal also demonstrates Thailand's restless effort to lead the group despite its economic difficulty.[61]

The peak of Thailand's proactive role in the region after Chatichai was during the premiership of Thaksin Shinawatra. Like Chatichai, Thaksin planned to pin Thailand as a hub for regional diplomacy and cooperation. Thaksin's strategy was to promote Thailand-led initiatives at two broad levels. ACD was set up to cultivate cooperation across Asia regionwide. ACD attracted eighteen participating countries and is currently expanding to thirty-five. One of Thaksin's tools for mobilizing this regional attention was to court Beijing as a core of the group. Thaksin wanted to reinvigorate Thailand's role in mainland Southeast Asia at the subregional level as well. Thaksin shared a common idea with broader Thai policy elites that this geographical area has been Thailand's sphere of influence and interest. Thaksin established a new subregional initiative, namely ACMECS.

On the one hand, ACMECS improved and secured Thailand's access to mainland Southeast Asia's markets and resources. Indeed, this continued Chatichai's plan on the eve of the Cold War. On the other hand, ACMECS helped institutionalize Thailand's economic and regional goals. ACMECS brought all mainland Southeast Asian nations to coordinate development strategies so that the subregion's development path would align with Thailand's direction. Thailand actively laid out the programs, including coordinating projects, mobilizing donors' funding, providing development assistance, and revamping Thailand's development agency to support the initiative.

Thaksin's grand strategy of strengthening its regional leadership failed to continue, thanks to decade-long political turmoil in Thai politics. The military intervened in politics twice in 2006 and 2014. At the same time Thai politics has been polarized into two broad spectrums between the conservative and the progressive groups. They took turns leading and dominating the government while facing street protests and counterprotests. The authoritarian turnaround, therefore, cripples Thailand's attempt to achieve this priority until today. Although some of Thaksin's ideas and initiatives continue to run, they lack the strong political will and a programmatic plan by the incumbent military-led government to realize the goal.

Certainly the Thailand-led initiative is not the only way Thailand could play a leading role in the region. ASEAN-led mechanisms since its birth have benefited Thailand in both security and economic terms. Therefore,

Thailand strongly supports ASEAN as a collective action to help supplement its foreign policy strategy, hence an essential element in Thailand's grand strategy. However, Thailand's role in strengthening ASEAN's mechanism is sometimes doubtful in the critical juncture of US-China competition. This is owing to the fact that Beijing has successfully consolidated its influence in both political and economic realms in Thailand, particularly since the military coup in 2014. Therefore, many observers view that Thai policy elites relatively sympathize with and tend to accommodate China.

Despite the constraints discussed previously, the new government led by the Pheu Thai Party under Paetongtarn Shinawatra, a daughter of former Prime Miniter Thaksin, announced that the government will revive the Asia Cooperation Dialogue (ACD), Thaksin's brainchild regional initiative initiated in 2002, by proposing to host the next ACD summit in Thailand in 2025.[62] Foreign Minister Marid Maris Sangiampongsa also emphasized Thailand's foreign policy strategy goal at a press conference in June 2024 that Thailand will return to playing an active role in the international stage. His statement captures Thailand's core grand strategy quite well:

> Thailand would like to demonstrate our role as a key player in the region. I would like to see our increased role in supporting humanitarian assistance for the benefit of mankind. Apart from our goal to restore Thailand's image after our "absence" from the international arena . . . We would like to have an increased role in the regional and sub-regional groupings, especially ASEAN, of which Thailand is a founding member.[63]

CONCLUSION

Thailand's grand strategy reflects its position in the international hierarchy as a small power; hence, its overarching strategy needs to maintain its survival and autonomy and minimize the interference of larger powers. This is what Thailand had experienced in its history of interaction with great powers, especially in the late nineteenth century and the Cold War. History taught Thai policy elites that choosing the wrong side in the conflict between great powers may have risked its independence. Therefore, skillful strategic calculation amid uncertainties enables the kingdom to walk on a tightrope throughout history.

By preserving Thailand's national integrity and independence, Thai policy elites gain political legitimacy to maintain their power domestically. Therefore, national survival and integrity became part of a major narrative in the construction of a grand strategy. It was the ultimate justification for Thailand's strategy in response to major events in history. These include Bangkok's centralization in the late nineteenth century, the support of the Japanese in the Pacific War, the formation of the Thai-US security alliance during the Cold War, and the normalization of Thai-Chinese relations against Vietnamese expansionism in the 1980s.

Economic development is also an undetachable goal in Thailand's grand strategy. Economic advancement helps improve the nation's material wealth and social stability in the policy elites' minds. The economic performance of the policy elites also sustains their political legitimacy. Elites from King Chulalongkorn in the late nineteenth century until the current ex-coup leader General Prayut Chan-o-cha have shared this same grand strategy to improve the country's economic well-being. This same goal can be called or propagated under different labels such as civilizing, modernizing, or economic upgrading.

Therefore, the most important operationalization of Thailand's grand strategy is to maintain stable relations with external powers. Balanced and omnidirectional diplomacy deems to be suitable to advance Thailand's national interests. The United States and China are currently the most significant external actors that offer the kingdom security and economic benefits. While Thai-US relations are mainly security-oriented based on the Cold War legacy, Thai-Chinese relations have grown steadily due to China's economic power. However, despite Thai-US security ties remaining a core to Thailand's strategy, history suggests that Bangkok cannot rely on Washington as it may risk abandonment. Therefore, expanding both security and economic relations with China and other nations also helps reduce this risk of US abandonment. Hedging against these uncertainties by diversifying relations with various counterparts is thus important to Thailand's grand strategy.

The space for maneuvering through a hedging strategy has narrowed amid the intensifying US-China competition. Any policy decision that favors one power risks straining Thailand's relationship with the other. Domestic factors often exacerbate this policy imbalance, with Thailand's closer ties to China over the past three decades and the military's return to politics increasing the risk of overdependence on Beijing. As a result, Thailand has recently made efforts to rebalance its strategy with major powers. The simultaneous pursuit of membership in both BRICS+ and the OECD exemplifies this balancing act, though it carries significant geopolitical risks and uncertainties.

While cooperation with China remains crucial, there has been a renewed emphasis on strengthening defense ties with Washington, particularly within the framework of the US Indo-Pacific strategy. Simultaneously, Thailand is reactivating its role in regional initiatives like the ACMECS and the ACD. These platforms are intended to coordinate regional economic development and serve as key elements of Thailand's grand strategy.

ACMECS is expected to help Thailand navigate the challenge of avoiding excessive dependence on China in mainland Southeast Asia, allowing the country to maintain its policy autonomy. Meanwhile, a revitalized role in the ACD aims to position Thailand as a regional leader, offering an alternative platform for cooperation that is not dominated by either the US or China. Ultimately, these strategic adjustments highlight the core objective of Thailand's grand strategy: to preserve its autonomy, safeguard its sovereignty, and ensure continued economic development.

NOTES

This chapter is part of the research project entitled "Great Power Rivalry and Thailand's Strategic Adjustment towards the United States and China" (Project No. 660090), approved on 20 March 2023.

1. Stephen D. Krasner, "An Orienting Principle for Foreign Policy," *Policy Review*, no. 163 (October 1, 2010), 3–13.
2. Kullada Kesboonchoo-Mead, *The Rise and Decline of Thai Absolutism* (RoutledgeCurzon, 2004), 32–37.
3. Thongchai Winichakul, *Siam Mapped: A History of the Geo-Body of a Nation* (University of Hawai'i Press, 1994), 115–27.
4. Patrick Jory, *A History of Manners and Civility in Thailand* (Cambridge University Press, 2021), 32–39.
5. Pongphisoot Busbarat, "A Review of Thailand's Foreign Policy in Mainland Southeast Asia: Exploring an Ideational Approach," *European Journal of East Asian Studies* 11, no. 1 (January 1, 2012): 1.
6. Shane Strate, *The Lost Territories: Thailand's History of National Humiliation* (University of Hawai'i Press, 2015), 24–36.
7. Thomas Frank Barton, "Siam: Buffer State or Gradual Piecemeal Consumption?," *Journal of Geography* 63, no. 7 (October 1964): 302–13, https://doi.org/10.1080/00221346408985096.
8. Office of the National Security Council, "National Security Policy and Plan (2023–2027)," 2023) 16, https://www.nsc.go.th/wp-content/uploads/2023/03/nsc_policy_66-70.pdf
9. Winichakul, *Siam Mapped*, 169–70.
10. Arne Kislenko, "A Not So Silent Partner: Thailand's Role in Covert Operations, Counter-Insurgency, and the Wars in Indochina," *Journal of Conflict Studies* 24, no. 1 (2004).
11. Wiwat Mungkandi, "The Security Syndrome: 1941–1975," in *A Century and a Half of Thai-American Relations*, ed. Wiwat Mungkandi and William Warren (Chulalongkorn University Press, 1982), 137–39.

12. Pongphisoot Busbarat, "Thai-US Relations in the Post-Cold War Era: Untying the Special Relationship," *Asian Security*, August 7, 2017, 1–19.
13. Thitinan Pongsudhirak, "An Unaligned Alliance: Thailand-U.S. Relations in the Early 21st Century," *Asian Politics & Policy* 8, no. 1 (2016), 63–74, https://doi.org/10.1111/aspp.12233.
14. Pongphisoot Busbarat, "Thailand in 2017: Stability without Certainties," in *Southeast Asian Affairs* (Singapore: ISEAS Publishing, 2018), 343–62.
15. "Thailand, China Progress Plan to Establish Joint MRO Facility," Janes.com, https://www.janes.com/defence-news/news-detail/thailand-china-progress-plan-to-establish-joint-mro-facility
16. Kullada Kesboonchoo-Mead, "A Revisionist History of Thai-US Relations," in *Asian Review 2003: Globalization and Hegemony* (Institute of Asian Studies, Chulalongkorn University, 2003), 45–67.
17. World Bank, "GDP Growth (Annual %)—Thailand | Data," https://data.worldbank.org/indicator/NY.GDP.MKTP.KD.ZG?locations=TH
18. Suchit Bunbongkarn, "The Military and Democracy in Thailand," in *The Military and Democracy in Asia and the Pacific*, ed. Ron May and Viberto Selochan (ANU Press, 2004), 53–54.
19. Sukhumbhand Paribatra and Suchit Bunbongkarn, "Thai Politics and Foreign Policy in the 1980s: Plus Ça Change, Plus C'est La Même Chose?," in *ASEAN in Regional and Global Context* (Institute of East Asian Studies, University of California, 1986), 52–76.
20. Busbarat, "A Review of Thailand's Foreign Policy in Mainland Southeast Asia."
21. Busbarat, "Thai–US Relations in the Post-Cold War Era."
22. World Bank, "GDP Growth (Annual %)—Thailand | Data."
23. U.S. Department of Commerce and 1, "Thailand—Trade Agreements," https://www.trade.gov/country-commercial-guides/thailand-trade-agreements.
24. Pongphisoot Busbarat, "'Bamboo Stuck in the Chinese Wind': The Continuing Significance of the China Factor in Thailand's Foreign Policy Orientation," *Contemporary Southeast Asia* 46, no. 1 (2024), 125–46.
25. "PM Pledges Economic Continuity, Soft Power Focus," https://thainews.prd.go.thnull
26. Reuters, "Thailand Kicks off First Phase of Digital Wallet Scheme," *Bangkok Post*, September 25, 2024, https://www.bangkokpost.com/business/general/2871923/thailand-kicks-off-first-phase-of-us-14-billion-digital-wallet-stimulus-scheme
27. "Thailand Plans Joint Arms Factory with China," *Bangkok Post*, November 16, 2017, https://www.bangkokpost.com/thailand/general/1361683/thailand-plans-joint-arms-factory-with-china
28. "Thailand Trade Summary 2014 | WITS Data," https://wits.worldbank.org/CountryProfile/en/Country/THA/Year/2014/Summary
29. "Thailand Trade Summary 2019 | WITS Data," https://wits.worldbank.org/CountryProfile/en/Country/THA/Year/2019/Summary
30. Thailand Exports by country and region 2022 | WITS Data, https://wits.worldbank.org/CountryProfile/en/Country/THA/Year/2022/TradeFlow/Export
31. "China Tops Foreign Investment in Thailand," https://news.cgtn.com/news/2020-02-14/China-tops-foreign-investment-in-Thailand-O4sD1dVGzS/index.html
32. T.A.T. Newsroom, "Thailand Welcomes First Group of Chinese Tourists Post Pandemic," *TAT Newsroom* (blog), January 9, 2023, https://www.tatnews.org/2023/01/thailand-welcomes-first-group-of-chinese-tourists-post-pandemic/

33. Bangkok Post Public Company, "Blinken Scraps Visit to Thailand after Journalist Tests Positive for Covid," *Bangkok Post*, accessed April 7, 2022, https://www.bangkokpost.com/thailand/general/2232511/blinken-scraps-visit-to-thailand-after-journalist-tests-positive-for-covid
34. "EEC-Government Initiative," https://www.eeco.or.th/en/government-initiative/
35. Eastern Economic Corridor Office, "EEC Annual Report 2019" (Eastern Economic Corridor (EEC), 2019), https://www.eeco.or.th/en/filedownload/1215/688f9dc8c810ec7a5322aa0274edf7cb.pdf
36. "Longthun EEC klai thalu pao 1.7 lan lan cho hai sitthi prayot mai mai samson BOI [Investment in EEC Nearly Hits the Target of THB 1.7 Trillion; Planning to Grant New Privileges Will Not Duplicate the Work of BOI]," *Prachachat Thurakij*, September 13, 2021, https://www.prachachat.net/economy/news-760205
37. John Blaxland and Greg Raymond, "Tipping the Balance in Southeast Asia? Thailand, the United States and China," November 2017, http://hdl.handle.net/1885/228741
38. Nigel J Brailey, "Chiengmai and the Inception of an Administrative Centralization Policy in Siam (II)," *Japanese Journal of Southeast Asian Studies* 11, no. 4 (1974), 439–69.
39. Michael S. H. Heng, "King Chulalongkorn as Builder of Incipient Siamese Nation-State," *East Asia* 36, no. 1 (March 1, 2019): 67–91.
40. Varatraya Hunchareon, "Rongrian nai samai ratchakan thi 5 lae ratchakan thi 6 (pho. so.2411-2468) [School Building in the Period of King Rama V and King Rama VI (1868–1925)" (Master Thesis, Bangkok, Silpakorn University, 2002), 27–28.
41. Gregory V. Raymond, "Strategic Culture and Thailand's Response to Vietnam's Occupation of Cambodia, 1979–1989: A Cold War Epilogue," *Journal of Cold War Studies* 22, no. 1 (February 1, 2020), 22–23.
42. Martin Wagener, "Lessons from Preah Vihear: Thailand, Cambodia, and the Nature of Low-Intensity Border Conflicts," *Journal of Current Southeast Asian Affairs* 30, no. 3 (September 1, 2011): 27–59,
43. Aurel Croissant, "Muslim Insurgency, Political Violence, and Democracy in Thailand," *Terrorism and Political Violence* 19, no. 1 (January 2007), 6–8, https://doi.org/10.1080/09546550601054485
44. Imtiyaz Yusuf, "The Southern Thailand Conflict and the Muslim World," *Journal of Muslim Minority Affairs* 27, no. 2 (August 2007), 319–39, https://doi.org/10.1080/13602000701536232.
45. Mongkol Bangprapa, "Blue Is the Colour as Senate Takes Centre Stage in Thailand," *Bangkok Post*, July 29, 2024, https://www.bangkokpost.com/thailand/politics/2837338/blue-is-the-colour-as-senate-takes-centre-stage-in-thailand
46. Busbarat, "Thailand in 2017: Stability without Certainties."
47. World Bank, "Trade (% of GDP)—Thailand | Data," The World Bank Data, https://data.worldbank.org/indicator/NE.TRD.GNFS.ZS?end=2020&locations=TH&start=1960&view=chart
48. Evelyn Goh, "Understanding 'Hedging' in Asia-Pacific Security," *PacNet*, no. 43 (2006), https://www.pacforum.org/analysis/pacnet-43-understanding-hedging-asia-pacific-security
49. Cheng-Chwee Kuik, Nor Azizan Idris, and Abd Rahim Md Nor, "The China Factor in the U.S. 'Reengagement' with Southeast Asia: Drivers and Limits of Converged Hedging," *Asian Politics & Policy* 4, no. 3 (2012), 317.

50. Cheng-Chwee Kuik, "How Do Weaker States Hedge? Unpacking ASEAN States' Alignment Behavior towards China," *Journal of Contemporary China* 25, no. 100 (July 3, 2016), 501–2.
51. Pongphisoot Busbarat, "'Bamboo Swirling in the Wind': Thailand's Foreign Policy Imbalance between China and the United States," *Contemporary Southeast Asia: A Journal of International and Strategic Affairs* 38, no. 2 (2016), 233–57.
52. Siemon T. Wezeman, "Arms Flows to South East Asia," n.d., 39–41.
53. Ian Storey, "Thailand's Military Relations with China: Moving from Strength to Strength," *Perspective* 2019, no. 43 (2019).
54. World Integrated Trade Solution, "Thailand Trade," World Integrated Trade Solution, 2019, https://wits.worldbank.org/countrysnapshot/en/THA
55. "Thailand Attempts to Strike a Balance with BRICS and OECD Bids," Nikkei Asia, https://asia.nikkei.com/Politics/International-relations/Thailand-attempts-to-strike-a-balance-with-BRICS-and-OECD-bids
56. "ACMECS Inaugural Senior Officials' Meeting with Development Partners," Ministry of Foreign Affairs of Thailand, https://www.mfa.go.th/en/content/107938-acmecs-inaugural-senior-officials%E2%80%99-meeting-with-development-partners?cate=5d5bcb4e15e39c306000683e
57. Busbarat, "'Bamboo Swirling in the Wind.'"
58. "Prime Minister of the Kingdom of Thailand to Attend the 3rd Belt and Road Forum for International Cooperation and to pay an official visit to the People's Republic of China on 16–19 October 2023," Ministry of Foreign Affairs of Thailand, https://www.mfa.go.th/en/content/preprbrf-2?cate=5d5bcb4e15e39c306000683e
59. Santander Trade, "Thailand: Foreign Investment," *Santander Trade*, 2020, https://santandertrade.com/en/portal/establish-overseas/thailand/foreign-investment
60. Olivier Languepin, "Thailand Joins Indo-Pacific Framework with 12 Other Countries—Thailand Business News," May 24, 2022, https://www.thailand-business-news.com/taiwan/90301-thailand-joins-indo-pacific-framework-with-12-other-countries.
61. Busbarat, "A Review of Thailand's Foreign Policy in Mainland Southeast Asia."
62. "*Thai prachum khui rangpatinyadoha nayokpoettua wethiraek ton tulakhomni*" ["Thailand Attends ACD Summit Discussing Doha Declaration, the First International Forum the PM will Attend in Oct This Year"], September 27, 2024, https://www.matichon.co.th/foreign/news_4814614
63. "Unofficial Translation of the Transcript (in Thai) of the Remarks given by H.E. Mr. Maris Sangiampongsa, Minister of Foreign Affairs at the 'Meet the Press #1' Event, 14 June 2024, Vithes Samosorn, Ministry of Foreign Affairs" (Ministry of Foreign Affairs of Thailand, June 14, 2024), https://image.mfa.go.th/mfa/0/mkKfL2iULZ/meet_the_press__1/EnglishTranslation.ThaiTranscript.FMRemarks.14June2024.pdf

CHAPTER 12

Vietnam

Dang Cam Tu

Over the past four decades, the evolution of Vietnam's grand strategy has pertained to the country's process of open-door reforms (widely known as *Doi Moi*). That process was necessitated by the task of post-war national reconstruction amid economic blockade and political isolation, and by fundamental changes in the international context that Hanoi faced in the 1980s. From a war-torn country, Vietnam emerged out of the Cold War and entered the 21st century as an increasingly proactive and trustworthy member of the international community, one whose socio-economic achievements and contributions to regional and global stability, prosperity, and cooperation is widely recognized. Such success was attributed to, among other things, an effective national defense and development strategy that Hanoi has been pursuing, with growing significance attached to foreign policies and relations. Foreign affairs and diplomacy were reckoned to be a crucial and regular task of the entire political system and major contributor to national construction, defense, and development.[1]

This chapter provides an analysis of the grand strategy of Vietnam from the international relations approach. In so doing, it examines the international and domestic dimensions of Vietnam's foreign policy formulation and implementation in its course of comprehensive *Doi Moi* that started in the mid-1980s. There was no formally labelled grand strategy in Vietnam. Yet, Hanoi's strategic responses to the contingencies of domestic and external environments over the last forty years, through its integrated scheme of foreign policy interests, objectives, principles, tools, and resources, suggest that it has made sense of external relations in grand strategic terms, and that it has employed what amounted to a grand strategy for the purpose of ensuring security and maximizing interests.

External factors informing Vietnam's foreign policy were largely associated with global and regional geo-political, security as well as geo-economic changes and trends after the Cold War. They included strategies and relations of major powers, particularly China and the United States, ASEAN, the prevalence of the East Asian model of economic development, the growth of globalization and regionalism, as well as traditional and non-traditional security challenges. Domestic factors included the need to shore up the legitimacy and leadership of the Communist Party of Vietnam (CPV), its new foreign policy and strategic thinking informed by new worldview, national interest and threat perceptions, and a greater role for diplomacy in the pursuit of national interests.

These factors brought about a grand strategy that highlighted the key elements including the pursuit of independence, strategic autonomy and development, the conduct of "being a friend to all, enemy to none" diplomacy, a growing sense of responsibility and credibility, the prioritization of relations with neighboring countries and big powers, extensive and comprehensive international integration, as well as pro-activism in multilateral arrangements (especially ASEAN and the UN).

The bottom line shows how the foreign policy of Vietnam since the 1980s has been greatly influenced by the classical concept of diplomacy as the first line of defense and the ability of policy makers in Hanoi to mobilize domestic resources and grasp opportunities presented by external conditions.

STRATEGIC PRIORITIES

The strategic priorities of Vietnam were preserving peaceful and stable external environment, safeguarding the homeland and national security, and accelerating international integration. These three priorities were cross-cutting, mutually reinforcing, and embedded in Hanoi's perception of national interest.

Preserving a Peaceful and Stable External Environment

A peaceful and stable external environment for economic development was first a desperate need for Vietnam in the immediate decade after its reunification in 1975. In the late 1970s and early 1980s, the country suffered from a grave domestic socio-economic crisis. The crisis was worsened by two concurrent wars on its borders with Cambodia and China and an ensuing political and diplomatic isolation and economic blockade. The severe hardship served as a driving force behind Hanoi's decision to launch its reforms (*Doi Moi*) at the Sixth National Congress of the CPV in December 1986.

Resolution No. 32 of the CPV Politburo adopted on 8 July 1986 identified peace and economic development as key features in the world and the highest priorities in Vietnam's foreign policy. The CPV Politburo Resolution No. 13 dated 20 May 1988 further emphasized that economic weaknesses, political isolation, and economic blockade were major threats to the country's national security and independence, and that preserving peace and developing the economy was the highest strategic objective and interest of Vietnam.[2]

Underlying this was the internal deliberation on redefining national interests in the context of changing great power politics and international economic relations characterized by the trends of co-existence, scientific-technological revolution, and growing interdependent economic transactions between the East and the West.[3] It signified the comprehensive security approach that increasingly embraced the economic development aspect and the role of foreign affairs in dealing with threats to national security and supporting economic development.[4]

Since the Cold War ended, Vietnam continued to attach strategic importance to preserving peace and stability for the pursuit of not only economic but also security interests, which became much intertwined. Subsequent National Congresses of the CPV since 1991 reaffirmed this as a prerequisite for national security and development. The Defense White Paper issued in 2009 read: "Vietnam always regards the maintenance of peaceful and stable environment for socio-economic development, industrialization and modernization, the building of a socialist-oriented market economy as the highest national interest, and the consistent goal of national defense policy."[5]

The prioritization of peace, stability and development was informed by the changed worldview and the new strategic thinking of leaders in Hanoi under *Doi Moi*.[6] It reflected a transformation from their view of the world divided into two exclusive camps of antagonistic contradictions to that of one interdependent world.[7] It manifested their recognition of the global mainstreams of peaceful co-existence, cooperation for economic development, globalization, and interdependence among countries. The 2019 Defense White Paper clearly stated: "Vietnam's National Defense Strategy is set to closely attach national peace and interests to regional and global peace, stability, and security."[8]

Safeguarding the Homeland and National Security

From the national defense approach, the emphasis on preserving favorable external environment was linked to that of protecting the Vietnamese Homeland in advance and from afar (*từ sớm, từ xa*). The idea of national defense "in advance and from afar" was traced back from Vietnam's tradition of defending the country before the real dangers came, given its long history of resistance against foreign aggression and domination. It was inferred from measures to promote good neighborliness, domestic stability and well-being, while enhancing an all-people and whole-government national defense posture. This approach was officially introduced in the documents of the Twelfth National Congress of the CPV in 2016.[9]

Safeguarding the Homeland in advance and from afar meant protecting the country within and beyond its territorial boundaries, creating contingency plans, taking early measures to prevent potential risks of war and armed conflict - i.e., exhausting all peaceful means and non-military channels to keep the homeland from being threatened in the first place.[10] Toward that goal, foreign policies and relations have been accredited with bigger roles to play, which represented an element of continuity in Hanoi's strategic thinking. The Politburo Resolution No.13 stated that the synergy of a strong economy, sufficiently strong national defense capacity, and expanded external relations were considered as the best course to protect national security.[11] This was, in essence, the broader recognition of the classic and conventional function of diplomacy as the first line of defense.

In Vietnam's security concept, national security and regime security went hand in hand. The Political Report at the Ninth CPV National Congress in 2001 read:

> To defend the socialist country is to defend the independence, sovereignty, unity, territorial integrity, national security, social order and safety, national culture, the Party, the State, the people, the socialist regime, as well as the cause of reforms, and national interests.[12]

The 2019 Defense White Paper further elaborated on Vietnam's Strategy to Safeguard the Homeland as enunciating the following views:

> To secure the leading role of the CPV, to promote the effectiveness of state management in the cause of Homeland protection; to determinedly uphold the goal of independence and socialism, maintaining a peaceful, stable environment for socio-economic development

> of the country, to closely combine the two strategic tasks of national defense and construction; to take internal strength as the decisive factor, economic development as the core, Party-building as the key, culture as the spiritual foundation of the society, and strengthening of national defense and security as the crucial and regular tasks.[13]

The nexus between regime security and national security in Vietnam well illustrated the nature of international politics in the Third World countries.[14] The history of struggling for national independence and reunification had reinforced the convergence between regime survival and that of the state. Being the force leading the state and society, the CPV's legitimacy and credibility depended on the effectiveness of its domestic and foreign policies. In fact, regime security was strengthened by the achievements that Vietnam attained in terms of national security, socio-economic development, and international prestige since *Doi Moi*. This did and continues to shape the way leaders in Hanoi identify the opportunities, threats, and courses of action in their grand strategy.[15]

International Integration

Underlined by the open-door orientation of *Doi Moi* and in pursuit of development, economic cooperation with other countries and international integration were identified as another key strategic priority. The rationale behind this choice was Hanoi's acknowledgement of the failure of the autarkic, closed economy model, and its perception about the necessity to expand international economic relations to take advantage of international markets and resources as well as tapping into the trends of globalization and cooperation in trade, investment, science, and technology for domestic socio-economic development.

In that process, growing importance was attached to economic diplomacy. In March 1989, the Party Central Committee tasked the Ministry of Foreign Affairs with shifting its focus from political to politico-economic diplomacy. Economic diplomacy started with economic engagement with western and East Asian countries. This was driven by Hanoi's awareness of the role of western advanced technology and capital investment, even in the Soviet Union and Eastern Europe in the late 1970s and early 1980s.[16] East Asian economic growth and successful developmental experiences in the mid-1980s and early 1990s also encouraged Hanoi to search for an alternative model of economic development fueled by expanded external economic relations and integration. On 10 February 2003, the Government issued a decree on the function of Vietnamese embassies and representative offices abroad of working at the service of national economic development. Since the Tenth Party National Congress in 2006, economic diplomacy has become a crucial focus in Vietnam's foreign strategy and comprehensive diplomacy.[17] Directive No. 15 issued by the CPV Secretariat on 10 August 2022 re-asserted that economic diplomacy was a fundamental task of Vietnam's foreign affairs and important driving force for national rapid and sustainable development. Localities, businesses, and the people were encouraged to take active participation in economic diplomacy.[18]

The strategic economic thinking of the CPV gradually evolved in response to the developments of the domestic, regional, and global economies with a view to maximizing the benefits that international integration could contribute to the domestic agenda of political stability and economic prosperity.[19] The Politburo Resolution No. 22 on international integration introduced in 2013 stated that pro-active international integration was a major strategic orientation of the Party, aiming at successfully implementing the task of building and protecting the socialist Fatherland of Vietnam.[20] Prior to 2016, international integration mostly had an economic connotation to Hanoi's efforts at ensuring Vietnam's place in the regional and international labor division.[21] At the Twelfth CPV Congress in 2016, domestic consensus was reached on expanding the scope of international integration to include all realms, other than economic, in a pro-active manner and comprehensive nature.[22] This reflected confidence in Hanoi that the country had attained adequate material and institutional capabilities as well as international credibility for embarking on a higher level of international integration.

The implications were twofold. One was the new priority for Vietnam to negotiate and enter into new-generation multilateral free trade agreements that include such non-trade aspects as environmental protection and labor rights. In the range of seven years since 2016, Hanoi managed to sign seven free trade agreements of the new generation.[23] The other was greater emphasis on the participation by the country's defense establishment in multilateral security and mil-to-mil cooperative arrangements at the regional and global levels. This resulted in Vietnam's greater participation in UN Peacekeeping Operations (PKO) and ADMM+.

The 2019 Vietnam's Defense White Paper reiterated: "Vietnam advocates developing defense cooperation with all nations, especially neighboring ones, strategic partners, comprehensive partners, building confidence and garnering international support and assistance to preclude and respond to the risk of wars of aggression," and "promotes multilateral defense cooperation with a view to contributing to ensuring national defense, security, and national sovereignty."[24] Accordingly, Vietnam's defense diplomacy would entail and prioritize the expansion of all forms of bilateral and multilateral cooperation, forming an integral part of the pro-active effort at national defense in advance and from afar, and contributing to the course of comprehensive international integration through the promotion of trust building, preventive diplomacy, and the rule of law.

However, it is noteworthy that Hanoi was not without cautions about the negative impacts of international integration and globalization, which explained the stressing of national interest as the underlining principle and ultimate objective of foreign affairs, including international integration.[25]

EXTERNAL FACTORS

Major Powers

Changes in the correlation of power, strategies, and relations among major powers informed fundamental turning points in Vietnam's foreign strategy. Against the context of rapprochement between the United States and the Soviet Union during the last phase of the Cold War, the collapse of the latter, and the dissolution of the socialist camp, the Seventh CPV National Congress in 1991 officially launched the foreign policy of independence, diversification and multilateralization of relations based on the principle of equal and mutually beneficial cooperation with all countries regardless of different socio-political systems, and peaceful co-existence.

Independence, autonomy, diversification, and multi-direction of external relations, accompanied by the effort at "being friend to all, enemy to none," has become the brand of Vietnam's foreign policy ever since, wherein relations with major powers and neighboring countries were of high priority. In the 1990s, Vietnam normalized and improved its relations with China and the United States, and promoted its ties with Russia, Japan, and European countries. By 2025, it has established strategic and/or comprehensive partnerships with all major powers, including all the P5 and G7.

Good relations with major powers were considered crucial for Vietnam's quest for peaceful and stable environment, enhancement of national security, development, as well as international status and prestige. They helped Vietnam to diversify the supply sources of economic resources, military equipment, and weapons to build up its national defense capacity. Deepened relations with major powers also created the state of intertwined interests that served as the foundation for bilateral relations, conditions for solving disagreements and disputes, and incentives for commitments to peace and stability, especially in its surrounding environment.

Economic cooperation with big partners, particularly Japan, China, the United States, and European countries, enabled Vietnam to mobilize huge resources for infrastructure development and sustainable economic growth to realize its goals of industrialization and modernization. Being strategic and/or comprehensive partners of all key players in the regional and global politics also brought about higher international recognition, respect, and support for Vietnam's economic integration and security policies, as well as greater strategic value in the formers' foreign strategies.[26]

The co-existence between cooperation and competition in the relations among major powers, most notably the United States and China, since the end of the Cold War largely informed the foreign strategy of Vietnam, similarly to other countries in East Asia. The choice of Hanoi was to stick to its policy of independence, autonomy, simultaneously deepening and delicately balancing relations with all the powers, particularly the two biggest ones, and seeing its relations with them in positive sum terms. Vietnamese leaders had practical reasons, born of their own historical experience, not to take side with any single power and avoid being dragged into the power politics game.[27] Growing competition among powers then compelled the quest for greater autonomy by Vietnam.

Whether Hanoi could avoid taking side depended to a large extent on its ability to perform the balancing act. To that end, the Eighth Party Central Committee Plenum in July 2003 adopted the Resolution entitled Strategic Directions of Defending the Fatherland in the New Situation, which introduced the concepts of "partner of cooperation" (*đối tác*) and "object of struggle" (*đối tượng*) to combine cooperation and competition in the conduct of foreign affairs, applying in any set of bilateral relations. Partners were identified as who respected Vietnam's independence and sovereignty, desiring to establish friendly, equal, and mutually beneficial relations with Vietnam, while objects of struggle were those going against the country's cause of national construction and defense.[28] Amid growing competition between the United States and China, Hanoi strictly applied this approach to Washington and Beijing, with a view to promoting all-rounded relations with both powers, while managing the areas of differences and utilizing the dynamics of its bilateral relations with each of them to promote those with the other.

In so doing, Vietnamese leaders believed that they could still enjoy opportunities to promote its relations with both competing powers without having to face the worst-case scenario of taking side.[29] The fact that both Washington and Beijing attached importance to promoting their relations with Vietnam in their strategic competition helped reinforce such belief in Hanoi. Vietnam's policies toward major powers suggested the primacy of pragmatic considerations of national interests over ideological ones in the formulation and implementation of its foreign policy under *Doi Moi*. They also indicated that Hanoi had almost discarded the binary friend-or-foe approach in its relations with other countries, including big partners, endeavoring to promote cooperation but at the same time resolutely safeguarding its national interests.[30]

ASEAN

For Vietnam to better do the balancing act in its relations with major powers, and to realize the strategic goals of peace, stability, national security, and international integration, ASEAN stood out to be most relevant and instrumental. Geo-political considerations and the awareness of interdependence between itself and the rest of the region in terms of both security and prosperity informed the importance of ASEAN. On that basis, Hanoi has made vigorous efforts to strengthen ties with regional countries, joined and played an increasingly active role in ASEAN since the end of the Cold War. It was facilitated by commonalities between Vietnam and ASEAN states in terms of size, historical experience, developmental goals, security concerns, especially in relations with big powers, the shared need for a peaceful, stable, and cooperative regional environment conducive to domestic political stability, national development, and resultant regime legitimacy, and more broadly the flourishing trend of regionalism.[31]

Vietnam's improving its relationship with ASEAN was a significant part of its endeavor to get out of political isolation and economic blockade in the late 1980s and early 1990s, and a breakthrough in the implementation of its new foreign policy designed on the concept of comprehensive security, diversification and multi-lateralization of international relations for the purpose of promoting national economic development, hence a bridge for integrating itself into the wider region and the world. This was expected to and did have mutually reinforcing effects on Hanoi's normalization and enhancement of its relations with major powers, particularly China and the United States.[32] ASEAN membership provided Vietnam with advantageous posture of collective capabilities, bargaining power, and strategic weight in conducting relations with bigger partners. Vietnam has been the only member in ASEAN who is strategic and/or comprehensive partner of all major powers in the Indo-Pacific and all the founding members of ASEAN. While key players are increasingly shifting their attention to the Indo-Pacific and enhancing their engagement with regional countries, Vietnam's role has become more salient in their strategic calculations, as seen in the policies of the United States, Japan, India, the EU, and Australia toward the region.[33]

A favorable external environment for development that Vietnam aimed to preserve meant, first and foremost, a peaceful and stable Southeast Asian neighborhood. The establishment of the ASEAN Community provided Vietnam with an effective vehicle for its strategy of enhancing national resilience, in terms of economic growth and strategic autonomy, and deepening regional integration. Furthermore, membership of the ASEAN Community put Vietnam in a better position of collective status for further integration beyond Southeast Asia. ASEAN also served as a good mechanism for proponents of the rules-based order and peaceful management and resolution of disputes that Vietnam had been pursuing, with particular reference to developments in its East Sea (South China Sea). Besides, Hanoi's efforts to forge a closer cooperative relationship with ASEAN states and seek ASEAN membership were largely linked with its search for a new state identity in the aftermath of the Cold War which was believed to be compatible to that of other ASEAN states.[34]

ASEAN has thus become one of the most important pillars of Vietnam's foreign strategy. It was emphasized by Vietnamese top leaders and reaffirmed in the documents of the CPV National Congresses that Vietnam would be "pro-actively and responsibly working with other ASEAN members to construct a strong ASEAN Community and maintain the ASEAN centrality in the regional security architecture."[35]

Threats and Opportunities

The threat perception of Hanoi, embedding internal and external dimensions, was shaped by the convergence between regime security and national security, and the growing level of integration between Vietnam and the world. As such, sources of internal threats were identified to be economic weaknesses and backwardness, unsustainable development, corruption, red-tape, inefficiency, political and ethical degradation of Party members through "self-evolution" and "self-transformation," and deviation of the socialist orientation.[36] These were the factors that could supposedly impede the performance of the CPV in providing security and development on which its legitimacy was solidified.

Sources of external threats included peaceful evolution to eliminate the leading role of the CPV and the socialist regime, power-based coercion, infringement upon Vietnam's sovereignty, sovereign rights, and jurisdiction as provided in international law, non-traditional security and global issues related to energy security, food security, climate change, terrorism, arms, drugs and human trafficking, maritime piracy, epidemics, natural and environmental disasters, and others.

Vietnam's perception of the external roots of threats evolved in correspondence with the process of its international integration. The more Vietnam integrated and exposed itself internationally, the greater number and new forms of external threats emerged, such as the gathering of national secrets and intelligence, disinformation, and cyberattacks, especially when its national security and development became increasingly intertwined with that of the region and the world.

In the face of permanent and increasingly sophisticated emerging threats and challenges, Vietnam's major foreign policy lines have been mostly unchanged and supported by the opportunities that Hanoi found in the developments in domestic and international situations. The favorable domestic conditions for the tendency of continuity stemmed from the fact that the foreign policy was a relatively successful one, wherein external relations made remarkable contribution to enhancing security, development, and international prestige of the country to which the CPV's legitimacy was highly credited.

Externally, the dynamic economic development of East Asia and the Asia-Pacific continued to provide conducive incentives for Vietnam's economic reforms and integration. It was acknowledged that cooperation remained the mainstream in international relations, conditioned by entrenched globalization, regionalism, and the advancement of the 4.0 technological revolution. There were also possibilities of big powers seeking areas for cooperation among themselves amid competition and courting other countries in their struggle for constellation of force and influence, hence those of coexistence and cooperation between and among countries of different political and economic systems and values. Therefore, the external environment, though increasingly complicated and fast changing, gave rise to no sense of urgency for Vietnam to change the *Doi Moi* main foreign policy discourse because, as Pham Binh Minh observed, it still provided "lights of opportunities and advantages."[37]

Type of Conflicts

Before the Cold War ended, under the ideologically-driven worldview informed by the binary structure of the world, Vietnam had emphasized four types of contradictions, namely between the socialist and the capitalist systems, the bourgeoisie and the proletariat, the oppressed people and colonialism, between and among imperialist countries. After the Cold War, conflicts between the socialist regime/state and hostile reactionary forces pertained, as reflected in Hanoi's perception of the threat of peaceful evolution. "Hostile forces conspiring with reactionaries and political opportunists inside the country have not given up their plots against the Vietnamese revolution . . . The hostile forces take full advantage of the technological advances, especially information and communication technologies, to stage information warfare and cyberwarfare against the Vietnamese revolution," stated the 2019 Defense White Paper.[38]

Possibilities of arms races and open armed conflicts were further prevented, according to strategic assessments in Resolution No.13 and other documents of the CPV, but not eliminated, while wars of aggression and partial conflicts were likely. Sources of future conflicts continued to be strategic rivalries between major powers and territorial disputes, mostly with the East Sea (South China Sea) connotation.

With the belief in the small likelihood of open armed conflicts, especially among big powers, the internal consensus on the approach to safeguarding the homeland in advance and from afar, as well as its advocacy of peaceful resolution of disputes, Vietnam's national defense strategy was implemented through a spectrum of political, economic, diplomatic, socio-cultural, and military activities aimed at eradicating the causes of armed conflicts and wars. The self-defense nature of Vietnam's national defense was meant to be conducted in close coordination with security and foreign affairs to effectively design and manage foreign relations of Vietnam guided by the strategic objective of peace, stability, economic development, and international integration, in the guise of the friend-to-all mantra.[39]

INTERNAL FACTORS

National Values

The new foreign policy thinking that Hanoi has adopted since the 1980s not only reflected changes in Vietnamese leaders' new worldview. More importantly, it took root from the national values that informed the strategic culture of the country.

Independence, autonomy, and war avoidance were the core values and principles of Vietnam's history of national defense and construction. In the context of fundamental changes brought about by the end of the Cold War and the contemporary world of growing connectedness and interdependence, they retained their merits as the most vital bases for Hanoi to pursue its national interests. It was more so given Vietnam's location next to an increasingly strong neighboring power and in a region of severe power strategic competition and rivalry.

Flexibility and adaptiveness as reflected in the process of reforms were also of strategic value. The fundamentally shifted conceptions and approaches from heavily military-oriented to comprehensive security, from ideology-based to interest-based foreign policy posture, and from the friend vs. foe to the "partner of cooperation" vs. "object of struggle" distinction served as valuable virtues, enabling Vietnamese policymakers to make close-to-reality assessments and, consequently, come up with a wide range of choices with greater flexibility and wisdom in their conduct of foreign affairs.

Furthermore, the remarkable achievements that Vietnam reaped in foreign affairs resulted from, and further promoted, the policy of "being friend to all, enemy to none." From endeavoring to make "more friends, fewer enemies" in the late 1980s, in order to promote peace, stability and overcome isolation, Vietnam showed growing willingness and capability to befriend and then to become "a friend and trustworthy partner, and responsible member of the world community." The element of responsibility had previously been demonstrated in Hanoi's perception of internationalist obligation. It featured high again in the new foreign policy which was translated into Vietnam's increasingly active role in and contribution to regional and global affairs.

Institutional Process

In the political system of Vietnam, the quinquennial National Congress of the ruling CPV is the most important event to officially adopt the country's national defense and development strategy in which foreign policy forms an integral part. Recent Party Congresses have reflected the formal institutionalization of Vietnam's collective decision making on national defense and development strategy, including foreign policy, in terms of actors and processes, on a broader premise of inputs, consultations, and recommendations.

The policy formulation went through a multi-phased process. It started from the work of think-tanks for inputs, then involved the participation of the Central Theoretical Council for recommendations on the implementation of Vietnam's overall socio-economic development and foreign policies. The recommendations were sent to agencies and ministries in the Party, National Assembly, and Government systems respectively as well as retired high-ranking officials for consultation.

At the highest level, the Party Central Committee and the Politburo played the core roles in policy and decision making. Under the guidance of the Politburo, sub-committees were established and tasked with drafting the documents of the CPV National Congress. They coordinated with think-tanks, ministries and agencies, provincial and local Party branches to organize conferences, seminars, field trips, and consultations with former high-ranking leaders of the Party and the Government, experts, and international organizations in preparation for the contents of the documents.

The Party spent approximately half a year for a nation-wide consultation on the full draft of the documents, especially the Political Report that included the foreign policy section, by means of mass media, to enable Vietnamese people from all walks of life to have access to contribute their opinions to the drafts. At the last phase, the final drafts of the documents were approved by the Central Committee before being introduced to the Party National Congress, where they were scrutinized by the delegates in various discussion sessions. The Congress, being the highest authority of policy and decision making, approved the documents by a show of hands in the plenary session.

The broadening of the participatory policy formulation process in Vietnam had its merits. It signified the efforts by the CPV to solicit as wide as possible the range of opinions from inside and outside of the Party. The endeavor to engage more actors, and thereby garnering more inputs, in foreign policy making was important for the CPV in at least two aspects. Firstly, it was the way to get the approval by the society on its conduct of the country's foreign affairs in terms of both form and substance. In this regard, the CPV was given high credit by the Vietnamese people for an effective foreign policy that helped create greater comprehensive national strength and international status for the country. Secondly, and more importantly, the CPV wanted to ensure wider consensus on foreign policy amid changing internal and external contexts.

Domestically, as Vietnam became more open to the rest of the world with more extensive and clearly felt impacts of international integration on every corner of the society, there was higher need to enhance consensus on the awareness and perception of national interest. With national interest being identified as the most important factor shaping the country's foreign policies and relations, the abstract idea of national interest ought to be operationalized in ways that foreign affairs, particularly economic diplomacy for national development, ultimately benefit all sectors in society, with the people, localities, and businesses at the center.[40] This benefit-based approach, in its turn, aimed at forging wider domestic support for and subsequently greater participation in the implementation of foreign policy.

There was also the need to have consensus on the identification and assessment of challenges and opportunities for Vietnam's foreign affairs in the external environment, which informed the country's foreign policy priorities. As the discussions and the final foreign policy texts showed, while greater importance was attached to the continuation of the foreign policy that the CPV had been pursuing for the last several decades, emphases were also made on the necessity of policy adaptation to changes in the regional and global environment that should be based on consensus in terms of both perception and action. The CPV's consensus-based and participatory approach to foreign policy formulation was, in essence, part of its whole-nation approach to foreign policy implementation.

Material Resources

Along the process of *Doi Moi* that brought about sustained economic growth, Vietnam was gaining more and more material resources for pursuing its foreign policy toward further reach. Enhanced economic strength also allowed Hanoi to invest more into developing human resources for the conduct of foreign affairs and building certain deterrent national defense capabilities, particularly for its navy and coast guard.

Better human resources in the form of a more capable foreign service resulted in higher confidence in Hanoi that Vietnam could be more visible in the regional and global arenas.[41] The institutional management of foreign policy implementation was also a contributing factor. Better collaboration was forged among various contingents engaging in foreign affairs, namely the three pillars of State, Party, and people-to-people diplomacy, in a wide range of areas within comprehensive diplomacy and a common regulation of foreign affairs management.[42]

In this regard, the participation of Vietnam in UN PKO missions and its effort to get elected to various positions in UN bodies including the UN Security Council, UN General Assembly, UN Human Rights Council, and UN Commission on International Trade Law, were notable cases in point. Pham Binh Minh highlighted the strength and solidarity of the entire political system, trust, companionship, and support of the people as well as the maturity and enthusiasm of those in charge of foreign affairs as solid premises for Vietnam to aim for higher goals in foreign affairs with new posture.[43]

OPERATIONALIZATION OF GRAND STRATEGY

Protection of Territorial Integrity

The East Sea (South China Sea) issue became increasingly salient in Vietnam's foreign policy. Policy makers in Hanoi were of the view that territorial and maritime disputes would be more intensified, complicated, and severe, and that peace, stability, security, safety, freedom of navigation and aviation in the South China Sea would face great challenges with potential risk of armed conflicts.[44]

Yet, this situation presented Hanoi with both challenges and opportunities. On the one hand, there were concerns about possibilities, though hypothetical, of either open military conflicts or secret compromises between major powers at the expense of the interests of smaller countries. On the other hand, expectations became higher about greater external constraints to future Chinese activities in the area, ASEAN's role in managing the situation in the South China Sea, and continued commitments by other powers to regional peace and stability.

While prioritizing the South China Sea issue, Hanoi could not lose sight of its most important task of preserving peaceful and stable environment for national economic development. The key to this was the reconfirmation of the approach of "resoluteness and persistence" (*kiên quyết, kiên trì*) in the pursuit of national interests.[45] The official posture remained that Vietnam would resolutely and persistently struggle against all acts of violating its independence, sovereignty, and territorial integrity, while endeavoring to promote peaceful resolution to territorial disputes as well as ensuring security, safety, freedom of navigation and aviation, and maritime cooperation.

This approach underlined several policy options that included urging for respect to the rules-based maritime order based on the 1982 UNCLOS and the 2016 South China Sea arbitral award by the Arbitral Tribunal instituted under Annex VII of the 1982 UNCLOS, conducting negotiations between ASEAN and China for an effective and substantial code of conduct (COC) while implementing in earnest the Declaration on the Conduct of Parties (DOC) in the South China Sea.

Greater weight was put on utilizing the ASEAN-led platforms to address the South China Sea issue, twining it into the greater context of regional peace and stability, and promoting international cooperation in such non-sensitive issues as environmental protection, anti-piracy, fish stock protection, and the likes. At the bottom line, the "resoluteness and persistence" approach was compatible with the effort to protect the country in advance and from afar, which Hanoi considered as the best course of action.[46]

Deepening Bilateral Relations

Deepening its bilateral relationships, particularly with neighboring countries and major powers, was a consistent focus, with a view to promoting intertwined interests, political trust, and consolidated institutional arrangements for bilateral relations. The intensifying Sino-US competition with resultant dynamics in the triangle relations involving Hanoi, Beijing, and Washington, the interest of a growing number of states in establishing bilateral partnership arrangements with Vietnam,[47] and its proactive membership in ASEAN and the UN all served to provide the context for Hanoi's emphasis on improving its bilateral relationships.

That Vietnam managed to establish and enjoy a good set of bilateral relations with foreign countries, especially all major powers, was one of the most prominent outcomes and illustrations of the success of its foreign policy. But as competition, even rivalry, between Washington and Beijing escalated, Hanoi found it increasingly difficult to perform the balancing act to avoid being trapped in great power politics and/or having to choose side. To effectively carry out this very delicate task of diplomacy, the following foreign policy emphases, therefore, prevailed in Hanoi's play book.

Vietnamese policy makers insisted on the policy of independence, autonomy, diversification, and multi-direction of Vietnam's external relations accompanied by the effort at being a trustworthy and responsible friend and partner of all other countries. In association to this was the pledge to follow the "four-no" principles of national defense: i.e., no military alliance, no foreign base on Vietnam's territory, no alignment with a second country against a third party, and no use of force or threat to use force in international relations. The country's Defense White Paper issued in 2019 stated, however, that depending on the circumstances and specific conditions, Vietnam would consider developing necessary, appropriate defense and military relations with other countries.[48]

The addition of "one-depending" to the "four-no" was viewed by analysts as underscoring the need for strengthening bilateral defense ties with countries who could support Vietnam's national interests. It also expanded the spectrum of its strategic choices and indicated a causal linkage between the sources of risks that deteriorate Vietnam's external peaceful and stable environment and its choice of partners to deepen defense cooperation.[49]

As a way of better doing the balancing act among powers, Hanoi also increasingly made use of ASEAN and the ASEAN-led platforms and relied on ASEAN's collective stance in dealing with emerging sensitive issues in relations with big powers. In addition to that, relations between Vietnam and medium-sized powers were forged to encourage the type of force alignment that was centered neither on Beijing nor Washington while promoting the centrality of ASEAN.[50]

Elevation of Multilateral Diplomacy

The identification of multilateral diplomacy as a strategic direction of foreign affairs was made official at the Twelfth Party National Congress in 2016. Two years later, the CPV Secretariat issued the Directive coded 25-CT/TW that provided the rationale and guidelines for the elevation of Vietnam's multilateral diplomacy up to the year 2030. Elevation was meant by Hanoi's endeavor to move beyond participation toward playing "a core, leading and/or mediating role" and contributing to shaping the rules of the game at the multilateral organizations and fora that were of strategic significance to the country–identified by measures of national interests.[51] Its greater pro-activeness in multilateral mechanisms provided the premise for Hanoi to pursue greater role and contribution with regards to multilateral diplomacy.

The elevation of multilateral diplomacy was conducted in line with the acceleration of international integration, thereby showing Vietnam's increasing engagement in and commitment to, in terms of institutional, human, and financial resources, a broader range of regional and global issues. This has been realized into Vietnam's commitment and participation within the framework of ASEAN Community building efforts that became increasingly comprehensive based on the three main pillars of politico-security, economic, and socio-cultural cooperation, that of the UN framework, as well as other multilateral security and military-to-military cooperative arrangements at the regional and global levels.

According to Vietnam's Deputy Prime Minister and Foreign Minister Bui Thanh Son, the promotion of multilateral diplomacy was mutually supportive of the deepening of Vietnam's bilateral relationships and the accelerating of international integration with a view to strengthening its comprehensive national power, improving its international status, and maintaining the peaceful and stable external environment.[52] The synergy of deepened bilateral relations, extensive and comprehensive international integration, and accelerated multilateral diplomacy were also meant to enlarge Vietnam's room for strategic maneuvering to achieve its goals of national security and development, especially in the context of changing great power politics largely associated with China's ambitions and Sino-US strategic competition.[53] Vietnam's new approach to multilateral diplomacy was demonstrated in various aspects that included ensuring the peaceful external environment beyond the regional scope, mobilizing more resources for national development, engaging in broader international security and development agendas, and developing the whole-nation and whole-government approach to foreign relations.[54] Yet, the elevation of multilateral diplomacy was also based on "specific needs, actual conditions, and available resources."[55]

In recent years, the driving force behind Hanoi's eagerness at multilateral diplomacy was growing domestic support for the promotion of Vietnam's nation branding as a middle power. It reflected the awareness of the opportunities in promoting its international status and striving for the rule of law through multilateralism, as means to respond to crude power politics in international relations, based on its newly accumulated resources and capacities after nearly four decades of reforms.

CONCLUSION

Vietnam's grand strategy, without being labelled as such, since the 1980s was reflection of unprecedented developments and fundamental changes in the geo-political and economic dynamism of East Asia, as well as the new foreign policy thinking and security approach as part of its domestic reforms. It provided a showcase of how smaller countries adapted to external upheavals, reidentified its strategic objectives and priorities, and brought together all the elements, both military and non-military, for the preservation and enhancement of long-term and core national interests.

National interest became the basis and point of reference for the design and conduct of foreign affairs of Vietnam in the post-Cold war era. A foreign policy of independence, autonomy, peace, cooperation, and development to secure the ultimate national interests, on the bases of the fundamental principles of international law, equal footing, and mutual benefit, has become the main and consistent posture of Vietnam for the past four decades and will continue to be so in the future. Its relevance and effectiveness for the country to respond to external developments and satisfy domestic needs has been proven.

More importantly, the success of Vietnam's *Doi Moi* process to which foreign policies and relations made essential contributions has brought about new comprehensive national power and international status for the country. Recently, Vietnam has been viewed as achieving certain criteria of a middle power, especially in terms of political will to participate actively in regional and global affairs.[56] This was evidenced by Hanoi's self-imaging as "a trustworthy friend and partner, and responsible member of the international community," having established strategic and/or comprehensive partnerships with more than thirty countries, actively participating in and contributing to major regional and global multilateral mechanisms, most notably ASEAN and the UN. As such, the formulation and execution of the resemblance of an official grand strategy of Vietnam is not only shaped by but promises to contribute to the regional and global geo-political, geo-economic, and security dynamics in increasingly significant ways.

NOTES

The views expressed in the chapter are entirely the author's own. They do not necessarily reflect those of the institution she works for.

1. Nguyen Phu Trong. 2023. *Xay dung va phat trien nen doi ngoai, ngoai giao Viet Nam toan dien, hien dai, mang dam ban sac "cay tre Viet Nam" (Building and Developing a Comprehensive, Modern Vietnamese Foreign Affairs and Diplomacy Imbued with the Identity of "Vietnamese Bamboo")*. Hanoi: Nha xuat ban Chinh tri Quoc gia Su that (National Politics Truth Publishing House). 56
2. Tran, Quang Co. 1992. "The gioi và chau A - Thai Binh Duong sau chien tranh Lanh." (The Post-Cold War World and Asia-Pacific). *Quan he quoc te (International Relations)*. 38. 13–14; Nguyen Co Thach. 1990. "Nhung chuyen bien tren the giọi va tu duy moi cua chung ta" (Changes in the World and Our New Thinking). *Quan he quoc te (International Relations)*. 3. 2–8
3. Path, Kosal. 2020. "The Origins and Evolution of Vietnam's Doi Moi Foreign Policy of 1986," *TRaNS: Trans-Regional and National Studies of Southeast Asia,* 8 (2), November, Seoul. 171–185
4. Tung, Nguyen Vu. 2011. "Vietnam's Security Challenges: Hanoi's New Approach to National Security and Implications to Defense and Foreign Policies," in *Asia Pacific Countries Security Outlook and Its Implications for the Defense Sector*. The National Institute for Defense Studies, Japan, NDIS Joint Research Studies (5), 409–410
5. Socialist Republic of Vietnam, Ministry of National Defence. 2009. *2009 Vietnam National Defence*. Hanoi: National Politics Publishing House, 11.
6. Minh, Pham Quang. 2012. *Chinh sach doi ngoai Doi Moi cua Viet Nam (Vietnam's Doi Moi Foreign Policy) 1986–2010*. Hanoi: Nha xuat ban The gioi, 56–57

7. Thayer, Carlyle A. "The Evolution of Vietnamese Diplomacy, 1986–2016," in Le, Hong Hiep. & Tsvetov, Anton. 2018. *Vietnam's Foreign Policy Under* Doi Moi. Singapore: Yusof Ishak Institute, 23–44
8. Socialist Republic of Vietnam, Ministry of National Defence (2019). *2019 Vietnam National Defence*. Hanoi: National Politics Publishing House, 6.
9. Communist Party of Vietnam. 2016. *Documents of the Twelfth Party National Congress*. Hanoi: Office of the Party Central Committee, 149; Nguyen, Manh Hung. 2016. New Context of Vietnam's National Security Challenges, *Trends in Southeast Asia* (17) Singapore: Yusof Ishak Iseas Publishing.
10. Do, Van Soan. 2017. "Bao ve To quoc tu som, tu xa - diem moi trong Van kien Dai hoi lan thu XII cua Dang." (Protecting the Fatherland in Advance and from Afar–A New Point in the Documents of the Twelfth Party National Congress) *Hai quan Viet Nam Dien tu (Vietnam Navy Online)* 1 January. Available at http://baohaiquanvietnam.vn/tin-tuc/bao-ve-to-quoc-tu-som-tu-xa-diem-moi-trong-van-kien-dai-hoi-lan-thu-xii-cua-dang (accessed on 28 August 2021); Nguyen, The Phuong. 2019. "Vietnam's 2019 Defense White Paper: Preparing for A Fragile Future," *AMTI Update*. 17 December.
11. Nguyen, Manh Cam. 1993. "Tren duong trien khai chinh sach doi ngoai moi," (On the Implementation of the New Foreign Policy). *Communist Review (Tap chi Cong san)*. 8 (448), 12; Vu, Quang Vinh. 2000. *Dang Cong san Viet Nam lanh dao hoat dong doi ngoai (Leadership of the Communist Party of Vietnam in Foreign Affairs)*. Hanoi: Nha xuat ban Thanh nien (Youth Publishing House), 44–45, 66–69.
12. Communist Party of Vietnam. 2016. *Documents of the Twelfth Party National Congress*. Hanoi: Office of the Party Central Committee, 117; See also Hoang, Xuan Lam. 2016. "Quan diem của Dang ve giu vung moi truong hoa binh, on dinh de phat trien dat nuoc," (The Party's Perception of Preserving Peaceful and Stable Environment for National Development). *Tap chi Quoc phong Toan dan (Journal of All-People National Defense)*. 23 May.
13. Socialist Republic of Vietnam. Ministry of National Defence. 2019. *2019 Vietnam National Defence*. Hanoi: National Politics Publishing House, 21.
14. Job, Brian. L (ed). 1992. *The Insecurity Dilemma: National, Regime, and State Securities in the Third World*. Boulder, Colo.: Lynne Rienner Publishers, 13; Ayoob, Mohamed. "The Security Predicament of the Third World State: Reflections on State Making in a Comparative Perspective," in Job, Brian L.(ed) 1992. *The Insecurity Dilemma: National Security of Third World States*. Boulder: Lynne Rienner, 77.
15. Tung, Nguyen Vu. 2011. "Vietnam's Security Challenges: Hanoi's New Approach to National Security and Implications to Defense and Foreign Policies," in *Asia Pacific Countries Security Outlook and Its Implications for the Defense Sector*. The National Institute for Defense Studies, Japan, NDIS Joint Research Studies (5), 107
16. Path, Kosal. 2020. "The Origins and Evolution of Vietnam's *Doi Moi* Foreign Policy of 1986," *TRaNS: Trans-Regional and National Studies of Southeast Asia,* 8 (2), November, Seoul, 171–185
17. Communist Party of Vietnam. 2006. *Documents of the Tenth Party National Congress*. Hanoi: National Politics Publishing House.
18. "Chi thi cua Ban Bi thu ve cong tac ngoai giao kinh te phuc vu phat trien dat nuoc den nam 2030," (The Party Secretariat Directive on Economic Diplomacy for National Development to the Year 2030). *Bao Dien tu Chinh phu (Online Government News)*. 23 August 2022. Available at http://baochinhphu.vn/chi-thi-cua-ban-bi

-thu-ve-cong-tac-ngoai-giao-kinh-te-phuc-vu-phat-trien-dat-nuoc-den-nam-2030-102220823181112802.htm (assessed on 10 September 2024)

19. To, Minh Thu. "Vietnam's International Economic Integration Under *Doi Moi*," in Le, Hong Hiep. & Tsvetov, Anton. 2018. *Vietnam's Foreign Policy Under* Doi Moi. Singapore: Yusof Ishak Institute, 235–259
20. Communist Party of Vietnam. 2013. *Nghi quyet so 22-NQ/TW ngay 10/4/2013 cua Bo Chinh tri ve hoi nhap quoc te* (Resolution No.22-NQ/TW on 10 April 2013 of the Politburo on International Integration). 10 April.
21. Bui, Thanh Son. 2015. *Hoi nhap quoc te va nhung van de dat ra doi voi Viet Nam (International Integration and Implications for Vietnam)*. Hanoi: Nha xuat ban Chinh tri quoc gia- Su that (National Politics–Truth Publishing House).
22. Communist Party of Vietnam. 2016. *Van kien Dai hoi Dang toan quoc lan thu XII (Documents of the Twelfth National Party Congress)*. Van phong Trung uong Dang (Office of the Central Party Committee). Hanoi.
23. Namely the Vietnam–Eurasian Economic Union Free Trade Agreement (VN-EAEU), Comprehensive and Progressive Trans-Pacific Partnership (CPTPP), the ASEAN–Hong Kong China Free Trade Agreement (AHKFTA), the EU–Vietnam Free Trade Agreement (EVFTA), the UK–Vietnam Free Trade Agreement (UKVFTA), the Regional Comprehensive Economic Partnership (RCEP), and the Vietnam - Israel Free Trade Area (VIFTA).
24. Socialist Republic of Vietnam, Ministry of National Defence. 2019. *2019 Vietnam National Defence*. National Politics Publishing House. Hanoi, 26–27
25. Communist Party of Vietnam. 2021. *Documents of the 13th National Congress*. National Politics Truth Publishing House: Hanoi, 162.
26. Thayer, Carlyle A. 2016. "Vietnamese Diplomacy, 1975–2015: From Member of the Socialist Camp to Pro-active International Integration," in the *International Conference on Vietnam: 40 Years of Reunification, Development, and Integration (1975–2015)*, 2–17
27. Rush, James R. "ASEAN's neighborhood," in Zasloff, Joseph J. (ed). 1989. *Postwar Indochina: Old Enemies and New Allies*. U.S. Department of State: Center for the Study of Foreign Affairs, Foreign Service Institute, 221
28. Ministry of Foreign Affairs. 2002. *Vietnam's Diplomacy 1945–2000*. National Politics Publishing House. Hanoi.
29. Do, Le Chi. 2020. *Viet Nam truoc tac dong cua cau truc an ninh tai khu vuc chau A - Thai Binh Duong (Vietnam Under the Impacts of Regional Security Architecture in the Asia-Pacific)*. Hanoi: Nha xuat ban Chinh tri Quoc gia Su that (National Politics Truth Publishing House).
30. Palmujoki, Eero. "Ideological and Foreign Policy: Vietnam's Marxist-Leninist Doctrine and Global Change, 1986–1996." in Thayer, Carlyle A. and Amer, Ramses (eds). 1999. *Vietnamese Foreign Policy in Transition*. Singapore: Institute of Southeast Asia Studies, 25–43.
31. Vu, Khoan. 1994. "Viet Nam va ASEAN," (Vietnam and ASEAN). *Communist Review (Tap chi Cong san)*. November. Hanoi, 31
32. Nguyen, Manh Cam. 1993. "Tren duong trien khai chinh sach doi ngoai moi," (On the Implementation of the New Foreign Policy). *Communist Review (Tap chi Cong san)*. 8 (448), 12; Goodman, Allan E. 1996. "Vietnam and ASEAN: Who Would Have Thought It Possible?" *Asian Survey*. XXXVI (6). June, 595
33. Thuy T. Do. 2015. "Vietnam's Moderate Diplomacy Successfully Navigating Difficult Waters," *East Asia Forum*, January 16

34. Nguyen, Vu Tung. 2021. *Flying Blind: Vietnam's Decision to Join ASEAN*. Singapore: Yusof Ishak Institute, 5
35. Communist Party of Vietnam. 2021. *Documents of the 13th National Congress*. Hanoi: National Politics Truth Publishing House.
36. Communist Party of Vietnam. 2021; 2016; 2011. *Documents of the Thirteenth, Twelfth, Eleventh Party National Congress*. Hanoi: National Politics Truth Publishing House; Socialist Republic of Vietnam. Ministry of National Defence. 2009; 2019. *Vietnam National Defence*. Hanoi: National Politics Publishing House.
37. Pham, Binh Minh. 2021. "Vietnam's Foreign Affairs in 2020: New Spirit and Posture." *Online Government News*. 1 January. Available at http://baochinhphu.vn/Doi-ngoai/Doi-ngoai-Viet-Nam-2020-Ban-linh-va-tam-the-moi/418602.vgp (accessed on 10 October 2021)
38. Socialist Republic of Vietnam. Ministry of National Defence. 2019. *2019 Vietnam National Defence*. Hanoi: National Politics Publishing House, 19
39. Tung, Nguyen Vu. 2011. "Vietnam's Security Challenges: Hanoi's New Approach to National Security and Implications to Defense and Foreign Policies," in *Asia Pacific Countries Security Outlook and Its Implications for the Defense Sector*. The National Institute for Defense Studies, Japan, NDIS Joint Research Studies (5), 122
40. Communist Party of Vietnam. 2021. *Documents of the 13th National Congress*. Hanoi: National Politics Truth Publishing House, 50
41. "Toan van phat bieu cua Tong Bi thu Nguyen Phu Trong tai Hoi nghi Ngoai giao 30." (Speech by Party Secretary-General Nguyen Phu Trong at the 30th Diplomatic Conference). 2018. *The gioi & Viet Nam (World & Vietnam)*, 13 August.
42. Quyet dinh so 272-QD/TW ngay 21/01/2015 cua Bo Chinh tri Khoa XI ve viec ban hanh Quy che quan ly thong nhat cac hoat dong doi ngoai (Decision number 22-QD/TW on 21 January 21, 2015 of the Eleventh Politburo on the Issuance of the common regulation on foreign affairs management).
43. Pham Binh Minh. 2021. "Vietnam's Foreign Affairs in 2020: New Spirit and Posture." *Online Government News*. 1 January. Available at http://baochinhphu.vn/Doi-ngoai/Doi-ngoai-Viet-Nam-2020-Ban-linh-va-tam-the-moi/418602.vgp (accessed on 10 October 2021)
44. Communist Party of Vietnam. 2021. *Documents of the 13th National Congress*. National Politics Truth Publishing House: Hanoi, 107
45. Le, Hai Binh (ed). 2020. *Tap hop luc luong trong the ky XXI: Xu huong, tac dong va doi sach cua Viet Nam (Force Alignment in the 21st Century: Trends, Impacts and Vietnam's Responses)*. Hanoi: Nha xuat ban Chinh tri Quoc gia Su that (National Politics Truth Publishing House).
46. Nguyen, Ngoc Hoi. 2021. "Quan diem "chu dong ngan ngua cac nguy co chien tranh xung dot tu som, tu xa" tai Dai hoi XIII cua Dang." (The perception of "proactively preventing risks of war and conflict in advance, from afar" at the 13th Party Congress). *Tap chi Quoc phong Toan dan (Journal of All-People National Defense)*. 26 May. Available at http://m.tapchiqptd.vn/vi/quan-triet-thuc-hien-nghi-quyet/quan-diem-chu-dong-ngan-ngua-cac-nguy-co-chien-tranh-xung-dot-tu-som-tu-xa-tai-dai-hoi-xiii-cua-dang-17139.html (accessed on 28 August 2021)
47. By early 2025, Vietnam has established strategic and/or comprehensive partnerships with 34 countries, including twelve comprehensive strategic partnerships with ten countries, namely China, Russia, India, Repubic of Korea, the U.S, Japan, Australia, France,

Malaysia, New Zealand, Indonesia, Singapore; strategic partnerships with eight countries, namely Spain, the UK, Germany, Italy, Thailand, the Philippines, Brazil, Czech Republic; and comprehensive partnerships with fourteen countries, namely South Africa, Chile, Venezuela, Argentina, Ukraine, Denmark, Canada, Myanmar, Hungary, Brunei, the Netherlands, Mongolia, United Arab Emirates, Switzerland.

48. Socialist Republic of Vietnam. Ministry of National Defence. 2019. *2019 Vietnam National Defence*. Hanoi: National Politics Publishing House, 24.
49. Grossman, Derek. and Sharman, Christopher. 2019. "How to read Vietnam's latest defense white paper: A message to great powers." *War on The Rocks*, 31 December. Available at https://warontherocks.com/2019/12/how-to-read-vietnams-latest-defense-white-paper-a-message-to-great-powers (accessed on 10 September 2021); Nguyen, The Phuong. 2019. "Vietnam's 2019 Defense White Paper: Preparing for a Fragile Future." *Asia Maritime Transparency Initiative, Amti Update*. 17 December.
50. Le, Hai Binh (ed). 2020. *Tap hop luc luong trong the ky XXI: Xu huong, tac dong va doi sach cua Viet Nam (Force Alignment in the 21st Century: Trends, Impacts and Vietnam's Responses)*. Hanoi: Nha xuat ban Chinh tri Quoc gia Su that (National Politics Truth Publishing House); Ngoc Lan. 2021. "EU voi vai tro can bang o An Do Duong -Thai Binh Duong." (EU as a balancer in the Indo-Pacific) *Cong an Nhan dan (People's Police Journal)*. 13 July.
51. Le, Hoai Trung. (ed) 2017. *Doi ngoai da phuong Viet Nam trong thoi ky chu dong va tich cuc hoi nhap quoc te (Vietnam's Multilateral Diplomacy in the Era of Proactive and Active International Integration)*. Hanoi: Nha xuat ban Chinh tri Quoc gia Su that (National Politics Truth Publishing House), 183
52. "Bo truong Ngoai giao Bui Thanh Son: Trien khai manh me, quyet liet va dong bo cong tac doi ngoai da phuong trong tinh hinh moi" (Foreign Minister Bui Thanh Son: Implementing Vigorously, firmly and Coordinatedly Multilateral Diplomacy in the New Context). *The gioi & Viet Nam (World & Vietnam)*. 9 July 2021. Available at https://baoquocte.vn/bo-truong-ngoai-giao-bui-thanh-son-trien-khai-manh-me-quyet-liet-va-dong-bo-cong-tac-doi-ngoai-da-phuong-trong-tinh-hinh-moi-150903.html (accessed on 8 November 2021)
53. Tran, Khanh. 2020. "On Vietnam's Foreign Strategic Space During Renewal (Doi Moi) Time, since 1986," *Global Policy and Governance*, Rome. 9 (2), 83–96
54. Phan Mich. 2020. "Tam the moi cua ngoai giao da phuong Viet Nam." (The New Posture of Vietnam's Multilateral Diplomacy). *The gioi & Viet Nam (World & Vietnam)*. 14 June.
55. Communist Party of Vietnam. 2021. *Documents of the 13th National Congress*. Hanoi: National Politics Truth Publishing House, 164.
56. Chen, Sharon and Ratnam, Gopal. 2013. "Vietnam Rises as Middle Power at Defense Summit: Southeast Asia." *Bloomberg*. 28 August; Kratiuk, Barbara. 2014. "Vietnam as a middle power in Southeast Asia." *Second International Conference on Asian Studies*. ICAS 2014: Sri Lanka; Emmers, Ralf. and Teo, Sarah. 2015. "Regional Security Strategies of Middle Powers in the Asia-Pacific." *International Relations of the Asia-Pacific* 15 (2): May.

Conclusion

Ramon Pacheco Pardo

With this edited volume, we set out to answer the following question: What is the grand strategy (GS) of each key power of East Asia? Contributors to the volume have answered this question by examining, respectively, the GSs of twelve key countries from the region: China, Japan, North Korea, South Korea, and Taiwan in Northeast Asia, and Indonesia, Malaysia, Myanmar, Philippines, Singapore, Thailand, and Vietnam in Southeast Asia. Making use of a framework of analysis laid out by Thierry Balzacq, Peter Dombrowski, and Simon Reich, the contributors to this volume have shown the goals, interests, and policies driving the GSs of countries across East Asia in the period between 1980 and the early 2020s.

In this concluding chapter, I first briefly discuss the design and implementation process of GS across East Asia. This links to the question discussed in the Introduction, regarding the degree to which East Asian GSs are formulated and applied more or less consciously. I then compare in more detail the external and internal factors driving the GSs of East Asian countries. As explained in the Introduction, understanding these factors is the basis of the analytical framework developed by Balzacq, Dombrowski, and Reich. Once these factors are understood, analysts can explain why states strategize to guarantee their security, for and against what states strategize, and the results of their choices. This, in a nutshell, is GS—as understood in this book. Thus, understanding the factors behind the GS of the countries in this region serves us to recognize what leads East Asian countries to behave in the way they do.

DESIGN AND IMPLEMENTATION OF GRAND STRATEGY

In the introductory chapter, we established that the design and implementation of GS may follow a well-defined process with a clear and centralized institutional framework making conscious decisions—or it may be the result of a looser process that may not even be conscious. After all, not all countries are US- and China-like great superpowers, fortunate enough to be able to think about long-term goals that they can try to attain by making use of a wide range of tools, in a way that would allow them to control the international system to their advantage. The contributors to this volume indeed show that East Asian countries exhibit both types of design and implementation processes: well-defined and led by a strong, central, institutional framework that may be more loosely defined and implemented subconsciously rather than intentionally.

Countries such as China, Japan, Myanmar, North Korea, Singapore, South Korea, Taiwan, or Vietnam have a more or less well-defined decision-making process, whereby centralized structures can be in charge of GS design and implementation. Thus, their respective GS can be traced by looking at key documents—speeches, national security strategies, white papers, and more. In contrast, Indonesia, Malaysia, the Philippines, and Thailand have a looser planning and execution process, and their actions are a better harbinger of their GS. This does not mean that these countries do not have any documents in which they lay out their GS. But it does mean they find it more difficult to act in ways that are laid out for them; there is thus the need to look at their actions.

It should be noted that, as per the East Asian cases presented in this book, the GS design and implementation process in operation does not portend whether one country's GS is "stronger" or "weaker" than the other, that is, whether the definition of a country's GS is clear or not, and whether its implementation is closer to the original design or not, and whether a country is able to achieve its goals or not. Thus, in principle, whether a country has a tighter or looser decision-making process, key foreign and security policy documentation or not, neither of these affect its ability to develop a GS. Any country can consciously or unconsciously formulate its own GS.

MAIN EXTERNAL FACTORS AFFECTING GRAND STRATEGIES ACROSS EAST ASIA

Logically, the main external factors affecting the GS of different countries across East Asia vary from each other. The differences are particularly stark when comparing countries located in Northeast Asia to those in Southeast Asia. Having said that, there are some factors that cut across the region, as shown by the contributors to this volume. Table C.1 summarizes the external factors informing the GS of countries across the region.

Table C.1. Main External Factors Affecting Grand Strategies across East Asia

	Third-Party Actors	Threats and Opportunities	(Potential) Conflicts
Northeast Asia			
China	United States	US hegemony, international economic landscape	US-China competition, domestic instability
Japan	United States, China, Russia, North Korea	Changing balance of power, territorial disputes, sea lines of communication (SLOC), Japan-US alliance	US-China competition, territorial disputes
North Korea	South Korea, China, United States, Japan, Russia	ROK-US alliance, relations with China and Russia, relations with Japan	US strike, domestic instability
South Korea	North Korea, United States, China, Japan, Russia	ROK-US alliance, China's rise	North Korean strike, US-China competition
Taiwan	China, United States	Taiwan-China-United States relations	Chinese invasion, US-China competition
Southeast Asia			
Indonesia	United States, China, Australia, ASEAN, Malaysia and Singapore	Territorial/maritime disputes, separatism, terrorism, natural disasters	Interstate conflict, domestic instability
Malaysia	ASEAN, Organisation of Islamic Cooperation, China, United States, Japan, South Korea, Taiwan	Defending national borders, territorial disputes, nontraditional security	Interstate conflict, nontraditional conflicts
Myanmar	China, United States, confluence of Northeast Asia-Southeast Asia-South Asia	Territorial disputes, separatism, terrorism	Domestic instability, nontraditional conflicts
Philippines	China, United States, US allies	Maritime disputes, Philippines-US alliance, Philippines-Japan partnership	Maritime conflict

Table C.1

	Third-Party Actors	Threats and Opportunities	(Potential) Conflicts
Singapore	Indonesia, Malaysia, China, United States	China's rise, relationship with US, territorial disputes	Territorial conflict, US-China competition
Thailand	United States, China	Thailand-US alliance, China's rise, ASEAN relations	Border disputes, US-China competition
Vietnam	United States, China, ASEAN, Soviet Union (Cold War)	Economic situation, nontraditional security threats	Armed conflict

Perhaps unsurprisingly, the two superpowers of the early twenty-first century are the main third parties influencing GS across East Asia. Both Northeast Asian and Southeast Asian countries have designed their GS by taking the behavior of the United States and China into consideration. In some cases such as Japan, the Philippines, South Korea, and Thailand, long-standing security ties with the United States has meant that their security and foreign policy actions necessarily need to take into consideration their respective relationships with Washington. In any case, all East Asian countries are impacted by the decisions taken by China and the United States.

In the case of Northeast Asia, other relevant third parties are other Northeast Asian countries and, to an extent, Russia—albeit, in the case of the latter, its influence has declined from the Cold War era and the disintegration of the Soviet Union. In the case of Southeast Asia, meanwhile, other predominant third parties are ASEAN and other Southeast Asian countries. It is logical that neighbors influence the behavior of actors in a given region. Yet it is interesting to note that few Southeast Asian countries seem to be influenced by their Northeast Asian counterparts other than China when designing their GS—while no Northeast Asian country seems to be affected by neighbors in Southeast Asia.

When thinking about the threats and opportunities that policymakers across East Asia focus on, the changing balance of power resultant from China's rise and the relative decline of the United States is a relevant consideration for multiple countries across the region. GSs across East Asia are affected by the economic, military, and diplomatic rise of one of their neighbors, which is seen as both as a threat and an opportunity. Similarly, the relative decline of a country that is an ally for several countries in the region and that, in any case, has strong economic, economic, and political ties across East Asia—the United States—is a threat that East Asian strategists have to grapple with.

In terms of Southeast Asia, external threats to sovereignty and territorial integrity are perceived as a threat for most countries in the region. This is logical when considering that most of Southeast Asia was colonized as recently as the first half of the twentieth century. As a result, the countries in the region, many of them postcolonial states, do not necessarily feel that external interference is a threat that they can ignore. After all, policymaking elites across Southeast Asia have memories of their countries' still recent lack of sovereignty at the hands of foreign actors.

As for potential conflicts that grand strategists across East Asia need to consider, Sino-American rivalry and the potential of interstate conflict stand out. In the case of Northeast Asia, the former is a common thread. In the case of the latter, interstate conflict may refer to rivalry between China and the United States, conflict among countries in the region, or both. Therefore, it can be argued that US-China rivalry glues the region together in that it is a potential conflict that grand strategists in different East Asian countries have to ponder. In the case of Southeast Asia, again the relative fragility concomitant to the relatively recent colonization of most countries across the region is seen as a potential source of problems if it leads to conflict among states displeased with their borders as currently marked.

MAIN DOMESTIC FACTORS AFFECTING GRAND STRATEGIES ACROSS EAST ASIA

The key internal factors influencing GS formulation and implementation across East Asian countries have similarities and differences. This makes sense given the different domestic characteristics, historical trajectories, and exact geographical location of each country. But it is also interesting to note that these differences do not preclude several similarities across the region. Table C.2 summarizes the internal factors that underpin the GS of countries across both Northeast and Southeast Asia.

The national values of East Asian countries vary widely, from the social stability of China, to the liberalism of Japan and South Korea, to the archipelagic component of Indonesia's and the Philippines's identity. It is interesting to note, however, that most postcolonial states across Southeast Asia greatly value cohesion. This again points to the importance that the still recent colonial experience has in informing the development of GS acrossing this subregion—a experience that cannot be underestimated in understand how policymakers in the region think about long-term foreign and security policy.

Table C.2. Main Internal Factors Affecting Grand Strategies across East Asia

	National Values	Influence of Values	National Policymaker Debates	Institutional Process(es)	Resources
Northeast Asia					
China	Social stability	Focus on internal stability	Importance of regime stability	Top-down, centralized	Economic power, diplomacy, military power
Japan	Pacifism, liberalism	Cooperation with like-minded partners	Strengthening relations with like-minded partners, deterring potential opponents	Horizontal with cabinet office on top	Economic power, diplomacy, values, military power
North Korea	Self-reliance	Personality cult	Personality-driven	Top-down, centralized	Military power
South Korea	Democracy, liberalism	Cooperation with like-minded partners	Reunification with North Korea, cooperation with like-minded partners	Horizontal, with president on top	Economic power, diplomacy, military power
Taiwan	Post-colonialism, split identities	Cooperation with like-minded partners, strengthening economic links with China	Relationship with China	Horizontal with strong influence of president	Economic power
Southeast Asia					
Indonesia	Cohesion, diversity, sovereignty, archipelagic outlook	National integration	Maintaining national unity, economic development	Top-down (dictatorship years), horizontal but with strong influence of president (democratic years)	Military power, economic power, diplomacy

(*continued*)

Table C.2 (*continued*)

	National Values	Influence of Values	National Policymaker Debates	Institutional Process(es)	Resources
Malaysia	Pragmatism, cohesion	Nation-building	Maintaining national unity, economic development	Top-down, centralized, horizontal characteristics	Economic power, diplomacy
Myanmar	Cohesion	Focus on internal stability	Stability	Top-down	Military power
Philippines	Archipelagic nature, diversity	Focus on cohesion, internal stability	Stability	Top-down, centralized	Military power
Singapore	Cohesion, sovereignty	Internal stability	Stability	Top-down, centralized	Diplomacy, economic power
Thailand	National integrity	Focus on sovereignty	Maintaining national unity, economic development	Top-down, centralized, horizontal characteristics	Military power, economic power
Vietnam	Indepen-dence, autonomy	Good diplomatic relations, war avoidance	Stability, economic development	Top-down, centralized, horizontal characteristics	Economic power, diplomacy

This results in values influencing GS across Southeast Asia in a similar way: by making decision-makers focus on cohesion, integration, and stability. These are sine qua non for Southeast Asian countries to be able to develop a GS that can withstand domestic instability. In the case of Northeast Asia, it is noteworthy that the three full democracies in the region—Japan, South Korea, and Taiwan—are influenced by their values in that they emphasize the centrality of cooperation with like-minded partners, whether within Northeast Asia itself or from other parts of the world. In a sense their values are influenced by their geographical location in a region in which full democracies are firmly in the minority.

When it comes to debates among policymakers, there is a wide range of them across East Asia. Having said that, the centrality of the colonial experience to understanding GS across Southeast Asia is once more inescapable. Indeed, national unity and/or stability are central debates that decision-makers have in the countries of the subregion. Economic development is another prominent debate in Southeast Asia. This is logical when considering that the countries in the region are still classified as middle income or low income by the World Bank, Singapore aside. In the case of Northeast Asia, policymaker debates mainly seem to focus on external threats, at least for the three full democracies present there.

Decision-making processes are remarkably similar among the different countries of East Asia. For the most part, these are elite-dominated, top-down, and centralized processes. Even in countries with more horizontal processes the leader of the country plays a crucial role in the formulation of GS, namely, Indonesia, Japan, South Korea, Taiwan, Thailand, and Vietnam. Arguably, this elite-driven process helps East Asian countries to be able to formulate fairly long-term GS.

When it comes to the resources at the disposal of policymakers, when thinking about and implementing GS, China, Japan, and South Korea are the only three that have the full range of resources at their disposal. These are the three biggest economies in East Asia, which strongly suggests that economic power gives access to a wider range of resources. Other countries in the region focus on specific resources. Yet it needs to be noted that military power remains a key resource for countries across East Asia, which seems sensical when considering that few feel that they live in a stable region.

GRAND STRATEGY IN EAST ASIA AND BEYOND

This is the first volume systematically analyzing the GS of countries across East Asia, with specific reference to the framework developed by Balzacq, Dombrowski, and Reich. As the scholarly study of GS moves beyond a narrow focus on the United States and China, this book offers a valuable contribution to our understanding of GS across great, middle, and small powers. In particular, there are three noteworthy implications from the findings of this edited volume beyond the case of East Asia.

To begin with, there is an important empirical implication that needs to be stressed: middle powers and small powers can have a grand strategy, which is thus not the exclusive domain of great powers. The focus of middle and small powers may be different. For example, they may not necessarily have a global focus—even if this should not be excluded—and instead focus on regional or even domestic affairs. Also, issues such as nation building, domestic stability, or economic development that (most) great powers do not need to worry about is a key focus for multiple middle and small counterparts. But their different focus should not be interpreted as an inability to formulate and implement GS.

Another relevant empiric-scholarly implication is that external and domestic factors are equally relevant when it comes to the design and execution of GS. Even in the case of neighbors sitting next to each other in a particular region, external factors affecting GS will be different and domestic values, processes, and resources will also differ. This matters insofar as it calls for the careful case-study analysis of each country in order to understand their GS. In other words, there may be some generalizable principles that apply across countries, but we should not assume that the GS of two neighbors or countries with similar positions in the international system will be the same.

Finally, an important scholarly implication of this volume is that there is a need to study GS beyond a small number of great powers and to extend this study beyond the West. As "the rise of the rest" gathers pace, scholars on international relations have embraced the study of countries across East Asia, Latin America, and North Africa, giving but three examples. This move should extend to the study of GS. This way, international relations scholarship will be able to shed light on still underexplored regions and enrich our understanding of how and why long-term foreign and security policy, as embodied by GS, has proceeded, and how it will evolve.

ABBREVIATIONS

ACD	Asia Cooperation Dialogue
ACMECS	Ayeyarwady-Chao Phraya-Mekong Economic Cooperation Strategy
ADB	Asian Development Bank
ADMM	ASEAN Defence Minister's Meeting
AFC	Asian financial crisis
AFTA	ASEAN Free Trade Area
AOIP	ASEAN Outlook on Indo-Pacific
APEC	Asia-Pacific Economic Community
APT	ASEAN-Plus-Three
ARF	ASEAN Regional Forum
ASEAN	Association of Southeast Asian Nations
AUKUS	Australia-United Kingdom-United States
BCP	Burma Communist Party
BN	Barisan Nasional
BRI	Belt and Road Initiative
BSPP	Burma Socialist Programme Party
BWS	Burmese Way to Socialism
CADC	Comprehensive Archipelagic Defense Concept
CCP	Chinese Communist Party
CFC	Combined Forces Command
CIA	Central Intelligence Agency
CSCAP	Council for Security Cooperation in the Asia Pacific
CVID	complete verifiable irreversible denuclearization
DCA	Defense Cooperation Agreement
DFA	Department of Foreign Affairs
DOE	Department of Energy
DPJ	Democratic Party of Japan
DMZ	Demilitarized Zone
DPP	Democratic Progress Party
DWP	Defence White Paper

EAO	ethnic armed organization
EAS	East Asia Summit
EDCA	Enhanced Defence Cooperation Agreement
EEC	Eastern Economic Corridor
EEZ	exclusive economic zone
EIU	Economist Intelligence Unit
ESF	Economic Support Fund
EU	European Union
FDI	foreign direct investment
FOIP	free and open Indo-Pacific
FOSS	Forum of Small States
FPDA	Five-Power Defence Arrangements
FMS	Foreign Military Sales
FTA	free trade agreement
GDP	gross domestic product
GMM	Global Movement of the Moderates
GMS	Greater Mekong Subregion
GS	grand strategy
GSOMIA	General Security of Military Intelligence Agreement
IA-CEPA	Indonesia-Australia Comprehensive Economic Partnership
ICBM	intercontinental ballistic missile
IMF	International Monetary Fund
IMS-GT	Indonesia-Malaysia-Singapore Growth Triangle
IPEF	Indo-Pacific Economic Framework
IR	international relations
JIIA	Japan Institute of International Affairs
JSP	Japan Socialist Party
KMT	Kuomintang
KNDO	Karen National Defence Organization
LDP	Liberal Democratic Party
LIC	low-intensity conflict
MAF	Malaysian Armed Forces
MAP	Military Assistance Program
MDT	Mutual Defense Treaty
MILF	Moro Islamic Liberation Front
MIRV	multiple independently targetable reentry vehicle
MNLF	Moro National Liberation Front
MSG	Melanesian Spearhead Group

MRCA	multirole combat aircraft
MRO	maintenance, repair, and overhaul
MRRV	multirole response vessel
NCA	National Ceasefire Agreement
NDC	National Defence College
NDSC	National Defence and Security Council
NEP	New Economic Policy
NGO	nongovernmental organization
NLD	National League for Democracy
NPA	New People's Army
NPT	Treaty on Non-Proliferation of Nuclear Weapons
NSS	National Security Strategy
ODA	Official Development Assistance
OECD	Organisation for Economic Co-operation and Development
OFW	overseas Filipino workers
OIC	Organisation of Islamic Cooperation
OPCON	operations control
OPM	*Organisasi Papua Merdeka*
OTMNC	Our Three Main National Causes
PGC	Philippine Coast Guard
PH	Pakatan Harapan
PLA	People's Liberation Army
PLAN	People's Liberation Army Navy
PMC	Philippine Marines Corps
PN	Perikatan Nasional
PNP	Philippine National Police
PRC	People's Republic of China
QD	Quadrilateral Dialogue
R&D	research and development
RC	Revolutionary Council
RCEP	Regional Comprehensive Economic Partnership
ROC	Republic of China
ROK	Republic of Korea
SAC	State Affairs Commission
SCS	South China Sea
SEANWFZ	Southeast Asia Nuclear Weapon-Free Zone
SIJORI	Singapore-Johore-Riau
SLOC	sea lines of communication
SLORC	State Law and Order Restoration Council

SLV	satellite launch vehicle
SPDC	State Peace and Development Council
SPV	Shared Prosperity Vision
TAC	Treaty of Amity and Cooperation
THAAD	terminal high altitude area defense
UAV	unmanned aerial vehicles
UNCLOS	United Nations Convention on the Law of the Sea
US	United States
USDP	Union Solidarity and Development Party
UU PSDN	*Undang-undang Pengelolaan Sumber Daya Nasional*
WMD	weapons of mass destruction
WTO	World Trade Organization
ZOPFAN	Zone of Peace, Freedom, and Neutrality

CONTRIBUTORS

RENATO CRUZ DE CASTRO is a professor at the International Studies Department of De La Salle University, Manila, and holds the Dr. Aurelio Calderon Chair in Philippines-American Relations. As member of the Board of Trustees of the Albert Del Rosario Institute of Strategic and International Studies (ADRI), he writes monthly opinion columns for the *Philippine Star* and *BusinessWorld*. He has written over a hundred articles on international relations and security, including most recently, "The Limits of Intergovernmentalism: The Philippines' Changing Strategy in the South China Sea Dispute and Its Impact on the Association of Southeast Asian Nations (ASEAN)" (*Journal of Current Southeast Asian Affairs*, 2020). He earned his PhD from the University of South Carolina.

DANG CAM TU is associate professor of politics and international relations and director-general of the Department of Science Information and Journal of International Studies at the Diplomatic Academy of Vietnam. She participated and served as Vietnam's national coordinator in several networks of think tanks in East Asia and the Asia-Pacific region. Recent publications include "Vietnam's Decision to Join ASEAN: The South China Sea Disputes Connection" (in *Vietnam's Foreign Policy under Doi Moi*, Cambridge University Press, 2018), "Understanding the U.S.-Vietnam Security Relationship, 2011–2017" (*The Korean Journal of Defense Analysis*, 2019) a "Decoding Vietnam's Foreign Policy After the Thirteenth National Party Congress: Process, Continuity, and Adjustment" (*TraNS: Trans-Regional and -National Studies of Southeast Asia*, 2023).

ANG CHENG GUAN is professor of the International History of Southeast Asia and associate dean, S. Rajaratnam School of International Studies (RSIS). His most recent publications include *Southeast Asia's Cold War: An Interpretive History* (Honolulu: University of Hawaii Press, 2018) and its sequel, *Southeast Asia after the Cold War: A Contemporary History* (Singapore: NUS Press, 2019), *The Southeast Asia Treaty Organisation* (London: Routledge, 2022), *Reassessing Lee Kuan Yew's Strategic Thought* (London: Routledge 2023) and *Singapore's Grand Strategy* (Singapore: NUS Press,

2023), *The Third Indochina War: An International History* (Cambridge: Cambridge University Press, 2024) and *The Five Power Defence Arrangements: From Origin to Fifty and Beyond* (London: Routledge, 2025).

PONGPHISOOT BUSBARAT is assistant professor at the Department of International Relations, Faculty of Political Science, and Fellow at the Institute of Security and International Studies (ISIS Thailand), Chulalongkorn University, Bangkok, Thailand. His research focuses on Thailand's foreign policy in Southeast Asia and its relations with the great powers, especially China and the United States. His publications include peer-reviewed articles in, for example, *Contemporary Southeast Asia, Asian Security,* and *European Journal of East Asian Studies.* He is working on a manuscript assessing the influence of Thailand's identities with China and the United States on Thailand's policy preferences toward these two powers. Dr. Busbarat received a PhD in political science and international relations from ANU.

MUHAMAD HARIPIN is political scientist at the Research Centre for Politics at the National Agency for Research and Innovation (BRIN), Indonesia. He is author of *Civil-Military Relations in Indonesia: The Politics of Military Operations Other Than War* (Routledge, 2020) and coauthor of *The Army and Ideology in Indonesia: From Dwifungsi to Bela Negara* (Routledge, 2021). His peer-reviewed articles and essays have been published in *Journal of Policing, Intelligence and Counter Terrorism, Defense and Security Analysis, Asian Journal of Comparative Politics, New Mandala, Kyoto Review of Southeast Asia,* and *The Jakarta Post,* among others. He holds a PhD from the Graduate School of International Relations, Ritsumeikan University, Japan.

YUICHI HOSOYA is professor of international politics at Keio University, Tokyo. Professor Hosoya was a member of the Advisory Board at Japan's National Security Council (NSC) (2014–2016). He was also a member of the Prime Minister's Advisory Panel on Reconstruction of the Legal Basis for Security (2013–14) and the Prime Minister's Advisory Panel on National Security and Defense Capabilities (2013). His publications include *Security Politics: Legislation for a New Security Environment* (JPIC, 2019); *History, Memory & Politics in Postwar Japan* (coeditor; Lynne Rienner, 2020); and "Japan's Security Policy in East Asia," in Yul Sohn and T.J. Pempel (eds.), *Japan and Asia's Contested Order: The Interplay of Security, Economics, and Identity* (Palgrave, 2018).

CHIUNG-CHIU HUANG is professor in the Graduate Institute of East Asian Studies at National Chengchi University (NCCU), Taipei, Taiwan. Her research focuses on Chinese foreign policy, Southeast Asian international politics (focusing on Vietnam, Cambodia, Laos, and Myanmar), and Sino-Mongolia relations. She published the book *Harmonious Intervention: China's Quest for Relational Security* (Ashgate, 2014) and the coauthored book *China and International Theory: The Balance of Relationships* (Routledge, 2019). She also published several articles in academic journals and edited books, including "Interpreting Vietnam's China Policy from the Perspective of Role Theory: Independent Role vs. Interactive Role" published in *International Relations* in February 2020.

YEW MENG LAI is associate professor of politics and international relations, and dean of the Centre for the Promotion of Knowledge and Language Learning (CPKLL), Universiti Malaysia Sabah. He is also a research fellow at the varsity's Small Islands Research Centre. His publications include *Security Studies: A Reader* (Routledge, 2011); *Nationalism and Power Politics in Japan's Relations with China: A Neoclassical Realist Interpretation* (Routledge, 2014); "Malaysia's Security Concerns: A Contemporary Assessment" in Meredith L. Weiss (ed.), *The Routledge Handbook of Contemporary Malaysia* (London, 2015); and "'Sea of Cooperation' or 'Sea of Conflict'?: The South China Sea in the Context of China-ASEAN Maritime Cooperation," *International Journal of China Studies* (2017).

MAUNG AUNG MYOE is dean of the Graduate School of International Relations and professor of international relations at the International University of Japan. His publications include *Building the Tatmadaw: Myanmar Armed Forces since 1948* (ISEAS, 2008); *In the Name of Pauk-Phaw: Myanmar's China Policy since 1948* (ISEAS, 2011); "The NLD and Myanmar Foreign Policy: Not New, But Different," *Journal of Current Southeast Asian Affairs* (2017); "Myanmar Foreign Policy: Principles and Practices," in *SAGE Handbook of Asian Foreign Policy* (SAGE Publication, 2020); and "The Military: Institution and Politics," in *Myanmar: Politics, Economy and Society* (Routledge, 2021). He earned his PhD in political science and international relations from Australian National University.

RAMON PACHECO PARDO is professor of international relations at King's College London and the KF-VUB Korea Chair at the Centre for Security, Diplomacy and Strategy (CSDS) of Free University of Brussels (VUB). His books include *South Korea's Grand Strategy: Making Its Own Destiny* (Columbia University Press, 2023); *Korea: A New History of South & North* (Yale University Press, 2023; with Victor Cha); *Shrimp to Whale: South Korea from the Forgotten*

War to K-Pop (Oxford University Press, 2022); and *North Korea-US Relations from Kim Jong Il to Kim Jong Un* (Routledge, 2019). His articles have been published in, among others, *Asian Survey, International Relations of the Asia-Pacific, Journal of Contemporary China,* and *New Political Economy.*

JUNG H. PAK was deputy assistant secretary in the US Department of State from 2021-2024. She concurrently served as the US deputy special representative for North Korea policy, and later as US senior official for North Korea policy. Prior to her work with the US Department of State, she was SK-Korea Foundation Chair in Korea Studies and Senior Fellow at the Brookings Institution. She is the author of *Becoming Kim Jong Un: A Former CIA Officer's Insights into North Korea's Enigmatic Young Dictator* (Ballantine, 2020). Pak was a senior analyst at the Central Intelligence Agency and the deputy national intelligence officer for the Koreas at the National Intelligence Council, Office of the Director of National Intelligence. She received her PhD in United States history from Columbia University.

SEONG-HO SHEEN is professor of international security and director of the International Security Center at the Graduate School of International Studies (GSIS), Seoul National University. His recent publications include "A Beginning of New Global Partnership? The ROK-US Relations under Biden and Moon," *Journal of International and Area Studies,* vol.29, no.1 pp.79-96. 2022 Available from: doi:10.23071/jias.2022.29.1.79, "US-China Mutual Vulnerability: A South Korean Perspective," US-China Mutual Vulnerability Perspectives on the Debate, ISSUES & INSIGHTS, VOL. 22, SR 2 | May 2022, *Pacific Forum,* "U.S. Coercive Diplomacy toward Pyongyang: Obama vs. Trump," *The Korean Journal of Defense Analysis,* Vol. 32, No. 4, December 2020, 517-538. He received his PhD from the Fletcher School of Law and Diplomacy, Tufts University.

KETIAN VIVIAN ZHANG is an assistant professor of international security in the Schar School of Policy and Government at George Mason University. She studies rising powers, coercion, economic statecraft, and maritime disputes in international relations and social movements in comparative politics, with a regional focus on China and East Asia. Her first book from Cambridge University Press examines when, why, and how China uses coercion when faced with issues of national security. Part of her research has appeared in *International Security, Journal of Strategic Studies,* and *Journal of Contemporary China,* among other venues. Ketian received her PhD in political science from the Massachusetts Institute of Technology.

INDEX